Nuggets of Wisdom

Some Pathbreaking Judgments of the Supreme Court

P.C. Hota
IAS (Retired)
Former Chairman
Union Public Service Commission

ATLANTIC
PUBLISHERS & DISTRIBUTORS (P) LTD

Published by
ATLANTIC
PUBLISHERS & DISTRIBUTORS (P) LTD
7/22, Ansari Road, Darya Ganj, New Delhi-110002
Phones : +91-11-40775252, 23273880, 23275880, 23280451
Fax : +91-11-23285873
Web : www.atlanticbooks.com
E-mail : orders@atlanticbooks.com

Branch Office
5, Nallathambi Street, Wallajah Road, Chennai-600002
Phones : +91-44-64611085, 32413319
E-mail : chennai@atlanticbooks.com

Printed in India at Nice Printing Press, A-33/3A, Site-IV, Industrial Area, Sahibabad, Ghaziabad, U.P.

Writing a book is an adventure. To begin with, it is a toy and an amusement; then it becomes a mistress, and then it becomes a master, and then a tyrant. The last phase is that just you are about to be reconciled to your servitude, you kill the monster, and fling him out to the public.

—Sir Winston Churchill

Foreword

This book contains observations of Hon'ble Judges of the Supreme Court of India in leading judgments on amendments of the Fundamental Rights and some other important constitutional issues.

Judges of the Supreme Court are so erudite that they cannot help writing scholarly judgments. Some of their judgments are also in complex prose. This poses a problem for lay readers and also for students of law. More often than not, they avoid reading the full text of the judgments reported in standard law journals. Instead, they rely on "help books". Admittedly, these books do not do justice to the brilliant logic and profound erudition of the judges. Against this background, summaries of some of the important judgments attempted by me, might bring out the logic and erudition of the judges and be easy to read by both lay readers as well as students of law.

In attempting to summarize important issues in the judgments, I have tried to adopt a simple prose style. The discerning reader will however appreciate that for centuries, legal language has been in a particular mould. Therefore, I might not have fully succeeded in my efforts to convey in simple prose summaries of the judgments.

A final word. Though for nearly five decades I have been reading standard law journals – both Indian and foreign – and commentaries on constitutional law – from De Smith to Denning – I have been an officer with an executive mindset. My professional compulsions have demanded of me certain "forward thrust" to achieve targets in key result areas. I must admit that because of professional compulsions, the temperament which an Executive functionary develops, is perhaps not the right one to understand and appreciate profoundly scholarly judgments of eminent judges who have pondered over legal and constitutional issues in slow-motion exercise.

For this book, I owe so much to so many: my only regret is, because of limitation of space, I would be able to acknowledge the help of only so few. Such an acknowledgement I have avoided for the simple reason that it might give rise to the charge of invidious discrimination on my part.

Place: New Delhi

P.C. Hota
Former Secretary to Government of India,
Ministry of Parliamentary Affairs;
Former Secretary to Government of India,
Ministry of Personnel, Public Grievances and Pension,
(Department of Personnel & Training);
Former Member & Former Chairman,
Union Public Service Commission

The Supreme Court of India: An Overview

Before I attempt to summarize a few important judgments of the Supreme Court of India, I may quote Lord Atkin who said, "Justice is not a cloistered virtue: she must be allowed to suffer the scrutiny and respectful, even though outspoken, comments of ordinary men."

I also like to recall the profound observation of Justice Oliver Wendell Holmes of the U.S. Supreme Court, that no one should understand him as speaking with disrespect for the law, because he criticizes it so frequently as, "One may criticize what one reveres."

Judgments of the Supreme Court of India are the only source of judge-made law in the country. Under Article 141 of the Constitution, it is only the Supreme Court which has powers to declare the law. The law so declared, is binding on all courts within the territory of India.

Salmond has written in his book, *Jurisprudence* that judge-made law is the most important source of law in a democracy. As a jurist has put it, the legislators enact the law in the wholesale: the courts by giving finishing touches to the law lay down what the law would be in retail.

Under Article 142 of the Constitution, only the Supreme Court has the power to pass such decree or make such order to do complete justice in any matter before it. Article 142, however, does not empower the Court to disregard the substantive law while doing complete justice.

In view of Article 32 of the Constitution, the Supreme Court is the ultimate protector of the Fundamental Rights. Under Article 136 of the Constitution, the Supreme Court has the power to grant special leave for appeal from any judgment, decree, determination, sentence or order passed by any court or tribunal in India. This plenary power is, however, not available to challenge any judgment, determination, sentence or order of any court or tribunal constituted under any law relating to the Armed Forces.

Under Article 131 of the Constitution, the Supreme Court has original jurisdiction in any dispute between the Government of India and any state or states, between two or more states and also between the Government of India and one state or states on one side and two or more states on the other.

The Supreme Court has acknowledged that it is not final as it is infallible, but it is infallible because it is final. Thus, the Court has been candid about its own limitations. Such a pronouncement inspires confidence in the Court as the sentinel on the *qui vive* to uphold the rule of law. Indeed, the Supreme Court of India occupies a pivotal position to uphold the Constitution and the law.

In course of its functioning, the Supreme Court has made pronouncements in different judgments, which have enhanced its power and authority. The first important landmark in this regard is the judgment in Kesavananda Bharati *versus* State of Kerala (1973). In this judgment, the Court laid down that under Article 368 of the Constitution, the Indian Parliament has powers to amend any provision of the Constitution, including the Fundamental Rights; but by such amendment, the Parliament cannot alter the basic structure of the Constitution. Though the Court has identified some components of the basic structure of the Constitution, such components are merely illustrative as the Court can lay down from time to time other components of the basic structure. This aspect of the power of the Court to identify new components of the basic structure of the Constitution has to be viewed in the light of observations of Justice K.K. Matthew, a distinguished former Judge of the Supreme Court, that the Fundamental Rights are only empty vessels. And into these vessels, each generation pours the contents of new rights which it wants to be considered as fundamental.

The next important judgment which has increased the power of the Supreme Court is Maneka Gandhi *versus* Union of India (1978). In this judgment, it was decided that the expression, "procedure established by law" in Article 21 of the Constitution did not mean any arbitrary or fanciful procedure, but a procedure which is just, fair and reasonable and not arbitrary, whimsical or oppressive. In other words, it is not any law which the court will uphold in its efforts to vindicate the rule of law.

The next important landmark has been introduction of Public Interest Litigation following the judgment of the Court in S.P. Gupta *versus* Union of India (1982). In this judgment, the Court relaxed the rule of *locus standi*. Such relaxation meant that if a legal injury has been caused to any person, who because of poverty, lack of education or any other disability has been unable to move the higher judiciary for enforcement of his rights, any public-spirited person or Non Governmental Organization, acting *bona-fide*, can approach the High Court and the Supreme Court for relief for the poor and the deprived. In S.P. Gupta's case (1982), the Supreme Court has believed that modern public law has carried forward "a culture of judicial assertiveness to repair the democratic process."

The next important landmark has been judgment of the Supreme Court in Visakha *versus* State of Rajasthan (1997). In the Visakha case, the Court did not wait for the legislature to enact a law to tackle the problem of sexual harassment at work place. Instead, the Court issued elaborate guidelines till the competent legislature came forward to fill the vacuum. The judgment in Visakha case is a good example of *pro-tem*, *ad hoc* judicial legislation.

Yet another important landmark in assertion of greater power by the Supreme Court has been the Vineet Narain case (1998). In it, the Court laid down that if the issue of a one-time writ of mandamus to a public authority may not be effective because of likelihood of inertia of the public authority, the Court may summon the authority to appear before it to report the progress of investigation. This is the doctrine of continuous mandamus – the latest addition to the armoury of writs which the Courts can issue – in case of investigation of offences committed by high-profile politicians, senior bureaucrats and corporate bigwigs.

The first judgment, I have summarized for this book, is that of A.K. Gopalan *versus* State of Madras delivered by the Supreme Court as early as 1950. In this case, out of six judges in the Bench presided over by Chief Justice Harilal Kania, four judges upheld the *vires* of the Preventive Detention Act 1950.

The four judges upheld the *vires* of the Preventive Detention Act minus Section 14 of the Act, which empowered the detaining authority to withhold the grounds of detention inter alia from scrutiny of the higher judiciary. Chief Justice Harilal Kania in his judgment pointed out the danger of shutting out judicial review of the grounds of detention. He mentioned that the detaining authority might give to the detenue three stanzas of a poem or three alphabets written differently as the grounds of detention and the detenue will have no effective remedy to challenge the grounds because of Section 14 of the Preventive Detention Act.

Chief Justice Harilal Kania made another significant observation when he said that the Court should not limit the power of legislature on the basis of what the Court considered as the spirit of the Constitution; as such a power in the hands of the judiciary "would be too great and too indefinite either for its own security, or for the protection of the private rights."

The Preventive Detention Act 1950 was allowed to lapse in the year 1969. In 1971, the Maintenance of Internal Security Act was passed by the Parliament to provide for a law of preventive detention. This Act was replaced in 1980 by the National Security Act, which is in force at present. Before 1980, the Parliament had already enacted a law of preventive detention known as Conservation of Foreign Exchange and Prevention of Smuggling Activities Act (COFEPOSA) in 1974. COFEPOSA is invoked by empowered officials of Government of India against economic offenders.

Various judgments of the Supreme Court have laid down guidelines, which the detaining authority must scrupulously follow while issuing order for preventive detention of any person.

The Supreme Court has held that even though it has no powers to substitute its own judgment for that of the detaining authority regarding sufficiency of the grounds of detention, it has the power to ensure that the grounds of detention are precise, pertinent and proximate to enable the detenue to represent against the order of detention. The Court has also held that the grounds of detention must be communicated in the language the detenue can understand so that his right to represent against the order of detention will not merely be an empty formality.

In Ram Manohar Lohia judgment (1966), the Supreme Court struck down the order of detention as the activities of the detenue were only prejudicial to law and order and not to public order. The Court held that as contrasted to law and order, activities prejudicial to public order are more serious as they disturb the even tempo of life of the community.

In 1982, the Supreme Court laid down in A.K. Roy's judgment that a detenue under a preventive detention law is not a convicted criminal and is entitled to better amenities and facilities during detention.

The Supreme Court has also held that a person serving a term in prison because of conviction and sentence by a court of competent jurisdiction can be arrested under a law of preventive detention immediately after release from prison if the detaining authority is satisfied that the released convict would again indulge in prejudicial activities relating to items at entry (9) of the Union List and entry (3) of the Concurrent List in the Seventh Schedule of the Constitution. The Court has also upheld the detention of a person under the preventive detention law, who was facing a criminal trial, where further prosecution was dropped by the competent authority if the Court was of the view that the detaining authority has acted *bonafide* in issuing the order of detention even after a pending criminal case on the same facts was dropped.

In A.K. Gopalan's case (1950), counsel for the petitioner argued that it was contrary to all notions of justice that the detenue will represent against the order of detention to the detaining authority. Even Justice Mehr Chand Mahajan had recorded his reservations against such a procedure which makes the detaining authority a judge of its own order of detention. It is however relevant to mention that during the Second War (1939-45) even in the United Kingdom the representation against detention was to be made to the Secretary of State who had passed the order of detention. The matter went upto the House of Lords where it was held in the famous case of Liversidge *versus* Anderson (1942) that it was perfectly legal for the Secretary of State to consider representation of the detenue even though the Secretary of State had earlier passed the order of detention against the detenue.

India is the only democratic country in the world with a constitutional provision for a law of preventive detention during peace time. It is relevant to mention that democracies such as the United Kingdom and United States of America had enacted a law of preventive detention only as a war-time measure.

What about the present status of preventive detention law in the major democracies of the world? In 2010, the newly set-up Supreme Court of the United Kingdom held as illegal arrest and detention of some terrorists allegedly involved in the attack on World Trade Centre at New York on 11 September 2001. The Court held that personal liberty of a person cannot be taken away in the United Kingdom by the Executive even on the basis of reasonable suspicion of the person having been involved in acts of terror; as such arrest violated the Human Rights Act of 1998. In 2008, the Supreme Court of the United States also ruled that the Al-Queda suspects captured by the American troops in Afghanistan and detained in Guantanamo, could not be denied the writ of Habeas Corpus.

Often the detaining authority is compelled to invoke the power of arrest and detention under a preventive detention law because some notorious law-breakers such as land grabbers, illegal timber traders, drug-peddlers, hawala agents, smugglers of valuable goods and Railway Wagon breakers are so prone to violence that ordinary citizens are afraid of deposing against them in a court of law. It often happens that the detaining authority is convinced that the only way to uphold the rule of law and ensure justice is to invoke the power of preventive detention against the notorious law-breakers.

While attempting summaries of judgments of the Supreme Court, I am reminded of what Justice Vivian Bose has said about dispensation of justice by the higher judiciary in India. Justice Vivian Bose was of the view that justice should be administered by the courts in a liberal way and be broad based on human values rather than on narrow considerations hedged around with hair-splitting technicalities.

To do justice based on common sense was also the approach of Lord Denning. Fali S. Nariman, the distinguished jurist, put it elegantly when he wrote that Denning executed some of his beautiful strokes while standing slightly outside the crease. Edmund Heward, the biographer of Denning, has said that Lord Denning believed that ultimately the power wielded by the judge is derived from faith of the people in transparency and fairness of the judiciary.

While eulogizing the role of the Supreme Court in upholding the rule of law, one may recall the observation of a distinguished jurist that laws are not always just and the judicial process is not always adequate to secure justice. The observations of the jurist become all the more relevant as the lower courts and the High Courts in India have huge backlog of pending cases. Inspite of the pendency of cases for years, unfortunately at any point of time there are large number of vacancies of judges in the lower courts and the High Courts.

The Federal Court – set up under the Government of India Act 1935 – heard only 151 appeals during its functioning from 1937 to 1950. The volume of litigations before the Supreme Court of India – the successor to the Federal Court – has increased enormously. Perhaps, the Court may like to screen out petitions filed before it at the admission stage. In the U.S. Supreme Court, pre-admission scrutiny is used extensively. Every year, the U.S. Supreme Court hears about 150 to 200 petitions, including appeals. This is perhaps one of the main reasons why the

U.S. Supreme Court has continued with only nine judges since its inception whereas the Indian Supreme Court started with a sanctioned strength of seven judges and the present sanctioned strength has increased to thirty-one judges.

As a measure of judicial reform, the U.S. Supreme Court allows only half-an-hour for each party to make oral submissions before the Court. In this context, it may be mentioned that in Kesavananda Bharati case (1973) the 13 Judge Constitution Bench heard the matter for as many as 65 days.

Justice is the objective of any responsible government. It is also the ideal of any civil society. But sadly enough, if a common man has no money to fight his case, "the court room becomes a place where Jesus Christ and Judas Iscariot are equals with betting odds in favour of Judas."

P.C. Hota

Contents

Foreword ... *iv*

The Supreme Court of India: An Overview ... *v*

1. A.K. Gopalan *versus* State of Madras (AIR 1950 SC 27) ... 1
2. RE: Delhi (Laws) Act 1912 (Special Reference One of 1951 under Article 143 of The Constitution of India) (AIR 1951 SC 332) ... 40
3. Shankari Prasad Singh Deo *versus* The Union of India and Others (AIR 1951 SC 458) ... 69
4. The State of West Bengal *versus* Anwar Ali Sarkar and Others (AIR 1952 SC 75) ... 74
5. Sajjan Singh *versus* State of Rajasthan (AIR 1965 SC 845) ... 82
6. I.C. Golaknath and Others *versus* State of Punjab (AIR 1967 SC 1643) ... 91
7. A.K. Kraipak and Others *versus* Union of India (AIR 1970 SC 150) ... 107
8. R.C. Cooper *versus* Union of India (AIR 1970 SC 564) ... 112
9. Kesavananda Bharati *versus* State of Kerala (AIR 1973 SC 1461) ... 129
10. Indira Gandhi *versus* Raj Narain (AIR 1975 SC 2299) ... 187
11. Additional District Magistrate, Jabalpur *versus* S.S. Shukla and Others (AIR 1976 SC 1207) ... 199

12. Maneka Gandhi *versus* Union of India (AIR 1978 SC 597) 212

13. Minerva Mills Limited *versus* Union of India (AIR 1980 SC 1789) 220

14. Union of India *versus* Tulsiram Patel (AIR 1985 SC 1416) 229

15. Supreme Court Advocates-On-Record Association and Another *versus* Union of India (AIR 1994 SC 268) 243

16. Managing Director E.C.I.L. *versus* B. Karunakara (AIR 1994 SC 1074)...................257

17. S.R. Bommai *versus* Union of India (AIR 1994 SC 1918) 263

18. Tata Cellular *versus* Union of India (AIR 1996 SC 11) 278

Author's Information..284

CHAPTER 1

A.K. Gopalan *versus* State of Madras (AIR 1950 SC 27)

[CHIEF JUSTICE HARILAL KANIA, JUSTICE FAZL ALI, JUSTICE PATANJALI SASTRI, JUSTICE MEHRCHAND MAHAJAN, JUSTICE BIJAN KUMAR MUKHERJEA AND JUSTICE SUDHI RANJAN DAS]

Case Summary

A.K. Gopalan, a leader of the undivided Communist Party of India, was detained under the Preventive Detention Act 1950 (in short, the impugned Act). He filed a petition under Article 32 of the Constitution, for a writ of *Habeas Corpus*. A Bench of six judges of the Supreme Court heard the petition and decided on a few important constitutional issues.

1. A majority of four judges upheld the order of detention. Justice Fazl Ali and Justice Mehr Chand Mahajan delivered dissenting judgments and held the detention illegal.
2. M.K. Nambiar, a constitutional lawyer of eminence, appeared for A.K. Gopalan. The State of Madras was represented by K. Rajah Ayyer, the Advocate-General for the State. M.C. Setalvad, Attorney-General for India, appeared for the Union Government.
3. Justice Harilal Kania, Chief Justice of India, delivered a separate judgment upholding the detention. The following are the salient points of his judgment:
   (i) A.K. Gopalan had challenged the order of detention as violative of Articles 19, 21 and 22 of the Constitution. He had also challenged it on the ground of *mala fides*.
   (ii) As without prior authorization of the Central or the State Government, as the case may be, Section 14 of the impugned Act made it an offence to disclose the grounds of detention, the question of *mala fides* could not be gone into by the Court in absence of facts constituting the grounds for detention.
   (iii) The Court, therefore, confined itself to the constitutional validity of the order of detention.
4. To appreciate the contention of the parties, it would be relevant to note the general scheme of the Constitution of India, which is as follows:

(i) Under Article 53, executive power of the Union vests in the President of India and is to be exercised by him, in accordance with the Constitution, either directly or through officers subordinate to him.

(ii) Under the Constitution, legislative power is divided between the Parliament and the legislatures of States. The ambit and limitation of the legislative power of the Parliament and the State legislatures are in Article 246 read with Article 245 and the Seventh Schedule of the Constitution.

(iii) The powers and jurisdiction of the Supreme Court are in Article 32 and Articles 124 to 147 of the Constitution.

5. Under the American Constitution, judicial power vests in the U.S. Supreme Court. In the Indian Constitution, there is no analogous provision.

6. The Preamble to the Constitution declares India as a Sovereign Democratic Republic to secure to its citizens, liberty and equality and to promote among them fraternity. [**N.B.:** The Constitution as it was originally enacted did not contain the expressions 'Socialist' and 'Secular'. By the Forty-Second (Constitution Amendment) Act 1976, the Preamble was amended to read, "Sovereign, Socialist, Secular and Democratic Republic". In S.R. Bommai *versus* Union of India (AIR 1994 SC 1918), Secularism has been held to be a basic feature of the Constitution.]

7. There was no chapter on Fundamental Rights in the Government of India Act 1935. In the chapter on Fundamental Rights in the present Constitution, the "State" includes both the Union and the State Governments. Article 13 stipulates that all laws in force at the commencement of the Constitution, to the extent of their repugnancy with any Fundamental Right, shall be void.

8. "Law" includes not only Acts of the Parliament and the State Legislature but also Ordinance, order, bye-law, rule, regulation, notification, custom or usage having the force of law. [**N.B.:** The Constitution (Twenty-Fourth Amendment) Act 1971 provided that "Law" in Article 13(2) shall not include any amendment of the Constitution under Article 368. The vires of the aforesaid Amendment Act has been upheld by the Supreme Court in Kesavananda Bharati *versus* Union of India (AIR 1973 SC 1461).]

9. In terms of legislative competence, the impugned Preventive Detention Act is covered by Entry 9 in the Union List and Entry 3 in the Concurrent List.

10. In the Chapter on Fundamental Rights, there is a distinction between the Rights of citizens and the Rights of non-citizens. Article 19 confers the Right mentioned therein on citizens only, whereas Articles 20, 21 and 22 confer Rights not only on citizens but also on non-citizens.

11. Inclusion of Article 13(1) and Article 13(2) in the Chapter on Fundamental Rights appears to be a matter of abundant caution. Even in their absence if any Fundamental Right is infringed by any law, the Court has the power to declare the law as void.

12. The Rights in Article 19 – which the petitioner has claimed have been infringed by the detention order – are as follows:

(a) to freedom of speech and expression,

(b) to assemble peaceably and without arms,

(c) to form associations or unions,

(d) to move freely throughout the territory of India,

(e) to reside and settle in any part of the territory of India; and

(f) to practise any profession or to carry on any occupation, trade or business.

13. Article 19 clearly means that the legislation, which is under attack, must be directly in respect of any of the Rights in Article 19. "The true approach is only to consider the directness of the legislation and not what will be the result of the detention otherwise valid, on the mode of detenu's life." On that short ground, the petitioner's argument that the detention order has infringed his Fundamental Right in Article 19 must fail.

14. The petitioner has urged that the detention order has directly affected his Right under Article 19(1)(d) to move freely throughout the territory of India.

15. Article 19(1)(d) has no application to a law providing for either punitive or Preventive Detention.

16. It has been argued that Article 19 and Article 21 have to be read together as they supplement each other.

17. The concept of the Right to move freely throughout the territory of India in Article 19(1)(d) is an entirely different concept than 'personal liberty' in Article 21.

18. Article 19(1) applies to a citizen in full possession of his personal liberty. A person detained under a law of Preventive Detention cannot claim to be in full possession of his personal liberty.

19. The American Constitution provides that "No person shall be deprived of his life, liberty or property except by due process of law." In Article 21, the Indian Constitution provides that "No person shall be deprived of his life or personal liberty except according to procedure established by law".

20. It was argued by counsel for the petitioner that "law" in Article 21, comprised the principles of Natural Justice. This contention is unacceptable. The Indian Constitution stipulates a procedure established by law. Once a validly enacted law sets out a procedure for deprivation of life or personal liberty, it cannot be questioned on the ground of violation of Natural Justice.

21. The general structure of the American Constitution has been described by Munro in his book, *The Government of United States*, in the following words:

"The architects of 1787 built only the basement. Their descendants have added walls and windows, wings and gables, pillars and porches to make a ramblings structure which is not yet finished. Or, to change the metaphor, the U.S. Constitution has a fabric, which to use the words of James Russel Lowell, is still being woven on the roaring loom of time."

22. In contrast to the American Constitution, the Indian Constitution provides in minute details the legislative powers of both the Parliament and the State legislatures.

23. There are points of distinction between the "due process" clause of the American Constitution and "procedure established by law" in the Indian Constitution. They are as follows:
   (i) In the U.S. Constitution, the word "liberty" is used whereas in the Indian Constitution the corresponding word is "personal liberty".
   (ii) In the U.S. Constitution, protection of "due process" is given to the Right to Property whereas in the Indian Constitution, the Right to Property is in Article 31. [**N.B.:** The Constitution (Forty-Fourth Amendment) Act 1978, has repealed Article 31 along with Article 19(1)(f). At present, the Right to Property is only a Constitutional Right in Article 300(A). The aforesaid Article 300A mandates that private property can be acquired only under a valid law for a public purpose.]
   (iii) In Article 21 there is no mention of due process of law as the Constituent Assembly chose to discard it in favour of the expression "procedure established by law", which refers to only procedural law.

24. Even in USA, the Supreme Court has interpreted due process of law differently in different periods. In his book, *Constitutional Limitations*, Willis has said that due process of law means reasonable law according to view of the majority of judges of the Supreme Court at a particular time. In USA, the doctrine of police powers has been brought in to control the meaning of due process of law. The doctrine of police powers stipulates that a law meant for the good of the people generally may entail surrender of some freedom by individuals.

25. The expression, procedure established by law, in Article 21 of the Indian Constitution has been borrowed from Article 31 of the Japanese Constitution of 1946.

26. In 1931, Lord Atkin had held that in British Jurisprudence, no member of the Executive can interfere with the liberty or property of a British subject except when he can support his act before a court of law.

27. In King *versus* the Secretary of State for Home Affairs (1923), Scrutton L.J. had observed that a man guilty of murder must yet be released if due forms of law have not been followed in his conviction.

28. The principles followed by the English Courts in the aforesaid judgment of Scrutton L.J. remain guaranteed in Article 21 of our Constitution.

29. Arrest and detention of a person contemplated by Article 22, although they may infringe personal liberty of an individual, will be legal because that becomes the legal procedure in respect of arrest and detention.

30. M.C. Setalvad, the Attorney-General, has stated that Preventive Detention dealt with in Article 22 does not fall under Article 21 as Article 22 is a complete code.

31. The contention of the Attorney-General cannot be accepted. In respect of arrest and detention under ordinary law, Article 22(1) and (2) provide safeguards, which stipulate that a person arrested cannot be detained without informing him as soon as may be, the grounds for such arrest. The person arrested also has the Right to consult and be defended by a legal practitioner of his choice. Moreover, a person, arrested has to be produced

before the nearest magistrate within 24 hours excluding the time taken for the journey from place of arrest to the place where the magistrate is located.

32. The safeguards provided in Article 22(1) and (2) are not available for a person, who is detained under any law of Preventive Detention because of Article 22(3).

33. It is, therefore, clear that Article 21 has to be read along with Article 22. On the points of procedure, which are not dealt with by Article 22, the operation of Article 21 will remain unaffected.

34. It is thus necessary first to look at Article 22(4) to (7) and next at the provisions of the impugned Act to determine if the impugned Act or any of its provisions are *ultra vires*.

35. In normal times, neither the American nor the Japanese Constitution has provision for a law on Preventive Detention. But in our country, Preventive Detention in normal times – even without any emergency as war – is recognized as a subject of legislation.

36. If the legislature prescribes a procedure by a validly enacted law on Preventive Detention and such procedure does not come in conflict with the provisions of the Chapter on Fundamental Rights including Article 22, the Preventive Detention Act must be held as valid notwithstanding that the Court may not fully approve of the procedure under such an Act.

37. Article 22(4) stipulates that a law providing for Preventive Detention for a period exceeding three months, shall contain a provision for an Advisory Board. In view of Article 22(7)(b), such detention beyond three months shall not exceed the maximum period of detention prescribed by Parliament by law.

38. Article 22(6) stipulates that the Authority passing the order of detention may withhold disclosure of facts, which such Authority considers against public interest to disclose. It is relevant to mention that Article 22(5) and Article 22(6) make a distinction between grounds, which have to be communicated to the detenue and the facts which such Authority may not disclose in the public interest.

39. Article 22(5) permits a detenue to make a representation against his detention. But it is not mandatory that the representation has to be made to any other body except the Detaining Authority. Even in case of Liversidge *versus* Anderson (1942 A.C. 206), the representation by the detenue was made to the Secretary of State of the United Kingdom, who had passed the order of detention.

40. Article 22(7) authorizes the Parliament to pass a law of Preventive Detention for a period exceeding three months without providing for an Advisory Board. The only stipulation is that the law must specify, the circumstances under which and the class or classes of cases in which, a person may be detained for a period longer than three months without obtaining opinion of an Advisory Board.

41. Under Article 22(7)(b), Parliament may prescribe the maximum period for which any person in any class or classes of cases is detained under any law of Preventive Detention. Article 22(7)(b) is permissive. It is not obligatory for the Parliament to prescribe a maximum period of detention in a law providing for Preventive Detention because of Article 22(7)(b). It has been argued that such a power gives the Parliament the Right to detain a person indefinitely. If that contention is correct, it springs out of the words of Article 22(7)(b) and the Court cannot help in the matter.

42. While dealing with arguments of the counsel for the petitioner, one must remember that a Constitution must not be interpreted in a narrow and pedantic manner.

43. Even though the words of a Constitution must be interpreted on the same principle of interpretation as is applicable to an ordinary law, we must remember that we are interpreting a Constitution – a mechanism under which laws are made and not a mere Act of a legislature which declares what law is to be. Sir Maurice Gwyer, Chief Justice of the Federal Court of India, had also endorsed this view. He had said that a broad and liberal spirit should inspire those whose duty it is to interpret the Constitution, specially when it is a Federal Constitution with its nice balance of jurisdictions.

44. Where the Constitution has not limited, either expressly or by necessary implication, the general powers conferred on the legislature, the Courts should not limit the powers of legislature on the basis of what the Courts think is the "spirit" of the Constitution. Such an approach would place in the hands of the judiciary power too great and too indefinite either for its own security or the protection of private Rights.

45. It was argued by Counsel for the petitioner that under Section 3 of the impugned Act, Parliament has delegated legislative power to the Executive to detain a person. The counsel argued that the satisfaction regarding the grounds of detention must be of the legislature and not of the Executive. This argument has been rejected in a number of cases by the Federal Court of India and also by the Courts in U.K.

46. Section 3 of the impugned Act has also been challenged on the ground that it does not provide an objective standard for the Courts for determining whether requirements for Preventive Detention of a person have been complied with. The counter argument is that no such objective standards can be prescribed for the Executive to use its discretion to detain a person.

47. Lord Finlay has observed in King *versus* Halliday (1917) that a Court is the least appropriate forum to investigate whether circumstances exist warranting preventive detention.

48. Before a person is held liable for an offence, he is supposed to know what he should not do to commit an offence. If he does an act forbidden by law, he is tried for the offence and depending on the evidence, he is convicted and punished according to law.

49. In Preventive Detention, the position is different as the purpose is to prevent an individual not merely from acting in a particular way but from achieving a particular object.

50. Section 7 of the impugned Act gives only the Right to the detenue to make a representation, but it does not state that such Right can extend to a Right to be heard orally and to lead evidence in rebuttal of the grounds of detention. Therefore, as argued by the petitioner's counsel, the provision of the impugned Act granting only the Right to the detenue to make a representation does not conform to an orderly procedure required by the Rules of Natural Justice.

51. But since the Constitution has not made any provision for the detenue to be heard orally, it would not be proper to read into Article 22(5) any such Right of the detenue.

52. Even Article 22(5) of the Constitution does not mandate that the detenu's representation against detention must be heard by an independent Tribunal.

53. Even a Right to judicial trial is not an absolute Right as held by the Supreme Court of United States of America. In a case before the Court, a Chinese who was a citizen of USA, was denied entry into the United States under an Exclusion Law passed by the U.S. Congress. The Supreme Court of the United States of America held that even though the Chinese is an American citizen and the Fifth Amendment applied to him, denial of the liberty to him to enter the United States did not require judicial trial and the decision of the Executive officer to deny his entry is also due process of law.

54. Even according to the principles of Natural Justice, a Right of being heard orally by a person against an order adverse to him is not mandatory. The House of Lords have decided in the Local Government Board *versus* Arlidge (1915) that the procedure of every Tribunal regarding oral hearing may not be the same.

55. As Article 22(6) prohibits even disclosure of facts which the Authority issuing the order of detention considers it against the public interest to disclose, the detenue cannot have the Right to lead evidence to contest the grounds of detention.

56. The provisions of the impugned Act, which excludes the Right of a detenue to appear either personally or through a lawyer before an Advisory Board is also constitutionally valid.

57. Article 22(7)(c) also gives power to the Parliament to enact a law relating to procedure of inquiry by the Advisory Board. Therefore, it cannot be argued that any law providing for Preventive Detention must provide for Right of a detenue to be heard orally. If Parliament enacts a law to provide Right of personal hearing to a detenue before the Advisory Board, such a law would be constitutionally valid because of Article 22(7)(c). But if the Parliament provides in a law only the Right of the detenue to make representation in writing against his detention, such a law cannot be challenged on the ground that it does not grant oral hearing.

58. Section 13(2) of the impugned Act was attacked by the petitioner on the ground that even if an order of detention was revoked, another order of detention could be passed on the same grounds. Section 13(2) is valid as it was inserted to prevent a man from being released if the original order of detention was invalid on some technical ground.

59. The principle of Natural Justice that a detenue must be furnished grounds for detention as soon as possible and shall be afforded the earliest opportunity of making a representation against the detention is incorporated in Article 22(5) of the Constitution. Every law providing for Preventive Detention must conform to this stipulation.

60. The petitioner has challenged Section 14 of the impugned Act as under Section 14, the Court is prevented from being informed of the grounds on the basis of which the order of detention was made.

61. In view of the aforesaid, Chief Justice Hari Lal Kania held that Section 14 of the impugned Act is clearly *ultra vires*. He went on to say that section 14 prevents the Courts from examining whether the grounds for detention are relevant to the order of detention. It must be understood that the Court is to inquire only regarding relevance of the grounds to the order of detention and not to the sufficiency of the grounds. In view of Section 14 of the impugned Act, the Court is prevented from doing it with the result that a Detaining Authority competent to detain a person can give to the detenue a piece of paper on which there are "written three stanzas of a poem or three alphabets written in three different ways" and the Court cannot strike down the order of detention for the total irrelevance of the grounds.

62. However, Section 14 can be severed from the Preventive Detention Act so that the impugned Act would be perfectly valid.

63. In view of the aforesaid, Chief Justice Harilal Kania held that there was no ground to interfere with the order of detention of A.K. Gopalan and the Preventive Detention Act 1950 without Section 14 is perfectly valid.

64. Justice Fazl Ali delivered a separate judgment. At the outset, he held that whether the order of detention of A.K. Gopalan was legal or not is a pure question of law and can be decided without referring to the long chain of facts in the petition. These facts have a direct bearing on the alleged *mala fides* of the Detaining Authority; but are not strictly relevant to decide whether the detention was *ultra vires*.

65. Counsel for the petitioner has argued that the detention has deprived A.K. Gopalan the Right to move freely throughout the territory of India guaranteed under Article 19(1)(d).

66. As held by Blackstone, freedom of movement is the essence of personal liberty. As a general proposition, this contention is well-founded in law.

67. Blackstone's views on personal liberty have never been challenged. It has been bodily incorporated by H.J. Stephen in his "Commentaries on the Laws of England". It has also been reproduced by Cooley, the American Jurist, in his well-known treatise "Constitutional Limitations".

68. The question whether Preventive Detention is an infringement of the Right to move freely throughout the territory of India has been considered by the Nagpur, Patna and Calcutta High Courts. The view adopted by these High Courts is that Preventive Detention is not a violation of the aforesaid Right.

69. Article 19(5) stipulates that nothing in Article 19(1)(d) shall affect the operation of any law imposing reasonable restriction on the Right of freedom of movement either in the interest of the general public or for the protection of the interests of any Scheduled Tribe.

70. The formulation of Article 19(1)(d) is very wide and means that a person can go at his will in any direction to any locality and upto any distance. Restraint on a freedom so wide in scope and extent may assume a variety of forms and may include internment or externment of a person, his confinement in a particular locality or within walls of a prison, his being prevented from visiting or staying in a particular area.

71. A reference to the Fifth Schedule of the Constitution and the corresponding provision of the Government of India Act 1935 as well as to certain laws made for Chota Nagpur, Santhal Parganas and other localities will show that great importance has been attached to protection and preservation of the Scheduled Tribes.

72. During the British Rule, Ordinance XIV of 1943 also provided for detention in custody of any person, who was likely to act in a manner prejudicial to public safety, the Defence of British India, the maintenance of public order, His Majesty's relation with foreign powers or Indian native States, the maintenance of peaceful conditions in tribal areas, or the efficient prosecution of the war. Thus, the concept of Preventive Detention is not new to the Indian sub-continent.

73. An argument has been advanced that if deprivation of personal liberty amounts to deprivation of the Right guaranteed under Article 19(1)(d) of the Constitution, any conviction for an offence involving a sentence of imprisonment will be subject to Judicial Review on the ground of reasonableness. Chief Justice Meredith of the Patna High Court has given expression to such apprehension in Rattan Roy *versus* The State of Bihar (AIR 1950 Patna 332) by saying that if provisions of the Penal Code will be subject to Judicial Review on the ground of reasonableness, it will place enormous powers in hands of the Courts.

74. But no Court will interfere with the Indian Penal Code which has been law of the land for about a century and the provisions of which are not in conflict with the basic principles of any system of law.

75. Moreover, the observations of Chief Justice Meredith may not also be correct in law. The Penal Code does not primarily impose restrictions on freedom of movement. Its primary object is to punish crime.

76. The scheme of the Chapter dealing with Fundamental Rights does not contemplate that each Article is a code by itself. It cannot be said that Articles 19 to 22 in the Chapter on Fundamental Rights do not to some extent overlap each other. Preventive Detention, dealt with in Article 22, also amounts to deprivation of personal liberty guaranteed under Article 21 and is also a violation of the Right under Article 19(1)(d) to move freely throughout the territory of India.

77. The expression 'personal liberty' and 'personal freedom' have both a wider and a narrower meaning. In the wider sense, they include not only immunity from arrest and detention but also other freedoms as freedom of speech and freedom of association. In the narrower sense, they mean immunity from arrest and detention.

78. In Halsbury's "Laws of England", the freedoms mentioned are the Right to personal freedom which is the same thing as immunity from detention. The other freedoms in Halsbury's "Laws of England" are the Right to property, the Right to freedom of speech, the Right of public meeting and the Right of association.

79. In the Constitution of the United States of America, Ireland and other countries where freedom is highly prized, Right of movement is not considered as something distinct from

personal liberty. The obvious explanation is that in law, no Right of free movement exists apart from what personal liberty connotes.

80. In the First World War (1914-1919), the British Parliament passed the Defence of the Realm Consolidation Act 1914. Regulation framed under the Act permitted the Secretary of State to subject any person to such obligation and restriction as hereinafter mentioned in view of his hostile origin or association. In Liversidge *versus* Anderson (1942 A.C. 206), Lord Atkin has observed that this Regulation gave the Secretary of State undisputed power to detain a suspected person under a law providing for Preventive Detention.

81. Under the Regulation, one Arthur Zadig, who was interned, moved the Kings' Bench in a writ of *habeas corpus* which was refused. The matter ultimately came before the House of Lords in Rex *versus* Halliday (1917). The House of Lords held that the Regulation was *intra vires* and did not infringe the Habeas Corpus Acts or take away any Right conferred by the Magna Carta (1215).

82. During the Second World War (1939-45), the British Parliament passed the Emergency Powers (Defence) Act 1939 under which a specified Regulation dealt with orders of detention.

83. Preventive Detention not only takes away the Right to move freely throughout the territory of India but also other Fundamental Rights in Article 19(1) except the Right to acquire hold and dispose of property [**N.B.:** It may be noted that the judgment of Justice Fazl Ali was delivered in the year 1950 much before Article 19(1)(f) containing the Right to acquire, hold and dispose of property was amended by the Constitution (Forty-Fourth Amendment) Act 1978 which came into effect from 20.06.1979.]

84. Whereas Preventive Detention operates on freedom of movement directly, its operation on the other Rights is indirect, consequential and notional.

85. The Attorney-General has argued that "law" in Article 21 means law enacted by the legislature. Counsel for the petitioner has, however, contested the stand of the Attorney-General and has argued that procedure established by law has been used in a much wider sense and approximates in meaning to the expression due process of law as in the U.S. Constitution.

86. The Attorney-General referred to the proceedings of the Constituent Assembly to show that Article 21, as originally drafted, contained the phrase, without due process of law but subsequently, the Constituent Assembly preferred the expression, except according to procedure established by law.

87. Debates in the Constituent Assembly may not be relevant to interpret the expression, procedure established by law; but the debates are relevant to show that the framers of the Constitution wanted to avoid the expression, "due process of law" in Article 21 of the Constitution.

88. In the beginning, the U.S. Supreme Court interpreted, due process of law, to cover matters of procedure only; but gradually the meaning of the expression was widened to cover substantive law also.

89. Our Constituent Assembly did not adopt the expression, "due process of law", on account of the very elastic meaning given to it; but preferred the expression, "procedure established by law", which occurs in the Japanese Constitution of 1946.

90. When the Japanese Constitution was being framed, instead of the Japanese Cabinet, General McArthur, the Supreme Commander of the Allied Forces in the Far East, played a dominant role.

91. Carl Brent Swisher has written in his book, *The Growth of Constitutional Power in the United States* that in USA, the expression, due process of Law, was understood for about a century as a restriction on procedure by which the Government exercised its power. During the second period – which extended through 1936 – due process of law, was understood not only as procedural due process but also was interpreted as a restriction on the substance of the activities in which the Government might engage. During the third period after 1936, the use of the expression, due process of law, as a substantive restriction has been largely suspended or abandoned, leaving it as a restriction on procedure only.

92. Against the background of dominant American influence, procedure established by law in the Japanese Constitution meant procedural due process.

93. The question to be decided is whether "law" means nothing more than statute law. In India, though it is not mandatory to adopt the construction put on the word "law" or due process of law by the U.S. Supreme Court, it is not correct to completely ignore the opinions of American Jurists in this regard. In the circumstances, it would be useful to refer to some of their decisions.

94. The U.S. Supreme Court has held as follows:

Although the legislature may at its pleasure provide new remedies or change old ones, the power is nevertheless subject to the condition that it cannot remove certain ancient landmarks, or take away certain Fundamental Rights which have been always recognized and observed in judicial procedures.

95. In another decision of the same Court, it was held that:

By the law of the land is most clearly intended the general law: a law which hears before it condemns, which proceeds upon inquiry and renders judgments only after trial.

96. It is clear that for the U.S. Supreme Court, "law" does not mean merely law enacted by the State. The word "law" does not exclude certain fundamental principles of justice which inhere in every civilized system of law and which are at the root of it.

97. Professor Willis has stated that the principles underlying the due process clause may assume different forms in different circumstances; but so long as they are conceded in principle, the requirement of law will be fulfilled. For example, a person cannot require any particular form or method of hearing, but all that he can require is a reasonable opportunity to be heard.

98. Similarly, an impartial Tribunal does not necessarily mean a judicial Tribunal. The real point is that the essentials of due process are really different aspects of the same Right, viz., the Right to be heard before one is condemned.

99. In regard to the Right to be heard before one is condemned, judicial opinion in England appears to be the same as that in USA. In England, it would shock one to be told that a man can be deprived of his personal liberty without a fair trial. Such a case can happen only if the British Parliament expressly takes away the Right in an Emergency as the Parliament did during the last two world wars.

100. The fundamental principle that a person, whose Right is affected must be heard has been observed not only in cases involving personal liberty but also in proceedings affecting other Rights. Cooper *versus* the Wandsworth Board of Works (1863) was a case under a law, which empowered the District Board to demolish a house where the builder had neglected to give notice of his intention to build seven days before proceeding to dig the foundation for the house. As the builder had not given the requisite notice, the District Board directed demolition of the building without giving the builder a notice to show cause. It was held that the District Board's action to demolish the building without notice was illegal even though the law did not specifically provide that the builder would be served a show-cause notice before demolition. It was held that justice of the common law that a party must be heard before any adverse action is taken against him would supply the omission of the legislature in not providing in the law that the delinquent builder would be heard before the building was demolished.

101. In Russell *versus* Russell (1881), George Jessel also said that persons other than Judges, who have judicial functions to perform, are bound by the maxim, "*audi alteram partem*". The maxim "*audi alteram partem*" (the Right of being heard) is not only confined to the conduct of strictly judicial Tribunals but is applicable to every Tribunal or body of persons invested with the authority to adjudicate upon matters involving civil consequences to individuals.

102. In Local Government Board *versus* Arlidge (1915), The House of Lords laid down the following principles:

(i) When a duty of deciding an appeal is imposed, those whose duty it is to decide must act judicially;

(ii) They must deal with the question referred to them without bias;

(iii) They must give to each of the parties an opportunity of presenting their case;

(iv) The decision of the Tribunal must be of a body, whose duty it is to do justice.

103. Even executive authorities and administrative Tribunals cannot pass an order affecting a person's Rights without giving a hearing to the person whose Rights have been adversely affected.

104. Lord Halsbury has said that in England, the Right of the subject to have any case affecting him tried in accordance with the principles of Natural Justice is well established.

105. The principle that no person shall be condemned without a hearing by an impartial Tribunal is not only deeply rooted in India's ancient history but is also the basis of trial of offences and preventive and quasi-administrative measures as contemplated under sections 107, 108, 109 and 110 of the Code of Criminal Procedure 1973. Therefore, in

India the Right of being heard in a fair manner is a part of the procedure established by law.

106. "Law" in Article 21 of the Constitution does not mean only law enacted by the legislature.

107. In a number of judgments of the higher judiciary, it has been held that though there may not be any specific provision in a statute for prior notice to the affected party, the provision for issue of a prior notice to parties must be read into it.

108. In the course of arguments, counsel for the petitioner, repeatedly asked whether the Constitution would permit a law being enacted abolishing the mode of trial permitted by the existing law and establishing the procedure of trial by battle which were in vogue in olden times in England.

109. The question posed by the counsel is something which is not likely to happen; but it does raise a legal problem.

110. To sum up, in Article 21 of the Constitution, the expression procedure established by law, means valid "law" and procedure means certain well-recognized and definite rules of procedure and not something which is a mere pretence of procedure.

111. Article 22 of the Constitution, which deals with Preventive Detention, does not exclude the operation of Article 19 or Article 21. Article 19 and Article 21 are also to be read subject to Article 22. The correct position is that Article 22 must prevail in so far as there are specific provisions therein regarding Preventive Detention but where there are no such provisions in Article 22, the operations of Article 19 and Article 21 cannot be excluded.

112. It was argued that Article 22 is a code by itself and the law of Preventive Detention was to be enacted within its four corners. This is not entirely correct as Article 22 provides for some matter of procedure but it does not exhaustively provide for all of them.

113. First, the Right to represent against the order of detention has been given to the detenue but it has been left to the legislature to provide the machinery to deal with the representation. Secondly, an Advisory Board has been provided for but such a Board can only act as a safeguard if the detention is beyond a period of three months. A close scrutiny of Article 22 indicates that ample latitude has been left to the Parliament and ample scope is there for Judicial Review to decide whether the law has transgressed the limits of reasonableness stipulated in Article19(5) of the Constitution.

114. Counsel for the petitioner has argued that section 3 of the impugned Act is unreasonable as it leaves the matter of detention of a person to the subjective satisfaction of the Detaining Authority. This argument is not sound as subjective satisfaction underlies the preventive measures even in the Code of Criminal Procedure of our country.

115. Section 10 of the impugned Act which provides that the Advisory Board shall make its Report within the stipulated period of three months is in conformity with Article 22(4) (a) of the Constitution.

116. Section 12 and Section 14 of the Preventive Detention Act are, however, *ultra vires*. Even if it is held that section 12 of the Act technically complies with the requirement of Article

22(7)(a), Parliament has acted unreasonably in exercising its discretionary power without applying its mind to essential matters and thus depriving a detenue of the safeguard of an Advisory Board.

117. All brother Judges in the Bench have declared Section 14 of the impugned Act as *ultra vires*. [**N.B.:** Since Justice Fazl Ali has agreed with his brother Judges, he did not repeat their arguments as to why Section 14 was *ultra vires*].

118. Section 12 of the impugned Act goes to the very root of the legislation in as much as it deprives a detenue of an essential safeguard viz. opinion of an Advisory Board. Therefore, the petitioner is entitled to a writ of *habeas corpus* on the ground that an essential provision of a law providing for Preventive Detention has not been complied with.

119. In our country, the impugned Act is a peacetime measure whereas in England, similar law was enacted only during the duration of the First World War (1914-19) and the Second World War (1939-45).

120. Two important cases in England which dealt with the war power of Preventive Detention are

(i) Rex *versus* Halliday (1917 A.C. 260)

(ii) Liversidge *versus* Anderson (1942 A.C. 206)

121. In Rex *versus* Halliday (1917), Lord Atkin held as follows:

"However, precious personal liberty of the subject may be, there is something for which it may well be to some extent, sacrificed by legal enactment, namely national success in war or escape from national plunder or enslavement."

122. There is a good substratum of sound law in the celebrated dictum of Lord Atkin in Liversidge *versus* Anderson (1942) that even amidst the clash of arms, the laws are not silent and that they speak the same language in war or in peace.

123. In the Regulations framed in England for Preventive Detention during the First World War (1914-19) and the Second World War (1939-45), there were elaborate provisions for Advisory Boards. This was a safeguard against improper detention of persons.

124. No great harm was likely to have been caused by setting up a machinery composed of either administrative or judicial authorities for examining the cases of detenues so as to satisfy the essentials of fairness and justice.

125. In U.K. and USA and many other countries, in certain matters, individual freedom is yielding to social control. Those who run the state have onerous responsibilities and it is not correct to say that in India emergency conditions have altogether disappeared.

126. Justice Patanjali Sastri delivered a separate judgment upholding the order of detention.

127. At the outset, Justice Patanjali Sastri said that it was the first case before the Supreme Court, where the petitioner has invoked protection of the Court as the guardian of the Fundamental Rights.

128. The petitioner had been under detention previously on the basis of orders by the Government of Madras under the Madras Maintenance of Public Order Act 1947. But as the Madras Act had been quashed by the Madras High Court, Parliament enacted a comprehensive Preventive Detention Act 1950 for the whole country. The impugned Act came into force on 25 February 1950. Immediately thereafter on 27 February 1950, the Government of Madras passed the order of detention of A.K. Gopalan.

129. Counsel for A.K. Gopalan has contended that the impugned Act takes away or abridges the Fundamental Rights in contravention of Article 13(2) of the Constitution and therefore is void.

130. The chapter on Fundamental Rights in the Indian Constitution is on the pattern of the Bill of Rights contained in the first ten amendments of the U.S. Constitution.

131. Article 12 of the Indian Constitution is the first Article in the chapter on Fundamental Rights. Article 12 defines the "State" as including the Government and the Parliament of India and the Government and the legislature of each of the state of the Indian Union and all local and other authorities within the territory of India or under control of the Government of India. [**N.B.**: The Supreme Court has expanded the definition of "state" in Article 12 to include public sector corporations and statutory bodies, who can issue directions which are binding on third parties. The expression, 'state' includes agency or instrumentality of the Government. The State Financial Corporations, the State Electricity Boards, the Indian Council of Agricultural Research and the Indian Standards Institute, which are societies under the Societies Registration Act 1860 and the Steel Authority of India, a Government company under the Companies Act 1956, have been held to be State within the meaning of Article 12 of the Constitution. The leading judgments of the Supreme Court in this regard are Ajay Hasia *versus* Khalid Mujib (AIR 1981 SC 487) and R.D. Shetty *versus* International Airport Authority (AIR 1979 SC 1628).]

132. Counsel for the petitioner, has advanced three main arguments which are as follows:

(i) The Right to move freely throughout the territory of India is the very essence of personal liberty. Detention of the petitioner was not a reasonable restriction which the Parliament could validly impose either in the interest of the general public or in interest of the Scheduled Tribes as stipulated in Article 19(5) of the Constitution.

(ii) Alternatively, the petitioner has a Fundamental Right under Article 21 not to be deprived of his personal liberty except according to procedure established by law. The impugned Act authorized detention otherwise than in accordance with proper procedure.

(iii) Finally, the impugned Act is *ultra vires* as the Parliament has overstepped the limitations on its legislative power.

133. The first argument leads to the question whether Article 19(1)(d) and Article 19(5) are applicable in the present case. A conjoint reading of Article 19(1)(d) i.e. freedom of movement throughout the territory of India, Article 19(1)(e) i.e. to reside and settle in any part of the territory of India and Article 19(5) (i.e. reasonable restrictions on these Rights in the interest of the general public or for protection of the interests of any Scheduled Tribe) make it clear that the Right guaranteed in Article 19(1)(d) and 19(1)(e) can be enjoyed by a citizen, who is enjoying personal freedom and has not lost it due to imprisonment.

134. A person imprisoned under any law, is not within the purview of Article 19 at all but is dealt with by Article 20, Article 21 and Article 22 of the Constitution. Briefly stated, Article 19 guarantees to all citizens certain civil liberties while they are not imprisoned under any law.

135. Counsel for the petitioner, has drawn a distinction between the Right of freedom of movement guaranteed by Article 19(1)(d) and Rights guaranteed by other sub-clauses in Article 19(1). Referring to Blackstone, the counsel has argued that personal liberty consists in moving one's person to whatever place one's inclination might direct.

136. The above argument has no substance as the Rights in Article 19(1) are equally essential elements of the liberty of the individual in any democratic society and imprisonment under any law operated as an extinction of all of them.

137. It was argued by the Counsel for the petitioner that Preventive Detention being a drastic restriction of the Right to move freely was in pith and substance within Article 19(1)(d) read with clause (5) of Article 19 and not within Article 21 which deals with offence, its punishment and prevention.

138. There is no room for the application of the rule of pith and substance in this case. The Privy Council has said that the rule of pith and substance was evolved to decide whether an impugned statute was in its true character, legislation with respect to matters within the jurisdiction of one legislature or another legislature in a federal constitution with divided legislative power. No such question arises in this case and hence the pith and substance rule is wholly irrelevant.

139. Debates in the Constituent Assembly also show that framers of the Constitution substituted the word "liberty" with "personal liberty" in Article 21. During the debates in the Constituent Assembly, it was pointed out by some Members that the word "liberty" was likely to be construed very widely so as to include the freedoms contained in Article 19 and hence the word personal should be put before the word liberty so that it would be clear that the personal liberty in Article 21 excludes the freedoms guaranteed in Article 19. Hence personal liberty in Article 21 is something distinct from the freedom to move freely in the territory of India guaranteed in Article 19(1)(d).

140. It was also argued that Article 19 declared the substantive Rights of personal liberty while Article 21 contained the procedural safeguards against their deprivation. This argument has found favour with some judges of High Courts.

141. The above argument establishing correlation between Article 19 and Article 21 does not take note that Article 19 is guaranteed to citizens only whereas Article 21 guarantees protection of life and personal liberty to all – citizens and non-citizens alike. Thus, the two Articles, Article 19 and Article 21 do not operate in a coterminous field and this is an important reason for rejecting the correlation between Article 19 and Article 21.

142. If Article 21 is understood to provide only procedural safeguards, where is the substantive Right to personal liberty of non-citizens to be found in the Constitution? If non-citizens have no Right of personal liberty, why is the procedural safeguard of Article 21 extended to them? Where is the Right to life provided in the Constitution? The Right to life – though the most fundamental of all – is one of the most difficult to define. The protection of the

Right to life generally takes form of a declaration that no person shall be deprived of it save by authority of law. The truth is that Article 21 – like its prototype in the Fifth and the Fourteenth Amendments to the Constitution of the United States of America – presents an example of the fusion of procedural and substantive Right to life.

143. Counsel for the petitioner, has argued that "law" in Article 21 should be understood not in sense of an enactment but as signifying the immutable and universal principles of Natural Justice – the *jus naturale* of the civil law – and procedure established by law, meant the same thing as due process of law in the Constitution of the United States of America.

144. Numerous decisions of the U.S. Supreme Court were cited to show that the expression, due process of law has the following basic requirements:

(i) an objective and ascertainable standard of conduct to which it is possible to conform;
(ii) notice to the party of the accusations against him;
(iii) a reasonable opportunity to the accused to establish his innocence; and
(iv) an impartial Tribunal capable of an unbiased judgment.

145. Under the Indian Constitution, certain Fundamental Rights have been made paramount. They have been, as it were, retained by the people of India when they delegated powers to three different organs of the state.

146. The language in the provisions of a Constitution should not be stretched to square with any constitutional theory. The cardinal rule of interpretation of any enactment is that its meaning should be gathered primarily from the natural meaning of the words used.

147. The term "law" in Article 21 of the Constitution does not mean the immutable and universal principles of Natural Justice. Procedure established by law in Article 21, must be taken to refer to a procedure with a statutory origin. In other words, procedure established by law in Article 21 means procedure established by state-made law or enacted law.

148. The due process clause in U.S. Constitution has an evolutionary history. Edward Coke identified due process of law with law of the land. Even in England, where supremacy of the Parliament has been fully established, Edward Coke meant by due process of law an inherent limitation on all legislation and ruled that the common law will control laws enacted by the Parliament. Though the doctrine of due process was later discarded in England as being a warning rather than an authority to be followed, the due process clause gained ground in the United States of America at first as a weapon in hands of the Revolutionists to resist the laws of the Congress. Later, it was an instrument in hands of the Judges for establishing supremacy of the Judiciary.

149. By giving Liberty and Property their widest meaning, the U.S. Supreme Court has made the due process clause a general restriction on all legislative power. And when the wide interpretation of the expression due process of law gave rise to certain problems, the U.S. Supreme Court formulated the equally vague and expansive doctrine of police power i.e. the power of Government to regulate private Rights in the public interest.

150. In the year 1877 – nearly a century after the phrase due process of law had been subject of judicial interpretation – a Judge of the U.S. Supreme Court held that due process of law was incapable of precise definition and its application could only be ascertained by the gradual process of inclusion and exclusion. Recently, a judge of the U.S. Supreme Court referred to the difficulty of giving definiteness to the vague contours of due process and of judging state action on the basis of such a gossamer concept.

151. Against this background, the Drafting Committee of the Constituent Assembly recommended that due process of law be substituted by the more precise expression, procedure established by law, which occurs in the Japanese Constitution of 1946.

152. The Attorney-General has argued that the procedure established by law in Article 21 means a procedure prescribed by law framed by a competent legislature, however, novel and ineffective the law might be to afford the accused person a fair opportunity for defending himself. The Attorney-General has also argued that the Constituent Assembly definitely rejected the doctrine of judicial supremacy, when it discarded the phrase, "due process of law". Thus, according to the Attorney-General, as long as some procedure is prescribed by law, the *vires* of the procedure in the law is beyond Judicial Review.

153. The Attorney-General also drew attention to speeches of Members of the Constituent Assembly for explaining the historical background of the expression, procedure established by law. But a speech made in course of debate in a Bill could at best be indicative of the subjective intent of the speaker; but it could not reflect the inarticulate mental process lying behind the majority vote which carried the Bill.

154. The arguments of the Attorney-General completely stultify Article 13(2) of the Constitution and the very concept of a Fundamental Right. It is the essence of any Fundamental Right that it is protected against infringement by the ordinary law.

155. It is not correct to say that the Indian Constitution has adopted the doctrine of Parliamentary Supremacy. On the other hand, the Constitution has accepted the view on Fundamental Rights of the U.S. Supreme Court.

156. It has also been argued that Article 31 has provided that no person shall be deprived of his property save by the authority of law and "law" in Article 31 meant enacted law. It was argued that if a person's property could be taken away by enacted law, his Right to life and personal liberty need not enjoy greater immunity. But this argument is misleading as Clause (2) of Article 31 of our Constitution provided for payment of compensation.

157. Even in U.K., the struggle between royal prerogative and the law has long since ended in favour of the law. Lord Atkin has said that in British Jurisprudence, no member of the Executive can interfere with liberty or property of a British subject except when he can support its legality before a Court of Law.

158. In view of the rival contentious, a satisfactory via media could be that, the procedure established by law in Article 21 could mean what the Privy Council had referred to in King Emperor *versus* Benoari Lal Sharma (AIR 1945 PC 48) as ordinary and well-established Code of Criminal Procedure. Even though the Code of Criminal Procedure provides for different procedures for different classes of cases, certain basic principles emerge as the factor common to these procedures. They form the core of the procedure established by law.

159. But even if the core of the procedure established by law is followed, the guarantee of life and personal liberty in Article 21 may not be immune from judicial interference if the core of the procedure of ordinary criminal law is changed by law enacted by a competent legislature.

160. To illustrate, if Article 22 was not in the Constitution, and the Parliament passed a law taking away the Right of an accused to be defended by a legal practitioner of his choice, according to counsel of the petitioner, the law passed by Parliament would be void as being contrary to immutable principles of Natural Justice embodied in Article 21. But as per the Attorney-General, such a law would be perfectly valid.

161. The correct view is that the Act of the Parliament would be valid if the denial to be defended by a legal practitioner of choice of the accused is made valid by the Parliament making it a normal feature of ordinary criminal law by amending the Code of Criminal Procedure. But in a democratic Republic as India such a drastic change in the normal law of criminal procedure would be difficult.

162. The Attorney-General has argued that protection under Article 21 is not available to a person detained under any law of Preventive Detention as clauses (4) to (7) of Article 22 provided a complete code of safeguards in respect of Preventive Detention.

163. The argument of the Attorney-General is not sound. If the framers of the Constitution would have wanted to deny the safeguard of Article 21 to a person detained under any law providing for Preventive Detention, they could have done so explicitly by incorporating a provision in Article 22 that protection of Article 21 will not be available to a detenue. There is also nothing in the language of clauses (4) to (7) of Article 22 to indicate that Article 21 is inapplicable to cases of Preventive Detention.

164. Clauses (4) to (7) of Article 22 only deal with certain aspects of Preventive Detention as

(i) duration of Preventive Detention;
(ii) constitution of an Advisory Board;
(iii) communication of the grounds of detention to the detenue;
(iv) provision for an opportunity to the detenue of making a representation against the order of detention.

165. It cannot be said that these provisions constitute an exhaustive code dealing with all matters relating to Preventive Detention.

166. Does the impugned Preventive Detention Act take away any of the Rights conferred by Articles 21 and 22 or infringe the protection afforded thereby? It has to be remembered that in India, Preventive Detention has a constitutional status. The provision for Preventive Detention is designed to prevent some grave abuse of freedom by anti-social and subversive elements. Clauses (4) to (7) of Article 22 might have to be viewed in this perspective so that these provisions can be harmonized with provision of Article 21.

167. Counsel for the petitioner, mentioned four essentials of the due process of law, which are as follows:

(i) an objective standard of conduct to which it is possible to conform;

(ii) notice to the party of the accusations against him;

(iii) a reasonable opportunity to the accused to establish his innocence; and

(iv) an impartial Tribunal capable of delivering an unbiased judgment.

168. These four essentials of the due process of law are part of the established procedures under the Code of Criminal Procedure in India. They are, however, not immutable and are not beyond legislative change.

169. Article 22 of the Constitution provides for notice to the detenue of the accusations against him and also the earliest opportunity to establish his innocence by making a representation to the Authority, who passed the detention order. Thus Article 22 conforms to one of the four essential elements of due process of law.

170. As argued by Counsel for the petitioner, an important requirement of an impartial Tribunal has not been provided for in Article 22. A Tribunal, which could give an unbiased judgment on justification for Preventive Detention, is a part of the protection afforded by Article 21. Therefore, the counsel has argued that the impugned Act, which did not provide for an impartial Tribunal contravened essential safeguards of personal liberty under Article 21.

171. The aforesaid argument is without merit as the Advisory Board has to pronounce upon the justification of the detention.

172. It is difficult to conceive how the Advisory Board could judge whether a person could be detained for more than three months without at the same time considering whether at the first instance there was sufficient grounds for his detention. Therefore, the Advisory Board is the prescribed impartial machinery for reviewing cases of Preventive Detention.

173. In view of the aforesaid, the petitioner has no Right of his representation against detention to be considered by any other impartial Tribunal.

174. Counsel for the petitioner pointed out that a law providing for Preventive Detention could authorize detention of a person for three months without providing for review by an Advisory Board and for a longer period beyond three months if Parliament passed a Preventive Detention Act as contemplated in sub-clause (a) of clause (7) of Article 22.

175. It can be said in reply that however deplorable such a result might be from the point of view of the person detained, there could be no remedy as the Constitution of India affords no higher protection for personal liberty.

176. It was also argued by counsel for the petitioner that Section 3 of the impugned Preventive Detention Act cannot be said to be a procedure established by law. It is so because section 3 prescribes no objective and ascertainable standard of conduct to which it will be possible to conform.

177. This argument of the counsel proceeds on the assumption that the procedure established by law is equivalent to the due process of law. This assumption is not correct.

178. Under the impugned Act, detention is ordered to prevent the person concerned from acting prejudicially in relation to certain matters. It would not be practicable to either indicate or enumerate in advance which acts or classes of acts would be regarded as prejudicial. The responsibility for security of the State and the maintenance of public order having

been entrusted to the Government, it must be left to that Government to exercise the power of Preventive Detention. Hence, Section 3 of the impugned Act is *intra vires*.

179. During the hearing, section 12 of the impugned Act came in for a good deal of criticism. Section 12, stipulates that any person detained in any of the following classes of cases or under any of the following circumstances may be detained, without obtaining opinion of the Advisory Board for a period longer than three months.

180. The following classes of cases and the following circumstances under Section 12 of the impugned Act have been enumerated:

(i) Defence of India;
(ii) Relations of India with foreign powers;
(iii) Security of the state;
(iv) Maintenance of public order.

181. Section 12(2) also provided for review of the order of detention within a period of six months by the Central Government or the State Government, as the case may be.

182. It was argued that clause (4) of Article 22 provided for ordinary cases of Preventive Detention where the detention of a person could not continue beyond a period of three months without opinion of the Advisory Board whereas clause (7) of Article 22 covered special cases of Preventive Detention for more than three months without the opinion of the Advisory Board. In view of the aforesaid, Section 12 of the impugned Act which only enumerates legislative items in Entry 9 of the Union List and Entry 3 of the concurrent list (except the entry relating to services and supplies essential to the community) hardly affords any guidance to the Detaining Authority regarding the class or classes of cases or the circumstances in which aggravated forms of prejudicial activities necessitate detention of a person beyond a period of three months without opinion of the Advisory Board.

183. The aforesaid argument is not sound as clause (7) of Article 22 deals with Preventive Detention which as Lord Atkin has observed in Rex *versus* Halliday (1917) must necessarily proceed in all cases to some extent, on suspicion as distinct from proof.

184. It would be difficult to mention the various circumstances, or to enumerate, except in broad outline, the various classes of cases exhaustively in which a person could be detained for more than three months.

185. In Rule 34 of the Defence of India Rules framed under the Defence of India Act 1939, "prejudicial acts" were mentioned by enumeration. Even in the Defence of India Rules, there was a sweeping residuary clause as acts likely to prejudice the efficient prosecution of war, the defence of British India or the public safety or interest.

186. In Section 12 of the impugned Act, five out of six matters or legislative items mentioned in the Union List and the Concurrent List have been incorporated as being the class or classes of cases or circumstances in which a longer period of detention beyond three months without opinion of the Advisory Board, is authorized. Section 12, therefore, enumerates a broad classification of cases or broad description of circumstances, where Parliament has provided in the law of Preventive Detention for detention upto the maximum period of one year without opinion of the Advisory Board. Therefore, Section 12 is not violative of clause (7) of Article 22 of the Constitution.

187. Section 14 of the impugned Act prohibits the disclosure of grounds of detention if such disclosure is against the public interest. It also prohibits disclosure of representation made by the detenue against the order of detention.

188. Counsel for the petitioner has argued that Section 14 of the impugned Act is violative of clause (5) of Article 22, which entitles the detenue to be communicated the grounds of detention to enable him to represent against the order. If the grounds for detention are too vague or if they are altogether irrelevant to his detention, or are such as to show that the order of detention was not *bona fide*, the detenue has the Right to move the Supreme Court under Article 32 of the Constitution to strike down the order of detention.

189. There is considerable force in this argument of the counsel for the petitioner.

190. There is not much force in the argument of the Attorney-General as the Federal Court had held that the Court could scrutinize the grounds of detention not to decide regarding their sufficiency but to examine their relevance to the order of detention. Section 14 of the impugned Act makes it impossible for the Court to examine the grounds of detention even for the limited purpose of their relevance to the order of detention. Therefore, Section 14 is violative of Article 13(2) of the Constitution and hence void. This, however, does not affect other provisions of the impugned Preventive Detention Act as without Section 14, the Act is *intra vires*.

191. As the petitioner did not disclose the grounds of detention to the Supreme Court, pending the decision of the Court on Section 14, the petitioner is now free to seek his remedy by disclosing to the Court the grounds of detention to enable the Court to decide whether they were relevant for the order of detention.

192. In the result, the writ petition of A.K. Gopalan fails and is dismissed.

193. Justice M.C. Mahajan delivered a separate judgment. He agreed with Justice Fazl Ali, and held both Section 12 and Section 14 of the impugned Act *ultra vires* and the detention of A.K. Gopalan illegal.

194. Justice M.C. Mahajan said that this is the first case in which the Supreme Court has been called upon to determine how far the Constitution has secured personal liberty to the citizens of the country.

195. The salient points of the judgment of Justice M.C. Mahajan are as follows: On 20 March 1950, A.K. Gopalan filed a petition under Article 32 of the Constitution praying for a writ of *habeas corpus* directing the State of Madras to set him at liberty as the impugned Preventive Detention Act infringed his Fundamental Rights.

196. Two points arise for consideration in deciding whether the impugned Act takes away or abridges the Fundamental Rights. These points are as follows:

(i) In what measure has the Constitution secured personal liberty to a citizen of India?

(ii) Has the impugned Act taken away or abridged the Fundamental Rights and if so, to what extent?

197. It is difficult on the basis of any general principle to limit the omnipotence of the sovereign legislative power by judicial pronouncements except in so far as the words of the Constitution expressly confer such power on the Court. An act of a competent legislature cannot be declared as void by the Court on the ground that it is opposed to the spirit of the Constitution.

198. Preventive Detention laws are repugnant to a democratic Constitution. They do not exist in peace time in any democratic country.

199. The Government of India Act 1935 conferred authority on the Central and provincial legislatures to enact laws providing for Preventive Detention and since then Preventive Detention laws have come to stay in India even in normal times.

200. The Constitution has also provided for some safeguards against Preventive Detention in Article 22. These safeguards are as follows:

(i) No law of Preventive Detention can provide for detention for a period beyond three months unless such detention is confirmed by an Advisory Board.

(ii) A law of Preventive Detention of a state legislature cannot authorize detention beyond the maximum period of detention prescribed by the Parliament.

(iii) Parliament also cannot enact a law authorizing detention of a person beyond three months without obtaining opinion of the Advisory Board.

(iv) Parliament also has to provide in the law of Preventive Detention the maximum period for which a person can be detained and the procedure to be followed by the Advisory Board for making an inquiry into justification for the detention. This is a safeguard against any arbitrary procedure.

201. Clause (5) of Article 22 also provides procedural safeguard to the detenu who has a Right to be informed of the grounds of detention and also a Right to submit a representation to the Detaining Authority.

202. No impartial machinery has, however, been provided to deal with the representation of a detenue. Consideration of representation of the detenue by an unbiased authority is a necessary consequence of the Right guaranteed to the detenue in clause (5) of Article 22 of the Constitution.

203. The Preamble of the Indian Constitution contains a solemn promise that the Constitution will secure, *inter alia*, justice. If the Right to submit a representation against the order of detention is a guaranteed Right to secure justice, no justice can be secured to the detenue unless an unbiased person considers merits of the representation. In a way, that would make the prosecutor in a case a judge in the same case. Admittedly, such procedure is repugnant to all notions of justice.

204. The Constitution has further curtailed the Right conferred on the detenue in Clause (5) of Article 22 (the Right to be communicated the grounds of detention and the Right to submit a representation to the Detaining Authority against the order of detention) by providing in clause (6) of Article 22 power of the Detaining Authority of withholding facts which the Authority considers against the public interest to disclose.

205. The Attorney-General, has argued that Article 22 – read with Entry 9 in the Union List and Entry 3 in the Concurrent List of the Seventh Schedule – provides a complete code on the subject of Preventive Detention and that being so, other Fundamental Rights need not be invoked for consideration of validity of the impugned Preventive Detention Act. If the provisions in Article 22 have dealt with all questions that are likely to arise on matters of procedure or on question of reasonableness of the period of detention, the inference of such an indication would be irresistible. Ordinarily, when a subject is expressly dealt with in a Constitution in some detail, it has to be assumed that the intention was to exclude application of the general provisions contained in the Constitution elsewhere. The Latin maxim, "*Expressio Unius Est Exclusio Alterius*" means that an express mention of one thing is an exclusion of the other. On examination of the whole scheme, it is evident that the framers of the Constitution intended that Article 22 of the Constitution—containing provisions to safeguard the Right of the detenue – is a complete code on the law of Preventive Detention.

206. There would have been no point in an elaborate procedure in Article 22 if the intention was that a law of Preventive Detention would be subject to provisions of Article 21 of the Constitution.

207. Article 19(5) is both a saving and an enabling provision. It empowers the Parliament to make a law imposing reasonable restrictions on the freedom of movement guaranteed in Article 19(1)(d). Article 22 is another enabling provision empowering the Parliament to enact a law of Preventive Detention.

208. In stating that Article 22 is a self-contained code, it should not be understood that the Drafting Committee while enacting Article 22 in any way overlooked the safeguards in Article 21.

209. Article 21 gives complete immunity against exercise of despotic power by the executive. It negatives the idea of fantastic, arbitrary or fanciful procedure. Therefore, the principles underlying Article 21 have been kept in view while incorporating Article 22 in the Constitution. A law of Preventive Detention properly made under Article 22, which lays down substantive and adjectival law on the subject, would fully satisfy the requirement of Article 21. Hence, there is no conflict between Article 21 and Article 22 of the Constitution.

210. Counsel for the petitioner has contended that clause (3) of the impugned Act, which gives power to order detention of a person, is bad in law as it gives no objective criteria – except the satisfaction of the Detaining Authority.

211. The stand of the counsel is not valid as by its very nature, the subject is such that the Detaining Authority has to exercise judgment *bona fide* to order detention of a person. The state is presumed to have a Government that conducts itself in a reasonable way. It is also presumed that the officers of the state, who have been vested with powers to order detention of a person are reasonable men. In view of the aforesaid, it cannot be said that in making satisfaction of the Detaining Authority as the standard for judging prejudicial acts of any person contravenes Article 22 of the Constitution.

212. The impugned Act gives full effect to Article 22(5) as it provides that the detenue can make a representation to the Detaining Authority against the order of detention. The

impugned Act however, is defective in the sense that it does not provide for an impartial machinery to consider the representation. But absence of such a provision would not make the impugned Act void.

213. Section 9 of the impugned Act provides for an Advisory Board. The procedure to be followed by the Advisory Board is laid down in the impugned Act. It was contended that the impugned Act had not provided for a personal hearing to the detenue before the Advisory Board nor has it provided for a Right to the detenue to lead evidence to establish his innocence. But it must be noted that the impugned Act has given powers to the Advisory Board to call for information it requires from the detenue himself. It has also the powers to examine the material placed before it in the light of facts and arguments in the representation of the detenue. It is admitted that the opportunity to the detenue to defend himself is not as full as a person gets under the normal judicial procedure. But when Article 22 contemplates a special procedure for Preventive Detention, validity of the impugned Act cannot be challenged on the grounds cited by the counsel for the petitioner.

214. Section 11 of the impugned Act was challenged on the ground that it violates the Constitution as it provides for Preventive Detention for an indefinite period. But as the impugned Act itself will cease to have effect with effect from 01 April 1951, the period of detention under the Act can only be till 01 April 1951.

215. Section 12 of the impugned Act has been assailed by counsel of the petitioner rather vehemently. Section 12 stipulates that Preventive Detention, for a period of more than three months but less than a year, can be made to prevent a person from acting in any manner prejudicial to:

(i) defence of India, relations of India with foreign powers or the security of India; or

(ii) the security of a state or maintenance of public order.

(iii) In cases of such detention for a period longer than three months and less than one year, it would not be necessary to obtain opinion of an Advisory Board.

216. Such a stipulation in section 12 goes against the stipulation in clause (7) of Article 22 where the Parliament by law prescribes the circumstances under which and the class or classes of case in which, a person can be detained for a period longer than three months without the opinion of the Advisory Board.

217. Section 12 – while purporting to comply with clause (7) of Article 22 of the Constitution – has actually failed to comply with any of the conditions. The real purpose of clause (7) of Article 22 was to provide for a contingency where requirement of an Advisory Board may defeat the purpose of the law of Preventive Detention. Clause (7) of Article 22 was incorporated to meet abnormal and exceptional cases where even an Advisory Board could not be taken into confidence.

218. It is correct – as the Attorney-General has argued – that "circumstances under which" referred to in clause (7)(a) of Article 22 means some situation extraneous to the detenue's own acts. It may be a situation of tense communal feelings or apprehended internal rebellion or the crisis of an impending war or other similar grave contingencies. These are situations extraneous to a detenue's own acts. In such situations, the machinery of Advisory Board may be dispensed with as it may become cumbersome to meet the grave situation. In view of the aforesaid, section 12 of the impugned Act enumerates no circumstances of grave nature but has only mechanically reproduced the items in Entry 9 of the Union List and Entry 3 of the Concurrent List of the Seventh Schedule of the Constitution (except the item 'supplies and services essential to the community' in the Concurrent List). This shows non-application of mind while drafting Section 12 of the impugned Act.

219. The provisions of Section 12 of the impugned Act also create a very anomalous situation. To illustrate, if a tense situation arises and there is a danger of the Indian railway network being sabotaged – which would adversely affect supplies and services essential to the community – it becomes necessary to pass detention order against certain persons, the procedure of reference to an Advisory Board for detention of such persons beyond a period of three months is mandatory whereas on the other hand, if there is apprehension of disturbance of public order by reason of wrong decision of an umpire in a cricket match or on account of conduct of some persons celebrating the festival of Holi, then by virtue of Section 12, detention beyond a period of three months is legal without reference to an Advisory Board. Such anomalous results would not have been in contemplated framers of the Constitution.

220. "Hurt" is an offence under Section 323 of the Indian Penal Code. "Hurt" has been classified as simple hurt, grievous hurt, grievous hurt with dangerous weapons, grievous hurt to extract a confession, grievous hurt to restrain a public servant from doing his duty, grievous hurt by a rash act and grievous hurt on provocation.

221. Similarly, the Constitution of India has dealt with Preventive Detention – detention for a period of three months in ordinary cases; detention for a period of more than three months with opinion of the Advisory Board in more serious cases and detention for a period beyond three months till the maximum period prescribed by Parliament by law in still more serious cases.

222. The wide construction of clause (7) of Article 22 brings within its ambit all items in Entry 9 and Entry 3 of the Union List and Concurrent List respectively in the Seventh Schedule except supplies and services essential to the community in Entry 3 of the Concurrent List. Such a wide interpretation seriously abridges the personal liberty of a citizen. A narrow and restricted interpretation is in accord with scheme of clause (7) of Article 22 of the Constitution. It operates on the whole field of legislative list in Entry 9 and Entry 3 of the Union List and Concurrent List respectively. It may be stated that Section 12 of the impugned Act treats the lamb and the leopard in the same class because they happen to be quadrupeds.

223. The requirement of an Advisory Board is the barest minimum that can make a law of Preventive Detention to some little degree tolerable under a democratic constitution. Such a law may also have some justification even without requirement of an Advisory Board to meet certain defined dangerous situations or to deal with a class of people, who are a grave danger to the state. But without such limitations, a law of Preventive Detention would be destructive of all notions of personal liberty.

224. In view of the aforesaid, Section 12 of the impugned Act is void. Section 14 of the impugned Act is also void as it prevents a Court from scrutinizing the grounds of detention to examine their relevance to the order of detention.

225. Article 32 of the Constitution guarantees to any person to move the Supreme Court for enforcement of Fundamental Rights. If grounds of detention are not disclosed to the Courts, the Supreme Court will not be able to exercise its power under Article 32.

226. In view of the aforesaid, Section 14 of the Preventive Detention Act is *ultra vires*.

227. Justice B.K. Mukherjea delivered a separate Judgment. The salient points in his judgment are summed up in the following paragraphs.

228. The Petitioner was initially arrested on 17 December 1947 on various criminal charges. During the trial, in April 1948, the petitioner was served with an order of detention under the Madras Maintenance of Public Order Act. This order was struck down by the Madras High Court. On the same day, a second order of detention was passed against the petitioner. On his moving the High Court again for a writ of *habeas corpus*, his application was dismissed on the ground that as he was not granted bail in three criminal cases pending against him, his detention was not unlawful. He was, however, given liberty to approach the High Court again when his period of detention, due to denial of bail in pending criminal cases against him, ceased.

229. In February 1949, in two criminal cases a magistrate imposed on A.K. Gopalan the punishment of rigorous imprisonment for six months. The orders of the magistrate in both the cases were set aside in appeal in September 1949. In the third criminal case, the petitioner was sentenced by the Session Judge to rigorous imprisonment for five years. On appeal, the Madras High Court reduced the sentence to rigorous imprisonment for six months. The Petitioner filed a fresh writ of *habeas corpus* before the Madras High Court against his detention order of April 1948. The writ petition was heard after the petitioner had served out his period of imprisonment under the punitive provisions of law in criminal cases referred to earlier. In January 1950, the Madras High Court dismissed the petition and upheld his detention order under the Madras Act. When the impugned Preventive Detention Act was passed on 25 February 1950 by the Parliament, the petitioner's earlier order of detention under the Madras Act was cancelled and a fresh order of detention under Section 3 of the impugned Preventive Detention Act was passed against him. It is against this detention order that the Petitioner has filed the present writ petition.

230. M.K. Nambiar, counsel for the petitioner, advanced the following arguments:

(i) Preventive Detention is a restriction on free movement of a citizen within the territory of India guaranteed under Article 19(1)(d) of the Constitution. It has to be seen by the Court whether the impugned Act is a reasonable restriction within the meaning of Article 19(5) of the Constitution.

(ii) The impugned Act is in conflict with Article 21 as it deprives a person of his personal liberty not according to procedure established by law. In Article 21, the word "law" does not mean a law enacted by a competent legislature but it means the general law of the land embodying the principles of Natural Justice and procedure considered fundamental in all systems of civilized jurisprudence.

(iii) Even though it is argued that the procedure in Article 22 of the Constitution for a valid law of Preventive Detention must override the general rules of procedure contained in Article 21 – both Articles 21 and 22 being in the chapter on Fundamental Rights – for any matter not provided for in Article 22, the provisions of Article 21 must apply.

(iv) The provision of Section 14 of the impugned Act is void as it renders completely nugatory the Fundamental Right under Article 32 of the Constitution.

231. Justice B.K. Mukherji said that the Indian Constitution has not accepted the English doctrine of absolute supremacy of the Parliament. In this respect, the Indian Constitution has followed the Constitution of the United States of America. In the American Constitution – as in the Constitution of India – there are certain limitations on powers of the Government. These limitations on powers of the Government act as a check on despotism of the majority. It was observed in a judgment of the American Supreme Court that "a government which holds the lives, the liberty and property of its citizens, subject at all times to the absolute disposition and unlimited control of even the most democratic depository of power, is after all but a despotism."

232. Under the Indian law, there is no authoritative definition of "Preventive Detention". As a topic of legislation, it occurred in the legislative lists of the Government of India Act 1935 and has been mentioned in item (9) of the Union List and item (3) of the Concurrent List in the Seventh Schedule of the Constitution.

233. The expression "Preventive Detention" has been used in contradistinction to the expression "Punitive Detention". Lord Finlay has said in Rex *versus* Halliday (1917 A.C. 260) that the law of Preventive Detention is not a punitive but a precautionary measure. As observed in Liversidge *versus* Anderson (1942 A.C. 206) the object of a Preventive Detention law is not to punish a person for having done something but to prevent him from doing it.

234. A law of Preventive Detention was only passed as a war measure in U.K. In no country of the World – except in the Republic of India – a law of Preventive Detention has been made an integral part of the Constitution during peace time.

235. This is undoubtedly unfortunate but the Court need not speculate on questions of policy.

236. The question to be considered is whether a law of Preventive Detention is justiciable on the ground of reasonableness under Article 19(5) of the Constitution.

237. Article 22 makes it clear that if a law of Preventive Detention conforms to the provisions in the clauses (4) to (7) of the Article, it is perfectly valid. There is nothing in Article 22 to suggest that such law must be reasonable and that it would be subject to Judicial Review on that ground.

238. Both Article 19 and Article 22 occur in the chapter on Fundamental Rights and both of them purport to lay down the Rights which the Constitution guarantees.

239. The principles for interpreting a statute are the same as principles for interpretation of a Constitution. As Lord Wright has observed in James *versus* the Commonwealth of Australia (1936) that the ultimate result must be determined upon the actual word used not *in vacuo* but as occurring in a single complex instrument in which one part may throw

light upon the other. The Constitution has been described as a federal compact and the Constitution must hold balance between all its parts.

240. Not only the Right of freedom of movement throughout the territory of India under Article 19(1)(d) but also other Rights under Article 19(1) remain suspended when a person is under Preventive Detention.

241. Blackstone writes in his "Commentaries on the Laws of England" that three absolute Rights are inherent in every Englishmen, namely,

(i) Right of personal security;
(ii) Right of Personal liberty; and
(iii) Right of private Property

242. According to Blackstone, the Right of personal security consists of a person's uninterrupted enjoyment of his life, his limb, his body, his health and his reputation; whereas personal liberty consists in the power of moving one's person to whichever place one's inclination may direct.

243. The Drafting Committee of the Indian Constitution had specifically suggested that "liberty" in Article 15 of the draft constitution – which became Article 21 of the Constitution – should be qualified by the expression "personal" lest "liberty" be interpreted widely so as to include "freedoms" in Article 13 of the draft Constitution corresponding to Article 19 of the Constitution. As the Constituent Assembly accepted the views of the Drafting Committee, the intention of the framers of the Constitution was obviously to exclude the "freedoms" in Article 19 from the concept of "personal liberty" in Article 21.

244. It is well-known that "liberty" has been given a very wide meaning by the U.S. Supreme Court. In the U.S. Constitution, "liberty" not only includes freedom from physical restraint but the Right to free use of one's property and the Right to enter into free contractual relations. In the Indian Constitution, "personal liberty" has been deliberately used in Article 21 to restrict it to freedom from physical restraint of a person by imprisonment. "Personal liberty" in Article 21 does not include the Right to move freely throughout the territory of India guaranteed in Article 19(1)(d). Therefore, the reasonableness of a Preventive Detention Act need not be tested on the ground contained in Article 19(5) of the Constitution.

245. The Attorney-General has argued that Parliament is fully competent to enact the impugned Act in view of Entry 9 of the Union List and Entry 3 of the Concurrent List. He also argued that the impugned Act has laid down a procedure of detention which is in conformity with Article 22 of the Constitution.

246. As against the arguments of the Attorney-General, counsel for the petitioner, has argued that "law" in Article 21 refers to procedural law only and not to substantive law. Moreover, "law" in the context does not refer to any "law" enacted by a competent legislature but to law in the abstract sense – in the sense of "jus" and not "lex". Accordingly, "law" means legal principles or fundamental rules that lie at the root of every system of positive law in civilized countries. Further, if "law" in Article 21 is interpreted as state-made law, Article 21 will not rank as a Fundamental Right imposing a check on the legislative authority of Government as the legislature can always pass a law containing irrational or arbitrary procedure and the people would have no protection at all against such a law. In support of his arguments, the counsel cited a number of decisions of the U.S. Supreme Court when the Court applied the due process clause to invalidate laws which appeared to the Court to be capricious, unfair and arbitrary.

247. Counsel for the petitioner has, however, argued that the expression, "procedure established by law" bears the same meaning as "due process of law" which stipulates that "due process" is limited to matters of procedure and does not extend to substantive law.

248. In this connection, it would be relevant to trace the background of the "due process" clause in the Constitution of the United States. It can be traced to the Magna Carta (1215), which states as follows: "No free man shall be taken or imprisoned or outlawed or exiled on in any way destroyed; nor shall we go upon him nor send upon him but by the lawful judgment of his peers and by the law of the land." Successive English monarchs confirmed the Magna Carta as a charter of English liberties. In one of the confirmations by a British monarch – known as "Statute of Westminster of the liberties of London", the expression, due process of law appeared for the first time. "Due process of law" has not been defined in any statute. Going by the authority of Sir Edward Coke, due process of law, means persons should not be imprisoned without proper indictment or trial by peers and property of a freeman should not be seized except in proceedings conducted in due form in which the owner would be served a notice to show cause why his property would not be seized. The exact phrase, due process of law came to be part of the constitution of USA by the Fifth Amendment (1791).

249. In 1858, by the Fourteenth Amendment of the U.S. Constitution, the expression "due process of law" already adopted by the Constitution of USA by the Fifth Amendment (1791), got also incorporated into the Constitution of the constituent States of USA.

250. There is no precise definition of "due process of law" in the Constitution of USA. In a leading judgment, the Supreme Court of USA observed that,

"Few phrases in Law are so elusive of exact appreciation as this. The Court has always declined to give a comprehensive definition of it and has preferred that its full meaning should be gradually ascertained by the process of inclusion and exclusion in course of decision on cases as they arise."

251. It is, however, clear that the due process clause has acted as a check in England against executive usurpation and royal tyranny whereas in USA it is bulwark against arbitrary legislation.

252. Daniel Webster stated in one of his famous arguments before the U.S. Supreme Court that:

"By the law of the land is most clearly intended the general law – a law which hears before it condemns, which proceeds upon inquiry and records judgment only after trial. The meaning is that every citizen shall hold his life, liberty, property and immunities under the protection of general rules which govern society."

253. No jurist has even attempted to enumerate comprehensively what these principles of general law are. But to a large extent, the principles of general law are principles of the English Common law and modes of judicial proceedings in United Kingdom. Sir Edward Coke's dictum of a supreme fundamental law – which referred to the English common law – did exercise considerable influence on minds of judges in the United States of America as stated by Willis in his book *Constitutional Law*.

254. The U.S. Supreme Court has held that there are limitations on powers of government which grow out of essential nature of free governments. In other words, these are implied reservations of Rights of individuals without which the social compact would not exist. It meant that the citizens of USA, when they formed themselves into a state, surrendered some of their Rights to the state while retaining certain other Rights of a fundamental character, which no law would take away.

255. Till the middle of the 19th century, the expression due process of law was considered by the U.S. Supreme Court not to have any bearing on substantive law at all.

256. The close of the Civil War in USA in 1861 led to a new period of industrial development and emergence of a capitalist and a working class. The capitalist class regarded some laws imposing limitations on private property, as encroachments on their vested Right to deploy capital in any manner they liked. In this background, the U.S. Supreme Court struck down a few substantive laws as being not in accordance with the due process clause. American authors have written that in doing so the Courts became a kind of negative third chamber.

257. In the Lochner case, when majority of judges of the U.S. Supreme Court struck down the law imposing a ceiling of 60 hours of work per week in some specified industries, Justice Oliver Wendell Holmes, who was in the minority, invoked "police power" of the Government to justify 60 hours per week in interest of health of workers.

258. Monroe in his book, *The Government of the United States* has defined police power as follows:

"The Right of a Government to regulate the conduct of its people in the interests of public safety, health, morals and convenience.

259. Under this authority of police power, a Government may make Regulations concerning safety of buildings, regulation of traffic, reporting of incurable diseases, inspection of markets, sanitation of factories, hours of work for women and children, sale of intoxicants and such other matters."

260. The extent to which the Courts in USA can interfere with the exercise of police powers by the state acting through the legislature, has not been clearly defined by judicial pronouncements. The generally accepted position is that while any enactment under the guise of police powers would not necessarily be constitutional, yet if the Regulation has a direct relation to a public purpose, it would be valid.

261. The decision of the Supreme Court of the United States – though not quite uniform – reveals the growing influence of the police power doctrine. Since 1936, in USA, there is a definite swing of the judicial pendulum in favour of police power. As Carl Brent Swisher

says in his book, *The Growth of Constitutional Power in the U.S.* that in the years after 1936, the due process clause has become a thing of the past and has been restricted to its original meaning of "procedural due process".

262. It is seen that the due process clause in the Constitution of United States of America has come to be used as a potent instrument in the hands of the judiciary for control over social legislation. But as the judgments, where due process clause was invoked to control social legislation, did not apply uniform principles of reasonableness of limits of police power, in each case before the Supreme Court, the doctrine of police power was used according to the social and economic philosophy of the Judges hearing the case.

263. While drafting the Constitution of India, the Drafting Committee suggested two modifications to Article 15 of the draft constitution, which corresponds to Article 21 of the Constitution. Article 15 read as follows:

"No person shall be deprived of his life or liberty without due process of law".

264. The Drafting Committee suggested that:

(i) The word 'personal' must precede the word 'liberty' to give a comparatively narrow interpretation to 'liberty'.

(ii) "Due process of Law", which has enabled the judiciary in USA to strike down laws as not conforming to either procedural or substantive due process, should be replaced by the expression "procedure established by law" occurring in the new Constitution of Japan.

265. The Attorney-General referred to speeches in the Constituent Assembly to establish that the Assembly was fully aware of the difference between Article 15 of the draft Constitution and Article 21 of the Constitution.

266. Jurists have been unanimous in their view that when the question is of true interpretation of the Constitution, reference to debates in the Constituent Assembly will be of limited relevance.

267. It will be difficult to hold that, procedure established by law, is the same as, due process of law. Counsel for the petitioner, has stated that the word "law" used in Article 21 of the Constitution refers to the procedural law only. He also held that "law" in Article 21 does not refer to any state-made law but refers to the fundamental principles of jurisprudence based upon the immutable doctrines of Natural Justice.

268. The above argument of the Counsel for the petitioner may not be valid. First, it is clear that the framers of the Indian Constitution did not desire to introduce into the Constitution elements of uncertainty and vagueness that have grown around the due process clause in Constitution of the United States of America.

269. The uncertainty and elasticity of the due process clause are in the doctrine itself, which is a hidden mine, the contents of which nobody knows and these contents are revealed from time to time to the conscience of the Judges. The framers of the Indian Constitution deliberately decided to discard the due process clause and substitute it by procedure established by law. [**N.B.:** The Drafting Committee was considering the first draft of the

Constitution, prepared by Sir B.N. Rau, I.C.S., the Constitutional Adviser, who had retained the due process clause. Justice Felix Frankfurter of the U.S. Supreme Court told Sir B.N. Rau, who visited USA, that the due process clause has given uncatalogued power to the Court in USA and the Indian Constitution should steer clear of the due process clause and adopt instead the expression, "Procedure established by law". Alladi Krishnaswamy Iyer, a leading Member of the Drafting Committee persuaded Dr. B.R. Ambedkar and other Members to accept the advice of Justice Felix Frankfurter].

270. Article 22 was not in the original draft constitution of India. After the due process clause was discarded by the Constituent Assembly in favour of procedure established by law in Article 21, Article 22 was inserted in the Constitution.

271. The question is whether section 12 of the impugned Act is *ultra vires* clause 7(a) of Article 22. Clause 7(a) empowers the Parliament to prescribe circumstances under which and the class or classes of cases, in which a person may be detained for a period longer than three months without obtaining opinion of the Advisory Board.

272. Section 12 of the impugned Act covers the entries in both the Union List and the Concurrent List as (i) Defence of India (ii) Relation of India with foreign powers (iii) security of India or (iv) security of a state (v) maintenance of public order. Section 12 only excludes, "the maintenance of services and supplies essential to the community", which is at Entry 3 of the Concurrent List.

273. Counsel for the petitioner has argued that mentioning five out of six legislative heads in Section 12 of the impugned Act does not amount to prescribing the circumstances under which or the classes or cases in which a person could be detained for more than three months as provided for in Article 22(7)(a) of the Constitution.

274. Justice B.K. Mukherji said that Section 12 of the impugned Act has been drafted in a rather clumsy manner; but just for that reason, it cannot be held that Section 12 is *ultra vires*.

275. The Indian Constitution has given powers to the Parliament in the matter of classification of cases and circumstances in which detention beyond a period of three months would be permitted without obtaining the opinion of the Advisory Board. It was open to the Parliament to adopt any method or principle for classification of "cases" and "circumstances" and the Parliament has done it by enumeration of five subjects in the legislative heads out of the total of six subjects. By doing so, it cannot be said that the Parliament has exceeded its power and Section 12 of the impugned Act is invalid.

276. Section 14 of the impugned Act prohibits any Court from evidence to be given before it of the grounds of detention of a detenue. Moreover, under Section 14, disclosure of the communications and documents prohibited against disclosure shall be punishable with imprisonment upto one year or with fine or with both. Such stipulations render utterly nugatory Article 32 of the Constitution. It would not be possible for the Court to decide whether the provisions of clause (5) of Article 22 of the Constitution have been duly complied with unless the grounds of detention are placed before the Court.

277. Section 14 of the impugned Act does materially affect the Fundamental Rights and for this reason is *ultra vires*. But Section 14, which is struck down, can be severed from the impugned Act and the whole Act cannot be, therefore, held to be *ultra vires*.

278. To sum up, the impugned Preventive Detention Act minus Section 14 – is *intra vires* the Constitution.

279. The writ petition of A.K. Gopalan is dismissed with the observation that he can submit a fresh petition, containing the grounds of detention for the Court to decide whether they are relevant for preventive detention.

280. Justice S.R. Das delivered a separate judgment agreeing with the majority of judges that the writ petition of A.K. Gopalan be dismissed. The salient points in his judgment are as follows:

281. The scope and ambit of powers of the Court are not the same under all Constitutions. In England, the doctrine of parliamentary supremacy prevails. A law duly enacted by the British Parliament cannot be challenged in any Court in U.K. as violative of Fundamental Rights of the British citizens. In U.K, the Court can only interpret and apply the law and has no powers to declare a law *ultra vires*.

282. In the United States of America, which has a written Constitution with a Bill of Rights, a law unnecessarily restricting a guaranteed Right, can be declared *ultra vires* by the Supreme Court.

283. Under Chief Justice Marshall, the U.S. Supreme Court asserted its power to declare any law as unconstitutional for not being in conformity with the due process of law.

284. In India, the position of the judiciary is somewhere in between the Courts in England and the Courts in the United States of America. While in India, the Parliament and the State Legislatures are supreme in their respective legislative fields, the Constitution has provisions, which prescribe limitations on legislative powers of the Parliament and the State legislatures. If the limitations have been transgressed, it is the duty of the Court to scrutinize the law and declare it *ultra vires*.

285. The Indian Constitution – unlike the American Constitution – does not recognize in all respects the absolute supremacy of the Court over the legislative authority. This is so as outside the restricted fields of constitutional limitations, the Indian Parliament and the State legislatures are supreme in their respective legislative fields.

286. In no country of the world, the Constitution permits a law of Preventive Detention during peace time. Such a law in India can be enacted even in peace time.

287. If there was no chapter on Fundamental Rights in the Constitution, the Parliament with respect to subjects in Entry 9 of the Union List and the Parliament and the State Legislatures with respect to subjects in Entry 3 of Concurrent List could make as drastic a Preventive Detention law as they pleased. Such a law might have authorized an ordinary policeman – not to speak of a District Magistrate, sub-divisional Magistrate or a Commissioner of Police – to take both a citizen and a non-citizen into custody and keep him in detention as long as the authority pleased.

288. It is needless to multiply instances of atrocious laws which Parliament or a State Legislature might have enacted under Article 246 read with the entries in different Lists in the Seventh Schedule of the Constitution if there was nothing else in the Constitution.

289. The Indian Constitution has not accepted the absolute supremacy of Parliament or of the State Legislatures. Under Article 245(1) of the Constitution, the legislative power is subject to provisions of the Constitution. Article 13(2) provides that the state shall not make any law which takes away or abridges the Fundamental Rights.

290. There are two principal limitations to the legislative powers of the Parliament, namely;

(i) the law must be within legislative competence of the Parliament.

(ii) such law must be subject to the provisions of the Constitution and must not take away or abridge the Fundamental Rights.

291. Civil Rights of a person are divided into two classes, namely, the Rights attached to the person (*Jus Personarum*) and the Right to property (*Jus Rerum*). Of the Rights attached to a person, the first and foremost is the Right to life. It means that the Right cannot be taken away except according to procedure established by law. Next to the Right to life is the Right to freedom, which means that one's body shall not be violated, and one shall not be arrested or imprisoned except under the authority of law.

292. Personal liberties may be compendiously summed up as the Right to do as one pleases within the law. Liberty is not unbridled license. It is what Edmund Burke called "regulated freedom".

293. Webster also has said that Liberty is the creation of law and is different from licentiousness. The working of our complex system, full of checks and restraints on legislative, executive and judicial power, is favourable to liberty and justice.

294. The Constitution has guaranteed some personal liberties in Article 19(1) but has put restraints on them by clauses (2) to (6) of the same Article. The Constitution has also put checks on legislative powers of the state under Articles 21 and 22. By providing for a law of Preventive Detention in Article 22, the Constitution has recognized that individual liberty may be subordinate to the larger social interest.

295. Article 21 guarantees to every person – citizen or non-citizen – the substantive Right to Life. The Right to Life can be taken away by procedure established by law and no particular procedure has been prescribed in that regard in the Constitution.

296. Under the Indian Constitution, some personal Rights have been guaranteed under Article 19(1). But this does not mean that a citizen has no other personal Rights except those under Article 19(1). Some of the Rights not mentioned in Article 19(1), but nevertheless enjoyed by every individual, have been enumerated by Chief Justice Trevor Harris of the Calcutta High Court in Kshitindra *versus* The Chief Secretary West Bengal (1950). They are the Right of a free man to eat what he likes subject to the rationing law, work as much as he likes or idle away his time as much as he likes, to drink as much as he likes subject to the licensing law and do a hundred and other things not included in the Rights under Article 19(1). These Rights, not enumerated in Article 19(1), are a necessary part of personal liberty under Article 21 of the Constitution.

297. The conclusion is irresistible that the Rights protected by Article 19(1) in so far as they are Rights attached to the person (*Jus Personarum*) are only those Rights which a free citizen – who is not under any detention or imprisonment according to law – can exercise. In view of the aforesaid, the validity of a law of Preventive Detention is not to be tested on the touchstone of Rights under Article 19(1).

298. To sum up, a citizen who loses his freedom by being lawfully detained – whether on conviction for an offence or under a law of Preventive Detention – loses his liberty to enjoy the Rights attached to the person (*Jus Personarum*).

299. Counsel for the petitioner has argued that Article 21 gives to any person only a procedural protection.

300. This argument of the counsel is not sound as the marginal note to Article 21 indicates that it guarantees to every person protection of life and personal liberty. It means that the Right to Life and personal liberty under Article 21 are substantive Rights.

301. Counsel for the petitioner has also argued that the procedure established by law in Article 21 refers to those fundamental and immutable rules of procedure established by the principles of Natural Justice and accepted in all countries and at all times. But such an interpretation is not valid as Article 21 uses the expression procedure established by law. Moreover, when Section 124A of the Indian Penal Code speaks of "Government established by law", it does not mean Government established by principles of Natural Justice.

302. In 1791, the American doctrine of due process of law was introduced by the Fifth Amendment to the U.S. Constitution. It was introduced in the State Constitutions of USA by the Fourteenth Amendment in 1858. The Constitution of USA was however silent as to who would be the umpire in case the legislature overstepped its limits. In 1803, the Supreme Court under Chief Justice Marshall, used the due process clause to assert the power of Judicial Review and act as the umpire.

303. The expression "due process of law" has been interpreted by the American Courts differently in different times. Carl Brent Swisher in his book, *Growth of Constitutional Power in the United States* says that during the first hundred years of the U.S. Constitution—the due process clause was interpreted as a restriction on procedure by which the Government exercised its powers. During the next hundred years the due process clause was interpreted as a restriction not only on procedure but also upon the substance of the activities in which Government might engage. After the year 1936, the due process clause has been interpreted again as it was interpreted in the first hundred years as restriction on procedure only.

304. In the guise of interpreting due process of law, the American Courts went much further than Lord Coke. By invoking the due process clause, the American Courts have gradually arrogated to themselves the power to review all legislations. In the words of Munro, due process of law became a sort of palladium covering all manner of individual Rights. All the while, the Supreme Court of USA refused to define due process of law, but used it to declare as *ultra vires* any law which it thought to be unreasonable. In the words of John Dickinson, the Judges began by setting aside laws and ended by making them.

305. To get over the difficulty created by the expression due process of law, the U.S. Supreme Court invoked the doctrine of police power to validate laws to promote public convenience, public health, public morals and public safety. The net result is that in USA, the all-inclusive and indefinable doctrine of due process of law has now been brought back to its original status of procedural due process by the new doctrine of police power – a peculiarly American doctrine.

306. Due process of law, which is a synonym for law of the land occurring in Magna Carta (1215), means a law which hears before it condemns, which proceeds upon inquiry and renders judgment only after trial.

307. Willis in his book on the American Constitution has enumerated the requirements of procedural due process as follows:

(i) issue of notice to the affected party;
(ii) opportunity to the affected party to be heard in response to the notice;
(iii) An impartial tribunal to adjudicate the matter;
(iv) An orderly course of procedure.

308. Counsel for the petitioner has argued that the American doctrine of due process of law need not be imported into the Indian Constitution in its full glory but it should be ensured that no person shall be deprived of his Right or personal liberty except by the observance of formalities required for justice and fair play.

309. The concessions in the Magna Carta (1215) were taken as guarantees against oppression by the King. It did not provide security to the common man in England by limiting the powers of the Parliament. Thus, Bills of Attainder, ex post facto laws, laws forfeiting estates and other arbitrary acts of legislation, which occurred frequently in English history, were never regarded as inconsistent with the laws of the land. In other words, the omnipotence of the English Parliament was absolute even against common law Rights. The practical security for English liberty against tyranny by the legislature was the power of free public opinion.

310. The Indian Constitution has imposed some limitations on the legislature; but subject to the limitations, it has left the Parliament and the State Legislatures supreme in their respective legislative fields. It will be incongruous to import the expression due process of law without the doctrine of police powers of the American Constitution and it is impossible to read the doctrine of police power into Article 21 of the Indian Constitution. Under Article 21, the Indian Constitution has provided for procedure established by law and has also prescribed some minimal procedure in Article 22. To add to them would be not to interpret the Constitution but to recast it according to judiciary's intellectual yardstick and the judiciary's predilection of what an ideal Constitution should be. If Parliament provides by law for death sentence to be executed by hanging by the neck or by a firing squad or by electric chair or even by boiling in oil, no objection can be sustained as it is a procedure established by law. A procedure laid down by the legislature by enacting a valid law may offend a court's sense of justice and fair play and a sentence provided by the legislature may outrage the court's notion of penology but that is a wholly irrelevant consideration. Protection against legislative tyranny, if any, lies in the ultimate analysis in a free and intelligent public opinion.

311. In many other Constitutions, supremacy of the legislature is recognized in the matter of depriving a person of his life, liberty and property. In U.K., it is clearly recognized in the doctrine of parliamentary supremacy.

312. The Attorney-General has urged that Article 21 has nothing to do with Preventive Detention at all and such detention is wholly covered by Article 22(4) to (7). In other words, Article 22 is the complete code for Preventive Detention. This is not the correct position because if there is no substantive Right to Life and personal liberty, which can be deprived by procedure established by law, there is no use for procedural protection of the Right of personal liberty contained in Article 22. Thus, the correct position is that Article 21 protects the substantive Rights of life and personal liberty by requiring a procedure and Article 22 gives the minimum procedural protection to the Right to personal liberty.

313. Clauses (1) & (2) of Article 22 of the Constitution lay down the procedure for arrest of a person. They ensure four safeguards, viz,

(a) a Right to be informed about grounds of arrest;

(b) a Right to consult and be defended by a legal practitioner chosen by the person arrested;

(c) a Right to be produced before a Magistrate within 24 hours of arrest;

(d) a Right to be free of detention beyond the said period of 24 hours except by orders of a magistrate.

314. These procedural safeguards are requirements of the procedural due process. These safeguards are also in the Code of Criminal Procedure of India.

315. Article 21 of the Constitution does not lay down any particular procedure but merely mentions procedure established by law and Article 22 lays down the minimum rules of procedure.

316. Clauses (4), (5), (6) & (7) of Article 22 relate to Preventive Detention. There are certain limitations on both the Parliament and a state legislature to make a law for Preventive Detention. These limitations to enact a law for Preventive Detention are as follows:

(a) No law of Preventive Detention shall authorize detention of a person for more than three months unless a duly constituted Advisory Board has reported before expiration of three months that there is sufficient cause for such detention.

(b) No law of Preventive Detention can authorize detention of a person beyond the maximum period prescribed by a law made by the Parliament.

(c) Although any state legislature may enact a law of Preventive Detention in terms of Entry 3 in the Concurrent List read with Article 246 of the Constitution, such a law cannot authorize detention for more than three months unless a duly constituted Advisory Board authorizes such detention or the circumstances under which and class or classes of cases in which a person can be detained without the opinion of the Advisory Board for more than three months are spelt out under a law of Preventive Detention.

(d) It is only the Parliament – and not the state legislature - which can decide regarding the maximum period of Preventive Detention.

(e) It is only the Parliament – and not the state legislature – which can prescribe the procedure to be followed by a duly constituted Advisory Board.

317. Counsel for the petitioner has argued that the detenue's representation against order or detention be considered by an impartial tribunal. This argument is not valid. Firstly, the Constitution only provides for communication to the detenue of the grounds of detention at the earliest and consideration of representation of the detenue by the concerned authority. Article 22 does not provide for a Tribunal – independent of the Government – to consider the detenue's representation. Secondly, there is no reason why the Government – which has high-level officials – cannot be trusted to consider the representation of a detenue in a fair manner. As most of the orders of detention would be passed by the District Magistrates or Commissioners of Police, the very fact that high level officials of the Government – other than the District Magistrate and Commissioners of Police who issued the order of detention – would consider the representation of the detenue, is sufficient safeguard for a fair consideration of representation of the detenue.

318. Counsel for the petitioner has argued that in enacting the impugned Act, Parliament has delegated its legislative power to the Executive. This argument is not sound as it overlooks the basic distinction between delegation of powers and vesting of discretion on officers to exercise the power.

319. Counsel for the petitioner has also argued that Section 12 of the impugned Act does not conform to clause (7) of Article 22 of the Constitution.

320. There is no strength in the aforesaid argument as clause (7) of Article 22 is only an enabling provision. As a matter of fact, the Calcutta High Court in Khsitindra Narayan *versus* Chief Secretary of West Bengal (1950) has held that the circumstances and the class or classes cases may coalesce as has been done in Clause (12) of the impugned Preventive Detention Act.

321. Counsel for the petitioner has, however, a good case when he challenges the *vires* of clause (14) of the impugned Act. Clause (14) can enable the Detaining authority to communicate to the detenue some scribblings which do not amount to any ground for detention and the detenue will have no remedy under Article 32 of the Constitution. Thus, the detenue's Right for enforcement of his important Fundamental Right of personal liberty is being abridged or abrogated by Section 14 of the impugned Act and hence Section 14 is *ultra vires*. Since it is a severable portion of the impugned Act, the impugned Act is a valid law after severance of Section 14.

322. In conclusion, the *vires* of the impugned Preventive Detention Act 1950 minus Section 14 is upheld and the writ petition of A.K. Gopalan stands dismissed.

CHAPTER 2

RE: Delhi (Laws) Act 1912 (Special Reference One of 1951 under Article 143 of The Constitution of India) (AIR 1951 SC 332)

[CHIEF JUSTICE HARILAL KANIA, JUSTICE S. FAZL ALI, JUSTICE PATANJALI SASTRI, JUSTICE MEHR CHAND MAHAJAN, JUSTICE B.K. MUKHERJEA, JUSTICE S.R. DAS AND JUSTICE VIVIAN BOSE]

Case Summary

In 1951, the President of India made a reference to the Supreme Court under Article 143 of the Constitution for advisory opinion on the following three issues:

(i) Is Section 7 of the Delhi Laws Act 1912 or any of provision thereof *ultra vires* the powers of the legislature which passed it?

[**N.B.**: Section 7 of the Delhi Laws Act 1912 is as follows:

"The provincial government may by Notification in the Official Gazette, extend with such restrictions and modifications as it thinks fit to the province of Delhi or any part thereof, any enactment which is in force in British India on the date of such Notification."]

(ii) Is the Ajmer-Merwara (Extension of Laws) Act 1947 or any of provision thereof *ultra vires* the powers of the legislature, which passed it?

[**N.B.**: Section 2 of the Ajmer-Merwara (Extension of Laws) Act 1947 is as follows:

"The Central Government may by Notification in the Official Gazette extend to the province of Ajmer-Merwara, with such modifications and restrictions it thinks fit, any enactment which is in force in any other province on the date of such notification."]

(iii) Is Section 2(C) of the Part (C) states (Laws) Act 1950 or any of the provisions thereof *ultra vires* the powers of Parliament, which passed it?

[**N.B.**: Section 2 of the Part 'C' states (Laws) Act 1950 is as follows:

"The Central Government may, by Notification in the Official Gazette, extend to any part 'C' state – other than Coorg and the Andaman – Nicobar Islands – or to any part of such part 'C' state, with such restrictions and modifications as it thinks fit, any enactment which is in force in a part 'A' state on the date of the notification and whether provision can be made in such enactment for the repeal or amendment of any corresponding law – other than a Central Act – which is for the time being applicable to a part 'C' state?"]

1. The three issues raise the main question of delegation of legislative power with reference to the three enactments which were passed by the legislature in three different stages of constitutional development of India.
2. The first issue covers legislative powers of the Indian Legislature during the period prior to the Government of India Act 1915.
3. The second issue covers legislative powers of the Indian Legislature after the Government of India Act 1935.
4. The third – and the last issue – is in respect of the legislative powers of the Indian Parliament under the present Constitution.
5. The three issues were considered by seven Judges of the Supreme Court viz. Chief Justice Harilal Kania, Justice S. Fazl Ali, Justice Patanjali Sastri, Justice M.C. Mahajan, Justice B.K. Mukherjea, Justice S.R. Das and Justice Vivian Bose. The issues were argued before the Court by legal luminaries including M.C. Setalvad, the first Attorney-General for India, N.C. Chatterji, Senior Advocate, C.K. Daphtary, Advocate-General for the state of Bombay and R. Somnath Iyer, Advocate-General for the State of Mysore.
6. The Chief Justice and each of the six other Judges recorded separate opinions.
7. Chief Justice Harilal Kania's opinion was as follows: When the Crown took over direct administration of India after the Sepoy Mutiny of 1857, the Indian Councils Act 1861 vested powers on the Governor-General-in-Council to make laws for the Indian empire.
8. The British Parliament is a sovereign legislative body. Its powers are recognized as absolute and unfettered. In Great Britain, the King-in-Parliament is all powerful. There is no Act which it cannot pass and which will not be valid within the ordinary limits of judicial interpretation. As a noted Jurist put it, even the Magna Carta is not inviolate."
9. The difference between powers of the Congress in the United States of America and powers of the Parliament in the United Kingdom is that whereas in USA powers of the Congress are limited by provisions of a written Constitution, in U.K. – which has no written Constitution – there is no such restraint.
10. In the United Kingdom, no law passed by the Parliament can be *ultra vires* as there is no touchstone of a written Constitution.
11. As against the sovereign British Parliament, the Governor-General-in-Council under the Indian Councils Act 1861, had no such plenary powers of legislation as the British Parliament. Because the Governor-General-in-Council derived powers of legislation from the Indian Councils Act, the powers of legislation of the Governor-General-in-Council was limited by provisions of the Indian Councils Act passed from time to time.
12. During 1861–1915, the Indian legislatures were subordinate legislatures – subordinate to the British Parliament – and not sovereign legislatures as the British Parliament was.
13. The legal position changed when the Government of India Act 1915 was passed by the British Parliament. The Act of 1915 did not set up a federation of British India but it introduced Dyarchy as it set up for the first time provincial legislatures in British India.

14. The Government of India Act 1935 set up a federation of British India with fields of legislation for the Central Legislature in List I and fields of legislation for the provincial legislature in List II and a List III, where both the Central and the Provincial legislatures could legislate. The Government of India Act 1935 placed the three lists (List I, II & III) in the Seventh Schedule of the Act.

15. But even under the Government of India Act 1935, the people of India had no role to alter or modify the provisions of the Act, which could only be done by the British Parliament. Under the Government of India Act 1935, the Government was also not responsible to the legislature.

16. The India Independence Act, 1947, abolished authority of the British Parliament to make any law for India. The Indian Central Legislature – elected by the people of India on the basis of a limited franchise – was empowered to enact laws for the Dominion of India. It also functioned as the Constituent Assembly to enact a new Constitution. But until the commencement of the Constitution of India on 26 January 1950, the Government of India Act 1935 was the Constitution or the basic law of India.

17. M.C. Setalvad argued that legislative power carries with it the power of delegation to any person the legislature may choose to appoint. Such delegation – the Attorney-General argued – must pass three tests viz.

   (i) it must be a delegation in respect of a subject or matter which is within the scope of legislative power of the legislature making the delegation;
   (ii) such power of delegation is not negatived by the instrument by which the legislature was established;
   (iii) the legislature does not create a parallel legislative body having the same powers and functions.

18. The Attorney-General also argued that in case of the United Kingdom, the Parliament can efface itself and even abdicate because it has the power to pass next day a law repealing the previous day's legislation.

19. Continuing the arguments, the Attorney-General said that when the British Parliament established legislative bodies in India, Canada and Australia by Acts of the Parliament, the legislatures so established were supreme with plenary powers. They could also delegate their legislative powers subject to the three stipulations mentioned earlier. The legislatures of India, Canada and Australia were not agents or delegates of the British Parliament. Therefore, the Latin maxim of '*delegata potestas non potest delegari*' (a delegate himself cannot further delegate) does not apply to these three legislatures of India, Canada and Australia. In view of this legal position, the Attorney-General argued that such delegation of legislative functions has been recognized for several years by the Privy Council. It was, therefore, urged that the decision of the Federal Court of India in Jatindra Nath *versus* Province of Bihar (1949) that such delegation was not permissible, required to be reconsidered.

20. The Attorney-General cited the judgment of the Privy Council in Queen *versus* Burah (1878). In that judgment, the Privy Council set aside the judgment of the Calcutta High Court which had held that the legislature in British India was an agent or delegate of the

British Parliament. Therefore, when the Governor-General-in-Council passed an Act in 1869 delegating to the Lieutenant – Governor of Bengal the power to remove the Garo Hills from the jurisdiction of the Tribunals established under the General Regulations and Acts of Legislature in British India and provided that hereafter the Lt. Governor of Bengal, by a Notification in the Official Gazette, was empowered to extend to the Garo Hills any law or any part of a law in force in other territories subject to the jurisdiction of the Lt. Governor, such an act of the Lt. Governor was perfectly valid. Similar provision was made in the Act of 1869 for extension of laws to Jaintia Hills, the Naga Hills and portions of the Khasi Hills.

21. The Privy Council held in Queen *versus* Burah (1878) that the Act 22 of 1869 conferring powers on the Lt. Governor of Bengal to exclude Garo Hills from operations of legislations in other parts of British India and to extend to the Garo Hills and other hilly areas such laws, which in the opinion of Lt. Governor should be extended, did not constitute delegated legislation. It was merely a case of conditional legislation as the authority of the Lt. Governor was not to pass new laws but only to extend laws which have been already passed by competent legislatures. The Privy Council stated in Queen *versus* Burah (1878) that:

"if what has been done is legislation within the general scope of the affirmative words which give the power, and if it violates no express conditions or restriction by which that power is limited............. it is not for any Court of Justice to enquire further, or to enlarge constructively those conditions and restrictions."

22. Similarly, in Emperor *versus* Benoari Lal Sarma (AIR 1945 PC 48) the Special Criminal Courts Ordinance 1942 was challenged on the ground that the Governor General delegated to the provincial Government the powers to decide whether an emergency existed on the outbreak of the Second World War (1939-45). The Privy Council rejected this argument by saying that the Governor-General has not delegated powers to decide whether an emergency existed, but has ensured that the local application of provisions of a statute was determined by a local administrative body as to its necessity. Accordingly, the Privy Council in Emperor *versus* Benoari Lal Sarma (AIR 1945 SC 48) did not agree with the Federal Court of India that the Special Criminal Courts Ordinance of 1942 was hit by delegation of essential legislative function by the Governor-General-in-Council.

23. Thus, the Privy Council's Judgments do not support the contention of the Attorney-General, that the power of delegation of the Indian Legislature is as wide as the power of legislation of the Indian legislature. In other words, the Indian legislature did not have unlimited power of delegation of essential legislative functions and the Indian Legislature can only delegate power to make Regulations ancillary to a legislation.

24. Cooley has stated in his book *Principles of Constitutional Law*, that in American Constitutional doctrine, no legislative body can delegate to another department of the Government or to any other Authority the power either generally or specially to enact laws. This high prerogative to enact laws has been entrusted to the legislators' own wisdom, judgment and patriotism and the legislature will act *ultra vires* if it delegates the task of legislation.

25. Whereas essential legislative function cannot be delegated by the legislature to any other Authority, subordinate legislation to implement the provisions of an enactment, may be vested in the Executive. Such subordinate legislation remains under parliamentary control and is lacking in the independent and unqualified authority which is an attribute of legislative power.

26. In so far as subordinate legislation to carry out the objectives of the main legislation are concerned, the noted jurist, Crawford has stated that for delegation of power to an Executive Agency or Administrative Board for framing subordinate legislation, the legislature must declare the policy of the law and fix the legal principles and provide a standard to guide the Executive Agency or Administrative Board to implement the law. Crawford summed up by saying that the filling in matter of details within the policy of legislative standards is essentially ministerial rather than legislative.

27. To conclude, a legislature cannot enact a law to delegate power to make a law, but it can enact a law to delegate its power to determine some facts or state of things upon which the law intends to make its own action depend.

28. In Jatindra Nath Gupta's case (1949), the Federal Court of India held that the legislature cannot delegate to the Executive or any other Authority to lay down the policy underlying a rule of conduct. The result will be that if the legislature does not choose to lay down detailed rules or regulations, such work maybe left to the Executive implementing the law, which has powers of subordinate legislation.

29. Regarding legality of Delhi Laws Act 1912, it may be noted that the province of Delhi was carved out of the province of Punjab. The province of Delhi was put under the administrative control of a Chief Commissioner. By Section 2 of the Delhi Laws Act 1912, all laws in force in the province of Punjab continued to operate in the province of Delhi, which had no separate legislative body. The power to legislate for the newly-created province of Delhi vested in the Governor-General-in-Council of India.

30. Section 7 of the Delhi Laws Act 1912 enables the Government to extend by Notification, with such restrictions and modifications it thinks fit, to the province of Delhi or any part thereof, any enactment which is in force in any part of British India on the date of such Notification. It means, any law in force in any part of British India – and not necessarily only in province of Punjab – can be made applicable in the province of Delhi with such adaptations and modifications as the Government might decide. It also applies not only to existing laws in force in any part of British India but any law which may be passed in future by any provincial legislature or the central legislature in British India.

31. At this stage, the Act 22 of 1869 – which the Privy Council had considered in Queen *versus* Burah (1878) – may be compared to the provisions of Delhi Laws Act of 1912. First, the Act 22 of 1869 permitted extension of the Acts which were enacted – or would be enacted – by the Governor-General-in-Council or the Lieutenant-Governor, both of whom were competent legislative authorities for the area under the administrative control of the Lt. Governor. Secondly, so far as Section 7 of the Delhi Laws Act 1912 empowered the Central Government to issue Notification to extend Acts passed by the Central legislature

to the province of Delhi, such Notification could be upheld on the ratio of the decision of the Privy Council in Queen *versus* Burah (1878).

32. But Section 7 of the Delhi Laws Act 1912 went further and empowered the Central Government to issue Notification extending any Act in any province of British India to the Chief Commissioner's Province of Delhi in respect of which only the Central Legislature was the competent Legislative body to enact laws. The result is that Acts of Provincial Legislatures – in respect of which the Central Legislature had not at all applied its mind – could be extended to the Chief Commissioner's Province of Delhi. This would be tantamount to the Central Legislature abdicating its legislative power in relation to the Chief Commissioner's province of Delhi as such legislative power would be exercised by the Central Government and not by the Central Legislature.

33. Therefore, to the extent Section 7 of the Delhi Laws Act 1912 permits the Central Government to extend to the Chief Commissioner's province of Delhi any provincial enactment, to that extent, Section 7 of the Delhi (Laws) Act 1912 is *ultra vires*.

34. Regarding legality of the Ajmer-Merwara (Extension of Laws) Act 1947. Section 2 of the Act states as follows:

"The Central Government may, by Notification in the official Gazette extend to the province of Ajmer-Merwara with such restrictions and modifications it thinks fit any enactment which is in force in any other province on the date of such Notification."

35. By the Government of India Act 1915, for the first time, provincial legislatures were given powers of legislation in respect of the concerned province and the unitary Government of India with Governor-General-in-Council as the sole legislative body for British India, came to an end. But by the Government of India Act 1915, there was no distribution of legislative power between the Central Government and the provinces.

36. Distribution of legislative power between the Central Government and the provinces was introduced for the first time in the Government of India Act 1935. Under the Government of India Act 1935, the Central Legislature was the only law-making authority for the Chief Commissioner's province and Ajmer-Merwara was a Chief Commissioner's province. Therefore, it was only the Central Legislature, which could legislate for Ajmer-Merwara and hence Section 2 of the Ajmer-Merwara Act 1947, which empowered the Central Government by Notification to extend to Ajmer-Merwara any provincial enactment, is *ultra vires*.

37. We have to now consider the third and the last issue referred to the Supreme Court by the President of India. To recapitulate, the issue is: Is section 2 of the Part C states (Laws) Act 1950 or any provision thereof *ultra vires*?

38. Section 2 of the Part C states (Laws) Act 1950 is as follows: "The Central Government may by Notification in the Official Gazette extend to any part 'C' state (except part 'C' states of Coorg and Andaman and Nicobar Islands) with such restrictions and modifications as it thinks fit, any enactment which is in force in a Part 'A' state of the Indian Union on the date of such Notification. Provision may also be made in any enactment so extended for the repeal or amendment of corresponding law – other than a Central Act – which is for the time being applicable to part "C" states.

39. In view of the reasons for declaring *ultra vires* Section 7 of the Delhi Laws Act 1912 and Section 2 of the Ajmer-Merwara Act 1947, Section 2 of the Part 'C' States Act 1950 is also *ultra vires* the Central legislature to the extent it empowers the Central Government to extend to a part 'C' state any law passed by the legislature of a Part 'A' State of the Indian Union.

40. But to the extent, the Indian Parliament – which is the competent legislature to pass laws for Part 'C' states – has passed any Act, which is applicable to a Part 'A' state, there can be no objection to the Central Government extending it to Delhi which was a part 'C' state under administrative control of a Chief Commissioner.

41. To sum up the views of Chief Justice Harilal Kania, Section 7 of the Delhi Laws Act 1912; Section 2 of the Ajmer-Merwara Act 1947 and Section 2 of the Part 'C' States Laws Act 1950 are *ultra vires*.

42. Justice Fazl Ali gave a separate opinion on the three issues as was done by the Chief Justice Harilal Kania and other brother Judges.

43. According to Justice Fazl Ali, answers to the three issues, depend upon answer to another important question, which may be stated thus:

"Can a Legislature which is sovereign or has plenary powers within the field assigned to it, delegate its functions to an executive authority or to another agency and if so, to what extent it can do so?"

44. It has been stated that delegated legislation is not possible because of certain well-known principles. The first such principle has been stated in a Latin Maxim viz. "*delegata potestas non potest delegare*" (a delegate cannot himself further delegate). But this argument may not be sound in the context of the Indian Legislature in British India as even when the Imperial Parliament set statutory limits on powers of the Indian Legislature, the Indian Legislature was not an agent or delegate of the British Parliament. This position was stated in Queen *versus* Burah (1878) by the Privy Council.

45. There have been some writers, who have suggested that a legislature is a delegate of the electors. But Lord Dicey has rejected this argument. In his *magnum opus*, "Laws of the Constitution", Dicey states that a legislature is neither an agent of the electors nor a trustee of its constituents. A legislature is legally the sovereign legislative power in the state.

46. Another argument against delegated legislation is the doctrine of separation of powers, which originated with Aristotle but got its prominence because of Locke and Montesquieu.

47. But in working of the U.S. Constitution, it was found that the rule against absolute delegation of legislative powers could not be sustained in practice. As early as 1825, Chief Justice Marshall said that the Congress might delegate powers which the Congress might rightfully exercise itself. By the year 1916, it was found that because of the variety and complexity of administration, the old doctrine prohibiting delegation of legislative power "has virtually retired from the field". But the higher judiciary in USA had not accepted this position and the U.S. Supreme Court struck down the National Industrial Recovery Act 1934 in so far as it conferred powers on the President of USA to adopt codes of fair

competition and impose the code on members of the industry for which such a code was approved. In this connection, Justice Cardozo of the U.S. Supreme Court held that in the National Industrial Recovery Act 1934, the delegated powers of legislation were not "canalized within banks that kept it from overflowing".

48. The American Judges have formulated the following guidelines for delegation of legislative power to the Executive.

(i) The distinction between executive and legislative action cannot be made with mathematical precision and the Executive and the Legislature cannot be divided into watertight compartments.

(ii) Too much effort to make the laws highly detailed would cause great confusion and would lead to problems in their execution.

(iii) The legislature cannot delegate its power to make a law but it can make a law to delegate its power to determine some facts or state of things upon which the law intends to make its own action depend. To deny this would be to stop the wheels of government.

(iv) Half the statutes in the United States of America depend upon discretion of some person or persons to whom the statutes give powers for execution. The exercise of such discretion by the administrative authorities is not tantamount to making the law.

(v) The legislature may declare its will and after fixing a primary standard, devolve upon administrative officers the power to fill up the details by prescribing administrative rules and regulations.

(vi) The Constitution of the United States has empowered the U.S. Congress by laying down policies and establishing standards, while leaving to selected instrumentalities the making of subordinate rules within the limits prescribed by the Congress.

49. The rule against delegation of legislative power is not so inelastic and judges in USA have tried to bring it in line with the needs of the present day administration. The opinion of Judges of the United States also shows that the rule against delegation of legislative power is not a necessary corollary of the doctrine of separation of powers.

50. In England – where Locke and Montesquieu advocated separation of powers for safeguarding liberty – the doctrine of separation of power has exercised very little influence on the course of judicial decisions. In England also, because of the cabinet system of government, the doctrine of separation of powers has come to mean only independence of the judiciary.

51. In USA, separation of powers has come to mean that the legislature cannot delegate to any other organ of government the power to legislate and if it does so, it will act *ultra vires*.

52. Moreover, each and every law passed by a legislature must answer the description of a law upon one or more of the subject matter contained in the Constitution. A law by which a legislature abdicates its law-making power to another body would be bad because it is not a law upon one or more of the subject matter in the Constitution. In 1919, Lord

Haldane correctly summed up the position when he said that even though the legislature of Ontario was entitled to entrust to a Board to enact Regulations relating to taverns, it could not endow any "authority" with legislative power.

53. In Queen *versus* Burah (1878), the Privy council held as follows:
   (i) The Governor-General-in-Council could not enact a law to create a new legislative authority for India as such a course was not authorized by the Indian Council Act passed by the British Parliament.
   (ii) In passing the Act 22 of 1869, the Governor-General-in-Council has not created a new legislative authority.
   (iii) The Governor-General-in-Council has enacted the Act 22 of 1869 with a provision to remove a particular district – Garo Hills in Assam – from jurisdiction of the ordinary courts and place it under new courts to be appointed by the Lt. Governor of Bengal. The Lt. Governor has also no discretion to frame laws for the Garo Hills but only has the power to apply by Notification in the Official Gazette to the Garo Hills any law already passed by any competent legislature in other territories in British India.
   (iv) The proper legislature has exercised its judgment as to place, person, laws, powers and the result has been to legislate conditionally as to all these things.
   (v) Where plenary powers of legislature exist as to particular subjects, those powers may be exercised either absolutely or conditionally. Conditional legislation on the exercise of a limited discretion entrusted by the legislature to persons in the executive is not uncommon. The statute books in England abound with several examples of conditional legislation.

54. The Privy Council considered the issue of delegated legislation in Russel *versus* Queen (1862) and Hodge *versus* Queen (1884) and upheld its decision that conditional legislation was permissible as it did not amount to delegation of legislative powers.

55. In Hodge *versus* Queen (1884), the question arose as to whether the legislature of Ontario had the legal competence to entrust to a local authority the power of framing detailed Regulations in regard to the Liquor License Act 1877. The Privy Council held that the legislature of Ontario – set up under the British North America Act – was supreme in its own sphere as the Parliament had the power to entrust to the Board of Commissioners the authority to frame detailed Regulations to operate and carry out the provisions of the Liquor License Act 1877.

56. The Privy Council also held that conditional legislation enacted by the Sovereign Legislature creating subordinate agencies to frame detailed Regulations for implementation of the law was ancillary to legislation and was perfectly legal as the subordinate agency derives its power from the sovereign legislature itself.

57. Conditional legislation has been recognized as a permissible form of legislation in view of the complexity of administrative laws on a multiplicity of subjects. Further, conditional legislation is subject to the following limitations:
   (i) the primary legislative function has to be discharged by the legislature and not by any other agency;

(ii) a sovereign legislature is free to legislate within its powers;

(iii) In order to freely legislate within its powers, the sovereign legislature may utilize any outside agency to frame the detailed Regulations for effective implementation of the law;

(iv) The sovereign legislature can create a subordinate agency to frame detailed Regulations to carry out the provisions of the law, but it cannot abdicate its sovereign legislative power to create a parallel legislative authority.

(v) The American Courts have applied the doctrine of separation of powers to check excessive delegation of legislative powers but in India, the Courts are not committed to the doctrine of separation of powers and cannot apply the doctrine in the same way it has been used to declare *ultra vires* the laws in America. In India, the main checks on delegation of powers by the legislature are two-fold viz.

(a) the good sense of the legislature;

(b) the legislature should not cross the line beyond which delegation amounts to abdication.

58. In view of the evolution of the concept of delegated legislation, it may be examined whether the Delhi Laws Act 1912 was *ultra vires*. Admittedly, by the Indian Council Act 1861, the Governor-General-in-Council was competent to exercise legislative authority over the whole of British India. In 1912, when the Delhi Laws Act was passed, the Governor-General-in-Council, which functioned as the legislature for British India, had the same plenary powers of the Governor-General-in-Council which enacted the Act 22 of 1869. In other words, the ratio of Queen *versus* Burah (1878) was applicable to the Delhi Laws Act 1912. Therefore, the provisions of the Delhi Laws Act 1912 that the Governor-General could extend by Notification, to the newly-carved province of Delhi, any law, which was in force in any part of British India on the date of such Notification, is *intra vires*.

59. As regards the *vires* of the Ajmer-Merwara (Extension of Laws) Act 1947, it may be noted that the Dominion Legislature under the Government of India Act 1935 could legislate on any matter for a Chief Commissioner's province. Since Ajmer-Merwara was a Chief Commissioner's Province, the Ajmer-Merwara (Extension of Laws) Act 1947 authorizing the Central Government to extend by Notification any law in force in any province in British India to the Ajmer-Merwara province was *intra vires*.

60. Section 2 of Part 'C' states (Laws) Act 1950 is perfectly *intra vires* as the Parliament is the legislature for the Part 'C' states, which have no separate legislatures. Therefore, the Central Government may by Notification extend to any Part "C' state – other than Coorg and the Andaman and Nicober Islands – any enactment which is in force in any Part 'A' state with such restrictions and modifications it thinks fit.

61. Thus Justice Fazl Ali differed from Chief Justice Harilal Kania and held that Section 7 of the Delhi Laws Act 1912, Section 2 of the Ajmer-Merwara (Extension of Laws) Act 1947 and Section 2 of the Part 'C' states Laws Act 1950 are *intra vires*.

62. Like the Chief Justice and other brother Judges, Justice Patanjali Sastri gave a separate opinion. The salient points of his opinion are as follows:

63. The President in making the reference to the Supreme Court had the following facts in the background. In Jatindra Nath Gupta *versus* the Province of Bihar (1949), the Federal Court held by a majority that the proviso to sub-section (3) of Section 1 of the Bihar Maintenance of Public Order Act 1947 was *ultra vires* as it conferred power on the provincial government to modify an Act of the provincial legislature and this amounted to delegation of legislative power to the provincial government. The aforesaid decision of the Federal Court raised doubts about validity of Section 7 of the Delhi Laws Act 1912, Section 2 of the Ajmer-Merwara Laws Act 1947 and Section 2 of the Part (C) States (Laws) Act 1950.

64. In Jatindra Nath Gupta *versus* the Province of Bihar (1949), Chief Justice Harilal Kania, Justice M.C. Mahajan and Justice B.K. Mukherjea of the Federal Court held that the relevant proviso to the Bihar Maintenance of Public Order Act 1947 was *ultra vires* as it amounted to delegation of legislative power to the provincial government. It is relevant to mention that the proviso empowered the provincial executive to extend the life of the Act for a specific period after its expiry and authorized the provincial government also to make modifications in the Bihar Maintenance of Public Order Act 1947 while extending its validity.

65. Justice Fazl Ali, while he was a Judge of the Federal Court, gave a dissenting judgment in Jatindra Nath Gupta *versus* the Province of Bihar (1949). He held that the power of the provincial government to extend life of the Bihar Maintenance of Public Order Act 1947, was a conditional legislation and hence valid though the power to modify the provisions of the Bihar Maintenance of Public Order Act 1947, while extending its validity beyond the period of expiry, was bad in law as it amounted to delegation of legislative power to the provincial government.

66. M.C. Setalvad attacked the majority judgment of the Federal Court in Jatindra Nath Gupta's case (1949) as being opposed alike to sound constitutional principles and the weight of authority. He cited numerous decisions of the Privy Council and of the American, Australian and Canadian Courts in support of the contention that legislative power includes a power to delegate it to other authorities.

67. It is now accepted by constitutional experts that a legislature created by a written Constitution must act within the limits of its power set out in the Constitution itself. In U.K., no such problem can arise as there is no written Constitution and no constitutional limitations on power of the sovereign British Parliament. In India, the position is different as in 1912, 1947 and 1950, when the impugned legislations were passed, India had a written Constitution. Hence, the proper approach to the three issues referred to the Supreme Court by the President is to find out whether the three enactments violated any express condition or restriction by which that power was limited.

68. There is no provision in the several Government of India Acts or the Constitution of India either authorizing or prohibiting in express terms delegation of legislative power. The question is: Can a provision against delegation of legislative power be derived inferentially from the terms of the several Government of India Acts or the present Constitution of India?

69. There are two main theories regarding delegated legislation. As already mentioned, because of the doctrine of parliamentary supremacy, no question of constitutionality of legislation can arise in England. But such questions of constitutionality of legislations has frequently arisen in British Commonwealth countries, which have written Constitutions. British Judges have evolved the doctrine that every legislature in a Commonwealth country, created by an Act of Parliament, is supreme within its allotted sphere and is no sense a delegate of the British Parliament. Therefore, the maxim of "*delegata potestas non potest delegare*" (a delegate cannot further delegate) is not applicable to such a legislature. A delegation of legislative function by such a legislature, however extensive, so long as they preserve their capacity to legislate cannot be challenged as unconstitutional. These propositions were laid down in no uncertain terms in Hodge *versus* Queen (1884) decided by the Privy Council. In the judgment, the Privy Council upheld the validity of an enactment by a provincial legislature in Canada entrusting authority on a Board of Commissioners to make Regulations in the nature of bye-law.

70. In Shannon's case (1938), the Privy Council endorsed extensive delegation of legislative power by passing a Marketing Act for setting up of a Board but leaving it to the Government to decide what powers and functions would be given to the Board.

71. In a reference on "the Natural Products Marketing Act 1937" the Privy Council approved extensive delegation of legislative power by stating that their judgment in the Queen *versus* Burah (1878) abounds with examples of delegation of legislative power to various persons and bodies on a variety of subjects.

72. The British approach to the problem of delegation of legislative power can be summed up as follows:

(i) Legislation by a duly – constituted legislature is not an example of exercise of delegated legislative power;

(ii) A duly – constituted legislature created by an Act of the British Parliament is not a delegate but a sovereign legislative body within limits set by the Act of the Parliament creating it;

(iii) The maxim of "*delegates potestas non potest delegare*" does not apply to such a legislature.

(iv) Legislatures have plenary powers of delegation of legislative powers subject to the stipulation that they cannot create a parallel legislative body. In other words, a legislature cannot either totally surrender or abdicate its legislative functions.

(v) Delegation of legislative power by the legislature is a revocable entrustment of power.

73. The American courts have approached the problem of delegation of legislative power along wholly different lines. In the 18th century, the American political scene was dominated by Locke and Montesquieu and the theory of rigid separation of legislative, executive and judicial powers. But the swift economic progress of USA and the resultant complexities of administration forced the American Judges to realize the inevitability of delegation of powers by the legislature. American decisions consist largely of disguising delegation by "veiling words". Bernard Schwartz has said in "American Administrative Law" that as

legislative powers cannot be constitutionally delegated by the Congress, it is essential that for smooth administration, certain powers be delegated by the legislature to administrative officers and regulatory commissions. The power thus delegated are not delegation of legislative powers but are mere ancillary powers, which can be delegated.

74. Recent judicial pronouncement of the U.S. Supreme Court support the view that after laying down the legislative policy or setting legislative standards, the legislature can delegate the power to frame appropriate rules and regulations to the executive. Such an arrangement can result in better implementation of the law.

75. After a brief survey of history of delegation of legislative power, Justice Patanjali Sastri held that: In 1912, when the Delhi (Laws) Act was enacted, the Indian Legislature was the Governor-General-in-Council. Section 7 of the Delhi (Laws) Act 1912 fell within the general scope of the affirmative words of clause (22) of the Indian Councils Act 1861, which conferred the law-making power on Governor-General-in-Council. Clause (22) also did not violate any of the provisions in the Indian Councils Act 1861 by which negatively that power was restricted.

76. The same approach can be justified in holding that Section 2 of the Ajmer-Merwara (Extension of Laws) Act 1947 was valid as it was fully covered by Section 99(1) of the Government of India Act 1935. This power of the Dominion Legislature to enact laws for the whole of the Dominion of India was also over the Chief Commissioners provinces of which Ajmer-Merwara was one.

77. A legal issue raised by Senior Advocate, N.C. Chatterji, was that Section 3 of the Ajmer-Merwara (Extension of Laws) Act 1947 enabled the Central Government by Notification in the Official Gazette, to extend with such restrictions and modifications as it thought fit to the Chief Commissioner's province of Ajmer-Merwara, any enactment in force in any province of British India. Such a delegation, argued N.C. Chatterji, was of undefined amplitude and was bad in law as it enabled the Central Government to alter or amend any law in its application to the province of Ajmer-Merwara.

78. M.C. Setalvad however rebutted the argument of N.C. Chatterji. He defended the legality of Section 2 of the Ajmer-Merwara (Extension of Laws) Act 1947 by citing the decision of the Privy Council in Queen *versus* Burah (1878) wherein it was held that the power vested in the local government to extend the Civil Procedure Code of 1869 "subject to any restrictions, limitations or proviso" was not bad in law on ground of excessive delegation of legislative power.

79. The Part C states (Laws) Act 1950, was enacted after commencement of the Constitution of India on 26 January 1950. Therefore, the decisions of the Privy Council in Queen *versus* Burah (1878) and in Benoari Lal Sharma's case (AIR 1945 P.C. 48) cannot be of binding nature but these decisions have laid down the correct approach to problems of this kind.

80. The correct way of resolving such problems is to look to the terms of the constitutional instrument and to find out whether the impugned enactment falls within the ambit of the law-making power conferred on the legislature.

81. Article 245 of the Indian Constitution confers law-making powers on the Parliament. The scheme of distribution of legislative power is contained in Article 246 read with the Union List, the State List and the Concurrent List in the Seventh Schedule of the Constitution. Article 246(4) of the Constitution states that Parliament has powers to make laws with respect to any matter for any part of the territory of India not included in any state notwithstanding that such matter is enumerated in the State List. Therefore, the Constitution has vested power on the Parliament to enact the Part 'C' states (Laws) Act 1950. There is also no provision in the Constitution which prohibits enactment of a law by the Parliament delegating legislative power to an agency of Parliament's choice.

82. N.C. Chatterjee has argued that the Preamble to the Constitution states that the People of India have resolved to adopt, enact and give to themselves the Constitution and therefore, the Indian Parliament is a delegate of the people of India as the U.S. Congress is a delegate of the people of the United States of America. Since a delegate cannot further delegate its powers, Parliament cannot delegate its legislative power to any other agency. The answer to this argument is that historically, the U.S. Constitution was framed in a political environment different from the political environment in which the Indian Constitution was framed. Moreover, the Indian Constitution has not established a Presidential form of Government as in the USA but it has a Parliamentary form of government on the Westminster pattern.

83. In USA, the maxim that a delegate cannot further delegate has been enforced by the Courts because it is a necessary corollary of the doctrine of separation of powers. But in India, where there is no rigid separation of powers in the Constitution, the Courts cannot strike down an Act of Parliament merely because the impugned Act has provision for delegation of legislative power to another instrumentality created by the Parliament.

84. N.C. Chatterjee has also argued that whenever the Constitution intends to delegate legislative power to the Executive, it has done so by making provision in the Constitution itself. For example, Article 357(1) of the Constitution provides for delegation by the President of India of the law-making power conferred on him by the Parliament in case of failure of constitutional machinery in a state. It can be said in reply to this argument that merely because the Constitution has in some contingency provided for delegation of legislative power, it does not mean that in appropriate cases, Parliament cannot delegate its legislative power. The Latin Maxim of "*expression unius est exclusion alterius*" is not of universal application. Moreover, in USA there have been many inroads in recent times into the Rule against delegation of legislative power.

85. In Queen *versus* Burah (1878), Lord Selbourne had rightly observed that, in adjudging a statute as constitutional, all that the Court has to see that the statute violates no express condition or restriction by which the law-making power conferred on the legislature is limited and it is not for the Court to enlarge constructively those conditions and restrictions.

86. In Benoarilal Sharma *versus* Emperor (AIR 1945 PC 48), the Privy Council held that the Indian legislature could do, in the matter of delegating its legislative power, what the British Parliament could do.

87. In the result, Section 7 of the Delhi Laws Act 1912, Section 2 of the Ajmer-Merwara (Extension of Laws) Act 1947 and Section 2 of the Part C States (Laws) Act 1950 are in their entirety constitutional and valid.

88. Justice M.C. Mahajan recorded a separate opinion. The salient points of his opinion are as follows: The Attorney-General has argued that legislative power without the authority to delegate is a futility and unless legislative power includes the power to delegate, power to administer law would be ineffective. It was also stated by the Attorney-General that legislative power of the Parliament includes the power to confer law-making power on authorities other than the Parliament and this is a natural corollary of the doctrine of supremacy of the Parliament. As stated by the Privy Council in Queen *versus* Burah (1878) the terms of the legal instrument by which affirmatively legislative powers are created and by which negatively legislative powers are restricted, have to be examined to pronounce upon the vires of a law providing for delegation of legislative power.

89. It is futile to ask in the year 1951 – when the President referred the three issues to the Supreme Court – whether delegated legislation is necessary. The necessity of delegation of rule-making power on the largest scale to administrative authorities is a basic fact of modern post-industrial society. The problem, however, is how delegated legislation and administrative discretion are conferred and controlled so as to comply with elementary principles of law in a democratic society.

90. Lord Dicey has said that it was futile for the Parliament to endeavour to work out details of large legislative enactments as such an endeavour would result in highly lengthy and extremely cumbersome statutes. Blackstone has also remarked that delegated legislation was essential for effective conduct of government. In U.K., delegated legislation could not be *ultra vires* as the Parliament is supreme. The British Parliament being "a large omnipotent despot" can delegate its legislative power or even create new bodies conferring on them powers to make laws.

91. But the constitutional position in India approximates more closely to the American model than to the English model. Hence, it would be worthwhile to find out what is the decision of the U.S. Courts on delegation of powers. It has also to be noted that in spite of the widest powers possessed by the British Parliament, it has adopted a policy of self-abnegation in matters of delegated legislation. The Donoughmore Committee to report on powers of Ministers in U.K. has set out limitations for delegation of legislative powers. It also recommended to keep a watchful eye on such delegated legislation. It discovered only a few instances where delegation was made to the Minister-in-charge in a limited way to modify Parliamentary statutes. In a case, where the Secretary of State had the power to modify and adapt a statute for a limited period of about a year and a half (May 1929 to December 1930) to bring the provisions of the Act in conformity with the provisions of other Acts, the power was given the nickname of Henry VIII Clause. The Donoughmore Committee recommended that the Henry VIII clause could be adopted in a very special case and that too to bring the Act into operation within a limited period of one year only. It is significant to note that since the recommendation of the Donoughmore Committee

(1931), the "Henry VIII Clause" has not been incorporated in any statute passed by the British Parliament.

92. The Dominion of Canada has a written Constitution. The decision of the Canadian Courts with regard to delegation of legislative power by the Canadian Parliament has not been uniform. Some instances of delegation of power by the Canadian Parliament have been justified under the War Measures Act and the exigencies of the First and the Second World Wars.

93. In Queen *versus* Burah (1878) the Privy Council was hearing an appeal from the High Court of Calcutta regarding the Act 22 of 1869 enacted by the Governor-General-in-Council which excluded the Garo Hills from jurisdiction of the ordinary courts of Civil and Criminal law.

94. The following aspects of Act 22 of 1869 may be noted:

(i) The Act did not empower the Lt. Governor to modify any provision of the Act in its application to the Garo Hills and any other areas as Jainita Hills, Naga Hills and Khasi Hills.

(ii) The Lt. Governor did not have power to select parts of an Act for local application in Garo Hills and the Khasi & Jaintia Hills.

(iii) By a majority judgment, the Calcutta High Court held the Notification by the Lt. Governor as void. The High Court held that the Indian Councils Act 1861 did not authorize the Council of Governor-General-of-India to delegate its legislative power to the Lt. Governor of Bengal which has been done by the Act 22 of 1869.

(iv) The Act 22 of 1869, which empowered the Lt. Governor of Bengal to issue Notification from time to time to extend *mutatis mutandis* all or any other provisions contained in the other sections of the Act 22 of 1869 to Jaintia Hills, Naga Hills and such portion of the Khasi Hills forming part of British India was an instance of delegation of power by the legislature and hence *ultra vires* the Indian Councils Act 1861.

(v) On appeal from the majority judgment of the Calcutta High Court, the Privy Council held in Queen *versus* Burah (1878) that:

(a) The Indian legislature i.e. Council of the Governor-General of India, has powers expressly limited by the Act of the Imperial Parliament, which created it. But while acting within its powers the Indian legislature is supreme as the British Parliament.

(b) The Courts may inquire into the terms of the written instrument by which affirmatively the legislative power was created and by which, negatively, they are restricted. If what would have been done is legislation within the affirmative scope of the general words which gave the power and if it violates no express restriction by which that power is limited, it is not for a Court to inquire further or to enlarge constructively those restrictions.

(c) The powers of the Lt. Governor of Bengal under the Act 22 of 1869 were vested entirely by the Council of the Governor-General of India. In other words, the Governor-General-in-Council, as the proper legislature, has exercised its judgment as to place, persons, laws and powers and the result has been to legislate conditionally as to all these things.

(d) Plenary powers of a legislature can be exercised absolutely or conditionally.

(vi) In spite of upholding the *vires* of the Notification of October 1871 issued by the Lt. Governor of Bengal in Queen *versus* Burah (1878), the Privy Council did not hold that the Indian legislature has full powers of delegation within the ambit of its legislative field.

(vii) The Privy Council justified the Act 22 of 1869 as an example of conditional legislation. They held that legislation of this kind was complete on fulfillment of those conditions and determination of those conditions could be left to an external agency. Even though the Privy Council did not hold that the Indian Legislature was an agent of the British Parliament, they held that a legislature cannot delegate its functions to an external agency and the external agency could at best do ministerial functions to efficiently implement the law passed by the competent legislature. It is difficult to conceive that the Privy Council would have hesitated to say that delegation of legislative power was a necessary corollary of the legislative power itself as argued by M.C. Setalvad. But the Privy Council did not say it.

95. In King Emperor *versus* Benoarilal Sharma (AIR 1945 PC 48) the Privy Council upheld the *vires* of the Ordinance of 1942 on the ground that it was a conditional legislation and not a delegated legislation. The facts of the case in brief were as follows: The ordinance of 1942 provided that Special Courts would be set up in any province if the provincial government was satisfied that an emergency existed because of either attack or imminence of an attack by a foreign power. It was argued that instead of the Governor-General deciding whether an emergency existed in a province, it was left to the provincial government to decide whether an emergency existed to set up special courts. Both the Calcutta High Court and the Federal Court had declared the Ordinance *ultra vires* because the Governor-General delegated his legislative power to the provincial governments to decide whether an emergency has arisen in a province to set up a special court. The Privy Council did not agree with the Calcutta High Court and the Federal Court and held that it was a conditional legislation in which the local application of the Ordinance was decided by a local administrative body.

96. A judgment of the Federal Court of India of importance in regard to delegated legislation is Jatindra Nath Gupta *versus* the Province of Bihar (1949). The Judgment held sub-section (3) of the Bihar Maintenance of Public Order Act 1947 *ultra vires* as it gave power to the provincial government to direct that the Act shall remain in force for a further period of one year beyond the period of one year of its commencement, with such modifications which the Provincial Government shall specify in the Notification. The Federal Court held that it was a case of delegation of legislative power by the legislature to the provincial government as the provincial government could modify any provision of the Act while extending its validity. It was a delegation of essential legislative power not permissible as laid down in Queen *versus* Burah (1878).

97. In the State of Bombay *versus* Narottamdas (AIR 1951 SC 69), the Supreme Court decided that Jatindra Nath Gupta's case (1949) was no authority for prohibiting the delegation of legislative power in case where the principle and policy of the law have been declared in the law itself. In other words, it was held that once policy of the law was declared in the law itself, ancillary powers could be delegated to the Executive for effective implementation of the Act.

98. The true solution to the problem of delegation of legislative power is to be found in the oft-quoted passage of Justice Ranney of the Supreme Court of Ohio in USA which states as follows: "The true distinction is between the delegation of power to make the law, which necessarily involves discretion as to what the law shall be, and conferring authority or discretion as to its execution, to be exercised under and in pursuance of the law. The first cannot be done; to the latter no valid objection can be made."

99. Justice Varadachariar of the Federal Court of India held in Benoarilal Sharma's case (AIR 1945 PC 48) that the constitutional position in India under the Government of India Act 1935 approximates more closely to the American model than to the English model and delegation of essential legislative power is not permitted under the Government of India Act 1935.

100. The Indian Councils Act 1861 also did not authorize the Governor-General to delegate legislative power to any other agency. That's why in Queen *versus* Burah (1878), the Privy Council upheld Act 22 of 1869 as a piece of conditional legislation.

101. Section 7 of the Delhi Laws Act 1912 has the following features:

(i) It gives a *carte blanche* to the Governor-General to extend to the newly-formed Chief Commissioner's province of Delhi any enactment in force in any province of British India.

(ii) It does not restrict itself to any enactment in force in any province of British India on the date of passing of Delhi (Laws) Act 1912. In other words, if any law is passed in any province of British India after the enactment of the Delhi (Laws) Act 1912 at a future date such enactment can also be extended to the Chief Commissioner's province of Delhi by a Notification.

(iii) As a necessary corollary, the principles and policy of the laws after enactment of the Delhi (Laws) Act 1912 would not be known to the legislature when it passed the Delhi (Laws) Act 1912.

(iv) The Governor-General held also power of modifying not only existing enactments but also future enactments after the year 1912 in its application to the Chief Commissioner's province of Delhi.

(v) Therefore, Section 7 of the Delhi (Laws) Act 1912 conferred a kind of wide, vagrant and uncanalised power on the Governor-General of India.

102. The conclusion is irresistible that by enacting Section 7 of the Delhi (Laws) Act 1912, the legislature virtually abdicated its legislative power in favour of the executive. Such an eventuality was not warranted either by the Indian Councils Act 1861 or by decision of the Privy Council in Queen *versus* Burah (1878). The net result is that Section 7 of the Delhi (Laws) Act 1912 declares that the legislature has no policy of its own and the Governor-General can decide such policy and lay down what laws would be applicable to the Chief Commissioner's province of Delhi. Therefore, Section 7 of the Delhi (Laws) Act 1912 is *ultra vires* the Indian Council Act 1861.

103. In regard to the second issue referred to the Supreme Court by the President, it may be relevant to recapitulate Section 2 of the Ajmer-Merwara (Extension of Laws) Act 1947 which states as follows:

"The Central Government may by Notification in the official gazette extend to the province of Ajmer-Merwara with such restrictions and modifications as it thinks fit any enactment in force in any other province at the date of such Notification".

104. It may be pointed out that under the Government of India Act 1935, different provinces of British India had the power to legislate in their allotted fields of legislation. But what policy was to be adopted in extending laws to the Chief Commissioner's province of Ajmer-Merwara was left to the Central Government. Therefore, Section 2 of the Ajmer-Merwara (Extension of Laws) Act is *ultra vires* the Government of India Act 1935.

105. Section 2 of the Part C states Laws Act 1950 is also *ultra vires* for similar reasons for which Section 7 of the Delhi (Laws) Act 1912 and Section 2 of the Ajmer-Merwara (Extension of Laws) Act 1947 have been held to be *ultra vires*.

106. Admittedly, the benefit of reasonable doubt about constitutional validity of a statute has to be resolved in favour of legislative action. But in this case, the legislative action has been of such a drastic and indefinite nature that it is not possible to hold any of the three enactments viz. Delhi (Laws) Act 1912, Ajmer-Merwara (Extension of Laws) Act 1947 and Part 'C' States (Laws) Act 1950 as constitutionally valid.

107. Justice B.K. Mukherjea recorded a separate opinion on the three issues referred to the Supreme Court. The salient points of his opinion are in the following paragraphs.

108. In all the three cases viz. Delhi(Laws) Act 1912; the Ajmer-Merwara (Extension of Laws) Act 1947 and the Part 'C' States (Laws) Act 1950, the legislature has conferred power on an outside authority and this delegation of power to the outside authority has been done empowering it to make any adaptation while extending the laws to the Chief Commissioner's Province of Delhi, the Chief Commissioner's province of Ajmer-Merwara and the Part 'C' States of the Republic of India. The Part 'C' States (Laws) Act 1950 expressly provided not only for such restriction and modification in the laws in Part A states as the Central Government would deem proper which in effect also empowered the Central Government to amend any provision of law in force in a Part A state in its application to a Part 'C' state.

109. The Attorney-General argued that a legislature, competent to legislate on a particular subject, has the power to delegate its power on that subject to any agent or external authority. There are only two limitations on the legislature in delegating its legislative power to an external authority. The first limitation is that a legislature cannot abdicate or surrender its powers altogether or bring into existence a new legislature. The second limitation is that if the constitutional document has distributed power to legislate among

different legislative bodies, one legislature cannot delegate to another legislature powers to legislate on subjects which are vested on it under the constitutional document.

110. The Attorney-General has argued that apart from these two limitations, there cannot be any other limitation on a legislature to delegate its legislative power. He also stated that the British model of Parliamentary Government does not recognize the rigid separation of powers of the U.S. Constitution.

111. A principle in support of the rule against delegation of legislative power is the maxim, "*delegatus non potest delegare*". Edward Coke had lent authority to this maxim.

112. The doctrine of separation of powers advocated by Montesquieu influenced the U.S. Constitution. They entrusted separate powers to the Executive, the Legislature and the Judiciary. Cooley says in his book, *Constitutional Limitations* that in the U.S. there is an implied limitation on each organ of Government for exercising functions conferred on the others.

113. The doctrine of "*delgatus non potest delegare*" (a delegate cannot further delegate) is based on the juristic theory that a legislature – elected by the people – is itself a delegate of the people themselves, who are the ultimate repository of all powers. And a delegate cannot further delegate its powers to an outside agency.

114. But these doctrines against delegation of power by the legislature operate in practice in a very limited way. Justice Story of the United States of America has stated that exercise of whole power by one entity of Government of the whole power of another entity of Government would subvert the principle of a free constitution. According to Justice Story, this is the real meaning of the doctrine of Separation of Powers.

115. In USA, vast complexities of social and economic conditions of the Modern Age have made it impossible for the legislature to frame laws, which are complete in all details. Therefore, in USA there are numerous rules and regulations passed by non-legislative bodies in exercise of power bestowed upon them by the legislature. Justice Cardozo in his dissenting judgment in the Panama Refining Company *versus* Ryan (1934) has aptly observed that the doctrine of separation of powers is "not a doctrinaire concept to be made use of with pedantic rigour" and there must be elasticity of adjustment in response to the practical necessities of Government.

116. In fact, in USA the rule of non-delegation of legislative power has so many exceptions that it is difficult to decide whether the rigid dogma of separation of powers or the exceptions engrafted upon it can be relied upon for an authentic interpretation of the doctrine of separation of powers.

117. The doctrine of rigid separation of powers has no place either in the present Constitution of India or in the system of Government during the British rule. In the Indian Constitution, the Executive is responsible to the legislature. The Council of Ministers both in the Union Government and the Government of different states is the "*hyphen which joins – a buckle which fastens the legislative part of the state to the executive part.*"

118. It is not a sound political theory that a legislature is merely a delegate of the people. In Queen *versus* Burah (1878), the Privy Council held that the Indian legislature under the Indian Councils Act 1861 was in no sense a delegate of the British Parliament. It was also held that the Indian legislature has powers expressly limited by the Act of the Imperial Parliament which created it, and it can, of course do nothing beyond the limits which circumscribe these powers. But when acting within those limits, it is not in any sense an agent or delegate of the Imperial Parliament, but has plenary powers of legislation. While acting within its powers, the Indian legislature has powers as large as the British Parliament itself.

119. The same observations were made by the Privy Council in Hodge *versus* Queen (1884) describing the position of the provincial legislature under the Canadian Constitution.

120. It is well established that the British Parliament has no constitutional limitations on its powers. It is both a legislative and a constituent body and as Lord Dicey says no Act of the British Parliament can be declared *ultra vires*.

121. But the Governor-General-in-Council, which was the legislative body for British India under the Indian Councils Act 1861 did not have the sovereign powers of the British Parliament, which Edward Coke had called transcendent and absolute. The legislative body of the Governor-General-in-Council had set the limits of the powers which were set by the Indian Councils Act 1861 passed by the British Parliament. The sovereign powers of the British Parliament are also not available to the Parliament of India, which has laid down powers and limits of those powers in the Constitution itself. The powers of the Parliament of India to confer on the President of India power to delegate law making power to any other authority has been provided for only in Article 357 of the Constitution of India as an emergency provision.

122. There is no other provision in the Constitution of India which permits the legislature to delegate power to any other authority. In Crawford's "Statutory Construction", it has been said that if a statute directs that certain acts shall be done in a specified manner or by certain persons, by necessary implication, performance of those acts in any other manner or by other persons is prohibited. Cooley also writes in his book, *Constitutional Law* that the high prerogative of legislation has been vested in the legislature and in framing laws, the legislature must exercise its own discretion and judgment. The legislative body will act *ultra vires* if it undertakes to delegate the trust instead of executing it.

123. The legislative bodies which enacted the Delhi (Laws) Act 1912 and the Ajmer-Merwara (Extension of Laws) Act 1947 did not have the power to delegate the essential law-making power to some other agency.

124. Delegation of legislative power could only be permitted as ancillary to, or in aid of, exercise of law-making powers by the proper legislature and not as a means of relieving itself of its duty of legislation.

125. In Queen *versus* Burah (1878), the Notification of the Lt. Governor of Bengal extending the Act XII of 1869 to some hill areas of Assam was upheld as an instance of conditional legislation and not as an instance of delegated legislation.

126. The same principle was applied by the Privy Council in Benoarilal Sharma's case (AIR 1945 PC 48). In that case, the validity of an emergency ordinance by the Governor-General of India was challenged, *inter alia*, on ground that it provided for setting up of special

courts for particular kinds of offences but the actual setting up of the Courts was left to the provincial government.

127. The Privy Council held that it was not delegated legislation, but it was an example of conditional legislation.

128. A legislature cannot delegate essential legislative functions. Essential legislative function consist in determination of legislative policy and of formally enacting the policy into a binding rule of conduct. It is open to the legislature to formulate that policy as broadly and with as little or as much details as it thinks proper. It may delegate the rest of the legislative work to a subordinate authority to work out the details within the framework of that policy.

129. In Panama Refinery Company *versus* Rayan (1934) – a judgment of the U.S. Supreme Court – it was held that a statute of the U.S. Congress was *ultra vires* as the Congress declared no policy, set no standard and laid down no rule for oil production in excess of permission. It was held that the delegation of power was uncanalized and vagrant and hence *ultra vires*.

130. During the emergency arising out of the First World War (1914–19), the Dominion War Measures Act 1914 was passed by the Dominion Parliament of Canada empowering the Governor-General to make Regulations for security, defence, peace, order and welfare of Canada. The question before the Supreme Court of Canada was whether the Governor-General could further delegate powers – conferred by the War Measures Act 1914 – to subordinate agencies. In 1918, when a reference was made to the Supreme Court of Canada, the Court held that the security of the country was the supreme law against which no other law would prevail.

131. There is perhaps no necessity of introducing the strained interpretation of law – following emergency and the War Measures Act – in India as the Indian Constitution has made adequate provision to tackle situations arising out of war and external aggression.

132. Against this background, the *vires* of Section 7 of the Delhi (Laws) Act 1912 may be examined. The Chief Commissioner's province of Delhi was carved out of the province of Punjab by a Notification issued on 17 September 1912. The laws in force in the province of Punjab were made applicable to the Chief Commissioner's province of Delhi by Section 2 of the Delhi (Laws) Act 1912. By Section 7 of the Delhi (Laws) Act, the Governor-General was authorized to extend to the province of Delhi or any part thereof, with such restrictions and modifications as the Governor-General thought fit, any enactment in force in any part of British India on the day of such Notification. In 1912, the Government of India was unitary in character and Section 22 of the Indian Council Act 1861 gave plenary powers to the Governor-General-in-Council to legislate for British India. Following the judgment in Queen *versus* Burah (1878), the Delhi (Laws) Act 1912 was passed within the scope of the affirmative words used in the Indian Council Act 1861 which gave the power. It also violated no express condition or restriction by which that power was limited. The policy behind the Delhi (Laws) Act 1912 seems to be that in Delhi, which had no local legislature and was small in size not to have a local legislature in near future, the Governor-General-in-Council decided that the laws validly passed and in force in other

parts of British India could be applied to the Chief Commissioner's province of Delhi with such restrictions and modifications as might be necessary.

133. The Delhi (Laws) Act 1912 is almost similar to Act 22 of 1869 which was declared *intra vires* by the Privy Council in Queen *versus* Burah (1878). The material difference is that under Act 22 of 1869, the Lt. Governor of Bengal in application of some laws to certain areas by Notification could not modify the law to suit the local condition. But in Delhi (Laws) Act 1912, the Central Government may extend to the Chief Commissioner's province of Delhi any law with such restrictions or modifications as the Central Government would consider necessary to adapt the laws to the local conditions of the Chief Commissioner's province of Delhi. But the "modification" in Section 7 of the Delhi (Laws) Act 1912 does not mean any substantial alteration inconsistent with policy of any Act which is sought to be extended to the Chief Commissioners' province of Delhi by Notification. The "modification" in Section 7 meant only such minor alteration as would make it appropriate to meet the local conditions. Such modifications cannot be called unwarranted delegation of legislative power.

134. **N.B.:** In Jatindra Nath Gupta's case (1949) the Federal Court – with Justice B.K. Mukherjea in the Bench – held "modification" of a statute by the Executive an exercise of legislative power by the Executive and hence *ultra vires*. [**N.B.:** In the present reference regarding Delhi (Laws) Act 1912, Justice B.K. Mukherjea, who became a Judge of the Supreme Court on commencement of the Constitution, has called the Delhi (Laws) Act 1912 an instance of delegation of ancillary power to a subordinate authority and hence *intra vires*.]

135. The second issue referred by the President of India to the Supreme Court is regarding the *vires* of Section 2 of the Ajmer-Merwara (Extension of Laws) Act 1947. It authorizes the Central Government to extend, by Notification, with such restrictions and modifications it thinks fit, to the Chief Commissioner's Province of Ajmer-Merwara any enactment in force in any other province of British India on the date of such Notification.

136. The ground which could be urged in support of *vires* of the Delhi (Laws) Act 1912 could be also urged for the *vires* of the Ajmer-Merwara (Extension of Laws) Act 1947. The modification which the Central Government could make in laws, which could be extended to the Chief Commissioner's province of Ajmer-Merwara, would be not radical changes in the law but such alteration as would suit the local conditions. If this limitation is transgressed, it would be a violation of section 2 of the Ajmer-Merwara (Extension of Laws) Act 1947.

137. The third – and the last – issue referred by the President of India to the Supreme Court is regarding *vires* of the Part C states (Laws) Act 1950 enacted by the Parliament of India after commencement of the Constitution.

138. The Part C State (Laws) Act confers powers on the Central Government far in excess of the Delhi (Laws) Act 1912 and the Ajmer-Merwara (Laws) Act 1947. By the Part C States (Laws) Act, power is given to the Central Government to abrogate or repeal any existing law – other than a Central Act – in force in Part 'C' State. It is an unwarranted delegation of legislative power to the Central Government. Therefore, the last part of

Section 2 of Part C States (Laws) Act 1950 is *ultra vires* the powers of the Parliament. It suffers from the vice of excessive delegation of legislative power.

139. Justice S.R. Das recorded a separate opinion on the three issues referred by the President of India to the Supreme Court.

140. The opinion of Justice S.R. Das may be summed up as follows: the reference to the Court has to be answered in the light of constitutional position in different countries. In the British Constitution, the Parliament is supreme. Dicey says in his book, *Law of Constitution* that the British Parliament can pass any law in its sovereign capacity. It can also amend or abrogate any law. No Court can pronounce law passed by the British Parliament as void. The British Constitution is the best example of a flexible Constitution where every part can be expanded, curtailed or amended with equal case.

141. Cecil Carr in his "Lectures in English Administrative Law" referring to the Sovereign power of the British Parliament, has said that even the Magna Carta (1215) is not inviolate. Even though Edward Coke has said that any statute passed by the Parliament contrary to the Magna Carta is void, in actual practice, nearly two-thirds of the Magna Carta have already been repealed by the British Parliament.

142. The reasons for the power of delegation as a necessary incident to the exercise of legislative power are as follows:

(a) Parliament has no time to shape legislative details in a law.

(b) Parliament, which has members with diverse background, may not have technical knowledge to fill up the details of law in a complex, fast-changing post-industrial society.

143. The Donoughmore Committee in U.K. (1931) which examined the extent of powers of the Ministers has not said that delegated legislation should be done away with altogether. It only recommended that reason for extensive delegation proposed must be mentioned in the memorandum attached to the Bill before the Parliament. A Select Committee on Statutory Instruments has since been appointed in U.K. for reporting on every Bill proposing to delegate law-making power. Thus in U.K., though the Parliament's power of delegation is unlimited, the Parliament keeps a watchful eye on delegation of legislative powers.

144. The U.S. Constitution was framed keeping in the forefront the theory of separation of powers advocated by John Locke and Montesquieu. The U.S. Constitution has vested legislative powers on the Congress, the executive power on the President and the judicial power on the Supreme Court and such inferior courts as the Congress may establish from time to time. In USA, the maxim "*delegata potestas non potest delegare*" (a delegate cannot further delegate) has been invoked to prohibit delegation of legislative powers to independent Boards or Commissions. But as Willoughby has said in his book *Constitutional Law of the United States*, the Central legislative body has delegated extensive legislative powers to local self-governments with reference to local matters.

145. In Field *versus* Clark (1891), Justice Harlan of the U.S. Supreme Court quoted an observation of Justice Ranney of the Supreme Court of Ohio which stated that: "The true distinction is between delegation of power to make the law which necessarily involves a discretion as to what it shall be and conferring authority or discretion as to its execution to be exercised under and in pursuance of the law. The first cannot be done; to the latter no valid objection can be made."

146. In other words, the legislature cannot delegate its power to make a law; but it can make a law to delegate its power to determine some facts or state of things upon which action under the law depends. To deny this would be to stop the wheels of government.

147. Professor Willis has summarized the exceptions to delegation of legislative powers as follows:

(a) There can be delegation of powers to local self-governments;

(b) The legislature may delegate the powers to determine the conditions under which a statute shall be operative;

(c) The legislature may delegate powers to make Regulations, to Boards of Health and Heads of Departments;

(d) Legislature may delegate power to ascertain facts and to apply rules of law in controversies.

148. After enumerating the exceptions to the delegation rule, Professor Willis has observed whether in USA, there is still a doctrine of separation of powers.

149. The Privy Council in Queen *versus* Burah (1878) has negatived the contention that the Indian legislature, under the Indian Councils Act 1861, was a delegate of the British Parliament. The Privy Council held that the Act 22 of 1869, passed by the Governor-General-in-Council for British India, was perfectly valid as it was enacted under the Indian Councils Act 1861. The Act 22 of 1869 did not create a new legislative body. It only exercised its judgment as to place, persons, law and powers and the result was to legislate conditionally and confer on the Lt. Governor of Bengal certain powers to extend to certain areas as the Jaintia Hills, the Naga Hills and some part of the Khasi Hills, some enactments by valid Notification.

150. The majority of the judges of the Calcutta High Court held that section 9 of the Act 22 of 1869 was *ultra vires* on ground of excessive delegation of legislative power. The Privy Council in Queen *versus* Burah (1878) negatived the above contention on the following two grounds:

(a) The Indian Legislature i.e. the Governor-General-in-Council was not an agent of the British Parliament but was a sovereign legislature within the limits of the Indian Councils Act of 1861.

(b) The Governor-General-in-Council had not delegated its power by enacting section 9 of the Act 22 of 1869. It was only a conditional legislation for which the Governor-General-in-Council had full powers.

151. The above two grounds relied upon by the Privy Council in Queen *versus* Burah (1878) did not mean that the Privy Council denied to the Governor-General-in-Council full delegation of legislative power. Actually, while denying to the Governor-General-in-Council powers to create a new legislative body, the Privy Council conceded the power of delegation to the Governor-General-in-Council but only set out the limits of such power.

152. The above line of argument finds support from another judgment of the Privy Council in Russell *versus* the Queen (1880), which considered the *vires* of the Canadian Temperance Act of 1878. The Privy Council held that the provision in the Canadian Temperance Act, 1878, that certain provisions of the Act will come into force only on a petition of the majority of electors in a city or a country, did not confer on the electors the powers to legislate. In passing the Canadian Temperance Act of 1878, the Canadian Parliament stipulated this condition of petition of majority of electors to enforce the Act and hence it was a case of conditional legislation.

153. Similarly, in Hodge *versus* the Queen (1884), the Privy Council decided that the Liquor License Act 1877 of the provincial legislature of Ontario in Canada authorizing the License Commissioner to make regulations, create offences and prescribe practices, was *intra vires*. The Privy Council held that by authorizing the License Commissioner, the legislature did not efface itself. On the other hand, it retained its power intact and could at any time abrogate the authority of the License Commissioner. Thus, the Privy Council supported delegated legislation as ancillary to the main legislation.

154. In King-Emperor *versus* Benorari Lal Sharma (AIR 1945 PC 48), the Privy Council considered the *vires* of the Special Criminal Courts Ordinance promulgated by the Governor-General in 1942 under the Government of India Act 1935 read with the India and Burma (Emergency Powers) Act 1940. The Ordinance was to come into force in any province of British India only if the provincial government was satisfied that an emergency has arisen in the province due to some disorder. The Ordinance was challenged on the ground that the Governor-General should have decided himself whether an emergency has arisen and not delegated the power to declare an emergency to the provincial government. The Calcutta High Court declared the ordinance *ultra vires*. A majority of judges of the Federal Court upheld the judgment of the High Court. The matter went up to the Privy Council, who did not agree with the High Court and the Federal Court and held that the ordinance was an example of the not uncommon arrangement by which local application of provisions of a statute is determined by judgment of the local administration.

155. The power of delegation is inherent in the legislative power itself and short of self-effacement, the legislature may exercise the widest power of delegation.

156. After the territory of the Chief Commissioner's province of Delhi was carved out of the province of Punjab in British India on 17 September 1912, there was urgent need for legislation for the Chief Commissioner's province of Delhi. As the Central Government was fully competent to administer the Chief Commissioner's province of Delhi, the Governor-General-in-Council passed the Delhi (Laws) Act 1912. Section 2 of the Delhi (Laws) Act saved the application of all laws of the province of Punjab, which were in force in Delhi when it was a part of the province of Punjab.

157. After the crown took over the administration of British India from the East India Company by the Government of India Act 1858, the Indian Councils Act 1861 was passed by the British Parliament. In 1912, the legislative power of the Governor-General-in-Council was the same as that of the Governor-General-in-Council when it passed the Act 22 of 1869 the *vires* of which was upheld by the Privy Council in Queen *versus* Burah (1878).

158. Since *vires* of the Act 22 of 1869 was upheld by the Privy Council as a piece of conditional legislation, the same logic could apply to the legality of Section 7 of the Delhi (Laws) Act 1912. Following the ratio of the judgment of the Privy Council in Queen *versus* Burah (1878) the Governor-General-in-Council, in enacting the Delhi (Laws) Act 1912, did not efface itself or abdicate all legislative power or set up a new legislative power. By enacting Section 7 of the Delhi (Laws) Act 1912, the Governor-General-in-Council acted within the ambit of the legislative power vested in him and hence Section 7 is not *ultra vires*.

159. Section 2 of the Ajmer-Merwara (Extension of Laws) Act 1947 is a piece of conditional legislation within the meaning of Queen *versus* Burah (1878).

160. The third issue referred by the President of India to the Supreme Court related to the *vires* of Section 2 of the Part C States (Laws) Act 1950.

161. The only difference between Section 2 of Part C States (Laws) Act 1950 and Section 7 of the Delhi (Laws) Act 1912 or section 2 of the Ajmer-Merwara (Extension of Laws) Act 1947 is that Section 2 of the Part C States (Laws) Act 1950 empowers the Central Government, while extending any enactment in a Part A state to a Part C State, to provide for repeal or amendment of any law in force (except Central Laws) in the Part C state. But even this difference does not prevent Section 2 of the Part C States (Laws) Act 1950 as being considered as a piece of conditional legislation. The Parliament of India thought it fit to give discretion to the Central Government to extend any enactment in a Part A state – which has already been passed by a competent legislature – to a Part C state with such alterations and modifications as would be suitable for local conditions in a part C state.

162. Even if it is agreed that Section 2 of the Part C States (Laws) Act 1950 is outside the ambit of conditional legislation, the section may be upheld as a permissible delegation of legislative power on two grounds. The first ground is that delegation of legislative power is inherent in the law-making power of the legislature. The second ground is that a law relating to delegation of legislative power can be passed under item (97) of the Union List, (i.e. residuary power of the Parliament) read with Article 248 of the Constitution.

163. To sum up, Justice S.R. Das upheld the *vires* of Section 7 of the Delhi (Laws) Act 1912, Section 2 of the Ajmer-Merwara (Extension of Law) Act 1947 and Section 2 (c) of the Part (C) States (Laws) Act 1950.

164. Justice Vivian Bose recorded a separate opinion on all three issues referred by the President. [**N.B.:** He upheld the *vires* of Section 7 of Delhi (Laws) Act 1912 and Section 2 of the Ajmer-Merwara (Extension of Laws) Act 1947 on the same ground on which some brother judges of the Supreme Court upheld their *vires*.]

165. On the third issue, Justice Vivian Bose held that the first part of the Part C States (Laws) Act 1950, passed by the Indian Parliament, authorised the Central Government to extend to any Part C state any law in force in any part A state of the Indian Union with such restrictions and modifications the Central Government thought fit. Only two Part C states as Coorg and the Andaman-Nicober Islands were excluded from the purview of this Act. Power was also given to the Central Government, when extending any law in Part A state to a Part C state for repeal or amendment of any corresponding law (except a Central

Act) applicable to a Part C state. This power given to the Central Government to repeal or amend any existing law in a Part C State while extending any law in a Part A state has given rise to a constitutional issue regarding the power of the Indian Parliament to delegate such legislative power to the Central Government.

166. The issue to be considered whether the Constituent Assembly in framing the new Constitution had decided to empower the Parliament to authorize the Central Government to amend or repeal any existing law in a Part C state while extending any law in force in a Part A state to a Part C state.

167. The Constituent Assembly had several models to follow in framing the Constitution of free India. On the one hand, they had before them the flexible British concept of the widest devolution of authority short of creating a new legislature as laid down by the Privy Council in Queen *versus* Burah (1878). The Constituent Assembly had also before it the American model with its rigid doctrine of separation of powers.

168. First, it has been seen from experience that functions of a modern state cannot be carried on without a large devolution of power and delegation of authority. Secondly, the practical application of the principle of delegation of legislative power has not been free from difficulties as is evident from experience of India, other parts of the British Empire and England itself. Finally, even in USA, the judges had to veer away from the rigidity of the doctrine of separation of powers in view of complexity of the tasks of modern governments.

169. But in India, under the new Constitution, the Parliament has not been left free. The provision for certain Fundamental Rights in the Constitution has placed fetters on powers of the Parliament to legislate. When Parliament legislates regarding the limitations on Fundamental Rights on grounds of reasonable restrictions on those Rights, it is the Parliament alone which can legislate and no other authority created by the Parliament. Parliament has powers only to legislate in respect of items in the Union List in the Seventh Schedule of the Constitution. It can legislate on items in the State List subject to the provisions in Article 249 of the Constitution, which authorizes the Parliament to legislate on items in the State List for a limited period pursuant to a resolution passed in the Council of States. Under Article 357 of the Constitution, the Indian Parliament has powers to legislate for a state when the state is under the President's rule under Article 356 of the Constitution.

170. The Indian Parliament can legislate along the lines of the decision in Queen *versus* Burah (1878) which means that it can leave to the Executive application of laws which are in existence at that time in any part of India which is subject to legislative control of the Parliament. This has been the past practice in India and does not seem to have been abrogated by the Constitution of India. But repealing or amending the laws in force in a Part C state can only be done by the Parliament in exercise of its legislative power and cannot be done by the Central Government even if the Parliament authorizes the Central Government to do so by a law. No decision of the Privy Council has been cited which authorizes the Executive to repeal the existing law in force. In the case of Sir John Gordon Sprigg *versus* Sigcau (1897) a case which arose from South Africa – the Privy Council held that amendment or repeal of any existing law cannot be done by the Executive even through duly authorized to do so by the legislature. "It is one thing to fill a void or a partial vacuum. Quite another to throw out existing laws enacted by a competent authority."

171. It is the main function of the legislature to legislate and not to leave it to others to legislate. But it may be difficult to adhere to this view because of the necessities of a modern state. But it is hoped that delegation of legislative power in the interest of administrative convenience in a modern state will be done sparingly. Even in England, where the Parliament has unfettered powers to legislate and delegate legislative power, the Donoughmore Committee (1931) has recommended that powers of the Parliament in this behalf be sparingly used.

172. In view of the aforesaid, the Part C States (Laws) Act 1950 is *intra vires* except the following:

"And provision may be made in any enactment so extended for the repeal or amendment of any corresponding law (other than a Central Act) which is for the time being applicable to a Part C state."

173. The power of the Central Government to restrict and modify as provided for in the Delhi (Laws) Act 1912 and the Ajmer-Merwara (Extension of Laws) Act 1947 are not meant to make essential changes in the enactments extended to the Chief Commissioner's province of Delhi or the Chief Commissioner's province of Ajmer-Merwara. They are meant to be alterations of a minor character to make a law enacted for one area applicable to another and to bring it in harmony with laws already in force in the Chief Commissioner's province. "To alter the essential character of an Act or to change it in material particulars is to legislate" and that power cannot be delegated by the Indian Parliament as the powers of the Parliament under the Constitution are not unfettered.

CHAPTER 3

Shankari Prasad Singh Deo *versus* The Union of India and Others (AIR 1951 SC 458)

[CHIEF JUSTICE HARILAL KANIA, JUSTICE PATANJALI SASTRI, JUSTICE B.K. MUKHERJEA, JUSTICE S.R. DAS, AND JUSTICE CHANDRASEKHAR IYER]

Case Summary

Under Article 32 of the Constitution, several petitions were filed before the Supreme Court challenging *vires* of the Constitution (First Amendment) Act 1951. The Amendment Act passed by the Provisional Parliament had inserted two new Articles viz. 31A and 31B after Article 31 containing the Fundamental Right to Property.

1. Article 31A provided for protection from challenge in Courts to the law for acquisition of "estates" for violation of Articles 14, 19 and 31.
2. Article 31B inserted the Ninth Schedule which stipulated that none of the Acts or Regulations specified in the Schedule shall be void for infringement of any Fundamental Right. It also provided that notwithstanding any judgment, decree or order of any Court or Tribunal to the contrary, each of the Acts and Regulations in the Ninth Schedule shall continue in force unless repealed by a competent legislature.
3. Against the above background, salient points of the unanimous judgment of the Court delivered by Justice Patanjali Sastri in Shankari Prasad Singh Deo case (AIR 1951 SC 458) are in the following paragraphs.
4. Parliament passed the Constitution (First Amendment) Act 1951 to protect laws of agrarian reform referred to as the Zamindari Abolition Acts. Some aggrieved Zamindars, filed writ petitions in different High Courts challenging the *vires* of the Abolition Acts.
5. The Patna High Court declared the Bihar Zamindari Abolition Act *ultra vires* whereas the High Courts of Allahabad and Nagpur did exactly the opposite.

6. Appeals from these decisions of the High Courts which were pending before the Supreme Court when the Constitution (First Amendment) Act 1951 was passed to protect the constitutionality of Zamindari Abolition Acts in different states.

7. The main grounds of challenge by Shankari Prasad Singh Deo were as follows:
   (i) Article 368 empowered the two Houses of Parliament as the designated body to amend the Constitution by following the laid down procedure but such power of amendment is not vested in the provisional Parliament, which meets only in a single chamber.
   (ii) The Constitution (Removal of Difficulties) order of January 1950 passed by the President of India under Article 392 of the Constitution referred to removal of difficulties in working of the Constitution. On 26 January 1950, when the President passed the Constitution (Removal of Difficulties) Order, no such difficulty in working of the Constitution had arisen.
   (iii) The Constitution (First Amendment) Bill 1951 was modified during discussion in the provisional Parliament and since Article 368 is a complete code by itself, it did not provide for any change in a Constitution Amendment Bill after it was introduced in either House of the Parliament.
   (iv) The Constitution Amendment Act 1951 is hit by Article 13(2) of the Constitution which mandates that the State shall not make any law which takes away or abridges any Fundamental Right.
   (v) The Amendment Act also makes changes in Article 32 relating to powers of the Supreme Court and in Article 226 relating to powers of the High Courts. Hence, the Constitution Amendment Bill 1951 required ratification by at least half of the state legislatures before the Bill was presented to the President for assent.
   (vi) The First Amendment Act is also *ultra vires* as it relates to matters in the State list in the Seventh Schedule on which Parliament is not competent to legislate.

8. In order to appreciate the issues raised by the petitioner, it is relevant to recapitulate the provisions of Articles 368, 379 and 392 of the Constitution.

9. Article 368 stipulates as follows:
   (i) A Bill for amendment of the Constitution may be introduced in either House of the Parliament;
   (ii) A Bill has to be passed in each House by a majority of total membership of the House and by a majority of not less than two-thirds of the members present and voting;
   (iii) After the Bill is passed by each House in the prescribed manner, it shall be presented to the President of India for assent;
   (iv) When the President gives assent to the Amendment Bill, the Constitution stands amended in terms of provisions of the Bill.

10. But if the amendment seeks to make any change in Articles in the "proviso" to Article 368, the Amendment Bill, duly passed by each of the Houses of Parliament, has to be

ratified by not less than half of the legislatures of the States by resolutions to that effect before the Bill is presented to the President for assent.

11. Article 379 of the Constitution provides that until both Houses of the Parliament have been duly constituted and summoned to meet for the first session, the Constituent Assembly shall be the provisional Parliament and shall exercise the powers and perform the functions of the Indian Parliament. [**N.B.:** Article 379 has since been repealed by the Constitution (Seventh Amendment) Act 1956.]

12. Article 392 stipulates that the President of India may for the purpose of removing difficulty in working of the Constitution direct by order that the Constitution shall, during the period specified in the order, have effect subject to such modification, addition or omission as the President may deem necessary. The proviso to Article 392 stipulates that no such order shall be passed by the President after the first meeting of the Parliament with both Houses.

13. The Constitution did not deliberately vest the power of amendment on the Parliament but vested it on each of the two Houses.

14. On behalf of the Court, Justice Patanjali Sastri held that the aforesaid argument has no substance as the power of amendment of the Constitution must be ascertained from the provisions of the Constitution itself and not on *a priori* grounds or on the analogy of Constitution of any other country.

15. The Indian Constitution provides for three categories of amendments. The first category can be made by a bare majority of Members of both Houses present and voting as in case of any ordinary legislation. The Constitutional amendments contemplated in Article 4, Article 169 and Article 240 fall in this category. These amendments are specifically excluded from the purview of Article 368. The second category are those that can be effected by a special majority as stipulated in Article 368. The third category comprise those which require not only a special majority but also ratification by resolutions of not less than half the state legislatures.

16. It is also not correct to argue that a Constitution Amendment Bill must be passed by each of the House only in the original form in which it was introduced in a House.

17. Article 368 is not a complete code for amendment of the Constitution. It has to be read with other provisions as Article 118 under which each House of Parliament can frame Rules for regulating its procedure and conduct of business.

18. There was some argument before the Court whether amendment is a legislative process. Assuming that it is not a legislative process and provisions of Articles 107 to 111 of the Constitution will not apply when Indian Parliament is dealing with a Constitution Amendment Bill, there may be no obvious reason why on such occasions Parliament cannot adopt its own normal procedure.

19. As early as 1915, Lord Haldane had observed that a Local Board – which has basically executive functions – if entrusted with judicial functions by a Statute, need not follow the procedure of a Court of Justice and could follow its own procedure.

20. The argument that the power of amendment under Article 368 having been entrusted to each House of Parliament – and not to Parliament as a collective body – the provisional Parliament with only a single chamber cannot consider any Constitution Amendment Bill, is also devoid of substance. [**N.B.:** Since a full-fledged Parliament with a Council of States and a House of People could not be constituted until the first General Election to the Parliament was held in the year 1952, the framers of the Constitution had provided for in Article 379 that the Constituent Assembly would function as the provisional Parliament to discharge all functions of the Parliament till a full-fledged Parliament, duly elected, was in place.] If the argument is accepted that the provisional Parliament, with one chamber, cannot consider any Constitution Amendment Bill, there would be no purpose behind Article 379 of the Constitution. Similarly, the provisions of Article 392 whereby the President can remove difficulties in relation to the transition from the Government of India Act 1935 to the present Constitution has also to be given a wider interpretation. The adaptation of Article 368 made by the President by order that till the first Parliament, duly elected, has its first session, the provisional Parliament, sitting in one chamber, can pass any Constitution Amendment Bill, is perfectly legal and valid.

21. A more plausible ground for attack of the Constitution (First Amendment) Act 1951 is that it is hit by Article 13(2) of the Constitution, which provides that,

"the State shall not make any law which takes away or abridges the Right conferred by this part and any law made in contravention of this clause shall to the extent of the contravention be void."

22. Counsel for the Petitioner has argued that "law" in Article 13(1) includes a constitutional amendment as the Constitution has put certain basic Rights in a separate chapter. Hence Fundamental Rights are immune from interference not only by ordinary law but also by any amendment under Article 368, which is "law" within the meaning of Article 13(2).

23. The Counsel argued that the framers of the Constitution had before them the American and the Japanese models. The Japanese Constitution characterized the Fundamental Rights, as "eternal and inviolate" whereas the U.S. Constitution stipulated that no amendment can be made to the Constitution depriving a state of the United States of America its equal suffrage in the Senate without specific consent of the concerned state. [**N.B.:** There is however no provision in the U.S. Constitution that the Bill of Rights – equivalent of Fundamental Rights – cannot be amended by the normal procedure of amendment laid down in Article V of the U.S. Constitution.]

24. The argument regarding inviolability of Fundamental Rights and its unamendability is attractive but there are weighty considerations to outweigh the otherwise attractive argument. Although "law" must ordinarily include constitutional law, there is a clear demarcation between ordinary law, in exercise of legislative power, and constitutional amendment, in exercise of constituent power.

25. If it was the intention of the framers of the Constitution that a Fundamental Right cannot be amended, they would have surely made a provision for it in the Constitution itself.

26. The principle of harmonious construction of Constitutional provisions mandates that in the context of Article 13, "law" must be taken to mean laws or Regulations made in

exercise of ordinary legislative power and not amendments made in exercise of constituent power. The result is that Article 13(2) does not affect amendments to the Constitution under Article 368.

27. Articles 31A and Article 31B have been attacked on the ground that these Articles were included in the Constitution without the Constitution Amendment Bill having been ratified by at least a majority of the State legislatures. It has been argued that before Article 31A and Article 31B were inserted in the Constitution, a High Court had powers to strike down an Estate Abolition law on ground of violation of the Fundamental Rights and if the High Court did not do so, the aggrieved party could come to the Supreme Court on appeal under Article 132 or on special leave under Article 136. But after the Articles 31A and 31B have been inserted, Estate Abolition legislations are immune from attack on the ground of unconstitutionality and thus change in power of the High Courts and the Supreme Courts have been made by the Constitution (First Amendment) Act 1951.

28. A close scrutiny of the Articles 31A and 31B would however indicate that they did not make any change in powers of the High Courts or the Supreme Court. Article 31A provides for saving of laws providing for compulsory acquisition of certain kind of property from operation of Article 31. Article 31B validates certain specified Acts and Regulations passed by the legislature which, but for such validation, would be liable to be impugned by the Courts. The powers of the High Courts and the Supreme Court – even after Article 31A and Article 31B have been inserted – remain just the same as they were before. Only a certain class of cases has been excluded from the chapter on Fundamental Rights and the High Courts and the Supreme Court will not be able to enforce Fundamental Rights in such excluded class of cases only because they are no longer a part of the Fundamental Rights.

29. An argument was advanced that Articles 31A and 31B relate to "land" and only the state legislatures are competent to legislate on "land" and not the Parliament. A close look at Article 31A and Article 31B would, however, indicate that they do not relate to "land" *per se*. They are amendments relating to laws of acquisition of land and other laws, which are put in the Ninth Schedule. The Ninth Schedule has been incorporated by the Constitution (First Amendment) Act 1951, which Parliament alone is competent to make.

30. It is also argued that Parliament could not validate a law, which it has no power to enact. But on close scrutiny, this argument also cannot be sustained. It is obvious that to make a law, which contravenes the Constitution, constitutionally valid, the Parliament alone has the power and the Parliament has exercised that power in passing the Constitution (First Amendment) Act 1951.

31. In view of the aforesaid, the petition challenging *vires* of the Constitution (First Amendment) Act 1951 is dismissed with costs.

CHAPTER 4

The State of West Bengal *versus* Anwar Ali Sarkar and Others (AIR 1952 SC 75)

[CHIEF JUSTICE PATANJALI SASTRI, JUSTICE FAZL ALI, JUSTICE M.C. MAHAJAN, JUSTICE B.K. MUKHERJEA, JUSTICE S.R. DAS, JUSTICE CHANDRASEKHAR AIYAR AND JUSTICE VIVIAN BOSE.]

Case Summary

The judgment is on constitutionality of the West Bengal Special Courts Act 1950 – in short, the West Bengal Act – enacted for speedier trial of offences. Seven Judges, including Chief Justice Patanjali Sastri, heard the appeal by the State of West Bengal against judgment of the Calcutta High Court quashing conviction of Anwar Ali Sarkar, under the West Bengal Special Courts Ordinance 1949. In March 1950 the Ordinance was replaced by the West Bengal Special Courts Act.

1. Chief Justice Patanjali Sastri did not agree with his brother judges and wrote a dissenting judgement. The salient points of his judgment are as follows:

2. Anwar Ali Sarkar and forty-nine others were charged with offences alleged to have been committed by them by armed raid on a factory at Dum Dum on the outskirts of the city of Calcutta. Under Section 5(1) of the West Bengal Special Courts Ordinance 1949, Government of West Bengal issued a Notification on 26 January 1950 that Anwar Ali Sarkar and his associates be tried by the Special Court.

3. Section 5 of the West Bengal Special Courts Ordinance 1949, provided as follows:

"A Special Court shall try such offences or classes of offences or cases or classes of cases as the State Government may by general or special order in writing direct."

4. The procedure of criminal trial by the Special Court distinguishing it from the normal procedure of criminal trial is as follows:

(i) Committal proceeding by a magistrate before trial of the accused in a Sessions Court as provided in the Code of Criminal Procedure 1898 was done away with;

(ii) Committal proceeding was substituted by the procedure of trial of warrant cases provided in the Code of Criminal Procedure;

(iii) Trial of case with jury was done away with;

(iv) Restrictions were imposed on powers of the special courts to grant adjournments of hearing;

(v) Provisions were made for dealing with a refractory accused;

(vi) Trial *de novo* was dispensed with on transfer of a case from one Special Court to another.

5. The Calcutta High Court held that Section 5(1) of the West Bengal Act, which vested in the State Government absolute power to refer any case to the Special Court which, in the opinion of the State Government, required speedier trial, was a source of arbitrary exercise of power and hit by Article 14 of the Constitution.

6. Chief Justice Patanjali Sastri conceded that Section 5(1) of the West Bengal Act did not seek to define the kind or class offences or cases which the State Government was empowered to assign to a Special Court. But as the object of the West Bengal Act was speedier trial with a simplified and shortened procedure, it is reasonable to assume that the state would refer to the Special Courts only cases requiring speedier trial.

7. The first part of Article 14 of the Constitution that the State shall not deny to any person "equality before law", appears to have been adopted from the Irish Constitution. The American Judges have called it the "basic principles of republicanism". The second part of Article 14 that the state shall not deny any person equal protection of the law, is based on the Fourteenth Amendment of the U.S. Constitution. In other words, the law must operate alike on all persons in like circumstances. This, however, does not mean that all laws must be general in character and universal in application. As pointed out in Chiranjit Lal Chowdhury *versus* Union of India (AIR 1951 SC 41), the State must of necessity make laws which could be different for groups or classes of persons within its territory. For that purpose, the state must have powers of classifying persons or things to be subjected to such laws. For a proper classification, a legislature may be allowed a wide measure of flexibility. Classification need not be by an exact or scientific exclusion or inclusion of persons or things. Therefore, it has been said that classification under Article 14 is justified if the classification is not palpably arbitrary.

8. The trend of recent decisions of the U.S. Supreme Court has been to lean strongly towards sustaining state action against attacks of hostile discrimination.

9. Whether a law conferring discretionary power on an administrative authority is valid or not should not be determined on the assumption that such authority will act in an arbitrary manner. As Justice Harilal Kania, former Chief Justice of India, had observed as early as 1950 that

"Abuse of power given by law sometimes occurs, but the validity of any law cannot be contested because of such apprehension."

10. On the contrary, it is presumed that a public authority will act honestly and reasonably in exercise of statutory powers.

11. A wide latitude must be allowed to a legislature in classifying persons or things to be brought under operation of a special law and such classification need not be based on exact or scientific inclusion or exclusion. Legislative judgment in such matters should not be challenged by Courts applying the doctrinaire "definite objective tests". The Courts should not insist in such cases, on what Justice Holmes called, as "delusive exactness". All that the Court is expected to see is whether the law, sought to be impugned, is palpably discriminatory.

12. Moreover, it is seen that not only Anwar Ali Sarkar's case but also five other cases of similar nature involving raid on the premises of the factory at Dum Dum, were notified by the Government of West Bengal for trial in the Special Court. The offences committed in these cases were not of ordinary type but arose out of serious disturbances in the nature of an armed attack on a factory by a large number of offenders. Thus, there were special features of these cases justifying speedier trial by the Special Court.

13. Justice Fazl Ali did not agree with Chief Justice Patanjali Sastri. Instead he agreed with the majority of Judges that the appeal by the state of West Bengal be dismissed because:

    (i) Provisions of the American Constitution, which corresponds to Article 14 of the Constitution of India, have greatly exercised minds of American Judges. The American Judges have struck down a number of laws and executive actions for violation of "equal protection of the law".

    (ii) Meaning and scope of Article 14 of the Constitution has been explained in two earlier judgments viz. Chiranjit Lal Chaudhury *versus* Union of India (AIR 1951 SC 41) and The State of Bombay *versus* S.N. Balsara (AIR 1951 SC 318). One of the principles common to both the judgments is that Article 14 is designed to protect all persons placed in similar circumstances against legislative discrimination.

    (iii) The West Bengal Act can be saved if it is shown that it is applicable to offences or persons in a well-defined class. But unfortunately, the Act does not apply to a well-defined class.

14. The Code of Criminal Procedure 1898 has also made provision for speedy trial in certain class of cases. The Code has made provision for summary trial of minor offences. It also provides for trial of summon cases, trial of warrant cases and trial by Court of Sessions. The classification of different trials, depends on gravity of the offence. In short, graver the offence, the more elaborate would be the procedure of trial under the Code of Criminal Procedure.

15. The West Bengal Act has completely ignored the principles of classification followed in the Code of Criminal Procedure. It lays down a new procedure without classifying the offences to which the new procedure of trial would apply. The result is that two procedures for criminal trial will exist side by side and for the sake of speedier trial, the executive can send persons charged with particular offence or offences to the Special Court for trial while for the same offence or offences some other persons may be tried under the normal procedure of trial under the Code of Criminal Procedure.

16. Admittedly, the Code of Criminal Procedure provides greater opportunities to the accused to defend himself than the West Bengal Act provides by its speedier procedure of trial.

17. Justice M.C. Mahajan also wrote a separate judgment agreeing with the majority of Judges.

18. The salient points of Justice M.C. Mahajan's judgment are as follows: Section 5(i) of the West Bengal Act 1950 is hit by Article 14 in as much as it does not lay down any basis for differential treatment for trial for certain offences by the Special Court.

19. M.C. Setalvad, the Attorney-General, has argued that the West Bengal Act has grouped cases requiring speedier trial as forming a class in themselves, differentiating that class from cases requiring ordinary trial.

20. The contention of the Attorney-General fails when tested on the anvil of Article 14. Article 14 is meant to prevent any person or a class of persons from being singled out for hostile and discriminatory treatment. In its application to legal proceedings, Article 14 assures to everyone similarly placed the same rules of evidence and modes of procedure.

21. Speedier trial of offences may be the motive for legislation but does not amount to a reasonable classification of offences. The necessity of a speedier trial is too vague and too uncertain a criterion to form the basis of a valid or reasonable classification. When certain persons accused of having committed some offences are sent for trial to the Special Court, they are entitled to ask why the "equal protection of the law" is denied to them and what objective criteria have weighed with the Government to decide that their offences require speedier trial. The West Bengal Act vests on the State Government unregulated discretion to send persons alleged to have committed some offences for trial before the Special Court only on subjective satisfaction of the state government that the offences deserve speedier trial. This is *per se* hit by Article 14.

22. The result is that the appeal by the state of West Bengal against the judgment of the Calcutta High Court fails and is dismissed.

23. Justice B.K. Mukherjea delivered a separate judgment agreeing with the majority of judges dismissing the appeal by the State of West Bengal.

24. The salient points of Justice B.K. Mukherjea's Judgment are as follows: In May 1949, the West Bengal government appointed the Sessions Judge of Alipore as the Special Judge and Anwar Ali Sarkar, the prime accused and 49 others were sent for trial before the Special Judge.

25. In March 1951, the Special Judge delivered the judgment sentencing Anwar Ali Sarkar and a few others to imprisonment for life. Some of the accused persons were also sentenced for varying terms of imprisonment.

26. Anwar Ali Sarkar filed a petition before the Calcutta High Court, praying for a writ of *certiorari* to quash his conviction.

27. Anwar Ali Sarkar's Counsel said that there are substantial points of difference between procedure of trial by the Special Courts and procedure of trial by ordinary Courts.

28. Article 14 states that the state shall not deny to any person "equality before law" or "equal protection of the laws" within the territory of India. It is based on the "equal protection clause" in the Fourteenth Amendment of the American Constitution.

29. Article 14 does not mandate that the same laws will be applicable to all persons within the territory of India. Article 14 only mandates that all persons similarly circumstanced shall be treated alike both in privileges conferred and liabilities imposed.

30. The entire problem under the "equal protection clause" is one of classification or drawing lines. In making the classification, the legislature cannot certainly be expected to provide "abstract symmetry". Classification can only recognize "degrees of evil" but the classification must never be arbitrary, artificial or evasive. Classification made without any reasonable basis has to be declared invalid. These propositions have not been controverted by the counsels of both parties while arguing this case. It has also not been disputed by the counsel for the respondent that the presumption is always in favour of constitutionality of a legislation and the burden is on him, who attacks the enactment, to prove that it is hit by violation of any constitutional provision.

31. The Attorney-General has argued that the respondent would invoke protection of Article 14 only if it is shown that the impugned law is a piece of hostile legislation. In reply it can be said that if a law is *per se* discriminatory, it is also a piece of hostile legislation.

32. If a legislation discriminates one person or class of persons in relation to others similarly situated, it is *per se* violative of Article 14.

33. The Attorney-General has rightly argued on the basis of a passage in Cooley's, "Constitutional Limitations" that inequalities of minor importance do not render a law invalid. But in this case, the West Bengal Act prescribes a procedure of trial materially different from the normal procedure of trial in the Code of Criminal Procedure.

34. The Attorney-General has argued that the principle of classification of criminal cases which could be notified by the State Government for trial by the Special Court is the Preamble of the West Bengal Act which states that, "whereas it is expedient to provide for speedier trial of certain offences".

35. The arguments of the Attorney-General have infirmities. First, while declaring the West Bengal Act *ultra vires*, Sir Trevor Harries, Chief Justice of the Calcutta High Court, has rightly held that the express provisions of an enactment cannot be curtailed or expanded with the aid of the Preamble.

36. Craies in his book *Statute Law* has said that it is only when the object or meaning of the enactment is not clear that recourse can be had to the Preamble to explain it. But in this case, language of Section 5(1) of the West Bengal Act is perfectly clear and free from any ambiguity. It vests an unrestricted discretion in the State Government to direct any case or class of cases to be tried by a Special Court in accordance with the special procedure.

37. The net result is that the present appeal by the State of West Bengal is bound to fail.

38. Justice S.R. Das delivered a separate judgment dismissing the appeal by the State of West Bengal.

39. The salient points in the judgment of Justice S.R. Das are as follows: Article 14 corresponds to the Fourteenth Amendment of the American Constitution.

40. While Article 14 is designed to prevent a person or class of persons from being singled out from other similarly situated for being subjected to discriminating and hostile legislation,

it does not insist on an "abstract symmetry". In other words, it does not insist that every legislation must have universal application. The state has powers to classify persons for purpose of legislation. But the classification cannot be arbitrary. First, the classification must be founded on some intelligible differentia which distinguishes those that are grouped together from others. Secondly, the differentia must have a rational relation with the object sought to be achieved by the legislation. Briefly stated, Article 14 forbids class legislation but does not forbid reasonable classification.

41. The Attorney-General, has argued that while a reasonable classification may be a test of a valid legislation, it is not the only test. He has urged that if there is inequality of treatment in a particular legislation and such inequality is not with an intention of causing prejudice to any person or class of persons but is made in the general interest of administration, there would be no infringement of Article 14. This test formulated by the Attorney-General, will mean adding to Article 14 of the Constitution the words, "except in good faith and in the general interest of administration". Such a modified formulation will reduce "equality before law" to a mere "rope of sand."

42. The Attorney-General has relied on Cooley's "Constitutional Limitations" to contend that inequalities of a minor nature do not render a law invalid. But a close scrutiny of the relevant passage in Coolery's book would show that perhaps Cooley did not intend such a conclusion to be drawn.

43. The Attorney-General put forward an argument that Article 14 is a protection against substantive law only and not against a procedural law. But he did not press his argument perhaps because a procedural law may easily inflict very great hardship on persons subjected to it.

44. It cannot be disputed that the West Bengal Act has prescribed procedure of trial different from the procedure laid down in the Code of Criminal Procedure. Sir Trevor Harries has brought out the difference between the procedure of trial in the Code of Criminal Procedure and the West Bengal Act very clearly in his judgment.

45. Section 5(1) of the West Bengal Act states as follows:

"A Special Court shall try such offences or classes of offences or cases or classes of cases as the State Government may, by general or special order in writing, direct."

46. The aforesaid provision makes no pretence of any classification on any basis whatsoever. It empowers the State Government to select particular cases against particular persons for being sent to the Special Court for speedier trial. As there is clear provision that the State Government can send up for trial by Special Court any case or class of cases, the State Government can make a purely arbitrary selection of cases for trial by the Special Court and such selection need not have any relation to the necessity of a speedier trial.

47. There is no intelligible differentia in the West Bengal Act distinguishing a criminal case from other criminal cases in matter of speedier trial by the Special Court.

48. In view of the facts of the case, Section 5(1) of the West Bengal Act is ultra vires.

49. Justice Chandrasekhar Aiyar delivered a separate judgment holding Section 5(1) of the West Bengal Act *ultra vires*. The salient points in the judgment are as follows:

50. The procedure for trial of criminal cases under the West Bengal Act is different in many important aspects from the procedure of trial under the Code of Criminal Procedure.

51. Sir Trevor Harries, Chief Justice of the Calcutta High Court, has enumerated in great detail the various items in procedure of trial under the West Bengal Act which are prejudicial to a fair trial.

52. The argument that changes in procedural law are not material and cannot be said to deny "equality before law" or "equal protection of the law" so long as substantive law remains unchanged, cannot be sustained as Article 14 covers both procedural and substantive law.

53. The Attorney-General, has argued that the object of the West Bengal Act is a laudable one and has the public purpose of speedier trial of some offences. This argument is devoid of merit as all laws are supposed to have a public purpose.

54. It does not, however, mean that "equality before law" guarantees abstract symmetry of treatments. Distinctions have to be made for different classes and groups of persons and a reasonable classification of such classes or groups of persons has to be permitted. Justice Oliver Wendell Holmes of the U.S. Supreme Court was of the view that the machinery of government would not work if it was not allowed a little play at its joints.

55. The real attack on the West Bengal Act is the absence of any pretence of classification of criminal cases on any basis whatsoever.

56. In view of the patent unconstitutionality of the West Bengal Act, the appeal of the Government of West Bengal deserves dismissal.

57. Justice Vivian Bose delivered a separate judgment agreeing with the majority of judges. His judgment is summarized in the succeeding paragraphs.

58. Article 14 does not guarantee equality in the abstract but only equality before the law. Law does differentiate between man and man. An example is that of different "Trusts" set up from which members of only one particular community might benefit. Another example is that places of worship are meant for a particular religious denomination only. There is also difference in personal law of different communities in matters of property, marriage and divorce.

59. As human society comprises men and women of different social standing and economic status, it is impossible to apply rules of abstract equality.

60. The provisions of a Constitution are not to be interpreted by simply taking the words of the Constitution in one hand and a dictionary on the other. Provisions of the Constitution are not mathematical formulae. They have their essence in not mere form. They constitute a framework of Government for men of different viewpoints. They are also means of ordering the life of a nation.

61. Classification into groups or classes for administration of different laws can be broad-based. Classification can also be broken down until one solitary unit is distinguished from the rest on the basis of some reasonable differentia. The main point is that a person or thing, if similar to another person or thing, must be treated as member of the same class for administration of the law.

62. We are not concerned with the motive of members of the legislature who passed an unequal law because even though the motive may be very good, an unequal law does discriminate in its operation.

63. The West Bengal Act has made substantial departures from the procedure for criminal trial in the Code of Criminal Procedure. These departures may be good in the sense that they promote the ends of justice. But such a value judgment is not the province of the judiciary.

64. Justice should not only be done but should be seen to be done. That cannot be when Ramchandra is tried by one procedure and Sakharam, similarly placed and facing equally serious charges, is tried by another procedure.

65. The Constitution is not for either those who govern or for the theorists. It is also for the common man. The Constitution must be interpreted in the sense in which the common man, not versed in the niceties of grammar and dialectical logic, can understand and appreciate so that he may have faith and confidence in the Constitution and the laws.

66. Judged from the common man's standpoint, it does not really matter whether the motive of the West Bengal Act is laudable or the Act is good for the society at large. It also does not matter to the common man whether the West Bengal Act has been enacted in good faith. The real test is: Can the West Bengal Act be regarded by fair-minded, reasonable, unbiased and resolute men, who are not swayed by emotion or prejudice as reasonable, just and fair. Can they regard the West Bengal Act as an example of that equal treatment and protection which is guaranteed by Article 14 of the Constitution?

67. On this short and simple ground, Justice Vivian Bose held the West Bengal Act *ultra vires* and dismissed the appeal of the Government of West Bengal.

CHAPTER 5

Sajjan Singh *versus* State of Rajasthan (AIR 1965 SC 845)

[CHIEF JUSTICE, P.B. GAJENDRAGADKAR, JUSTICE K.N. WANCHOO, JUSTICE M. HIDAYATULLAH, JUSTICE RAGHUBAR DAYAL AND JUSTICE J.R. MUDHOLKAR]

Case Summary

Sajjan Singh *versus* State of Rajasthan (AIR 1965 SC 845) was decided by a Constitution Bench of five judges presided over by Chief Justice P.B. Gajendragadkar. The judgment pronounced upon the validity of the Constitution (Seventeenth) Amendment Act 1964 by which Article 31A of the Constitution was again amended to include 44 Acts passed by different state legislatures in the Ninth Schedule to protect them from challenge for violation of Fundamental Rights.

1. The petitioners in the writ petitions before the Supreme Court and the intervener were affected by one or the other of the 44 Acts passed by different state legislatures which were included in the Ninth Schedule. They prayed before the Court for re-consideration of the judgment in Sankari Prasad Singh Deo's Case (AIR 1951 SC 458).
2. Chief Justice P.B. Gajendragadkar, delivered the majority judgment on behalf of himself and Justice K.N. Wanchoo and Justice Raghubar Dayal. Justice M. Hidaytullah and Justice J.R. Mudholkar, however, delivered separate judgments agreeing with the majority judgment that the petition challenging the Constitution (Seventeenth) Amendment Act 1964 be rejected but at the same time expressing no final opinion on some of the issues decided in the majority judgment.
3. The salient points in the majority judgment delivered by Chief Justice P.B. Gajendragadkar are in the following paragraphs.
4. The impugned Constitution (Seventeenth) Amendment Act 1964 consists of three sections, which are:
   (a) Section 2(i) of the Amendment Act which has added a proviso to clause (1) of Article 31A. The proviso stipulated that where any law provides for acquisition of any estate, if any land not exceeding the ceiling limit laid down in the law of

estate abolition, is held by the owner of the estate under his personal cultivation – including any building or structure standing on such land – such land or building shall not be acquired by the state without compensation at the market rate.

(b) Section 2(ii) of the Amendment Act which provided for enlargement of the meaning of the expression "estate".

(c) Section 3 of the Amendment Act which amended the Ninth Schedule to include the 44 Acts.

5. The validity of the Constitution (Seventeenth) Amendment Act 1964 can be decided on the basis of interpretation of Article 368.

6. Article 368 stipulates a procedure under which a Bill to amend the Constitution can be introduced in either House of the Parliament. The Bill has to be passed by a majority of members of the House and also by a majority of not less than two-thirds of members of the House present and voting. But if the Parliament intends amendment of any provision contained in the proviso to Article 368, such Amendment Bill has to be also ratified by the legislatures of not less than one-half of the states by Resolutions to that effect. The procedure of ratification is an additional safeguard against amendment of certain provisions.

7. Fundamental Rights in the Constitution are not included in the proviso to Article 368. Therefore, if any Fundamental Right is amended, the additional safeguard of ratification is not provided in Article 368.

8. But if Article 226 of the Constitution dealing with powers of High Courts is to be amended, the safeguard of ratification by at least one half of legislatures of states is required.

9. In dealing with constitutional questions of this character, the courts generally adopt the pith and substance test laid down in Attorney-General for Ontario *versus* Reciprocal Insurers and Others decided by the Privy Council in the year 1924. The impugned Constitution (Seventeenth) Amendment Act 1964 in pith and substance does not amend Article 226 and hence the safeguard of ratification by one-half of legislatures of states is not attracted.

10. In Sankari Prasad Singh Deo's Case (AIR 1951 SC 458) Justice Patanjali Sastri held that Article 31A and 31B, inserted by the Constitution (First) Amendment Act 1951, did not make any change in Article 226 relating to power of the High Courts and Articles 132 and 136 relating to power of the Supreme Court.

11. Regarding the argument that the decision in Sankari Prasad Singh Deo's Case (AIR 1951 SC 458) required re-consideration, it is pertinent to note that the doctrine of *stare decisis* may not be invoked to perpetuate a wrong decision by the Court; but the normal principle that the judgment of the Supreme Court is final cannot be ignored unless cogent reasons of a compelling character make it necessary to re-consider the earlier judgment. Therefore, the plea to re-consider the ratio of Sankari Prasad Singh Deo's Case (AIR 1951 SC 458) is wholly unjustified.

12. In Sankari Prasad Singh Deo's Case (AIR 1951 SC 458) it was held that the harmonious rule of construction requires that "law" in Article 13 should be taken to exclude constitutional amendments under Article 368. This view is sound and needs no re-consideration by this Court.

13. If the framers of the Constitution would have intended to subject any amendment of a Fundamental Right to the prohibition in Article 13(2) of the Constitution, they would have made a clear provision in this regard.

14. The question is: can the Fundamental Rights be considered as eternal and inviolate in the sense that they can never be abridged or amended. It is true that in the case of A.K. Gopalan *versus* State of Madras (AIR 1950 SC 27), Justice Patanjali Sastri had held that the people of India adopted the democratic ideal and reserved for themselves certain Fundamental Rights. This hypothesis *prima facie* may tend to show that power to amend the Fundamental Rights vested not in the Parliament but in the people of India themselves. Subsequently, Justice Patanjali Sastri had occasion to consider the question more elaborately in *in re* The Delhi Laws Act 1912 (AIR 1951 SC 332) where he held that the Indian Parliament, while acting within its legislative competence, has plenary powers as large as that of the British Parliament. He also held that the maxim *delegatus non potest delegare* (a delegate cannot further delegate) is not a part of the constitutional law of India. Therefore, whether the Parliament can amend the Fundamental Rights must be answered in the affirmative in view of the provisions of Article 368 and not on the basis of any theoretical concept that sovereignty vests with the people of India and the legislatures are only delegates of the sovereign people.

15. It is legitimate to assume that the Parliament is competent to amend any Fundamental Right to meet new challenges. Such challenges are faced in course of socio-economic progress and development of the country.

16. The argument that Fundamental Rights are beyond the power of amendment can be met by pointing out that even Article 368 can be amended by the Parliament by following the procedure of ratification by at least one-half of legislatures of states. By such amendment of Article 368, the Parliament can provide that under Article 368 the Parliament can amend any Fundamental Right. Therefore, the argument regarding immutable character of the Fundamental Rights is not well-founded and deserves to be rejected.

17. In *in re:* the Berubari Union and Exchange of Enclaves (AIR 1960 SC 845) the Supreme Court had held that amendment of Article 1 of the Constitution, consequent upon transfer of any part of the territory of India in favour of a foreign state, does not attract the safeguard of the proviso to Article 368 as neither Article 1 nor Article 3 of the Constitution is included in the proviso to Article 368. There is also an anomalous situation as any amendment of Article 226 attracts the safeguard of the proviso to Article 368 but such safeguard is not available if the Parliament amends Article 32 of the Constitution which guarantees the Right to Constitutional remedies by the Supreme Court. Parliament may like to consider whether the anomaly can be removed by including the Fundamental Rights in the proviso to Article 368.

18. The salient points of the judgment of Justice M. Hidaytullah, who delivered a separate judgment in Sajjan Singh *versus* State of Rajasthan (AIR 1965 SC 845) are in the following paragraphs.

19. Justice M. Hidaytullah agreed with the majority judgment of Chief Justice P.B. Gajendragadkar that the Constitution (Seventeenth) Amendment Act 1964 did not

require for its validity ratification of the Amendment Bill by at least one-half of legislatures of the states.

20. Justice M. Hidaytullah also held that in Sankari Prasad Singh Deo's Case (AIR 1951 SC 845) the effect of the Constitution (First) Amendment Act 1951 on Article 226 was considered. It was held by the Court that the Constitution Amendment Act 1951 did not make any change in Article 226 so as to attract the proviso to Article 368. The reasoning in Sankari Prasad Singh Deo's Case (AIR 1951 SC 458) on this point applies to the impugned Constitution (Seventeenth) Amendment Act of 1964.

21. Justice M. Hidaytullah said that he chose to write a separate judgment as he found it difficult to accept a part of the reasoning in the judgment in Sankari Prasad Singh Deo's Case (AIR 1951 SC 458).

22. Elaborating his arguments, Justice M. Hidaytullah held that it would have been easy for the framers of the Constitution to provide specifically that "law" in Article 13(3) does not include constitutional amendments but they have not done so. If a constitutional amendment would be held as "law" in Article 13(3), the Fundamental Rights become "eternal and inviolate" to borrow the language of the Japanese Constitution.

23. The Articles in the chapter on Fundamental Rights use the language of permanency. This can be illustrated by having a close look at Article 32. If Article 32 would have been included in Part XX (chapter on Amendment of the Constitution), it would have made the guarantee in Article 32 more secure against any amendment. It is a matter for consideration whether the guarantee in Article 32 in any less because the Article is in Chapter III of the Constitution dealing with the Fundamental Rights. The first clause in Article 32 contains a guaranteed remedy. The guarantee is against both legislative and executive action. Part III containing the chapter on Fundamental Rights is full of declarations of what the legislature can do and what it cannot do. If it be held that the guarantee in Article 32 is inviolable, would not the guarantee of the Constitutional Remedies make the Fundamental Rights equally protected?

24. The Preamble of the Constitution is equally vital to our body politic. In *in re*: the Berubari Union and Exchange of Enclaves (AIR 1960 SC 845) the Court held that though the Preamble is the key to the minds of the framers of the Constitution, it is not a part of the Constitution. "Perhaps in one sense it does not but in another sense it does." Our Preamble is more akin in nature to the American Declaration of Independence of July 1776 than to the Preamble of the Constitution of the United States. The Preamble of our Constitution does not make any grant of power; but it gives a direction and purpose to the Constitution which is reflected in the chapter on Fundamental Rights and in the chapter on Directive Principles of State Policy. Is it to be imagined that a two-thirds majority of the two Houses at any time is all that is necessary to alter it without even consulting the States? It is difficult to think that an amendment of Fundamental Rights does not have even the protection of the safeguard in the proviso to Article 368.

25. In A.K. Gopalan *versus* State of Madras (AIR 1950 SC 27) Chief Justice Harilal Kania had said that inclusion of Article 13(1) & 13(2) in our Constitution has been done as a matter of abundant caution as even without such inclusion, the Court had always the power to strike down any law, which abridged or infringed any Fundamental Right.

26. Chief Justice Harilal Kania did not make the observation to belittle the importance of Article 13. Rather, he made the observation to emphasize the importance and commanding position of the Fundamental Rights.

27. Justice M. Hidaytullah said that he would require stronger reasons than those in the judgment in Sankari Prasad Singh Deo's Case (AIR 1951 SC 458) that the Fundamental Rights were not really fundamental but were intended to be within the power of amendment in Article 368 in common with other parts of the Constitution and that too without ratification by at least half of the legislatures of states of the Indian Union.

28. In view of clauses (2) to (6) in Article 19, curtailment of the Right to Freedom can be made in the public interest by enacting a law. This shows that Fundamental Rights are not static. It visualizes change and progress but at the same time it preserves the individual Right. There is hardly any reform which cannot be introduced reasonably in the Republic of India the guarantee of individual liberty notwithstanding. Even the agrarian reform could have been carried out without Article 31A & 31B but such reforms could have cost more to the public exchequer.

29. Restricting the Fundamental Right guaranteed in Article 19 by resort to clause (2) to (6) of Article 19 is one thing but removing the Right in Article 19 from the Constitution or debilitating it by an amendment is quite another. This is the implication of Sankari Prasad Singh Deo's Case (AIR 1951 SC 458). It is true that such things would never be, but one is concerned to know that such a thing is possible.

30. Article 368 does not give power to amend any provision of the Constitution. At least the Article does not say so. As per the accepted canons of interpretation, it lays down the procedure of amendment of the Constitution.

31. Article 368 lays down the manner of amendment and the effective condition for such amendment. The contrast between the opening part of Article 368 and the proviso in the Article does not show that what is outside the proviso is necessarily within the powers of amendment under Article 368. The proviso to Article 368 puts outside the power of the Parliament to amend those provisions on which our federal structure rests. It makes it obligatory that at least one-half of the state legislatures must agree with the Constitution Amendment Bill amending the Articles in the proviso. The proviso also protects our higher judiciary vital to a written Constitution and to a Democracy such as ours. But Article 368 nowhere says that the Preamble and every single Article of the Constitution can be amended despite any permanency in the language and despite any historical fact or sentiment.

32. The Indian Constitution gives so many assurances in the chapter on Fundamental Rights that it would be difficult to think that they were mere playthings of a special majority. To hold this would mean *prima facie* that the most solemn parts of our Constitution stands on the same footing as any other part of the Constitution.

33. The anomaly that Article 226 cannot be amended only by the Parliament in view of the fact that Article 226 is contained in the proviso to Article 368 but Article 32 can be amended by the Parliament without the safeguard of ratification by majority of the states must give us pause. Article 32 erects a shield against the conduct of the state including that of the legislature. The question is: can the legislature take away the shield by amendment of Article 32? One can agree with such a view if one makes a literal construction of Article 368. But the Court should not play a grammarian's role. The power of amendment of the Constitution in Article 368 ought not ordinarily be a means of escape from absolute constitutional restrictions.

34. Justice M. Hidaytullah concluded his judgment by saying that though he agreed with the Chief Justice and his two brother judges regarding the *vires* of the Constitution (Seventeenth) Amendment Act 1964, he would not like to be understood to have expressed a final opinion on different aspects of the case.

35. Justice J.M. Mudholkar also delivered a separate judgment. At the outset, he stated that he agreed with the majority to dismiss the writ petitions challenging the *vires* of the Constitution (Seventeenth) Amendment Act 1964.

36. The separate judgment of Justice J.M. Mudholkar is summarized in the following paragraphs.

37. In Sankari Prasad Singh Deo's Case (AIR 1951 SC 458) the Court upheld the *vires* of the Constitution (First) Amendment Act 1951 on two grounds:

(a) An amendment of a Fundamental Right is not "law" within the meaning of Article 13(2) of the Constitution and any Fundamental Right can be amended by following the procedure in Article 368.

(b) Articles 31A and 31B do not make changes in Articles 32, 136 or 226 and hence ratification of the Constitutional amendment by at least one-half of the state legislatures is not necessary.

38. In taking the view that "law" in Article 13(2) does not include an amendment of the Constitution, the Court has not borne in mind some important considerations. The language of Article 368 is plain enough to show that action of the Parliament in amending the Constitution is a legislative act done in exercise of legislative power. The only difference is that in amending the Constitution – except the Articles in the proviso to Article 368 – the Parliament has to pass it by a majority of Members of each House and a two-thirds majority of Members of the House present and voting. Inspite of this provision for special majority in both Houses to pass a Constitutional amendment, the result of a legislative action by the Parliament in passing a Constitutional amendment cannot be other than "law". Article 368 does not say that when Parliament passes a Bill amending the Constitution, it performs a constituent act. By passing a constitutional Amendment Bill, the Parliament does not become a Constituent Body. Justice M. Hidaytullah was right when he said that it is open to doubt whether Article 368 confers any such power on the Parliament. Even assuming that it does, it can be regarded as an additional legislative power.

39. Whether an amendment has become a part of the Constitution is a matter subject to Judicial Review. The Court is also competent to do Judicial Review in regard to any other law, which is challenged before the Court. This is an issue which has not been considered in the earlier decision of Sankari Prasad Singh Deo *versus* The Union of India (AIR 1951 SC 458).

40. In A.K. Gopalan *versus* State of Madras (AIR 1950 SC 27) Justice Patanjali Sastri had held that Fundamental Rights are those Rights which the people of India have reserved for themselves. Subsequently, *in re*: The Delhi Laws Act 1912 (AIR 1951 SC 332), Justice Patanjali Sastri has held that Parliament acting within the limits of its legislative power, has plenary powers of legislation, which are as large as those of the British Parliament. In The Delhi Laws Act 1912 (AIR 1951 SC 332) Justice Patanjali Sastri has rejected the argument that the Parliament of India is the delegate of the people of India.

41. That the Parliament of India has plenary powers of legislation within the limits of its legislative power and cannot be regarded as a delegate of the people, while exercising its legislative power, is a well accepted position. The fact however remains that unlike the British Parliament, the Indian Parliament can only function within the limits of power granted by the Constitution. This would also be so when in exercise of legislative power, it makes an amendment to the Constitution. It would , therefore, appear that the earier observation of Justice Patanjali Sastri in A.K. Gopalan *versus* State of Madras (AIR 1950 SC 27) cannot be said to be inconsistent with what he said in The Delhi Laws Act 1912 (AIR 1951 SC 332). At any rate, this is an aspect of the matter which requires further consideration.

42. It is true that by virtue of Section 8 of The Indian Independence Act 1947, sovereignty devolved upon the Constituent Assembly. But both the Objective Resolution of 22 January, 1947 and the Preamble to the Constitution show that the Constituent Assembly framed the Constitution of India in the name of the people of India and by virtue of the powers derived from them. In the circumstances, it has to be considered whether Justice Patanjali Sastri was not right in saying that the Fundamental Rights are the Rights reserved by the people of India and hence these Rights are unalterable.

43. It is true that the Constitution does not directly prohibit amendment of the Fundamental Rights. But it would indeed be strange that Rights which are considered to be fundamental should be more easily capable of being abridged or restricted than any of the matters referred to in the proviso to Article 368, some of which are less vital than the Fundamental Rights.

44. As observed by Justice M. Hidaytullah, it is possible that Article 368 merely lays down the procedure to be followed in making amendments to the Constitution and does not confer a power to amend the Constitution.

45. An argument has been advanced that if Fundamental Rights cannot be amended, it may hamper legislation for the changing needs of a dynamic society. This is a weighty argument. But an answer to the argument is that Article 19 of the Constitution is already subject to reasonable restrictions as stipulated in clauses (2) to (6) of the Article itself and the other Fundamental Rights – at least many of them – can perhaps be adapted to meet the needs

of a changing society with the aid of the Directive Principles of State Policy. Article 37 of the Constitution imposes a duty on the state to apply the Directive Principles in making laws. The Directive Principles must be interpreted harmoniously with the Fundamental Rights.

46. The Constituent Assembly could have set up a sovereign Parliament in the British model. But instead the Constituent Assembly enacted a written Constitution with the following stipulations:

(a) The Executive, the Legislature and the Judiciary were set up with defined powers;

(b) The Union Executive and the Executive in the states were made responsible respectively to the Union Parliament and the State Assemblies;

(c) A federal structure was set up with distinct legislative powers for the Union and the States;

(d) A chapter on Fundamental Rights was incorporated in the Constitution which also provided for its guaranteed enforcement;

(e) Prescribed forms of Oaths of office with the stipulation that those who are required to subscribe to them bear true allegiance to the Constitution;

(f) Stipulation that the Supreme Court and the High Courts are bound to uphold the Constitution by virtue of the Oath of office of the Judges.

(g) A Preamble, which is an epitome of the basic features of the Constitution.

47. It perhaps can be said that these are indicia of the intention of the Constituent Assembly to give permanency to basic features of the Constitution.

48. It may also be considered whether making a change in a basic feature of the Constitution can be regarded merely as an amendment, or it be in effect re-writing a part of the Constitution. If it is the latter, can amendment of a basic feature of the Constitution be made under Article 368?

49. A Member of Parliament is required to take an oath of allegiance to the Constitution. If upon a literal interpretation of power of amendment under Article 368 it can be held that the basic feature of the Constitution can be amended, the issue is how to harmonize the oath of allegiance to the Constitution of a Member of the Parliament with the power to make amendment to its basic feature?

50. It would be of interest to mention that the Supreme Court of Pakistan has held in Fazlul Quader Chowdhury *versus* Mohd. Abdul Haque (1963) that franchise and form of government are fundamental features of a Constitution and the power of the President of Pakistan to remove difficulties in working of the Constitution does not extend to making an alteration in a fundamental feature of the Constitution.

51. As long as the expression, "Sovereign Democratic Republic" is in the Preamble of our Constitution, can the Constitution be amended to depart from its democratic or republican character? If it cannot be done, as long as the expression, "Justice, social, economic and political" are contained in the Preamble of our Constitution, would it be legally valid to take away the Rights guaranteed in Articles 14 to 19 and Articles 21, 25, 31 and 32?

If the Rights guaranteed in these Articles cannot be taken away, it is for consideration whether those Rights can be modified by amendment under Article 368?

52. It has been held by the Court that the Preamble is not a part of the Constitution. But the Preamble of our Constitution – which has the stamp of deep deliberation and is marked by precision – is an epitome of the broad features of our Constitution.

53. Justice J.R. Mudholkar felt reluctant to express a definite opinion whether "law" in Article 13(2) excludes an Act of Parliament amending the Constitution and also whether the Parliament is competent to make any amendment to any Fundamental Right.

54. Justice J.R. Mudholkar also held that even if it is assumed that the Parliament was competent to enact the Constitution (First) Amendment Act 1951 to insert Article 31A and expand the definition of "estate", the question still remains whether the Parliament could validate a law enacted by a state legislature on "land", which is a state subject in the Seventh Schedule. A legislature, which has power to enact a law, only has the power to validate the law. Since the agrarian laws sought to be protected by the Ninth Schedule in Article 31B could not have been enacted by the Parliament, would it be right to say that the Parliament could validate them? These issues were not dealt with in Sankari Prasad Singh Deo's Case (AIR 1951 SC 458). They have also not been urged before the Constitution Bench in the present case of Sajjan Singh *versus* State of Rajasthan (AIR 1965 SC 845). Justice J.R. Mudholkar however held that he agreed with the majority judgment of Chief Justice P.B. Gajendragadkar that no case has been made out for striking down the Constitution (Seventeenth) Amendment Act 1964.

55. Justice J.R. Mudholkar further held that if the effect of an amendment is to curtail substantially, though indirectly, the jurisdiction of the High Courts under Article 226 or of the Supreme Court under Article 136, without recourse to the safeguards of ratification of the proposed amendment by at least one-half of the legislatures of the states, the question whether it was a colourable exercise of power by the Parliament could be considered by the Court.

56. Justice J.R. Mudholkar concluded his judgment by stating that what he had held in his judgment was not an expression of his final opinion on the subject. But his views are an expression of the doubts which have assailed him regarding a question of paramount importance to citizens of the country to know whether the basic features of the Constitution will endure for a long time or at least for the foreseeable future or whether the basic features are no more enduring than the subordinate features of the Constitution.

CHAPTER 6

I.C. Golaknath and Others *versus* State of Punjab (AIR 1967 SC 1643)

[CHIEF JUSTICE K. SUBBA RAO, JUSTICE K.N. WANCHOO, JUSTICE M. HIDAYTULLAH, JUSTICE J.C. SHAH, JUSTICE S.M. SIKRI, JUSTICE R.S. BACHAWAT, JUSTICE V. RAMASWAMI, JUSTICE J.M. SHELAT, JUSTICE VASISHT BHARGAVA, JUSTICE G.K. MITTER, AND JUSTICE C.A. VAIDIALINGAM]

Case Summary

This is a landmark judgment of the Supreme Court where the majority of judges, including the Chief Justice K. Subba Rao, held that the Indian Parliament has no powers to amend any Fundamental Right so as to abridge it. They held that an amendment under Article 368 is "law" within the meaning of Article 13(2) of the Constitution. As any "law" abridging a Fundamental Right is void under Article 13(2) and an amendment of the Constitution is "law", amendment of any Fundamental Right is also void.

1. The judgment overruled earlier judgments in Sankari Prasad Singh Deo *versus* Union of India (AIR 1951 SC 458) and in Sajjan Singh *versus* State of Rajasthan (AIR 1965 SC 845) where the Court had held that under Article 368, the Parliament could amend any Fundamental Right as a constitutional amendment was not "law" within the meaning of Article 13(2).
2. In I.C. Golaknath (AIR 1967 SC 1643) the Court laid down the "doctrine of prospective overruling" to protect amendments of Fundamental Rights already made by the Parliament.
3. [**N.B.**: The ratio of I.C. Golaknath (AIR 1967 SC 1643), is no longer good law because of the judgment in Kesavananda Bharati *versus* State of Kerala (AIR 1973 SC 1461), where a larger Bench of 13 Judges by majority laid down that the Parliament under Article 368 can amend any Fundamental Right and any other provision but cannot by such amendment alter the "basic structure" of the Constitution.]
4. [**N.B.**: At present, the constitutional position is that the Court can subject any amendment of the Constitution to Judicial Review to decide whether it violated the basic structure. The Supreme Court have held in Minerva Mills *versus* Union of India (AIR 1980 SC 1789) that Judicial Review is a part of the basic structure of the Constitution.]

5. [**N.B.:** From time to time, the Court may lay down that apart from the federal and the Republican character of the Constitution and the Parliamentary system of Government, other provisions of the constitution could also be included as parts of the basic structure.]

6. Chief Justice K. Subba Rao delivered the majority judgment in I.C. Golaknath *versus* State of Punjab (AIR 1967 SC 1643) on behalf of himself and four other judges viz. Justice J.C. Shah, Justice S.M. Sikri, Justice J.M. Shelat and Justice C.A. Vaidialingam.

7. The salient points in the majority judgment, delivered by Chief Justice K. Subba Rao, are set out in the succeeding paragraphs.

8. I.C. Golaknath and others, who are the son, daughter and grand-daughter of one Henry Golaknath – who passed away in 1953 – filed a writ petition in the Supreme Court under Article 32 of the Constitution that the provisions of the Punjab Security of Land Tenure Act 1953, under which a little over 418 standard acres of the petitioner's lands were declared surplus, were void as the Punjab Act violated the petitioner's Fundamental Rights under Article 19(1)(f) and 19(1)(g) of the Constitution.

9. Some other petitioners also filed analogous writ petitions challenging constitutionality of the Mysore Land Reforms Act 1962.

10. The States of Punjab and Mysore took the stand that the Punjab and the Mysore Acts were placed in the Ninth Schedule by the Constitution (Seventeenth Amendment) Act 1964 and hence were immune from attack on the ground of their constitutionality.

11. Broadly speaking, the contention of the petitioners are as follows:

   (i) The Constitution is intended to be permanent. It cannot be amended in a way which would "injure or destroy its indestructible character".

   (ii) 'Amendment' means a change in the Constitution, which can carry out better the purpose for which the Constitution was framed.

   (iii) The Fundamental Rights are a part of the basic structure of the Constitution and the power of amendment can only be exercised to preserve the essence of those Rights.

   (iv) The expression "amend" in Article 368 has a limited meaning.

   (v) Speeches in the Constituent Assembly establish that framers of the Constitution never intended to invoke powers under Article 368 to amend the Fundamental Rights.

   (vi) The chapter on the Fundamental Rights is a self-contained code and its provisions are elastic enough to meet reasonable requirements of a changing situation.

   (vii) Power to amend the Constitution is located in Articles 245, 246 and 248 and Article 368 only lays down the procedure of amendment;

   (viii) "Law" in Article 13(2) of the Constitution includes every branch of law, statutory and constitutional. Hence amendment of the Constitution is also "law" within the meaning of Article 13(2).

12. In reply, the arguments of the states of Punjab and Mysore are as follows:

   (i) An amendment of the Constitution is not an exercise of legislative power by the Parliament but is an exercise of sovereign powers of the State. Therefore, an amendment partakes the character of the Constitution itself.

(ii) As the provisions of Article 368 are clear, there is no scope to invoke the implied limitations on exercise of powers of Parliament.

(iii) India has a flexible constitution which empowers the Parliament to amend the Constitution to express the will of the people from time to time.

(iv) If implied limitations are read into Parliament's power to amend the Constitution, it would take away the safety – valve of the Constitution and result in violent revolution.

(v) There is no artificial distinction in the Constitution between the basic features and not-so-basic features.

(vi) Debates in the Constituent Assembly cannot be relied upon to hold that the Fundamental Rights cannot be amended under Article 368.

(vii) Even if the debates are relied upon, there is nothing to show in them that the Fundamental Rights are beyond the powers of amendment under Article 368.

(viii) Article 13(2) cannot control the clear, categorical and imperative language of Article 368.

(ix) To implement the Directive Principles of State Policy, the Constitution has been amended from time to time affecting some Fundamental Rights. Thus the burden is very heavy on the petitioners to establish that the Fundamental Rights cannot be amended under Article 368.

(x) Article 31A of the Constitution and the Ninth Schedule of the Constitution under Article 31B do not affect the powers of the courts and hence the proviso to Article 368 of the Constitution does not apply to them.

13. In Sankari Prasad Singh Deo *versus* Union of India (AIR 1951 SC 458), the Constitution (First Amendment) Act 1951 – which introduced Article 31A & 31B of the Constitution – was sought to be quashed. The court held unanimously that the provisional Parliament had the power to amend any Fundamental Right as the word "law" in Article 13(2) was "law" enacted by the Parliament in exercise of legislative power and not in exercise of constituent power under Article 368.

14. In Sajjan Singh case (AIR 1965 SC 845), Chief Justice, P.B. Gajendragadkar, speaking for the majority, upheld the "ratio" in the earlier judgment in Sankari Prasad Singh Deo's case (AIR 1951 SC 458); but Justice M. Hidaytullah in his separate judgment in Sajjan Singh's case (AIR 1965 SC 845) held that the Fundamental Rights gave so many guaranteed Rights that it would be difficult to think that "they are only the playthings of a special majority."

15. In I.C. Golaknath (AIR 1967 SC 1643) the majority of judges, speaking through Chief Justice K. Subba Rao, held that the Preamble of the Constitution contains in a nutshell its ideals and aspirations. The Preamble is worked out in detail in the Constitution where no Authority created under the Constitution is supreme as the Constitution alone is supreme.

16. The Constitution does not implicitly believe the representatives of the people for "uncontrolled and unrestricted power might lead to an authoritarian state." It, therefore, preserves certain Rights against encroachment by the state and the higher judiciary is the sentinel for protection of the Rights.

17. The chapter on the Fundamental Rights and the chapter on the Directive Principles constitute an integrated scheme forming a self-contained code. The scheme is so elastic that the Directive Principles can reasonably be enforced without abridging a Fundamental Right.

18. The Constitution itself provides for suspension or modification of the Fundamental Rights in special circumstances. For example, Article 33 empowers the Parliament to modify these Rights in relation to members of the Armed Forces. Article 34 empowers the Parliament to impose restrictions on the Fundamental Rights while Martial Law is in force in an area.

19. Article 32 makes the Right to constitutional remedies for enforcement of any Fundamental Right also a Fundamental Right. Even during promulgation of Emergency under Article 352, only Article 19 is automatically suspended and all other Fundamental Rights remain intact unless suspended by the President by Notification in that regard. [**N.B.:** By the Constitution (Forty-Fourth Amendment) Act 1978, the Rights under Article 20 and Article 21 cannot be suspended even by a Notification during the period of Emergency promulgated under Article 352].

20. Granville Austin has called the Fundamental Rights and the Directive Principles of State Policy as "the conscience of the Constitution."

21. While proposing for adoption of the Interim Report on the Fundamental Rights, Jawaharlal Nehru had said in the Constituent Assembly that the Fundamental Rights are to be viewed as a permanent feature of the Constitution whereas other provisions may be looked at from "more temporary point of view." Even Dr. B.R. Ambedkar had told the Constituent Assembly how the Fundamental Rights were a permanent feature of the Constitution.

22. Even the Supreme Court had noticed the paramount character of the Fundamental Rights in A.K. Gopalan *versus* The State of Madras (AIR 1950 SC 27).

23. The minorities in India regard the Fundamental Rights as the bedrock of their political existence and the majority consider the Rights as the guarantee for their way of life.

24. The incapacity of the Parliament in exercise of its amending power to modify, restrict or impair the Fundamental Rights arises from the scheme of the Constitution and the nature of the freedoms.

25. A "law" amending the Constitution is a constitutional law. Article 13(2) which states that any law which takes away or abridges any Fundamental Rights is void gives an inclusive definition of "law" and such inclusive definition does not exclude constitutional law.

26. The decision of the Privy Council, in Mc Cawley *versus* The King (AIR 1920 PC 91), also supports the view that an amendment of a Constitution is a "law".

27. Again, the decision of the Privy Council in Bribery Commissioner *versus* Ranasinghe (1965 AC 172) supports the view that amendment of the Constitution is also a "law".

28. The fact that Fundamental Rights cannot be amended under Article 368 is clear from a comparative study of major constitutions of the world, which provide for amendment

of the Constitution but which do not have any provision comparable to Article 13(2) of our Constitution.

29. An argument was advanced that the power of amendment of a Constitution is a supreme power and is not subject to any implied limitation. The advocate of such an opinion is Lester Orfield who has written the book *The Amending of the Federal Constitution*. Orfield has said that under Article V of the U.S. Constitution, there is no implied limitation on the power of amendment and the only express limitation in Article V is that no state of USA could be deprived of its equal representation in the Senate of the Congress without consent of that state. Thus under Article V, even the Bill of Rights can be amended by following the laid-down procedure.

30. It has been argued that "amendment" in Article 368 has both a positive and a negative content and in exercise of the power of amendment, Parliament cannot destroy the basic structure of the Constitution.

31. Since it is held that the Parliament cannot amend any Fundamental Right, what will be the fate of amendments to Fundamental Rights already made?

32. Chief Justice K. Subba Rao invoked the doctrine of prospective overruling to protect the amendments already made. He also held that the doctrine of prospective overruling has the support of American jurists as John Henry Wigmore and Benjamin Cardozo. The doctrine is also consistent with Articles 32, 141 and 142 of our Constitution.

33. The judgment of Chief Justice K. Subba Rao on behalf of the majority of judges, may be summed up as follows:

(i) An amendment of Fundamental Right, being "law" is hit by Article 13(2) of the Constitution.

(ii) Power of the Parliament to amend the Constitution is derived from Articles 245, 246 and 248 of the Constitution.

(iii) Article 368 is not the source of power of amendment but only lays down the procedure of such amendment.

(iv) Amendment of the Constitution under Article 368 is a legislative process.

(v) The three Constitution Amendment Acts viz. the Constitution (First Amendment) Act 1951, the Constitution (Fourth Amendment) Act 1955 and the Constitution (Seventeenth Amendment) Act 1964 abridge Fundamental Rights but on basis of earlier judgments of the Supreme Court they are valid.

(vi) On application of the "doctrine of prospective overruling", these amendments as aforesaid shall continue to be valid.

(vii) As the Constitution (Seventeenth Amendment) Act 1964 is valid on the basis of "the doctrine of prospective overruling", the two impugned Acts as the Punjab Security of Land Tenures Act 1953 and the Mysore Land Reforms Act 1962, cannot be struck down as violative of Articles 13, 14 and 31 of the Constitution.

34. Justice K.N. Wanchoo delivered a separate judgment in I.C. Golaknath case (AIR 1967 SC 1643) on behalf of himself, Justice Vasisht Bhargava and Justice G.K. Mitter.

35. The important issues decided by Justice K.N. Wanchoo and his two brother judges are in the succeeding paragraphs.

36. The Constitution (First Amendment) Act 1951, inter alia, provided for two new Articles viz. 31A and 31B in the chapter on Fundamental Rights. Article 31A stipulated that no law providing for acquisition by the state of any estate or of any Rights therein or the extinguishment or modification of any such Right shall be deemed to be void on the ground that it abridged or abrogated any Fundamental Right. Article 31B provided for validation of certain Acts and put such Acts in the Ninth Schedule to protect their constitutionality.

37. The Constitution (First Amendment) Act 1951 was immediately challenged by the affected parties.

38. The Supreme Court decided the matter in Sankari Prasad Singh Deo's Case (AIR 1951 SC 458) and rejected the contention that the Constitution (First Amendment) Act 1951 was hit by Article 13(2) of the Constitution.

39. By the Constitution (Seventeenth Amendment) Act 1964, forty-four new Acts were put in the Ninth Schedule to protect them from judicial Review. The above amendment was challenged in Sajjan Singh's Case (AIR 1965 SC 845). By a majority of three to two, the Supreme Court upheld the Constitution (Seventeenth Amendment) Act 1964 and reiterated their decision in Sankari Prasad Singh Deo's case.

40. Inter alia, it was argued by the Union of India that the doctrine of *stare decisis* has to be invoked not to disturb the earlier decisions in Sankari Prasad Singh Deo's Case (AIR 1951 SC 458) and Sajjan Singh Case (AIR 1965 SC 845). It was urged that after Sankari Prasad Singh Deo's Case (AIR 1951 SC 458) many states of the Union of India went for agrarian reform and millions of acres of ceiling surplus land have been taken from landowners and distributed among the landless.

41. There was also some argument that Article 368 provides only the procedure of amendment but not the power of amendment. This argument has not much force. Article 368 states *inter alia* that, "the Constitution shall stand amended in terms of the Bill." This shows that Article 368 provides for "the power to amend after the procedure has been followed". It is true that the marginal note to Article 368 is "procedure for amendment of the Constitution." But a marginal note cannot control the Article itself.

42. Moreover no entry in the Union List in the Seventh Schedule mentions "amendment of the Constitution" as an item which empowers the Parliament to amend the Constitution. Therefore, the important power of amendment of the Constitution need not be located in entry 97 of the Union List, which deals with "residuary power" of the Parliament. In no major Constitution of the world, the power of amendment of the Constitution is located in the residuary power of legislation.

43. There is a vital distinction in a written constitution between the fundamental law – which is the Constitution itself – and the ordinary law. This view has the support of the famous Constitutional expert, W. Ivor Jennings.

44. Power for amendment of the Constitution is a constituent power and is different from ordinary legislative power. Therefore, under Article 368 Parliament has the same powers as the Constituent Assembly had while framing the Constitution.

45. An argument was advanced that amendment means a change. Such a change is usually an improvement over the original provision; but such an argument has no support even in plain dictionary meaning of the word 'amendment'.

46. As pointed out in Sajjan Singh's Case (AIR 1965 SC 845) amendment will include any change whether by way of addition or alteration or deletion of any provision of the Constitution.

47. A question was raised whether under Article 368, Parliament has power to abrogate the Constitution and substitute it by a new one. This is a theoretical question. But it can be said that short of abrogating the Constitution and substituting it by a new one, the Parliament has powers to add or alter, modify or delete any provision of the Constitution.

48. The next question is: whether there are some limitations on Parliament's power to amend the Constitution. A plain reading of the Article 368 indicates that there are no express limitations. Regarding the implied limitations, neither the Supreme Court of USA nor the noted jurists of USA have accepted any implied limitation on power of amendment in Article V of the U.S. Constitution.

49. If the Indian Constitution could have certain implied limitations on power of amendment of the Constitution, it would have provided for it expressly. Moreover, it is not clear what are the basic features in the Indian Constitution, which are beyond powers of amendment of the Indian Parliament.

50. It is, therefore, clear that the power of amendment under Article 368 can reach any part of the Constitution and any provision of the Constitution can be amended provided the procedure laid down in Article 368 is followed.

51. It was urged that the debates in the Constituent Assembly may be referred to for appreciation of implied limitation on powers of the Parliament to amend the Constitution. Noted experts on construction of statutes have held that legislative debates might not be referred to by the Courts to ascertain the legislative intent. The debates are only relevant to understand the historical background in which the law was enacted.

52. The Preamble of the Constitution cannot be interpreted to provide for implied limitation on amending powers of the Parliament. In the Presidential reference under Article 143 in the matter of Berubari Exchange of Enclaves (AIR 1960 SC 845), the Court held that even though the Preamble provides the key to the minds of the framers of the Constitution, the Preamble forms no part of the Constitution. The Preamble also is not the source of any substantive power.

53. The Court had taken the correct view in both Sankari Prasad's Case (AIR 1951 SC 458) and Sajjan Singh's case (AIR 1965 SC 845) that "law" in Article 13(2) does not mean constitutional amendment but means only ordinary law.

54. Unanimous judgments of five judges of the Supreme Court as in Sankari Prasad Singh Deo's case (AIR 1951 SC 458) should not be overruled unless there were compelling reasons. Though the Court should be prepared to review earlier judgments in the public interest, the normal principle that judgments of the Supreme Court are final could not be ignored.

55. Justice M. Hidaytullah delivered a separate judgment. The main points in his judgment are set out in the succeeding paragraphs.

56. In Sankari Prasad Singh Deo's case (AIR 1951 SC 458), the Supreme Court unanimously upheld the *vires* of the Constitution (First Amendment) Act 1951. The Court held that power under Article 368 is a constituent power and a constitutional amendment was not "law" within meaning of Article 13(2).

57. Whether a constitutional amendment affecting any Fundamental Right was "law" arose when the Constitution (Seventeenth Amendment) Act 1964 was challenged in Sajjan Singh *versus* State of Rajasthan (AIR 1965 SC 845). But this time, unlike in Sankari Prasad Singh Deo's case (AIR 1951 SC 458) the Court was not unanimous though it upheld by majority the *vires* of the Seventeenth Amendment Act.

58. The majority judgment in Sajjan Singh's case (AIR 1965 SC 845) was delivered by Chief Justice P.B. Gajendragadkar on behalf of himself and Justice K.N. Wanchoo and Justice Raghubar Dayal. Justice M. Hidaytullah and Justice J.R. Mudholkar delivered separate judgments. Justice M. Hidaytullah on his part found the reasons in Sankari Prasad Singh Deo's case (AIR 1951 SC 458) to be totally unacceptable though he refrained from expressing himself finally on the broader question whether a constitutional amendment was "law" within the meaning of Article 13(2) of the Constitution.

59. Justice M. Hidaytullah had said in his separate judgment in Sajjan Singh's case (AIR 1965 SC 845) that he required stronger reasons than those contained in the judgment in Sankari Prasad Singh Deo's case (AIR 1951 SC 458) to accept that Fundamental Rights could be amended in common with other parts of the Constitution. He had further held as follows:

(i) Clauses (2) to (6) in Article 19 of the Constitution permit a curtailment of the Fundamental Rights in the public interest. The courts could decide whether any such curtailment was justified in the public interest.

(ii) There was hardly any measure of reasonable socio-economic reform which could not be implemented in spite of the Fundamental Rights.

(iii) Even the agrarian reforms as abolition of the zamindari system and the land ceiling laws could have been introduced without the Constitution (First Amendment) Act 1951. However, such reforms would have cost more to the public exchequer in terms of higher monetary compensation to the affected parties.

(iv) The Constitution gives so many assurances in the chapter on Fundamental Rights that it would be difficult to think that the Rights would be mere playthings of a special majority.

60. The proviso to Article 368 indicates that ratification by half of the state legislatures is not mandatory for amendment of Article 32, which is a Fundamental Right. Such an anomaly could not have been intended by the framers of the Constitution.

61. Article 32 erects a shield against action of the state including action of the legislature. Justice M. Hidaytullah asked whether the Parliament can take away the shield by amendment of the Constitution?

62. Conflicting constitutional provisions cannot be harmonized with each other by a priori view of the omni-competence of Article 368.

63. If there are two provisions in the Constitution, which seem to be hostile to each other Juridical hermeneutics require the Courts "to interpret them by combining them but not by destroying one with the aid of the other."

64. No part of a Constitution is superior to another part unless the Constitution itself says so. There is no accession of strength to any provision by calling it a *Code Portalis*. Even the French Jurist, who drafted the Code Napoleon, had said that among different provisions of the Constitution, there should be harmony.

65. Justice M. Hidaytullah went on to say that the Indian Constitution is not merely a document containing the structure and mechanism of Government but is a social document containing relationship of Government to both individuals and the society. It also contains the Rights of the Minorities and the Backward Classes. The concepts in the Preamble have been expanded into the Fundamental Rights and the Directive Principles of State Policy.

66. The origin of the chapter on Fundamental Rights can be traced to the demand for certain basic Rights in the Constitution of India Bill 1895 framed by the Indian National Congress. Annie Besant's Commonwealth of India Bill 1925, with its seven Fundamental Rights, is the precursor of Article 19 of the Constitution. The Jawaharlal Nehru Report emphasized importance of Fundamental Rights in the Constitution of free India.

67. The dictum of de Tocqueville that the English Constitution does not exist is far from accurate. There is a vast body of statutory laws in England, which provide the constitutional framework of the British Government but these statutes are not contained in one document called the Constitution of England.

68. Article 368 does not contain the complete code on powers of amendment by Parliament as under Articles 4, 11 and 169, certain provisions can be amended without invoking Article 368.

69. A statute and a Constitution, though of unequal dignity, are both laws and rest on the will of the people. A Constitution is a law which is difficult to change and is not subject to impulses of the majority, popular caprice and passion.

70. Democracy may be lost if there is no liberty based on law and if there is no law based on Equality. The protection of Fundamental Rights by the ordinary process of amendment of the Constitution is necessary if the citizen have not to walk in fear of democracy itself.

71. Eminent jurists have acknowledged that there could be implied limitations on power of the Parliament to amend the Constitution. Cooley had said,

"There never was a republican Constitution which delegated to functionaries the latent powers which lie dormant and are boundless in extent and incapable of definition."

72. In modern parliamentary democracies, the cabinet has attained a position of dominance over the legislature. The Executive uses the legislature to pass laws which the Executive wants. This has happened in the Weimar Republic of Germany after Hitler came to power as the Chancellor in the year 1933. Many jurists as Ivor Jennings have admitted that if

a Government had the majority in the Parliament, it could secure any law. Therefore, it would not be expedient to assume that the Parliament could be wholly trusted not to abridge any Fundamental Right by way of amendment.

73. In recent times, major countries of the world have come to realize importance of the Fundamental Rights. On December 10, 1948, the General Assembly of the United Nations unanimously adopted the "Universal Declaration of Human Rights". A European Commission on Human Rights has been set up to investigate individual cases of violation of the Rights.

74. Some thinkers would like to give higher place to the Directive Principles than to the Fundamental Rights. Such thinkers always think of freedom as a by-product of social justice. In their scheme of things, Fundamental Rights become an "*epitheton Ornans*" (i.e. ornamental epithet). These thinkers have scant regard for liberty, dignity and freedom of the individual. In the Indian Constitution, liberty of the individual is fundamental. Today's Parliament is a constituted body and is not the same as the Constituent Assembly. Can a political party with two-third majority in the Parliament and simple majority in at least half of the states of the Indian Union amend Article 368 and provide that a constitutional amendment does not require a special majority as in Article 368 but can be done by simple majority of members as is required for enacting ordinary law? Since the answer to this question is in the affirmative, can it be held thereafter that there is no difference between ordinary law and constitutional amendment and a constitutional amendment is also "law" within the meaning of "law" in Article 13(2) of the Constitution?

75. The English and American precedents do not lay down any principle applicable to amendment of the Indian Constitution. In U.K. whether a constitutional amendment is valid or not cannot arise as the King-in-Parliament is supreme. The example of the U.S. Constitution cannot also serve any useful purpose for understanding powers of the Indian Parliament.

76. The power of amendment of the U.S. Constitution flows from Article V of the Constitution.

77. Article V stipulates that no state, without its consent will be deprived of its equal suffrage in the Senate.

78. The provision for amendment of the American Constitution is different from the provision for enactment of ordinary law by the U.S. Congress.

79. Though no provision is there in Article V about the time limit of ratification of a proposed amendment to the U.S. Constitution, the Supreme Court of USA has ruled that the ratification could be within seven years of the proposed amendment.

80. Orfield, the noted Constitutional expert, is of the view that when the U.S. Congress is involved in amending the Constitution, it is not legislating but is exercising a peculiar power.

81. In the U.S., the Constitution works because the Supreme Court does the work of remoulding the Constitution to keep it abreast of new conditions and new times.

82. In the U.S., there is no provision in the Constitution similar to Article 13(2) of the Indian Constitution.

83. The guarantee of Fundamental Rights in the Indian Constitution is unique as the power to more the Supreme Court for enforcement of Fundamental Right is a guaranteed Right. This guarantee will be practically useless if the Fundamental Rights can be taken away by amendment.

84. It has been argued that if the Fundamental Rights are beyond amendment, society will become static and a revolution will be the only method for any change. This argument is not correct as in India, Parliament can pass a law under item 97 of the Union List to call another Constituent Assembly. Such Constituent Assembly can abrogate any Fundamental Right. To take away any Fundamental Right, a constituted body, as the Parliament of India, has no powers. It is only a new Constituent Assembly which will have such powers.

85. The Romans were the first to separate the legal personality of an individual from his membership of the state. Cicero was the first to declare that the primary duty of the state was to secure to each individual his private property. This was the beginning of the concept of Right to Property as a Fundamental Right. John Locke developed this concept of Right of Property as one of the primary duties of any Government. Blackstone gave unstinted support to the Right to Property as the backbone of English Society. The Right to Property appeared in the Magna Carta (1215) and the American Declaration of Independence (1776).

86. Article 31 of the Constitution, as it stood originally, mandated payment of compensation for acquisition of private property. The Constitution (First Amendment) Act 1951, which inserted Article 31A and Article 31B, restricted the Court's jurisdiction in matters of acquisition of zamindaries by of the state. The Constitution (Fourth Amendment) Act 1955 further limited the powers of the Court by prescribing that the amount provided by the law for acquisition of private property cannot be questioned by the Court on the ground that it is not adequate.

87. *Inter alia*, the Constitution (Seventeenth Amendment) Act 1964, adds as many as forty-four enactments of different state legislatures to the Ninth Schedule and protects them from Judicial Review. The power under Article 368 was to empower the Parliament to amend the Constitution. Giving protection to the forty-four enactments, which offend the Constitution can hardly merit the description of amendment of the Constitution. The intention behind the Ninth Schedule is not to amend the Constitution but to silence the Courts. The Indian Constitution is the only Constitution in the world which protects a long list of state legislations against the Constitution itself. In the result, the provision in the Constitution (Seventeenth Amendment) Act 1964 which protects forty-four state Acts by putting them in the Ninth Schedule is *ultra vires*.

88. A provision for amendment in a Constitution is a safety valve. It adjusts the movement of the machinery when it is out of order and is in danger of self-destruction. But the provision for amendment of a Constitution is not an open valve to let out that which was meant to be retained.

89. As K.C. Wheare has pointed out, the people – or a Constituent Assembly acting on behalf of the sovereign people – has authority to enact a Constitution and a portion of

the Constitution placed outside the amendatory process by one Constituent Body can be amended by another Constituent Body convoked by the people themselves.

90. Justice M. Hidaytullah summed up his observations as follows:

(i) The Fundamental Rights are outside the power of the Parliament to abridge them under Article 368.

(ii) The earlier judgments in Sankari Prasad Singh Deo's case (AIR 1951 SC 458) and Sajjan Singh's case (AIR 1965 SC 845) were based on an erroneous view of Article 13(2) and Article 368 of the Constitution.

(iii) The First, Fourth and the Seventeenth Amendments, being part of the Constitution by acquiescence for a long time, cannot now be challenged. [**N.B.:** Justice M. Hidaytullah invoked the doctrine of acquiescence to protect the Amendments of the Fundamental Rights prior to the year 1967 whereas Chief Justice K. Subba Rao had invoked the doctrine of prospective over-ruling for protection of those Constitutional Amendments.]

(iv) As the Supreme Court have now laid down that Fundamental Rights cannot be amended under Article 368 of the Constitution, any further inroads into Fundamental Rights by constitutional amendments would be *ultra vires*.

(v) For amendment of any Fundamental Right with a view to abridge it, a new Constituent Assembly has to be convoked.

91. Justice R.S. Bachawat delivered a separate judgment upholding the power of the Parliament to amend any Fundamental Right under Article 368. He also held that the power of amendment of the Constitution and the procedure thereof are to be found in Article 368 itself. The following are the salient points in the judgment of Justice R.S. Bachawat.

92. The contention that Article 368 contains only the procedure of amendment of the Constitution cannot be accepted.

93. In the Constitution, Article 248 read with Entry 97 in the Union List and Article 246 of the Constitution do not contain the power of amendment. No law made under the residuary power in Entry 97 of the Union List can derogate from the Constitution and amend it.

94. Like other Constitutions of major countries, clear provision in Article 368 of the Indian Constitution has been made to amend the Constitution.

95. The note on the margin of Article 368 that it is "procedure for amendment of the Constitution" need not be read literally.

96. Article 128 of the Australian Constitution has a note similar to the note on the margin of Article 368 of the Indian Constitution. No doubt has however been expressed by jurists that Article 128 of the Australian Constitution does not contain the power of amendment of the Constitution.

97. Article 368 has empowered the Parliament to amend any provision of the Constitution including any Fundamental Right.

98. It has been argued that a Constitution Amendment Act is a "law" and therefore the power of amendment under Article 368 is limited by Article 13(2) of the Constitution.

99. A constitutional amendment is not "law" within the meaning of "law" in Article 13(2). "Law" in Article 13(2) has been defined to include any "ordinance, order, bye-law, rule, regulation, notification, custom or usage having in territory of India the force of law." The distinction between the Constitution and the "law" is so fundamental that the Constitution is not regarded as a law.

100. The procedure of amendment under Article 368 is not an ordinary law-making procedure. It is only to be found in Article 368 and not in Articles 245, 246 and 248 of the Constitution, which lays down the procedure of enacting ordinary law.

101. Even in the U.S. Constitution "law" does not include a constitutional amendment. In *Corpus Juris Secundum*, it has been said that the term "Constitution" is ordinarily employed to designate the organic law in contradistinction to statue law.

102. The Constitution (First Amendment) Act 1951 introduced Article 31A and Article 31B and the Ninth Schedule to give effect to the policy of agrarian reforms. Such a measure was in conformity with Article 39 of the Directive Principles of State Policy. The (First Amendment) Act 1951 was upheld in Sankari Prasad Singh Deo's case (AIR 1951 SC 458). The Constitution (Fourth Amendment) Act 1954 amended Article 31(2) to supersede the decision in Bela Banerji's case (AIR 1954 SC 927) that private property can be acquired for a public purpose by payment of compensation at market rate.

103. By the Constitution (Fourth Amendment) Act 1954, "Compensation" was substituted by the word "amount" and it was stipulated that the amount was not justiciable. The Constitution (Sixteenth Amendment) Act amended Article 19 to enable imposition of reasonable restriction on the specified Fundamental Rights in the interest of sovereignty and integrity of India. The Constitution (Seventeenth Amendment) Act 1964 enlarged the definition of "estate" in Article 31A to supersede the decision in K.K. Kochuni *versus* State of Kerala (AIR 1962 SC 723). The validity of the Seventeenth Amendment was upheld in Sajjan Singh's case (AIR 1965 SC 845). All the aforesaid constitutional amendments would be invalid if it is held that under Article 368, the Parliament cannot amend any Fundamental Right.

104. It has been argued that the chapter on Fundamental Rights incorporates the objectives in the Preamble of the Constitution and as the Preamble cannot be amended, the Fundamental Rights also cannot be amended.

105. To counter this argument, it may be stated that the Preamble is secured not only by the chapter on Fundamental Rights but also by the chapter on the Directive Principles of State Policy.

106. Those who have argued that Parliament cannot amend any Fundamental Right have quoted the observations of Justice Patanjali Sastri in A.K. Gopalan's case (AIR 1950 SC 27) that the people of India, after delegating powers to the Executive, the Legislature and the Judiciary have "reserved to themselves certain Fundamental Rights so-called". But the same Judge held in Sankari Prasad Singh Deo's case (AIR 1951 SC 458) that the Fundamental Rights can be amended under Article 368.

107. In the case of Rhode Island *versus* Palmer – popularly known as the National Prohibition Case (1919) – the U.S. Supreme Court totally negatived the contention that an amendment

of the Bill of Rights must be confined in its scope to an improvement of that which is already contained in the Constitution and cannot include new grants of power.

108. Regarding the doctrine of implied limitation on the power of amendment of a Constitution, it can be said that such a doctrine is based on distrust of powers of Parliament. Possibility of abuse of power is no reason in law for limiting the force of the language vesting such power.

109. The historical background of framing of the Indian Constitution shows that the Fundamental Rights in the Constitution were not meant to be immutable.

110. The Constituent Assembly was elected on the basis of limited franchise. The provinces in India elected their representatives to the Constituent Assembly by members of the lower Houses of provincial Assemblies. The princely states sent their own representatives to the Constituent Assembly. After the draft of the Constitution of India was released on 26 February 1948, it was decided that in future, the Parliament would be elected by universal adult suffrage. Such a provision was incorporated later in Article 326 of the Constitution. Both politically and economically when the Constitution was being drafted, India was in a state of flux. Conditions in India were changing so fast that Sir B.N. Rau, the Constitutional Adviser to the Drafting Committee, recommended that for the first five years after commencement of the Constitution, any provision in the Constitution could be amended by the ordinary law-making process. This suggestion was, however, not accepted by the Drafting Committee.

111. The Constituent Assembly, which was elected on basis of a limited franchise, was conscious that in future, Parliaments elected on basis of universal adult suffrage would be more representative and Article 368 of the Constitution provided a sufficiently flexible machinery for amending the Constitution.

112. Justice R.S. Bachawat justified his stand by quoting an article published on the Independence Day (15 August 1947). The author of the article was Sir B.N. Rau, the Constitutional Adviser, who wrote that it would be illogical if a Constitution settled by a simple majority by a Constituent Assembly, elected indirectly on the basis of a very limited franchise, cannot be amended by the Parliament under Article 368 by a special majority of each of the Houses of the Parliament even when the elections to the Parliament for the Lower House would be held on the basis of universal adult suffrage.

113. The Constituent Assembly did not discuss any proposal that any provision of the Constitution including the Fundamental Rights was beyond the power of amendment of the Constitution. The debates in the Constituent Assembly indicate that there was a proposal by a Member of the Assembly that the Right to Property should not be amended; but later he withdrew the proposal.

114. Since commencement of the Constitution on 26 January 1950, there has been a rare unanimity of views among lawyers, judges and legislators that Fundamental Rights could be amended by the Parliament under Article 368.

115. If amendment of a Fundamental Right is interpreted as "law" under Article 13(2) of the Constitution, even if a Constitutional convention set up by the Parliament amends

a Fundamental Right, such an amendment could still be struck down on the ground that it is "law". The net result would be that even if the whole adult population of the country wants a change in the Fundamental Rights, it cannot be done even by a special Constitutional Convention elected for the purpose as Article 13(2) would always stand on the way. Such a deadlock can be resolved only by a violent Revolution.

116. The power of amendment of the Constitution, as held in Sankari Prasad Singh Deo's case (AIR 1951 SC 458), is a constituent power of the Indian Parliament.

117. There is no permanence about any Constitution. Thomas Jefferson, who played a big role in drafting the Constitution of USA, said that each generation is a distinct nation and cannot bind a succeeding generation. Therefore, each generation must decide whether the Fundamental Rights require any modification.

118. Justice R.S. Bachawat concluded his judgment by agreeing with Justice K.N. Wanchoo that the petition challenging amendment of the Fundamental Rights in the Constitution deserves to be dismissed.

119. Justice V. Ramaswami delivered a separate judgment agreeing with Justice K.N. Wanchoo. The salient points in the judgment of Justice V. Ramaswami are as follows:

120. Had it been the intention of framers of the Constitution that the Fundamental Rights could not be amended, the Constitution could have provided for it in as many words.

121. The expression Fundamental Rights means that such Rights are fundamental vis-à-vis the laws enacted by the legislature and the acts of the Executive. The expression, "Fundamental" does not lift the Fundamental Rights above the Constitution itself. Similarly, the expression, "guaranteed" in Article 32 means the Right to move the Supreme Court to enforce any Fundamental Right without exhausting the channel of the High Court under Article 226.

122. It is not correct to say that Article 368 only provides for the procedure for amendment. Actually, Article 368 contains both the power and procedure of amendment of the Constitution as Article 368 is the sole Article in Part XX of the Constitution dealing with amendment of the Constitution.

123. There is also no force in the argument that there are implied limitations on power of amendment of the Constitution. If the framers of the Constitution would have wanted to insulate certain basic features of the Constitution from amendment by the Parliament, they would have provided for it in the Constitution itself.

124. So far as the federal character of the Indian Constitution is concerned, it was held in State of West Bengal *versus* Union of India (AIR 1963 SC 1241) that as there was no compact between the constituent states and the Union and no provision for citizenship of a state and a separate citizenship of India, the federal structure was not a basic feature of the Constitution. The Preamble to the Constitution also cannot limit the power of the Parliament to cede some portion of Indian territory to Pakistan as held by the Supreme Court in the Berubari Union case (AIR 1960 SC 845).

125. The proper approach is to look upon the Fundamental Rights of individuals by balancing of interests and not as pre-ordained private Rights.

126. Harold J. Laski has observed that the struggle for liberty has been transferred from political to economic Rights. The roots of liberty are held to be in ownership and control of the means of production by the state and equitable distribution of the material goods.

127. As pointed out by Lord Dicey, the power of amendment of a Constitution is an adjunct of sovereignty. It does not admit of any limitation. Lord Bryce also held a similar view regarding the absence of any implied limitation on power of the Congress to amend any part of the Constitution.

128. The U.S. Supreme Court held in the National Prohibition Case (1919) that the U.S. Constitution does not provide any limitation on the U.S. Congress to amend the Constitution except that a state, without its consent, may not be deprived of equal representation in the Senate.

129. In the ultimate analysis, the doctrine of implied limitation will not be able to protect the people from their representatives in the Parliament. The perpetuity of democratic institutions would ultimately depend not on a special mechanism in the Constitution but on the character, intelligence and good conscience of the people themselves. As Justice Felix Frankfurter of the U.S. Supreme Court has held, a democracy need not depend upon the Courts to save it from its own unwisdom and ultimately it is the alertness of the people which can save democracy.

130. It is true that the principle of *stare decisis* may not strictly apply to a decision of the Supreme Court on a constitutional issue. There is no prohibition for the Supreme Court to review in the public interest its earlier judgment on a constitutional issue. But the Court has to ensure that its earlier decision on a constitutional issue is not frequently reviewed and departed from.

131. After due consideration of all aspects, it is necessary to follow the principle of *stare decisis* and hold that Parliament has powers under Article 368 to amend any Fundamental Right. In the result, the petition fails and is dismissed.

CHAPTER 7

A.K. Kraipak and Others *versus* Union of India (AIR 1970 SC 150)

[CHIEF JUSTICE M. HIDAYATULLAH, JUSTICE J.M. SHELAT, JUSTICE VASISHT BHARGAVA, JUSTICE K.S. HEGDE AND JUSTICE A.N. GROVER]

Case Summary

This is a unanimous judgment of a Constitution Bench of five Judges of the Supreme Court. The judgment was delivered by Justice K.S. Hegde.

1. This is a landmark judgment on how "Natural Justice", with its expanding ambit, is applicable to not only judicial orders but also to purely administrative decisions. The judgment lays down that the principles of Natural Justice may not be always in form of embodied rules. It also lays down that even administrative decisions are to be fair and unbiased and not arbitrary or unreasonable.
2. In this case, some officers of the J&K State Forest Service challenged the Notification of the Ministry of Home Affairs regarding initial constitution of the Indian Forest Service in 1966 as the third All-India service.
3. Regulation (3) of the Indian Forest Service (Initial Recruitment) Regulations 1966 provided for a Special Selection Board for each state to select officers of the State Forest Service for initial constitution of the Indian Forest Service.
4. The Special Selection Board's composition was as follows:

   Chairman, Union Public Service Commission or a Member of the Commission nominated by the Chairman – Chairman

   Inspector – General of Forest, Government of India – Member

   An officer of the Government of India not below the rank of a Joint Secretary – Member

   Chief Secretary of the State Government or Secretary of the State Government dealing with Forests – Member

   Chief Conservator of the concerned State Government – Member
5. The Special Selection Board was to recommend a list of officers of the State Forest Service, who on basis of their records of service, were suitable for appointment to the Indian Forest Service on initial constitution. It was provided that the list of names recommended and list

of names not recommended shall be sent along with records of service of the State Forest Service Officers to the Union Public Service Commission along with the observations, if any, of the Ministry of Home Affairs. The Union Public Service Commission shall send its final recommendation to the Government of India.

6. The Special Selection Board for the state of J&K had one Naquishbund, the Acting Chief Conservator of Forests of J&K, who participated in selection of suitable officers of J&K State Forest Service. The Special Selection Board, with Naquishbund as a Member, recommended name of Naquishbund himself at the top of the list of the officers of the J&K State Forest Service as suitable for appointment to the Indian Forest Service.

7. Three forest officers of the J&K Government – including one Basu who was senior in service to Naquishbund – had appealed to the State Government when Naquishbund was appointed as the Acting Chief Conservator of Forests in 1964 superseding their claims. The representation of Basu against his supersession was still pending with the Government of J&K when the Special Selection Board, did not recommend Basu for appointment to the Indian Forest Service. Two other officers viz. Baig and Kaul, who were Conservators of Forests and were rivals of Naquishbund, were also overlooked and not recommended for appointment to the Indian Forest Service. Naquishbund participated in the proceedings of the Special Selection Board, which did not recommend Basu, Baig and Kaul. Naquishbund, however, absented himself from meeting of the Special Selection Board when his name was considered for appointment to the Indian Forest Service.

8. It is true that the Special Selection Board was a high-powered body. It is also true that the list of names prepared by the Board was not the last word in matter of appointment of Forest Officers of J&K to the Indian Forest Service. It is also true that the Union Public Service Commission would have reviewed records of service of all officers of the J&K Forest Service before making final recommendation of names. But obviously, the names recommended by the Special Selection Board would have weighed with the Union Public Service Commission.

9. The petitioner had argued that the power of the Special Selection Board was a quasi-judicial power as they had to adjudge suitability of officers of the J&K Forest Service. The Special Selection Board, it was argued, was a statutory body and its action in not selecting an officer would adversely affect career prospects of the officer ignored for selection.

10. The Attorney-General for India, however, took a contrary view and argued that "adjudge" meant worthy of selection and the Special Selection Board was exercising not a quasi-judicial, but an administrative power.

11. Justice K.S. Hegde held that the dividing line between an administrative power and a quasi-judicial power is quite thin and is being gradually obliterated. In order to determine whether a power is administrative or quasi-judicial, one has to look at the following:

(i) nature of the power;
(ii) person on whom the power is conferred;
(iii) consequences of exercise of that power;
(iv) manner in which the power is expected to be exercised.

12. Under the Indian Constitution, the Rule of Law pervades the entire field of administration. The concept of the Rule of Law would lose its vitality if instrumentalities of the state do not discharge their functions in a fair and just manner. The requirement of acting judicially is nothing but a requirement to act justly and fairly and not arbitrarily or capriciously. The procedures, which are considered inherent in the exercise of judicial power, are merely those which facilitate a just and fair decision.

13. In recent years, the concept of quasi-judicial power has been undergoing a radical change. A few years ago, what was being considered as an administrative power is now being considered as a quasi-judicial power.

14. With the increase of power of administrative bodies, it has become necessary to provide guidelines for exercise of that power to ensure justice and fair play. To prevent the abuse of that power and to see that it does not become a new despotism, Courts are gradually evolving principles for exercise of such powers.

15. For purposes of the present case, we assume that the powers exercised by the Special Selection Board was an administrative power and test the validity of the impugned recommendations.

16. It is true that ordinarily the Chief Conservator of Forests of a State should be the most appropriate person to be a member in the Special Selection Board. He is expected to know his officers and their weaknesses as well as their strengths. His opinion as regards their suitability for appointment to the Indian Forest Service is entitled to great weight. But in the circumstances, it was improper to have included Naquishbund, the Acting Chief Conservator of Forests of J&K, as a member of the Special Selection Board as he was also one of the officers to be considered for appointment to the Indian Forest Service.

17. It is against all cannons of Justice to make a man judge in his own case. It is true that Naquishbund did not participate in deliberations of the Selection Board when his case was considered. But the very fact that he was a member of the Selection Board must have had its impact on the decision of the Board. Naquishbund admittedly participated in deliberations when claims of his rivals in service viz. Basu, Kaul and Baig were considered. At every stage of participation of Naquishbund in deliberations of the Special Selection Board, there was a conflict between his duty and his interest. In the circumstances, it is difficult to believe that Naquishbund acted impartially. The real question is not whether he was biased. The Court has to see whether there is reasonable ground for believing that he was likely to have been biased.

18. The Court agrees with the Attorney-General that a mere suspicion of bias is not sufficient to invalidate recommendations of the Board. There must be a reasonable likelihood of bias to invalidate its recommendations. In deciding the question of bias, the Court has to take into consideration human probabilities and ordinary course of human conduct. Judged by this yardstick, it was in the interest of Naquishbund to keep out his rivals from the list of names of suitable officers.

19. The members of the Special Selection Board, other than Naquishbund, have filed affidavits that in no manner Naquishbund influenced their decisions to recommend names of suitable officers. This contention cannot be sustained as each Member of the Board was bound to influence the others. The bias of Member of the Board as Naquishbund, who has special knowledge, was likely to operate in a subtle manner. It is no wonder that other Members of the Board were unaware of the extent to which opinion of a Member of the Board with special knowledge influenced their conclusions. The Court is unable to accept the contention that in judging the suitability of officers for appointment to the Indian Forest Service, Members of the Selection Board did not have any discussion. It is not as if the records of service of officers of the J&K Forest Service spoke for themselves. The Court is unable to believe that Members of the Selection Board functioned like computers. At the time names were recommended, Members of the Selection Board other than Naquishbund were not likely to have known that Basu's representation against his supersession was still pending for a decision by the State Government. Therefore, there was no occasion for Members of the Selection Board to distrust the opinion of Naquishbund about Basu's unsuitability for selection.

20. The Attorney-General quoted several judgments in support of his contention that principles of Natural Justice have no application to administrative proceedings. It is not necessary to examine the ratio of these judgments as there has been a great deal of fresh thinking of the subject. The horizon of Natural Justice has been constantly expanding. The question how far the principles of Natural Justice govern administrative inquiries came up before the Queen's Bench Division when in the year 1967, Lord Parker pronounced upon the validity of action taken by an Immigration Officer. Lord Parker said that even if an Immigration Officer is not a judicial or a quasi-judicial authority, he must give the immigrant an opportunity of satisfying him of the matters in the sub-section and let the immigrant know what the Immigration Officer's immediate impression is so that the immigrant can disabuse him of his impression. This is not acting or being required to act judicially but of being required to act fairly.

21. Justice Blain, who was in the Bench with Lord Parker, agreed that acting fairly meant that the Immigration Officer must apply his mind dispassionately to a particular problem and information available to him. If an Immigration Officer was not doing so, a writ or mandamus would lie against him.

22. In State of Orissa *versus* Dr Binapani Dei (AIR 1967 SC 1269), Justice J.C. Shah said that an enquiry by the Government of Orissa regarding correct age of a Government Servant must follow the principle of Natural Justice. Even though the inquiry by the Government was administrative in character, an administrative order which visits a Government Servant with civil consequence, must be made consistently with the principle of Natural Justice. In other words, the Government Servant would be informed about the case against him to enable him to make a representation and exercise the Right of being heard before any action is taken.

23. The rules of Natural Justice are to secure justice or to put in negatively to prevent miscarriage of justice. These rules can operate only in areas not covered by law validly made. In other words, they do not supplant the law but supplement the law.

24. The concept of Natural Justice has undergone a great deal of change. In the past, the concept included just two rules, viz.,

(i) No one shall be judge in his own case. (*nemo debet esse judex propria causa*)

(ii) No decision shall be given against a party without a hearing (*audi alteram partem*). Very soon, a third rule was added which envisaged that quasi-judicial enquiries must be held in good faith, without bias and not arbitrarily or unreasonably.

25. In course of years, many more subsidiary Rules were added to the Rules of Natural Justice. Until recently, the Courts had held that unless the Authority concerned was required by law to act judicially, there was no room for application of the principles of Natural Justice. The validity of such a proposition is now being questioned. If the purpose of the principles of Natural Justice is to prevent miscarriage of justice, one fails to see why they should not be made applicable to administrative inquiries. Often, it is not easy to draw the line that demarcates administrative inquiries from quasi-judicial inquiries. Arriving at a just decision is the aim of both quasi-judicial and administrative inquiries.

26. In Suresh Kosy George *versus* The University of Kerala (AIR 1969 SC 198), the Court held that rules of Natural Justice are not embodied rules. What particular rule of Natural Justice should apply to a given case must depend to a great extent on facts and circumstances of the case, the framework of the law under which the inquiry is held and the constitution of the tribunal or body of persons appointed for the purpose. Whenever, a complaint is made before a Court that some principle of Natural Justice has been contravened, the Court has to decide whether observance of the principle of Natural Justice was justified for a just decision in the case.

27. Looking at the composition of the Special Selection Board and the nature of duties entrusted to it, it cannot be denied that its recommendations would have carried considerable weight with the Union Public Service Commission. If the recommendation of the Special Selection Board is held to have been vitiated, the final recommendation of the Union Public Service Commission must also be held to have been vitiated.

28. The Attorney-General argued that whereas Naquishbund should not have participated in deliberations of the Special Selection Board while the Board considered the suitability of Basu, Baig and Kaul, there is no ground for the Court to set aside selection of other officers of the J&K State Forest Service to the Indian Forest Service. The Attorney-General submitted that in the interest of justice, cases of Basu, Baig and Kaul could be reconsidered by another Special Selection Board without Naquishbund participating. He also submitted that there is no ground for the Court to set aside the selection of at least the Junior Scale Officers of the J&K Forest Service for appointment to the Indian Forest Service.

29. It would be difficult to agree with the Attorney-General because selection of junior scale officers and also of senior scale officers were made from the same pool of officers of the J&K State Forest Service. Every Officer of the J&K Forest Service who had put in at least eight years of regular service was eligible for being considered for selection for the senior scale of the Indian Forest Service. The Board selected some of them for the junior scale of the Indian Forest Service whereas some others were selected for the senior scale of the Service. Hence, it was not possible to separate the two sets of officers.

30. In view of the aforesaid, the Court set aside the entire selection and directed the Central Government and the State Government of J&K to pay the cost of litigation to the Petitioners.

Chapter 8

R.C. Cooper *versus* Union of India (AIR 1970 SC 564)

[JUSTICE J.C. SHAH, JUSTICE S.M. SIKRI, JUSTICE J.M. SHELAT, JUSTICE VASISHT BHARGAVA, JUSTICE G.K. MATHUR, JUSTICE C.A. VAIDIALINGAM, JUSTICE K.S. HEGDE, JUSTICE A.N. GROVER, JUSTICE I.D. DUA, JUSTICE P. JAGANMOHAN REDDY AND JUSTICE A.N. RAY]

Case Summary

This is a judgment of a Constitution Bench of eleven Judges of the Supreme Court. The judgment, by a majority of ten judges, was delivered by Justice J.C. Shah. The judges, who agreed with Justice J.C. Shah, are Justice S.M. Sikri, Justice J.M. Shelat, Justice Vasisht Bhargava, Justice G.K. Mathur, Justice C.A. Vaidialingam, Justice K.S. Hegde, Justice A.N. Grover, Justice P. Jagmohan Reddy and Justice I.D. Dua. The lone dissenting judgment is of Justice A.N. Ray.

1. The majority judgment, delivered by Justice J.C. Shah, held as follows: Under Article 32 of the Constitution, R.C. Cooper, a former Director of the Central Bank of India who had shares in four out of the 14 commercial banks nationalized by the Government, filed a petition before the Supreme Court with a prayer for quashing the Banking Companies (Acquisition and Transfer of Undertaking) Ordinance promulgated by the Acting President of India on 19 July 1969 and the Banking Companies (Acquisition and Transfer of Undertaking) Act of 09 August 1969, which replaced the Ordinance. R.C. Cooper alleged that the Ordinance and the Act violated his Fundamental Rights under Articles 14, 19 and 31.

2. The history of legislation relating to Banking Companies indicates that till the year 1949, there was no comprehensive legislation governing banking business. In 1949, the Central Legislature, enacted a comprehensive legislation called the Banking Companies Act 1949, which was later called the Banking Regulation Act. The Act defined 'Banking' and 'Banking Companies'. Section 6 of the Act stipulated that the Banks in addition to the business of banking can also do some other specified business only. *Inter alia,* the Act stipulated minimum paid-up capital and reserves to be held by each Bank. It contained provisions for voting Rights of stakeholders and modalities for election of Board of Directors of

Banks. It also contained various other provisions. The Act also empowered the Reserve Bank of India to issue directions to commercial Banks.

3. In the year 1968, the Banking Regulation Act 1949 was amended to give effect to the policy of social control over the Commercial Banks. In the year 1955, the State Bank of India Act had been enacted to take over management of the Imperial Bank of India. To sum up, in June 1969, there were as many as 14 scheduled commercial Banks in the country with each Bank having deposits of more than Rs. 50 crore.

4. On 19 July 1969, the Acting President of India, promulgated an ordinance under Article 123 of the Constitution vesting the undertakings of 14 named commercial Banks in corresponding new Banks set up under the Ordinance.

5. The named 14 Commercial Banks which were taken over by the Ordinance – later replaced by the Act 22 of 1969 – were as follows:
   - The Central Bank of India Ltd.
   - The Bank of India Ltd.
   - The Punjab National Bank Ltd.
   - The Bank of Baroda Ltd.
   - The United Commercial Bank Ltd.
   - Canara Bank Ltd.
   - United Bank of India Ltd.
   - Dena Bank Ltd.
   - Syndicate Bank Ltd.
   - The Union Bank of India Ltd.
   - Allahabad Bank Ltd.
   - The Indian Bank Ltd.
   - The Bank of Maharashtra Ltd.
   - The Indian Overseas Bank Ltd.

6. *Inter alia*, it was provided that the Chairman of the 14 named Banks shall be custodians of the new Banks. The general supervision and direction of affairs of new Banks vested in the custodians of the new Banks, who became the Chief Executive officers.

7. It was stipulated that the Central Government shall give compensation to the 14 nationalized Banks according to the following principles:
   (a) where the amount of compensation can be fixed by agreement, the compensation shall be as per the agreement;
   (b) where no agreement could be reached, the Central Government was to refer the matter to a Tribunal;
   (c) compensation was to be paid in the form of Central Government securities.

8. Under the Ordinance, the entire undertaking of every named 14 Commercial Bank was taken over by the new Banks and all assets, contractual rights and obligations, to which the named Commercial Banks were subject, stood transferred to the corresponding new

Bank. The Chairman and Directors of the Commercial Banks were deemed to have vacated their office which they held before nationalization of the Banks. The services of the administrative and other members of the staff also stood transferred to the new Banks.

9. As stated earlier, the Ordinance promulgated by the Acting President in July, 1969 was replaced by the Act, in August, 1969.

10. R.C. Cooper challenged the Ordinance and the Act on the following grounds:
   (i) The Ordinance was invalid because the conditions precedent to promulgate it did not exist.
   (ii) Parliament had no legislative competence to enact the Act of 1969 as the Act encroached upon items in the State list.
   (iii) The Act infringed the Fundamental Rights of the petitioner under Articles 14, 19(1) (f) and (g) and 31(2).
   (iv) The Act violated the freedom of trade, commerce and intercourse guaranteed under Article 301 of the Constitution.
   (v) The retrospective operation of the Act of 1969 was invalid.

11. Niren De, Attorney-General for India, argued that no Fundamental Right of the petitioner was directly infringed as the petitioner was merely a shareholder, depositor and Director of a Bank and not the owner. He argued that a Company under the Companies Act 1956 is a distinct legal person and is separate from its members. A shareholder has merely an interest in the Company arising under its Articles of Association, measured by a sum of money for the purpose of liability and a share in the profit. A Director of a Company is not the owner of the Company; but merely its agent for management of the Company. A person who has a deposit in a Banking Company is only its creditor. Therefore, a shareholder, a Director or a depositor of a Banking Company is not entitled to move a petition under Article 32.

12. But the contention of the Attorney-General is not valid because if action of the State impairs the right of a shareholder, the courts will not deny relief. Moreover, the petitioner has stated that by nationalization of the named Banks in which he has shares, value of his shares has been substantially reduced and his Right to receive dividend has been adversely affected. Moreover, his Right to carry on business through agency of the Banking company has been impaired and he has suffered substantial financial loss.

13. In Charanjit Lal Chaudhury *versus* the Union of India (AIR 1951 SC 41) the Supreme Court had held that a preference shareholder of a Company is competent to file a suit challenging the Sholapur Spinning and Weaving Company (Emergency Provision). Ordinance 1950 as it directly affected the shareholder.

14. The Attorney-General cited judgment of the Supreme Court in the State Trading Corporation of India Ltd. *versus* the Commercial Tax Officer, Visakhapatnam (AIR 1963 SC 1811) in support of his claim. But Justice J.C. Shah held that the judgment has no relevance for case of the Petitioner, as in the judgment, the Court held that the State Trading Corporation, not being a citizen, cannot claim infringement of the Right to hold

property and to carry on business under Article 19(1)(f) and (g) of the Constitution. For similar reasons, the Supreme Court also did not permit the Tata Engineering and Locomotive Company Ltd. (TELCO) to file a petition under Article 32 for violation of the Fundamental Right to property, which can be enforced by a citizen only.

15. In view of the aforesaid, the preliminary objection raised by the Attorney-General against maintainability of the petition under Article 32, must fail as the petitioner is a citizen of India.

16. One of the issues urged by the petitioner is the validity of the Ordinance of July 1969. The Petitioner has contended that under Article 123 of the Constitution, the President has to be satisfied that circumstances which render it necessary for him to take immediate action and the Court must be satisfied that these preconditions for promulgation of the Ordinance did exist.

17. In reply, the Attorney-General stated that satisfaction of the President as regards the necessity to take immediate action is purely subjective and the Union of India was under no legal obligation to disclose the circumstances to justify immediate action to promulgate the Ordinance. The Attorney-General cited decisions of the Privy Council and the Federal Court in support of his argument.

18. N.A. Palkhivala, Counsel for the Petitioner, did not agree with the Attorney-General and said that the Court was competent to scrutinize whether the circumstances were such as to justify promulgation of an Ordinance as otherwise powers to promulgate an Ordinance might be invoked for a collateral purpose.

19. Justice J.C. Shah held that as the Ordinance of July 1969 has been repealed and replaced by an Act in August 1969, the issue of validity of the Ordinance at this stage is purely academic.

20. N.A. Palkhivala argued that the Act of 1969 was not within the legislative competence of the Parliament and to the extent to which the Act vests in the corresponding new Banks the assets of business other than Banking, it trenches upon the authority of the state legislature and is therefore void.

21. Before the Constitution (Seventh Amendment) Act 1956, Entry 33 in the Union List conferred on the Parliament the power to enact laws with respect to acquisition or requisition of property for purpose of the Union and Entry 36 in the State List conferred on the state legislature the power for acquisition or requisition of property for other purposes. These entries were deleted by the Constitution (Seventh Amendment) Act 1955 and a single Entry 42 of the concurrent list vested the power on the Parliament and the state legislatures for acquisition and requisitioning of private property.

22. The position is that, after the Constitution (Seventh Amendment) Act 1956, power to legislate for acquisition and requisition of property can only be exercised under Entry 42 of the Concurrent List.

23. Article 19(1)(f) of the Constitution is a positive declaration in the widest terms of the Right to acquire, hold and dispose of property. The Right is only subject to restrictions imposed by law in the interest of the general public. As held by the Supreme Court Article

19(1(f) does not merely protect an abstract Right to Property; it extends to concrete Right to property as well.

24. Article 31(1) stipulates that no person shall be deprived of his property save by authority of law. Under Article 31(2) no private property shall be compulsorily acquired or requisitioned save for a public purpose and save by authority of law. Such law must fix an amount for acquisition of property or must set out the principles for fixing the amount for acquisition of property and given in such manner to the owner of the property as may be specified in such law. It further stipulates that no such law can be questioned in any Court on the ground that the amount so fixed is not adequate or the whole or part of such amount is to be given to the owner otherwise than in cash. The proviso to Article 31(2) stipulates that a law providing for acquisition of property of a minority educational institution, referred to in Article 30 of the Constitution, shall be such as not to restrict or abrogate the Right of a minority to set up and administer an educational institution. The Constitution also stipulates that where a law does not provide for transfer of the ownership or Right of possession of any property to the state or a corporation owned or controlled by the State, it shall not be deemed to provide for compulsory acquisition or requisition of property notwithstanding that it deprives any person of his property. The Constitution also stipulates that no law providing for acquisition or requisition of property passed by any state legislature shall have effect unless such law having been reserved for consideration of the President, has received his assent.

25. Protection against impairment of the guarantee of Fundamental Rights is determined by the following:
   (a) nature of the Fundamental Right;
   (b) interest of the aggrieved party;
   (c) degree of harm resulting from action by the state;
   (d) impairment of the Right of the individual and not the object of state action in taking the impugned decision;

26. Validity of state action must be adjudged in the light of its operation upon the Right of the individual and groups of individuals in all their dimensions.

27. Early in history of the Supreme Court, the question of inter-relationship between provisions regarding protection of Fundamental Rights fell to be determined. In A.K. Gopalan *versus* State of Madras (AIR 1950 SC 27), the majority of judges held that Article 22 of the Constitution being a complete code relating to Preventive Detention, validity of an order of detention must be determined within the four corners of the Article 22 itself.

28. Justice Fazl Ali, however, took a different view when he held that the scheme of the chapter dealing with Fundamental Rights did not contemplate that each Article in the chapter is a code by itself and is independent of other Articles in the same chapter. He held that Preventive Detention, which has been dealt with in Article 22 of the Constitution, also amounts to deprivation of personal liberty referred to in Article 21 and is also a violation of the Right to freedom of movement referred to in Article 19(1)(d).

29. The principle underlying the mutual exclusiveness of the Fundamental Rights laid down in A.K. Gopalan's case was extended to the Right of Property when in Charanjit Lal Chaudhury's case (AIR 1951 SC 41) it was held that the Right to Property guaranteed in Article 19(1)(f) would continue until the owner was deprived of the Right by authority of law. The ratio of Charanjit Lal Chaudhury's case was reiterated in State of West Bengal *versus* Subodh Gopal Banerji (AIR 1954 SC 92) and in State of Bombay *versus* Bhanji Munji (AIR 1955 SC 41).

30. The case of State of Bombay *versus* Bhanji Munji (AIR 1955 SC 41) arose under Article 31 before it was amended by the Constitution (Fourth Amendment) Act 1955. It was held in that case that clause (1) and clause (2) of Article 31, as they then stood, dealt with the same subject matter of compulsory acquisition of property.

31. After the Constitution (Fourth Amendment) Act 1955 it was held by the Supreme Court – Justice K. Subba Rao delivering the majority judgment in K.K. Kochuni's case (AIR 1960 SC 1080) – that clause (2) of Article 31 only dealt with compulsory acquisition of property and not clause (1) of Article 31. In K.K. Kochuni's case (AIR 1960 SC 1080), the Court also held that the expression "authority of law" in Article 31(1) meant authority of a valid law seeking to deprive a person of his property and the law could be tested on the ground of violation of other Fundamental Rights including the Right to acquire, hold and dispose of property under Article 19(1)(f).

32. The theory that the object and form of state action determines the extent of protection, which an aggrieved party may claim, is not consistent with the scheme of our Constitution where each freedom has different dimensions. Article 19(1)(f) deals with the Right to acquire, hold and dispose of property and Article 19(5) authorizes imposition of restrictions upon those Rights. Article 19(5) and Article 31(1) and (2) prescribe restrictions on state action subject to which the Right to Property may be exercised. If the acquisition of property is for a public purpose, substantial reasonableness of the restriction may be presumed but inquiry into reasonableness of the procedure of acquisition cannot be barred. To illustrate, if a Tribunal is set up by law to determine the amount of compensation for property fixes the amount of compensation without hearing the owner of the acquired property, the law, can be struck down for violation of Article 19(1)(f). In other words, compliance with the conditions under Article 31(2) alone is not sufficient to negative the protection of the guarantee to Right to Property. The law providing for compulsory acquisition of property must be within competence of the legislature and should not impair the guarantee of the Fundamental Rights. Thus, Article 19(1)(f) and Article 31(2) are not mutually exclusive.

33. In view of the foregoing analysis, the assumption in A.K. Gopalan's case (AIR 1950 SC 27) that certain Articles in the chapter on Fundamental Rights exclusively deal with specific matters is not the correct interpretation. It is also not correct, as held in A.K. Gopalan's case (AIR 1950 SC 27) that in determining whether there is infringement of Fundamental Rights, the object and form of the state action alone need be considered and effect of the laws enacted by the state on the Fundamental Rights of individuals in general shall be ignored by the Courts.

34. A citizen may claim that the law authorizing compulsory acquisition of property imposes fetters upon his Right to hold property under Article 19(1)(f) and such fetters are not reasonable restrictions.

35. Against this background, the Court has to consider whether Sections 4 and 5 of the Act of 1969 adversely affect the Fundamental Rights under Article 19(1)(f) and 19(1)(g) of the Constitution.

36. It is relevant that under Section 4 of the Act of 1969, the entire undertaking of each of the 14 named Banks vests in the Union of India and the Bank – prohibited from engaging in business of Banking in India – may engage in other forms of business. But it may be appreciated that each of the named Banks has no assets with which it can carry on other forms of business. It cannot engage also in non-Banking business in its old name. A named Bank deprived of its entire assets, its managerial and other members of the staff, its premises, and its name may have a theoretical Right to carry on non-banking business, but it will not be able to do so especially when a fraction of the market value of the named Bank, payable to it as compensation, is not paid to it in cash immediately after compulsory acquisition of the Bank.

37. By the Constitution (First Amendment) Act 1951, Article 19(6) was inserted to provide that the state can create a monopoly in its own favour in respect of any trade or business. In dealing with a law creating a state monopoly, in Akadasi Pradhan *versus* State of Orissa (AIR 1963 SC 1047), the Supreme Court unanimously held that validity of law creating a state monopoly, cannot be challenged on the ground that it imposes unreasonable restrictions in the interest of the general public. But if the law contains other incidental provisions, which do not constitute an essential and integral part of the monopoly created by it, its validity can be challenged. It was, however, stated in Akadasi Pradhan's case (AIR 1963 SC 1047) that state monopoly in respect of any trade or business must be presumed to be reasonable so far as Article 19(1)(g) of the Constitution is concerned.

38. It is clear that the Act of 1969, which prohibits the 14 named Banks from carrying on banking business is not liable to be challenged because of Article 19(6) introduced by the Constitution (First Amendment) Act 1951.

39. N.A. Palkhivala argued on the basis of published documents of the Reserve Bank that the performance of the named Banks compared favourably with the government controlled State Bank of India and there was no need for nationalizing the 14 named Banks when the social control – introduced by the Banking Laws (Amendment) Act of 1968 – had achieved the desired results.

40. The Attorney-General however rebutted the arguments by stating that the 14 named Banks had to follow a conservative policy as they had to protect the interest of their shareholders. The conservative policy deprived free flow of bank loans to the weaker section of the society. The Attorney-General also pointed out that in spite of social control of the named Banks, only 24 percent of towns in India had branches of the 14 named Banks.

41. The Supreme Court is, however, not the forum for resolution of the conflicting claim made by N.A. Palkhivala, counsel for the petitioner, and Niren De, the Attorney-General for India. The following issues cannot be decided by application of known judicial parameters:

(i) whether there is a genuine need for banking facilities in rural areas;

(ii) whether certain sections of the community are not able to make progress because of lack of free flow of bank loans;

(iii) whether commercial Banks taken over by the Government will be able to function properly;

(iv) whether Government by being not driven by profit motive can help the deprived section of the society through banking services;

(v) whether undue emphasis on banking as a means of social regeneration, specially in backward areas, is a doctrinaire approach.

42. To put it briefly, whether the policy followed by the Government or the policy propounded by the opponents of the Government policy may reasonably attain the national objectives are matters which have little relevance in determining legality of nationalization of the 14 named Banks. What is relevant for the Court is that the Parliament in India has the competence to legislate in respect of Banking and other commercial activities of the named Banks because of Entry 45 in the Union List. Similarly, Parliament has powers to legislate for acquiring the undertaking of the named Banks under Entry 42 of the Concurrent List.

43. It is also not relevant for the Court to consider whether under the Banking Laws (Amendment) Act 1968, the Reserve Bank could control the named Banks and achieve the objectives of the Act 22 of 1969.

44. The Court has the power to strike down a law on the ground of want of legislative competence but the Court will not sit in appeal over the policy of the Parliament in enacting a law.

45. By the Act of 1969, the named Banks are entitled to do only non-banking business; but the provisions of the Act are such that they cannot carry on even such business. A named Bank cannot use its name and the compensation for acquisition can be paid to the named Banks in government securities and not in cash. The government securities will mature after a few years and hence none of the named Banks may have cash to enable them to carry on their non-Banking business. Where restrictions imposed on carrying on a business are so stringent that in practice, the business cannot be carried on, the Courts will not regard the restrictions as reasonable.

46. The next issue to be considered is whether the Act of 1969 is hit by Article 14. Article 14 forbids class legislation but not reasonable classification. In a catena of decisions as Charanjit Lal Chaudhury's Case (AIR 1951 SC 41), State of Bombay *versus* F.N. Balsara (AIR 1951 SC 318), the State of West Bengal *versus* Anwar Ali Sarkar (AIR 1952 SC 75) and R.K. Dalmia *versus* Justice S.R. Tendolkar (AIR 1958 SC 538) the Supreme Court have held that

(a) classification in any law must be founded on an intelligible differential distinguishing persons, transactions or things grouped together from others left out of the group;

(b) the differentia must have a rational nexus with the object sought to be achieved by the law;

(c) the legislature is free to recognize the degree of harm and to restrict the operation of a law only to those cases where the need is the clearest;

(d) Courts will assume that there is reasonable classification in the impugned law and it is for the party challenging the law as discriminatory to establish discrimination.

47. The ground for selection of the 14 named Banks for nationalization is that these Banks on a specified date in June 1969 had deposits of not less than Rs. 50 crore each.

48. Hostile discrimination against the 14 named Banks may be established on the ground that Banks other than the 14 named Banks may carry on banking business and new Banks may be floated for carrying on Banking business.

49. The other ground in support of hostile discrimination is that selection of 14 named Banks has penalized efficiency and good management and other Banks, which did not have efficient management and had deposits of less than Rupees Fifty crore on the specified date in June 1969, were allowed to carry on Banking and non-Banking business.

50. Section 15(2) of the Act of 1969 which prohibits the named Banks from carrying on Banking business is, therefore, liable to be struck down as violative of Article 14 of the Constitution.

51. The next issue to be considered is whether the Act of 1969 has infringed the guarantees in Article 31(2) of the Constitution.

52. Article 31(2) places two restrictions on power of the state for compulsory acquisition of property. The first restriction is that private property can be acquired only for a public purpose. The second restriction is that acquisition of property for a public purpose must be under authority of law and such law shall either fix an amount as compensation or specify the principles on which and the manner in which the amount is to be determined and given. Further, no Court can question whether the amount given to the owner for acquisition of his property is adequate.

53. The petitioner has argued through his counsel that compensation means a "just equivalent" in money of the property acquired. Opposing the contention of the petitioner, the Attorney-General said that "compensation" in Article 31(2) of the Constitution did not mean a "just equivalent" of the property acquired. He argued that a law for compulsory acquisition of property, if it is not confiscatory or the principles it sets out for determining the amount as compensation are not irrelevant, cannot be challenged on the ground of propriety of principles of fixation of the amount or adequacy of the amount as compensation.

54. What is the true meaning of "compensation" in Article 31(2)? The dictionary meaning of compensation means anything of equal value. In all countries, where the Rule of Law prevails, the Right to compensation is inextricably linked to the Right to property.

55. In the United States of America, the Right of "eminent domain" has been circumscribed by the Fifth Amendment of the Constitution as follows:

"Nor shall private property be taken for public use, without just compensation."

56. Similar guarantees exist for compulsory acquisition of private property in the Japanese Constitution and the Constitution of the Commonwealth of Australia.

57. Blackstone in his "Commentaries of the Laws of England" has stated the principles for payment of compensation for compulsory acquisition of private property. He has said that the owner of private property should not be deprived of his Right to property by compulsory acquisition in an arbitrary manner and the owner must be given "a full indemnification and equivalent amount for the injury sustained."

58. Even though the British Parliament is supreme in law, it has always acquired property for a public purpose under a law providing for cash value in the market of the acquired property.

59. Section 299(2) of the Government of India Act 1935 also did not empower either the federal or any provincial legislature to enact a law for compulsory acquisition of private property without either fixing the amount of compensation or specifying the principles on which and the manner in which compensation was to be determined.

60. Prior to the Constitution (Fourth Amendment) Act 1955, the Supreme Court had observed in State of West Bengal *versus* Bela Banerjee and Others (AIR 1954 SC 170) that compensation for compulsory acquisition of property by law for a public purpose must be a just equivalent of what the owner had been deprived of.

61. The Constitution (Fourth Amendment) Act 1955, which came into force from 27 April 1955, provided that no law for compulsory acquisition or requisition of property shall be called in question in any Court on the ground that the amount paid to the owner of property for acquisition is not adequate.

62. In Shantilal Mangaldas case (AIR 1969 SC 634), it was held that compensation for compulsory acquisition of property under a law may not be a "just equivalent" of the property acquired. But it has to be ensured that the amount paid is not illusory or is determined on application of principles not relevant for the purpose.

63. Section 6(1) of the Act of 1969, which lays down that compensation for acquisition of the named Banks shall be determined according to principles specified in the Act can be successfully challenged on the ground that the principles specified are not relevant for fixing the amount as compensation for acquisition of a Banking Company. The Act of 1969, does not provide for valuation of the Banking Undertaking reduced by the liabilities of the Undertaking. In determining compensation, some important assets of Banks have not been taken into consideration. Moreover methods adopted for valuation of lands and buildings of the acquired Banks have not been based on the relevant principles to determine the amount of compensation with the result that the value determined thereby has been illusory. Moreover, goodwill of a named Bank has not been taken into account to determine the compensation. Moreover, premium paid for unexpired period of lease of the properties on rent to the named Banks has not been taken into account to fix the amount of compensation.

64. There is also force in the argument of N.A. Palkhivala that cash in Bank could not have been acquired under the Act of 1969. Acquisition of cash of the Banks with provision

for payment of compensation through government bonds at some future date amounts to levying a long-term "forced loan".

65. The Supreme Court had already held in State of Bihar *versus* Maharajadhiraj Kameswar Singh of Darbhanga (AIR 1952 SC 252) that cash and choses in action are not capable of acquisition.

66. In the present case, the Court is of the view that the provision in the Act of 1969 that compensation for land and building of a named Bank shall be paid as per the "ascertained value" is based on twelve times the value of annual rent of the land and building. If for the land and building, no rent is paid by a named Bank as the property belongs to the Bank as owner thereof, the rent will be calculated at twelve times the annual rent for which the land and building may be reasonably expected to be rented out from year to year. In the opinion of this Court, this is not a relevant principle to determine compensation for acquisition of the Banks as property values have gone up in the last few years. Moreover, some state Rent laws have pegged down the rent of buildings to that prevailing in the year 1940. In the present day property market, these are unrealistic low returns. Moreover, no higher monetary value has been provided for vacant land of the Banks in urban areas. In opinion of this Court compensation for vacant land in urban areas owned by the Banks can be ascertained by ascertaining market value of comparable land in urban areas and not by capitalizing the annual rental value of the land. Even though vacant premises in urban areas have a considerably larger value than buildings occupied by tenants, the Act of 1969 did not take into account value of vacant premises and took recourse to a method of valuation not relevant for acquisition of lands and buildings of Banking companies. Moreover in determining compensation for lands and buildings of Banking Companies, as a multiplier of the annual rent of such lands and buildings, the Act has reduced the actual amount of annual rental by several unjustified outgoings. To illustrate, irrespective of whether a building of a Banking Company is old or new, one-sixth of the annual rent has been deducted towards repairs and maintenance. Moreover, if a building has been acquired, constructed, repaired, renewed or re-constructed with borrowed capital, the amount of interest payable on such capital is deducted before capitalization of the annual rental and the capitalized value of the building is again reduced by the amount of borrowing. Thus by the method prescribed in the Act of 1969 for determining the amount of compensation to named Banking Companies for their assets as lands and buildings, a single debt is debited twice – first in commuting the value of assets and again in calculating the liabilities.

67. An error has also crept into the method of calculation of compensation for the buildings of the named Banking Companies as "plinth area" of buildings of the Banks has been treated as if it is the "floor area" vitiating the formula for calculation of amount of compensation.

68. The Act of 1969 has also prescribed some mechanism for determination of amount to be paid for vacant land with no buildings thereon. The mechanism is substantially more liberal than the mechanism for determination of compensation for land with buildings thereon.

69. The Act of 1969 has provided for a method of valuation of buildings which is not relevant and amount determined on basis of such principles cannot be called as compensation for compulsory acquisition of assets as land and building of a Banking Company.

70. Though compensation may be provided under a statute otherwise than in cash i.e., by Government Bond, the rate of interest on the Government Bond, which on maturity is payable to the holder of the Bond after a lapse of a few years must be comparable with prevailing commercial rate of interest or else compensation for acquisition of property would be a long-term forced loan by the owner of the acquired property.

71. In view of the reasons as aforesaid, the majority of ten judges speaking through Justice J.C. Shah held as follows:

(i) the Act of 1969 is within legislative competence of the Parliament;

(ii) the Act makes hostile discrimination against the fourteen Banks as it prohibits them from carrying on Banking business whereas other Banks – both Indian and foreign – are permitted to carry on the Banking business. Even there is no prohibition in the Act for new Banks to be licensed to carry on Banking business;

(iii) the Act restricts the named Banks from carrying on business other than Banking business;

(iv) the Act also violates the guarantee of compensation for compulsory acquisition of property as in Article 31(2) of the Constitution as it provides for payment of certain amount to the Banks determined according to principles not relevant for such determination.

72. The net result is that the Act of 1969 is *ultra vires*.

73. Justice A.N. Ray – the only Judge who did not agree with the majority of ten judges – delivered a dissenting judgment.

74. Justice A.N. Ray stated that there are as many as 89 commercial Banks in our country of which 73 are scheduled Banks including the State Bank of India and its seven subsidiaries. Out of the 89 commercial Banks 14 are foreign Banks. The State Bank of India and its subsidiaries have 27 percent of the aggregated deposits of the 89 commercial Banks whereas the 14 commercial Banks taken over by the ordinance of June 1969 had 56 percent of total deposits of the 89 commercial Banks. The 36 scheduled Banks outside purview of the Act of 1969, have a deposit of Rs. 269 crore which worked out to only 6.3 percent of total deposits with the 89 commercial Banks.

75. N.A. Palkhivala contended that the Act of 1969, could not have retrospective operation from July 19, 1969 as it affected the Fundamental Right to property. This argument of N.A. Palkhivala cannot be sustained as the Supreme Court have already held that there could be retrospective legislation for acquisition of property.

76. N.A. Palkhivala argued that compulsory acquisition of property under Article 31(1) and Article 31(2) would have to be tested in relation to Article 19(1)(f) read with Article 19(5) of the Constitution.

77. In State of Gujarat *versus* Shantilal Mangaldas and Others (AIR 1969 SC 634) the Supreme Court considered applicability of Article 19(1)(f) in relation to acquisition or requisition

of property under Article 31(2). The Court held that where a competent legislature has passed a law for acquisition of property and has fixed the amount for such acquisition or laid down the principles for determining the amount payable, Article 19(1)(f) has no application.

78. Justice Mehr Chand Mahajan speaking for the Supreme Court in State of Bihar *versus* Maharajadhiraj Kameswar Singh of Darbanga (AIR 1952 SC 252) dealt with "public purpose" in the background of Article 39 of the Directive Principles. Article 39 lays down that the state shall direct its policy to secure that ownership and control of the material resources of the community are so distributed as best to subserve common good and the operation of the economic system does not result in concentration of wealth.

79. In the present case, the Act of 1969 was enacted to acquire the 14 Banks for the public purpose of strengthening the national economy. It is intended to confer benefit on the weaker sections and the weaker sectors.

80. N.A. Palkhivala has raised the issue of legislative competence of the Parliament in regard to the Act of 1969. He argued that Parliament was incompetent to enact the Act of 1969 as there was no entry in either the Union List or the Concurrent List of the Seventh Schedule for 'Nationalisation of a Bank'.

81. This argument has no force as Entry 42 of the Concurrent List and entry 45 of the Union List provide for legislative competence of Parliament to enact the Act of 1969. The doctrine of pith and substance used in Union Colliery of British Columbia *versus* Bryden (1899 A.C. 580) is nothing but an illustration of the principle that when a legislation is referable to one or more entries, the Courts try to find out what the pith and substance of the legislation is. If according to the pith and substance of a legislation, a law can be related to an entry in the field of legislation, the Courts will uphold competence of the legislature to pass such a law.

82. N.A. Palkhivala has contended that the provision in the Act of 1969 permitting, the Banks to carry on business other than Banking was an empty promise as the assets of the 14 Banks have been acquired and there was no capital with them to carry on non-Banking business. Such a contention of N.A. Palkhivala fails to carry conviction as the Banks will get compensation for such acquisition. Constitutionally of the Act of 1969 cannot be impugned on ground of lack of resources to carry on business.

83. Another argument of N.A. Palkhivala was that Section 1 of the Act of 1969 suffered from the vice of excessive delegation. This argument cannot stand scrutiny as the Act of 1969 contained enough guidelines.

84. The Preamble to the Act of 1969 states that the object is to "serve better the needs of development of the economy in conformity with national policy and objectives". In Harishankar Bagla *versus* The State of Madhya Pradesh (AIR 1954 SC 465) the former Chief Justice, Mehr Chand Mahajan, had stated that:

"The preamble and the body of the sections sufficiently formulate the legislative policy and the ambit and character of the Act is such that the details of that policy can only be worked out by delegating them to a subordinate authority within the framework of that policy".

85. N.A. Palkhivala, has attacked the Act of 1969 as being violative of Article 14. The arguments of N.A. Palkhivala are as follows:

(i) the Act discriminated against the 14 Banks as it spared other scheduled commercial Banks;

(ii) selection of the 14 Banks had no reasonable connection with the object of the Act;

(iii) scheduled commercial Banks which were inefficient were not acquired by the Act of 1969 but the 14 commercial Banks, which were efficiently carrying on their Banking operations were subjected to acquisition.

(iv) the 14 commercial Banks could no longer carry on Banking business whereas there was no restriction on new Banking Companies to carry on the Banking business.

86. Justice A.N. Ray held that the aforesaid arguments of N.A. Palkhivala could be rebutted by stating that the 14 Banks were chosen as on the specified date each of them had deposits of above Rs. 50 crore. These 14 Banks had not only deposits of Rs. 50 crore or more but they also had greater coverage, better managerial and manpower resources. Parliament enacted the Act of 1969 to take over the 14 Banks on the basis of intelligible criteria relevant to the objects of the Act. The Parliament also in making the classification and treating the 14 Banks as belonging to a separate category, is the best judge of what should subserve the public interest.

87. Article 14 of the Constitution came to be considered comprehensively in Sri Ram Krishna Dalmia *versus* Justice S.R. Tendolkar and Others (AIR 1958 SC 538). It was held in the judgment that there is a presumption in favour of constitutionality of a legislation. It was also held that in enacting a law, the Court would take into consideration the history of the times and facts existing at the time of legislation.

88. The Supreme Court also held in R.K. Dalmia case (AIR 1958 SC 538) that any reasonable classification for the purpose of legislation would have to satisfy two tests, viz. there should be an intelligible differentia which distinguishes persons of things grouped from others left out and the differentia must have a rational relation to the object sought to be achieved. Moreover, the legislature is free to recognize the degree of harm and to confine its restrictions to those cases where the need was deemed to be the greatest.

89. N.A. Palkhivala attacked the *vires* of the Act of 1969 on the ground that the compensation for acquisition of 14 Banks was not the just equivalent and hence violated Article 31(2) of the Constitution. Rebutting the contention of the counsel, the Attorney General has argued that after the Constitution (Fourth Amendment) Act 1955, no law could be called into question on ground that compensation was not adequate.

90. In Vajaravelu Mudaliar *versus* Special Deputy Collector (AIR 1965 SC 1017), two broad principles were laid down by the Supreme Court. These principles are as follows:

(i) if principles for fixation of amount for acquisition of property are not relevant to fix value of the property, the fixation of amount to be paid for acquisition of property could be questioned.

(ii) if a law fixes an amount as compensation for acquisition of property and such amount is illusory, the Courts can also question it.

91. The Act of 1969 had laid down that the value of land and building of the 14 Banks shall be determined for purpose of calculation of the amount as compensation on the basis of market value of such land and building but where such market value exceeded the ascertained value of the land and building determined in the manner fixed in Explanation (2) of the Act, the amount to be paid shall be the "ascertained value". This method finds support in Vajravelu Mudaliar *versus* Special Deputy Collector (AIR 1965 SC 1017) where the amount to be paid for acquisition of property was market value on the date of notification of acquisition or average market value during the past five years preceding the date of notification of acquisition, whichever was less.

92. N.A. Palkhivala argued that the Act of 1969 had laid down that the amount to be paid for acquisition of building would be calculated as 12 times the annual rent of the building. He argued that such a mode of calculation would make the amount to be paid as totally illusory.

93. The aforesaid argument is not correct as the standard rent of a building necessarily takes the value of the land on which the building stands and hence the amount fixed as 12 times the standard annual rent is a relevant principle.

94. The objection raised by N.A. Palkhivala that the amount required for repair of a building of one of the Banks should not be deducted against capital value also is not sound as amount towards repair and maintenance is always deducted in the capitalization method of fixing value of a building.

95. There is provision in the Act of 1969 to find out "ascertained value" of a building. The "ascertained value" has been fixed as 12 times the annual rent or the rent at which the buildings is expected to be let out, less deductions mentioned. These deductions are permissible under the capitalization method. Interest on mortgage or borrowed capital will be one of the deductions in calculating outgoings under the capitalization method.

96. There is also no merit in argument of N.A. Palkhivala that goodwill of an acquired bank was not taken into account while determining the amount to be paid for such acquisition. Goodwill has been defined as the probability that the old customers will always go to the old place. Whether or not goodwill has a saleable value is a question of fact to be determined in each case. The 14 Banks were carrying on Banking business as they were licensed under the Banking Regulation Act 1949. The concept of "sale" in such a situation is unreal. It is a doubtful proposition whether goodwill can also pass after a property as a Banking Company is acquired under law. Moreover, any challenge as to compensation for goodwill falls within the area of adequacy of compensation. Such a concept is not valid as adequacy of amount was no more justiciable after the Constitution (Fourth Amendment) Act 1955.

97. The principles set out in the Act of 1969 are relevant for determination of compensation. It may be that adoption of one principle may confer lesser sum of money than another but that will not be a ground for saying that the principle is not relevant. The criticism

that the compensation for acquisition of the 14 Commercial Banks is illusory is utterly devoid of merit.

98. The scheme of social control of the Banks is in pursuance of the Directive Principles of State Policy. In India, the commercial Banks before the take-over of the 14 Banks, gave about 80 percent of their loans and credit to commerce and industry and only one percent of loan and credit to agriculturists. It is said that small borrowers did not get any credit from commercial Banks. In most of the rural areas, commercial Banks had no branches as only about 5000 out of about 5,64,000 villages in the country were covered by branches of commercial Banks. Moreover, only five major cities in the country enjoyed 65 percent of loans and credit by commercial Banks.

99. Agriculturists in rural areas get only five percent of credit requirements from commercial Banks and 34 percent of credit requirements from co-operative Banks and co-operative credit societies. The balance credit requirement of the agriculturists were met by private moneylenders. The 14 Banks, after takeover, will have to look to the credit needs of agriculturists and small-scale industries, who employ about 40 percent of the total workers in the country.

100. Counsel for the petitioner argued that the ordinance of 1969 could be challenged as circumstances did not exist to enable the acting President of India to promulgate an ordinance in July 1969.

101. The answer is: Both the President of India and Governor of a State are empowered to promulgate ordinance on matters for which the Parliament and the State Legislatures are competent to legislate. Ordinances can be promulgated if the Parliament and the State Legislatures are not in session and in the opinion of the President or the Governor of a State circumstance exist for taking immediate action.

102. The power of the executive head of the state to promulgate ordinances having the force of law is of historical antiquity. When India was under the East India Company, under Section 46 of the Regulating Act of 1773, the Governor-General could promulgate an ordinance. Under Section 23 of the Indian Councils Act 1861, the Governor-General could promulgate an ordinance in case of urgency for peace and good government. Section 72 of the Government of India Act 1915 also vested similar powers on the Governor-General. The Government of India Act 1935, also vested powers to promulgate an ordinance on the Governor-General on matters within legislative competence of the Dominion Parliament. The Government of India Act 1935 also vested powers to promulgate ordinance on the Governors of provinces for matters on which the provincial legislatures were competent to legislate.

103. N.A. Palkhivala argued that the Court had powers to go into the question whether satisfaction of the President of India that circumstances existed to promulgate an ordinance under Article 123 of the Constitution.

104. In the English case of Liversidge *versus* Anderson (1942 A.C. 206) it was held that the expression "if satisfied" meant subjective satisfaction.

105. In two other English cases viz. Ayar Collieries (1943) and Carltona (1943) the Court considered the import of the expression "if it appears" occurring in statutes. It was held in these two cases that the expressions "if it appears" means subjective satisfaction of the designated authority and such satisfaction was immune from scrutiny by the Courts.

106. The powers of the President under Article 123 of the Constitution concern a matter of policy when an immediate action is necessary. Since the President acts on the advice of the Council of Ministers, if satisfaction of the President to promulgate an ordinance is subjected to judicial scrutiny, it may lead to disclosure of advice of the Council of Ministers to the President. Such advice is protected under Article 74(2) of the Constitution.

107. Counsel for the petitioner relied on the decisions of the Supreme Court in the Barium Chemicals *versus* Company Law Board (AIR 1967 SC 295) and the Rohtas Industries Ltd. case (AIR 1969 SC 707) where Section 237(b) of the Companies Act 1956 came up for consideration. It was held by the Supreme Court in these two cases, that whereas the opinion of the Central Government that the affairs of the company was not being properly conducted was subjective, the Courts could enquire into whether circumstances existed for the opinion of the Central Government that the affairs of the company were not properly conducted. But these cases did not deal with satisfaction of the President to promulgate an ordinance.

108. The only way in which satisfaction of the President to promulgate an ordinance could be challenged is to establish bad faith or corrupt motive of the President in having promulgated an ordinance. But in this case no bad faith or corrupt motive on part of the President has either been alleged or proved.

109. It was also argued on behalf of the Petitioner that the ordinance was promulgated in a hasty manner on 19 July 1969 when Parliament had already been summoned to meet on 21 July 1969. But this argument is devoid of substance as it was for the President to decide whether in view of urgency the ordinance was to be promulgated even two days before the Parliament was to meet. The promulgation of the ordinance shortly before the session of the Parliament began did not prove any *mala fide*.

110. There is no reason to give a finding on *locus standi* of the Petitioner to file the petition under Article 32 of the Constitution as the petition has been heard on merits.

111. The result is that the petitions fail and are dismissed.

112. The order of the Supreme Court was as per the majority decision of the ten judges, who held that the Banking Companies (Acquisition and Transfer of Undertakings) Act 1969 was invalid and the action taken or deemed to be taken in exercise of the powers under the Act was unlawful.

CHAPTER 9

Kesavananda Bharati *versus* State of Kerala (AIR 1973 SC 1461)

[CHIEF JUSTICE S.M. SIKRI, JUSTICE J.M. SHELAT, JUSTICE K.S. HEGDE, JUSTICE A.N. GROVER, JUSTICE A.N. RAY, JUSTICE P. JAGANMOHAN REDDY, JUSTICE D.G. PALEKAR, JUSTICE H.R. KHANNA, JUSTICE K.K. MATHEW, JUSTICE M.H. BEG, JUSTICE S.N. DWIVEDI, JUSTICE A.K. MUKHERJEE AND JUSTICE Y.V. CHANDRACHUD]

Case Summary

Kesavananda Bharati *versus* State of Kerala (AIR 1973 SC 1461) was decided by a Constitution Bench of 13 Judges presided over by Chief Justice S.M. Sikri. The judgment, delivered on 24 April 1973, is a *locus classicus* on constitutional law.

1. The issue whether under Article 368, Parliament can amend any Fundamental Right was already examined in three other judgments of the Supreme Court. These judgments are dealt with briefly as follows:
   (i) In Sankari Prasad *versus* Union of India (AIR 1951 SC 458), it was held that Parliament can amend any Fundamental Right and such amendment is not "law" within meaning of Article 13(2) of the Constitution as an amendment under Article 368 is not a legislative but a constituent measure.
   (ii) About 16 years later, the Supreme Court affirmed the ratio of Sankari Prasad case (AIR 1951 SC 458) in Sajjan Singh *versus* State of Rajasthan (AIR 1965 SC 845).
   (iii) However, in I.C. Golaknath *versus* State of Punjab (AIR 1967 SC 1643) the Court overruled the aforesaid decisions and held that under Article 368, Parliament had no power to amend any Fundamental Right. The Court held that the "Law" in Article 13(2) would not only cover a legislative measure but also a constituent measure.
2. Following the judgment in I.C. Golaknath case (AIR 1967 SC 1643), Parliament passed the Constitution (Twenty-fourth Amendment) Act 1971 which added clause (4) to Article 13 of the Constitution. The new clause (4) stipulated that nothing in Article 13 shall apply to any amendment of the Constitution under Article 368. The Constitution (Twenty-fourth Amendment) Act 1971 also clarified that Article 368 contained both the power and the procedure to amend the Constitution.

3. In Kesavananda Bharati (AIR 1973 SC 1461), the Constitution Bench upheld the *vires* of the Constitution (Twenty-fourth Amendment) Act 1971 and overruled the ratio of I.C. Golaknath case (AIR 1967 SC 1643). Briefly stated, in Kesavananda Bharati (AIR 1973 SC 1461) the Court upheld the power of the Parliament under Article 368 to amend any Fundamental Right and any other provision of the Constitution but held that by such amendment, the Parliament could not alter the basic structure of the Constitution. The basic structure was identified as supremacy of the Constitution, the principle of Secularism, the Rule of Law, the democratic character of the polity, the federal structure and the Separation of Powers between the Executive, the Legislature and the Judiciary.

4. After the judgment in the Kesavananda Bharati case a summary of views of majority of judges was issued under signature of nine out of the 13 judges including the Chief Justice of India, Justice S.M. Sikri. (Chief Justice S.M. Sikri demitted office on attaining 65 years of age soon after he signed the summary of views.)

5. The summary of views was as follows:
   (i) I.C. Golaknath *versus* State of Punjab (AIR 1967 SC 1643), is overruled with prospective effect.
   (ii) Article 368 does not enable the Parliament to amend the Constitution so as to alter its basic structure.
   (iii) The Constitution (Twenty-fourth Amendment) Act 1971 is valid.
   (iv) Section 2(a) and Section 2(b) of the Constitution (Twenty-fifth Amendment) Act 1971 are valid. The aforesaid provisions stipulated that for acquisition of private property the owner shall be paid an amount and the law in fixing the amount or the principles of payment of an amount, shall not be called into question on the ground of its adequacy. The Constitution (Twenty-fifth Amendment) Act 1971 also inserted a new Article 31C which provided that laws giving effect to certain Directive Principles shall not be void on ground of repugnancy with any Fundamental Right. Exclusion of Judicial Review on the basis of a mere declaration in the law that it seeks to give effect to clauses (b) and (c) of Article 39 of the Directive Principles of State Policy was held to be unconstitutional and Article 31C was struck down as *ultra vires*.
   (v) The Constitution (Twenty-ninth Amendment) Act 1971 – which put two Kerala Acts dealing with land reforms in the Ninth Schedule of the Constitution – is valid. But the Court has to decide whether the two Kerala Acts abrogate any "basic structure" of the Constitution.
   (vi) The Court will also decide regarding validity of the Constitution (Twenty-sixth Amendment) Act 1971 relating to repeal of Article 291 providing for privy purse to erstwhile rulers of princely states and repeal of Article 362 guaranteeing some privileges to the erstwhile rulers.

6. In Kesavananda Bharati case (AIR 1973 SC 1461) eleven judgments were delivered by the 13-Judge Constitution Bench. Each of the judgments ran into several pages and testified to the erudition of the Judges, who heard the matter for as many as 65 days.

7. Chief Justice S.M. Sikri, who presided over the Bench and delivered a separate judgment, held as follows: there is clear demarcation between ordinary law enacted in exercise of legislative power and constitutional law enacted in exercise of constituent power. As "law" referred to in Article 13(2) refers to ordinary law – and not constitutional amendment – the stipulation in the Constitution (Twenty-fourth Amendment) Act 1971 that nothing in Article 13 applies to any amendment of the Constitution under Article 368, is valid.
8. Harilal Kania, the first Chief Justice of India, was right when he said in A.K. Gopalan *versus* State of Madras (AIR 1950 SC 27) that Article 13 of the Constitution was by way of abundant caution as even in its absence, any ordinary law infringing a Fundamental Right, could be *ultra vires*.
9. In I.C. Golaknath case (AIR 1967 SC 1643), a Constitution Bench of eleven Judges, again went into the question whether Fundamental Rights could be amended by the Parliament. Six out of eleven Judges, including Chief Justice K. Subba Rao, held that Parliament could not amend any Fundamental Right because of Article 13(2) of the Constitution. The other five Judges held that the earlier decisions in Sankari Prasad case (AIR 1951 SC 458) and Sajjan Singh's case (AIR 1965 SC 845) were correct and Parliament has full powers under Article 368 to amend any provision of the Constitution including any Fundamental Right.
10. The majority of Judges in I.C. Golaknath case (AIR 1967 SC 1643) held that Fundamental Rights could be amended only by a new Constituent Assembly.
11. Justice V. Ramaswami, one of the Judges in I.C. Golaknath case (AIR 1967 SC 1643), not only differed from the majority of Judges but also held that the Fundamental Rights are not above the Constitution itself. He also held that both the power to amend the Fundamental Rights and the procedure thereof could be located in Article 368 and there was no implied limitation on Parliament's power to amend the Constitution.
12. The Privy Council in Bribery Commissioner *versus* Ranasinghe (1965 AC 172) had inferred implied limitations on Parliament's powers under the Constitution of Ceylon to amend certain basic Rights. The Privy Council held that the implied limitations represent the solemn balance of Rights between the citizens of Ceylon and the fundamental conditions under which they accepted the Constitution.
13. In the context of the Indian Constitution, the Constituent Assembly did not use the word 'amend' in its widest sense. In other words, the basic features of the Constitution cannot be amended by the Parliament under Article 368 so as to erase the identity of the secular and democratic Constitution of India based on the Rule of Law.
14. Therefore, amendment in Article 368 means any addition or change in any provision of the Constitution within the broad contours of the Preamble and the Constitution to carry out the objectives in the Preamble and the Directive Principles. It would mean that while Fundamental Rights cannot be abrogated, reasonable abridgements of such Rights can be made by law in the public interest.
15. The basic structure of the Constitution, which cannot be amended under Article 368, comprises the following:

(a) Supremacy of the Constitution;
(b) Republican and democratic form of Government;
(c) Secular character of the Constitution;
(d) Separation of Powers between the Executive, Legislature and the Judiciary;
(e) Federal character of the Republic.

16. Parliament has the power to amend Article 368 but it does not mean that Parliament could so amend Article 368 as to change the amending power beyond recognition. Parliament – a creature of the Constitution – cannot through an amendment enlarge its power over the Constitution, while purporting to act under it.

17. Section 3 of the Constitution (Twenty-fourth Amendment) Act 1971 lays down as follows:

"Notwithstanding anything in this Constitution, Parliament may in exercise of its constituent power amend by way of addition, variation or repeal any provisions of this Constitution in accordance with the procedure laid down in this Article". The expression "notwithstanding anything in this Constitution" does not really widen the meaning of the expression "Amendment of the Constitution". It only states that the source of power of amendment of the Constitution is in Article 368 itself and not in Article 248 read with Entry 97 of the Union List.

18. Section 2 of the Constitution (Twenty-fifth Amendment) Act 1971 stipulated that private property can only be compulsorily acquired or requisitioned for a public purpose and that too only by authority of law. Such law may fix an amount to be paid for such acquisition or requisition. The law can also lay down that the amount has to be in accordance with some principles and be paid to the owner in certain manner to be prescribed in the law itself. The Constitution (Twenty-fifth Amendment) Act 1971 stipulated that such law for acquisition or requisition of property would not be challenged in any court on the ground that the "amount" was not adequate and the stipulation that either whole or part of the "amount" would be paid to the owner not in cash. The Constitution (Twenty-fifth Amendment) Act 1971 also stipulated that in the law to be enacted for compulsory acquisition of property of an educational institution administered by a "minority" ('minority' based on language or religion referred to in Article 30 of the Constitution), the State shall ensure that the amount to be paid, is such as would not restrict or abrogate the Right of the minority to administer educational institutions of its choice.

19. Admittedly, the Constitution (Twenty-fifth Amendment) Act 1971 was passed by the Parliament to modify the ratio in the judgment in R.C. Cooper's case (AIR 1970 SC 564) where the Court held that the Banking Companies (Acquisition & Transfer of Undertakings) Act 1969 nationalizing 14 Commercial Banks, violated Article 31(2) of the Constitution. The Court held that the Act of 1969 provided for "amount" determined according to some principles not relevant for acquisition of the Banks.

20. Parliament has no power to abrogate the Fundamental Rights but has power only to regulate or adjust them. Parliament cannot amend the Right to Property to provide for an illusory amount or an amount fixed arbitrarily. Such an amendment would amount to confiscation of private property.

21. If the amount or the procedure for fixing the amount for acquisition of private property for a public purpose, is arbitrary and has no rational connection with value of the property, it can be struck down as violative of Article 14 of the Constitution.

22. Clauses (b) and (c) of Article 39 of the Directive Principles of State Policy lay down that the State shall direct its policy towards securing that:
   (i) ownership and control of the material resources of the community are so distributed as best to subserve the common good and
   (ii) operation of the economic system does not result in concentration of wealth and means of production to the common detriment.

23. Article 31C, inserted by the Constitution (Twenty-fifth Amendment) Act 1971, provided that notwithstanding anything contained in Article 13, no law giving effect to the policy of the State towards securing the principles specified in clause (b) or clause (c) of Article 39 shall be deemed to be void on the ground of inconsistency with the Rights under Articles 14, 19 and 31 of the Constitution. It also stipulated that no law containing a declaration that it has been enacted to give effect to provisions in clauses (b) and (c) in Article 39 shall be called into question in any Court on the ground that the law does not give effect to such a policy. The Constitution (Twenty-fifth Amendment) Act 1971 however stipulated that any law passed by a state legislature to give effect to provisions in clauses (b) and (c) in Article 39 of the Directive Principles must receive the President's assent before the law can claim the constitutional immunity of the new Article 31C.

24. In Article 31C, the sky is the limit for the Parliament or any state legislature to pass any law to implement provisions in clauses (b) and (c) of Article 39 of the Constitution. In effect, Article 31C empowers the Parliament and the State legislatures, to abridge Fundamental Rights in Articles 14, 19 and 31. Article 31C, therefore, is in excess of power of amendment of the Constitution under Article 368 as it enables also the State Legislatures to amend the Constitution. Therefore, Chief Justice S.M. Sikri held that clause (3) of the Constitution (Twenty-fifth Amendment) Act 1971 – which inserted Article 31C of the Constitution – is void.

25. Chief Justice S.M. Sikri also held that the validity of the Constitution (Twenty-sixth Amendment) Act 1971, which deals with abolition of privy purse of former Rulers of princely states, will be decided by the Court.

26. Justice J.M. Shelat and Justice A.N. Grover jointly delivered a separate judgment. They held that the real issue is the scope, ambit and extent of power of the Parliament under Article 368.

27. N.A. Palkhivala had urged that Article 368 gives limited power to the Parliament to amend the Constitution. He argued that Parliament cannot amend the essential features, basic elements and fundamental principles of the Constitution. The power to amend these features, said N.A. Palkhivala, vests with the people of India.

28. The Respondents – through Niren De, the Attorney – General for India and eminent Counsel, H.M. Seeravai – argued that there was no "implied limitation" on power of the

Parliament to amend the Constitution. They held that the Constitution can be amended by way of variation, addition or repeal so long as no vacuum is left in governance.

29. Justice J.M. Shelat and Justice A.N. Grover held that the Indian Constitution is unique as it is not only the longest written Constitution in the world but it is meant for a country with the second largest population in the world with the people speaking different languages and professing different religions.

30. Historically speaking, for the first time in the year 1934, the Indian National Congress demanded a Constituent Assembly to draft the Constitution of free India. The Constituent Assembly was elected in July-August 1946. When the partition of the country was announced on 03 June 1947, some changes were made in composition of the Constituent Assembly.

31. The India Independence Act 1947 empowered the Constituent Assembly to frame the Constitution of free India. Pandit Jawaharlal Nehru, Prime Minister in the interim government, moved the "Objective Resolution" in the Constituent Assembly spelling out the aims and objectives of the new Constitution.

32. On 22 January 1947, the Constituent Assembly passed the "Objective Resolution" and declared that the power and authority of Government in independent India are derived from the people of India.

33. The Constitution of India is a controlled Constitution. India is a federation. It is also a secular state. The Rule of Law has been guaranteed by providing for Judicial Review. Adult suffrage is recognized as the basis of popular participation in Government. In State of Madras *versus* Champakam Dorairajan (AIR 1951 SC 226) and in Mohammad Hanif Quereshi *versus* the State of Bihar (AIR 1958 SC 731), it was held that the Directive Principles must conform – and run subsidiary to – the Fundamental Rights. In answering the reference of the Kerala Education Bill under Article 143 of the Constitution (AIR 1958 SC 956) Chief Justice S.R. Das, reiterated that the Directive Principles are fundamental in governance of the country and it shall be the duty of the state to apply these principles in making law.

34. The issue is validity of the Constitution (Twenty-fourth Amendment) Act 1971, which made the following changes:

(a) The marginal heading of Article 368 which was "procedure for enactment of the Constitution" has been changed to read, "power of Parliament to amend the Constitution and procedure thereof".

(b) The amended Article 368 provides that, notwithstanding anything in the Constitution, Parliament may, in exercise of its constituent power, amend by way of addition, variation or repeal any provision of the Constitution in accordance with the procedure laid down in this Article.

(c) Before the Constitution (Twenty-fourth Amendment) Act 1971, Article 368 stipulated that when a Bill is passed in each House by a majority of total membership of that House and by a majority of not less than two-thirds of the Members of the House present and voting, it shall be presented to the President for assent and upon such assent being given, the Constitution shall stand amended in terms of the Bill. After the Constitution (Twenty-fourth Amendment) Act 1971, the amended provision reads that "it shall be presented to the President who shall give his assent to the Bill."

(d) By the Constitution (Twenty-fourth Amendment) Act 1971, clause (3) was added to Article 368 to provide that nothing in Article 13 shall apply to any amendment of the Constitution. To put the matter beyond doubt, the same stipulation was made in the new clause (4) to Article 13 of the Constitution that nothing in Article 13 shall apply to any amendment of the Constitution.

35. N.A. Palkhivala did not seriously dispute the provision of the Constitution (Twenty-fourth Amendment) Act 1971 insofar as it overturned the majority judgment in I.C. Golaknath's case (AIR 1967 SC 1643).

36. N.A. Palkhivala, however, argued that by the Constitution (Twenty-fourth Amendment) Act 1971, the Indian Parliament has clothed itself with legal sovereignty which only resided with the people of India. If Parliament amends the Constitution and takes away its "essential features", such an amendment will be void as the Fundamental Rights are an "essential feature" of the Constitution.

37. Niren De, the Attorney-General for India, however, argued that the Constitution (Twenty-fourth Amendment) Act 1971 only made explicit what was already implicit in Article 368.

38. Justice J.M. Shelat and Justice A.N. Grover said in their common judgment that the 'proviso' to Article 368 of the Constitution mandates a special procedure for amendment of the following Articles:

(i) Article 54 (the President of India shall be elected by members of an electoral college comprising elected Members of both Houses of the Parliament and elected members of legislature of States).

(ii) Article 55 (manner of election of the President of India, which stipulates detailed procedure for securing uniformity in scale of representation of various states in election of the President and the system of proportional representation by means of single transferable vote by secret ballot).

(iii) Article 73 (extent of executive power of the Union).

(iv) Article 162 (extent of executive power of a state in the Indian Union).

(v) Article 241 (High Courts for Union Territories).

(vi) Chapter IV of Part (V) of the Constitution (the Union Judiciary i.e. the Supreme Court of India).

(vii) Chapter V of the Part VI of the Constitution (the High Courts in the States).

(viii) Chapter I of the Part XI (Legislative relation between the Union and the States i.e. Distribution of Legislative powers between the Union and the States).

(ix) List I, II and III of the Seventh Schedule of the Constitution i.e. Union List, State List and Concurrent List.

(x) Representation of states in the Parliament.

(xi) Article 368 dealing with amendment of the Constitution.

39. When the above provisions are sought to be amended under Article 368, the Amendment Bill, duly passed by the two House of Parliament, shall be required to be ratified by legislatures of not less than one half of the states by resolutions to that effect before the Amendment Bill is presented to the President for assent.

40. Both the judges held that the proviso to Article 368 does not indicate that even with ratification of a Constitution Amendment Bill by not less than one-half of the legislatures of the States, the basic structure of the Constitution can be changed or modified or repealed. To illustrate, the provision of Article 52 (there shall be a President of India) and Article 53 (executive power of the Union shall be vested in the President) are not mentioned in the proviso to Article 368. It is incomprehensible that the framers of the Constitution provided for ratification for any amendment to Articles 54 and 55 of the Constitution relating to manner of election of the President of India leaving Articles 52 and 53 – relating to office of the President and vesting of executive power of the Union on him – to the ordinary mode of amendment. There are also other 'important matters as office of the Vice-President of India, office of Governor of states of the Indian Union, terms of office of the Governors, Constitution and functions of Council of Ministers in States of the Indian Union, the subordinate judiciary below the High Courts, administrative relations between the Union and the States have not been mentioned in the proviso to Article 368 even though they are important matters. Similarly for any amendment of Fundamental Rights no ratification by the legislatures of States has been provided.

41. The Fifth Schedule of the Constitution, which deals with administration of the Scheduled areas and the Scheduled Tribes in States other than the states of Assam, Meghalaya, Tripura and Mizoram can be amended by way of addition, variation or repeal by law passed by Parliament. Such amendment shall not be deemed to be amendment of the Constitution under Article 368. Similarly, the Sixth Schedule providing for administration of tribal areas in states of Assam, Meghalaya, Tripura and Mizoram provides that provisions of the Schedule can be amended by way of addition, variation or repeal by a law of Parliament and such amendment shall not be deemed to be amendment under Article 368.

42. In the Constituent Assembly, H.V. Kamath had proposed that the word "amend" in Article 304 of the draft Constitution – corresponding to Article 368 of the Constitution – should be qualified by the expression, variation, addition or repeal; but the Constituent Assembly did not accept it. Therefore, N.A. Palkhivala argued that "amendment" in Article 368 had been deliberately given a narrow meaning, which is sought to be changed by the wider meaning of the expression "amendment" in the Constitution (Twenty-fourth Amendment) Act 1971.

43. N.A. Palkhivala submitted that there can be only three possible meanings of the word "amendment", which are as follows:

(a) To improve or remove error and such improvement or removal of error can be considered from the standpoint of basic philosophy of the Constitution and its essential features.

(b) To make changes – which may not be improvement or removal of error – but which do not alter or destroy the basic features of the Constitution.

(c) To make any change whatsoever in the Constitution.

44. N.A. Palkhivala argued that Article 368 permits only amendments as at (a) and (b) above but amendment as at (c) above is completely ruled out. Moreover, for any amendment of Fundamental Rights no ratification by legislatures of at least half the States have been provided for in the "proviso" to Article 368.

45. The wider meaning given to the word "amendment" in paragraphs (7) and (21) of the Fifth and the Sixth Schedule respectively was meant to ensure that at an appropriate time the Fifth and the Sixth Schedule would be repealed and the Scheduled areas and the Scheduled Tribes covered by them could be administered like the rest of the country.

46. Counsels for the respondents did not agree with the contention of N.A. Palkhivala that 'amendment' in Article 368 is amendment *simpliciter* and must have a narrow meaning. They argued that, Article 368 is the only Article which appears in part XX of the Constitution. Secondly, Articles 4, 169, paragraphs (7) of the Fifth Schedule and paragraphs (21) of the Sixth Schedule – which contain wider powers for amendment of the Constitution – can themselves be amended only by the Parliament under Article 368.

47. Counsel for the respondents also argued that the Constituent Assembly had used the word 'amendment' in the sense it has been used in Article V of the American Constitution. But debates in the Constituent Assembly indicate that the Constituent Assembly had in view apart from the U.S. Constitution, the Constitutions of Canada, Australia, Ireland, USA, Switzerland and Japan while framing our Constitution. Moreover, Article 368 is different from Article V of the U.S. Constitution as in the United States of America the people are associated in some manner with amendment of their Constitution. The people of India, however, do not play any role either for initiating or for ratifying any amendment of the Constitution.

48. A cardinal principle of interpretation of a Constitution is that it is not to be construed in a narrow and pedantic sense. To quote Sir Maurice Gwyer, a Chief Justice of the Federal Court of India, a Constitution is "a mechanism under which laws are to be made and not a mere Act which declares what the law is to be".

49. In the year 1936, Lord Wright had said that "the question, then is one of construction of the Constitution and the ultimate result must be determined upon the actual words occurring in a single complex instrument, in which one part may throw light on another".

50. It is not without significance that the Constituent Assembly first considered and adopted the Articles and the Schedules of the Constitution. Thereafter in the light of the provisions in the Constitution, the Constituent Assembly adopted the Preamble, which was different from the original draft Preamble suggested by Sir B.N. Rau ICS, the Constitutional Adviser. The draft Preamble suggested by Sir B.N. Rau was as follows:

"We, the people of India, seeking to promote the common good, do hereby through our chosen representatives, enact, adopt and give to ourselves this Constitution."

51. The Constituent Assembly finally adopted the Preamble in a totally different form, which is as follows:

"We, the people of India, having solemnly resolved to constitute India into a sovereign democratic Republic and to secure to all its citizens Justice, social, economic and political; liberty of thought, expression, belief, faith and worship; equality of status and of opportunity; and to promote among them all fraternity assuring the dignity of the individual, in our Constituent Assembly this twenty-sixth day of November 1949, do hereby adopt, enact and give to ourselves this Constitution."

[**N.B.**: By the Constitution (Forty-second Amendment) Act 1976, the words 'socialist' and 'secular' were added after the expression 'sovereign' and before the expression 'democratic republic'. The expression 'unity and integrity of the nation' was also added after the expression 'dignity of the individual'.]

52. In D.S. Nakra *versus* Union of India (AIR 1983 SC 130), it was held that the expression 'socialist' in the Preamble meant that the State will strive to eliminate inequality in income and achieve its equitable distribution. The expression 'socialist' in the Preamble is a blend of Marxism and Gandhian Socialism leaning heavily towards Gandhian Socialism.

53. The Preamble of our Constitution is unique as:

(a) it did not "walk before the Constitution" as the Preamble to the U.S. Constitution.

(b) the Preamble was finally approved after the draft Constitution was approved by the Constituent Assembly.

(c) the Drafting Committee of our Constitution was of the view that the Preamble incorporated "the essential features of the new state".

(d) the Preamble embodied the fundamental concept of sovereignty being with the people of India.

54. The Supreme Court have given the Preamble a "transcendental position". The Presidential reference in the Kerala Education Bill 1957 (AIR 1958 SC 956) referred extensively to the Preamble and observed that the chapter on Fundamental Rights was provided to implement the Preamble.

55. In Berubari Union and Exchange of Enclaves case (AIR 1960 SC 845), it was held that the Preamble is a key to open minds of the framers of the Constitution but is not by itself a source of power.

56. As the Indian Constitution has an identity, an amendment, under Article 368, cannot be such as would denude the identity. Moreover, the effect of unlimited amending power under Article 368 – as stipulated in the Constitution (Twenty-fourth Amendment) Act 1971 – cannot be conducive to survival of the Constitution. After the Twenty-fourth Amendment Act 1971, the power of amendment of the Constitution can itself be taken away and the Constitution made virtually unamendable by providing for an impossible majority in both Houses of the Parliament to pass a Constitution Amendment Act.

57. The basic theory of our Constitution is that the constituent power is vested in the people and was exercised for and on their behalf by the Constituent Assembly.

58. In a written Constitution, where sovereignty resides in the people, there is no question of the Parliament being sovereign.

59. Counsels for the respondents relied upon wide powers of amendment in Article V of the U.S. Constitution to justify that the powers of amendment under Article 368 is very wide and admits of no limitation.

60. The U.S. Constitution provides for participation by the citizens of USA in the process of amendment of the Constitution and it is substantially different from the procedure of amendment of our Constitution.

61. In Bribery Commissioner *versus* Ranasinghe (1965 AC 172) the Privy Council held that it is the form and manner of amendment of the Constitution which is material and the Bribery Amendment Act, 1958 is *ultra vires* as it had not been enacted in accordance with provisions of the Constitution of Ceylon.

62. Citing the decision of the Privy Council, counsels for the respondent argued that if form and manner of amendment in Article 368 is complied with, there can be no other implied limitations on powers of the Parliament to amend the Constitution.

63. N.A. Palkhivala questioned this interpretation of counsels of the respondent that the Constitution of Ceylon had authorized the Parliament of Ceylon to amend or repeal the Constitution – a power far wider than the power of amendment *simpliciter* conferred by Article 368 of our Constitution. As pointed out by N.A. Palkhivala, the Ranasinghe case (1965 AC 172) is a direct authority against the argument of the counsels for the respondent since it held that religious and racial Rights guaranteed in the Constitution of Ceylon could not be subjected to any amendment.

64. N.A. Palkhivala, rightly argued that it is the Constitution which is supreme and not any of the three organs of the state. Moreover, if there is no limitation on the amending power under Article 368, the Parliament can bend the Constitution at its will. He also pointed out that the argument that there cannot be any implied limitation on power of amendment under Article 368 because there are no express limitations stipulated in Article 368 is a contradiction in terms as implied limitation can only arise when there are no "express limitations".

65. Both Justice J.M. Shelat and Justice A.N. Grover held that the basic structure of the Constitution is not a vague concept. Keeping in view the historical background, the contents of the Preamble, the relevant provisions of the Constitution including Article 368, the following can be considered as the basic structure of the Constitution. However, these elements of the basic structure cannot be fully catalogued but can only be illustrated. They are:

(a) The supremacy of the Constitution.
(b) Republican and Democratic form of Government.
(c) Sovereignty of India.
(d) Secularism.
(e) Federal character of the polity.

(f) Separation of power between the Legislature, the Executive and the Judiciary.
(g) Dignity of the individual secured by the Fundamental Rights.
(h) A welfare state on basis of the Directive Principles of State Policy.
(i) Unity and integrity of the Nation.

66. Amending power, under Article 368, is neither narrow nor unlimited. The Constitution (Twenty-fourth Amendment) Act 1971 is valid if it is understood that the power under Article 368 is wide enough to permit amendment of the Constitution by way of addition, variation or repeal so long as its basic structure is not abrogated.

67. The Constitution (Twenty-fifth Amendment) Act 1971 amended Article 31(2) of the Constitution to provide that when private property is acquired or requisitioned by the State under a law for a public purpose, the owner shall be paid an amount only. This substitution of the expression "amount" for "compensation" was necessitated as in the State of West Bengal *versus* Bela Banerji (AIR 1954 SC 170), the Supreme Court held that compensation for acquisition of private property for a public purpose was the market value of the property. But inspite of the Constitution (Fourth Amendment) Act 1955, the Supreme Court in Vajravelu Mudaliar's case (AIR 1965 SC 1017) and in Union of India *versus* Metal Corporation of India's case (AIR 1967 SC 637), interpreted the expression "amount" in Article 31 as just equivalent of value of the property acquired.

68. Though in State of Gujarat *versus* Shantilal Mangaldas (AIR 1969 SC 634) the Supreme Court overruled its earlier decisions in Vajravelu Mudaliar case (AIR 1965 SC 1017) and in Metal Corporation of India case (AIR 1967 SC 637), in R.C. Cooper *versus* Union of India (AIR 1970 SC 564), the Supreme Court overruled its own decision in Shantilal Mangaldas case (AIR 1969 SC 634). The decision in R.C. Cooper's case (AIR 1970 SC 564) – popularly known as the Bank Nationalisation Case – led to the Parliament passing the Constitution (Twenty-fifth Amendment) Act 1971, which amended Article 31(2) to say that where private property is acquired by law for public purpose, the law may decide the amount to be paid to the owner for such acquisition or may lay down the principles on the basis of which the amount is to be paid. The Constitution (Twenty-fifth Amendment) Act 1971 further stipulated that, the law providing for acquisition of private property shall not be questioned in a Court on the ground that the amount to be paid to the owner was not adequate or on the ground that the whole or part of the amount shall be paid to the owner otherwise than in cash.

69. In Shantilal Mangaldas case (AIR 1969 SC 634), the Supreme Court had already held that the amount to be paid for acquisition of private property could not be fixed according to principles, which were not relevant for the purpose. Such irrelevant principles would grant a charter of arbitrariness.

70. Though the Constitution (Twenty-fifth Amendment) Act 1971, amending Article 31(2), put the adequacy of the amount beyond Judicial Review, it was held that the Court can decide whether the amount is wholly illusory or the principles for fixing the amount are totally irrelevant for the purpose.

71. Both Justice J.M. Shelat and Justice A.N. Grover struck down Article 31C as it gave a charter not only to the Parliament but to all state legislatures to amend the Constitution.

72. Justice K.S. Hegde and Justice A.K. Mukherjea jointly delivered a separate judgment.

73. Both the judges observed that in Sankari Prasad Singh Deo case (AIR 1951 SC 458), the Supreme Court laid down that the expression "law" in Article 13(2) did not apply to amendment of any Fundamental Right. This ratio was affirmed by the Court in Sajjan Singh *versus* State of Rajasthan (AIR 1965 SC 845).

74. But in I.C. Golaknath *versus* State of Punjab (AIR 1967 SC 1643) six out of the eleven judges in the Constitution Bench held that both Sankari Prasad and Sajjan Singh were not decided correctly. But the six judges did not strike down earlier Constitutional Amendment Acts. Out of the six judges, who delivered the majority judgment, five judges (Chief Justice K. Subba Rao, Justice J.C. Shah, Justice S.M. Sikri, Justice J.M. Shelat and Justice C.A. Vaidialingam) relied on the "doctrine of prospective overruling" and the sixth Judge, Justice M. Hidaytullah relied on the "doctrine of acquiescence" to save the earlier three Constitutional Amendment Acts from being declared *ultra vires*.

75. Justice K.S. Hegde and Justice A.K. Mukherjea did not agree with the majority judgment in I.C. Golaknath (AIR 1967 SC 1643) and held that the power as well as the procedure for such amendment were in Article 368.

76. Both the Judges quoted from the *Corpus Juris Secundum* to hold that the provisions of Article 13(2) and Article 368 have to be interpreted harmoniously. They also held that the Constitution has made a distinction between the "Constitution" and the "Law" as Article 60 of the Constitution stipulates that the President of India is required to take an oath to preserve, protect and defend the Constitution and the law.

77. Justice K.S. Hegde and Justice A.K. Mukherjea referred to the argument of N.A. Palkhivala that an amendment was moved by K. Santhanam in the Constituent Assembly, that the expression "law" in Article 13(2) did not include constitutional amendments. The amendment was accepted by Sardar Patel, Chairman of the Advisory Committee on Fundamental Rights. But the Drafting Committee did not agree and rejected the proposed amendment. It showed the intention of the Constituent Assembly to bring constitutional amendments within the scope of the expression "law" in Article 13(2) of the Constitution.

78. Both the Judges stated that as the Constitution is expected to endure for a long time and as the needs of the society change with time, the Constitution must be elastic. Again, to give effect to the Directive Principles, it may be necessary to amend some Fundamental Rights. They referred to the Constitution (First Amendment) Act 1951 which incorporated a new clause (4) to Article 15 of the Constitution to enable the State to make special provisions for any socially and educationally backward classes of citizens or for the Scheduled Castes and the Scheduled Tribes. They also referred to how the Constitution (First Amendment) Act 1951 also imposed some reasonable restrictions on the Rights to Freedom in Article 19 of the Constitution in the interest of security of the state, friendly relations with foreign states, public order, decency or morality or in relation to contempt of court, defamation or incitement to an offence.

79. Both Justice K.S. Hegde and Justice A.K. Mukherjea held that the power of amendment under Article 368 must be given a broad and liberal interpretation. They held that as the Constitution (First Amendment) Act 1951 was enacted by the Provisional Parliament – which comprised those who were also Members of the Constituent Assembly – it cannot be said that the Constituent Assembly did not empower the Parliament to amend any Fundamental Right.

80. Both the Judges held that as the word "amendment" takes its colour from the context in which it is used, it cannot be interpreted *in vacuo*. They quoted Justice Oliver Wendell Holmes who had said that,

"a word is not a crystal, transparent and unchanged; it is the skin of a living thought and may vary greatly in colour and content according to the circumstances and the time in which it is used."

81. In our Constitution, the word 'amendment' – unlike the same word in the Constitution of the United States of America – has been used to convey different meanings in different places. For example, Article 4 of the Constitution – which provides for laws to amend the First Schedule (names and extent of territories of the states and union territories) and the Fourth Schedule (allocation of seats in the Council of States to the states and the Union Territories) are not to be taken as amendment of the Constitution under Article 368. Again, very wide powers have been conferred on the Parliament to amend by way of addition, variation and repeal the Fifth Schedule – under paragraph (7) of the Schedule – and the Sixth Schedule – under paragraph (12) of the Schedule.

82. For the first time in I.C. Golaknath's case (AIR 1967 SC 1643), the question of implied limitations on power to amend the Constitution was discussed but there was no unanimity among the Judges. Even Chief Justice, K. Subba Rao and four other Judges – while recognizing force of the contention that there are implied limitations on power of Parliament to amend the Constitution – did not make any definitive pronouncement on the issue.

83. Justice K.N. Wanchoo and two other Judges in the I.C. Golaknath case (AIR 1967 SC 1643) said that even though under Article 368, power of amendment of the Constitution is very wide, it cannot be invoked to abrogate the Constitution.

84. The Heydon's Rule has been that while interpreting a law, it must be decided what mischief the framers of the law sought to remedy. Such an interpretation required that a brief survey be made of the demand of India's independence from the colonial rule since 1885. Within a few years of the founding of the Congress party in 1885, the Constitution of India Bill was drafted in 1895 by some eminent Indians. In 1918, in the Bombay Session of the Indian National Congress, it was resolved that the new Government of India Act 1919 should contain, "Declaration of Rights of the people of India as British Citizens". In 1927, in the Madras Session of the Congress, a resolution was passed that the future Constitution of India must have a chapter on Fundamental Rights. In 1928, the Nehru Report also made a similar recommendation. The demand for a new Constitution for India with a chapter on Fundamental Rights was adopted on 22 January 1947 in the Objective Resolution.

85. The Objective Resolution is a precursor to the Preamble of our Constitution. The Preamble indicates that the Constituent Assembly had the primary objectives before it as:
    (a) to constitute India into a Sovereign Democratic Republic.
    (b) to secure to its citizens certain basic Rights. Against this background – and keeping in view the Heydon's rule – it is difficult to accept the contention that framers of the Constitution made provision in Article 368 to destroy these ideals. Therefore, both Justice K.S. Hegde and Justice A.K. Mukherjea said that the identity of the Constitution must remain unchanged even after an amendment of the Constitution under Article 368 as the Parliament cannot amend the basic structure of the Constitution.
86. The people of India are not associated with the amendment of the Constitution under Article 368; but the Preamble says that the Constitution was framed by the people of India acting through the Constituent Assembly. Though the Constituent Assembly was elected on basis of a narrow franchise, it cannot be questioned at this stage that it did not represent the will of the people of India.
87. Under Article 368, the power to amend has been given to both Houses of the Parliament; but even a majority of members of each House and a two-thirds majority of members present and voting in each House cannot reflect the majority opinion in the country because of our electoral system, where a person who secures the highest number of votes gets elected to the legislature.
88. Both Justice K.S. Hegde and Justice A.K. Mukherjea held that implied limitations on powers constitute a general feature of all statutes.
89. Most of the commentators have held that in USA there are no implied limitations on power of amendment of the Constitution. But it has to be noted that Article V of the U.S. Constitution is substantially different from Article 368 of our Constitution.
90. The Judgment of the Privy Council in Queen *versus* Burah (1878) is of no assistance to support the argument that there can be no implied limitation on the power of amendment. The issue in Queen *versus* Burah (1878) was regarding conditional legislation and not regarding implied limitation on power of amendment of a Constitution.
91. Both the Judges held that it is a fallacy that every time the Constitution is amended, the amendment necessarily reflects the will of the people. For example, it is theoretically possible for the Parliament under Article 368 to amend the Constitution to extend its life indefinitely or to use Article 368 to make such an amendment as would make the Constitution virtually unamendable.
92. After an exhaustive analysis of the provisions for amendment of the Constitution in different countries, both Justice K.S. Hegde and Justice A.K. Mukherjea agreed with the contention of N.A. Palkhivala, that Article 368 has certain implied limitations on the power of amendment.
93. Both the Judges held that the Constitution (Twenty-fourth Amendment) Act 1971 was valid.

94. They also held that substitution of the expression "amount" for compensation in Article 31(2) of the Constitution providing for acquisition of private property in the public interest is valid. But the "amount" to be paid to the owner of the private property cannot be illusory and the principles for determining such "amount" cannot be irrelevant to value of the property. Both the Judges held that the decision in R.C. Cooper's case (AIR 1970 SC 564) is valid that any arbitrary fixation of the "amount" is liable to be struck down as an abuse of power. But otherwise the Constitution (Twenty-fifth Amendment) Act 1971 amending Article 31(2) has to be upheld as the adequacy of the "amount" to be paid for acquisition of property is beyond Judicial Review.

95. Article 31C, introduced by the Constitution (Twenty-fifth Amendment) Act 1971, is *ultra vires* as by this device, the Parliament permits the State Legislatures to amend the Constitution. Therefore, the new Article 31C destroys the basic features of the Constitution and is void.

96. Justice K.S. Hegde and Justice A.K. Mukherjea summed up their stand as follows:

(a) Even before the Constitution (Twenty-fourth Amendment) Act 1971, Parliament had powers under Article 368 to amend each Article and every part of the Constitution.

(b) "Law" in Article 13(2) of the Constitution even before the Constitution (Twenty-fourth Amendment) Act of 1971 did not include a constitutional amendment.

(c) Though the power to amend the Constitution under Article 368 is very wide, it does not include the power to destroy or emasculate either the basic elements or the fundamental features of our Constitution.

(d) The Constitution (Twenty-fourth Amendment) Act 1971 did not enhance the power of the Parliament to amend the Constitution under Article 368. It only made explicit what was implicit in Article 368 itself.

(e) The new Article 31(2) – introduced by the Constitution (Twenty-fifth Amendment) Act 1971 – does not destroy the Right to property as the "amount" to be fixed for acquisition of private property will have reasonable relationship with value of the acquired property.

(f) If the amount is not fixed by law providing for such acquisition of private property but only the principles or fixing the amount are laid down in the law, it has to be ensured that the principles fixed in the law are relevant for acquisition of private property.

(g) The amount to be paid for acquisition of private property should not be illusory and cannot be fixed arbitrarily.

(h) Whether the amount fixed by law or arrived at by application of principles laid down in the law is adequate is not open to Judicial Review.

(i) The new clause 31C is *ultra vires* as it permits destruction of basic features of the Constitution. It permits the Parliament and the State Legislatures to amend the Fundamental Rights by a declaration in their laws that the laws are meant to implement Articles 39(b) and 39(c) of the Directive Principles of State Policy.

(j) The Constitution (Twenty-ninth Amendment) Act 1971 is valid but whether the two enactments relating to land reforms in Kerala included in the Ninth Schedule abrogate the basic features of the Constitution shall be decided by the Constitution Bench.

97. Justice A.N. Ray delivered a separate judgment not only upholding validity of the Constitution (Twenty-fourth Amendment) Act 1971 and the Constitution (Twenty-fifth Amendment) Act 1971 but also holding that under Article 368, the Parliament can amend even the basic features of the Constitution. He also held that Article 31C, incorporated by the Constitution (Twenty-fifth Amendment) Act, is valid.

98. At the outset, Justice A.N. Ray raised the following questions:

(a) Can there be any implied limitation on the face of express power to amend the Constitution under Article 368?

(b) Can a distinction be made between the essential and non-essential features of the Constitution?

(c) Who is to decide what are the essential as distinguished from non-essential features of the Constitution?

99. Justice A.N. Ray also said that democracy proceeds on faith of the people to elect their representatives and faith in the representatives to represent the people. He also observed that in the history of mankind, if any power has been more potent than any other, it is that of faith of the people in themselves. He quoted Grote, a historian of ancient Greece, to say that the diffusion of constitutional morality is not merely among the majority of any community but is throughout the whole community.

100. In Sankari Prasad *versus* Union of India (AIR 1951 SC 458), the unanimous view of the Judges was that there is clear demarcation between law made in exercise of legislative power and constitutional law made in exercise of constituent power. It was reiterated – though not unanimously – in Sajjan Singh *versus* State of Rajasthan (AIR 1965 SC 845).

101. In I.C. Golaknath case (AIR 1967 SC 1643), it was held by a majority of six out of eleven judges that any constitutional amendment is "law" within the meaning of Article 13(2) and hence amendment of any Fundamental Right would be void as violative of Article 13(2) of the Constitution.

102. In I.C. Golaknath (AIR 1967 SC 1643), the majority of judges overruled the earlier two Judgments – Sankari Prasad and Sajjan Singh.

103. Justice A.N. Ray differed sharply from the majority judgment in I.C. Golaknath case (AIR 1967 SC 1643) because:

(a) In a federal Constitution, there is a fundamental difference between the power to amend the Constitution and the ordinary legislative power. When Parliament is engaged in the process of amendment of the Constitution, it is exercising a power which is *sui generis*. The amendment of the Constitution under Article 368 is a constituent law and not "law" within the meaning of Article 13(2) of the Constitution.

(b) Under Article V of the U.S. Constitution, the Congress does not function as a legislature but functions as a Constituent Assembly.

(c) In the Indian Constitution, the procedure of passing a constitutional amendment under Article 368 makes the procedure of amendment distinctly different from the procedure for passing ordinary law.

(d) Parliament of India, while enacting ordinary law, has no connection with the State legislatures. But for amendment of specified Articles of the Constitution Parliament does not act as the Union Legislature as ratification by at least one half of the state legislatures is required to pass the Constitution Amendment Bill.

(e) The Constituent Assembly enacted Article 368 as a single Article and included it in a separate chapter in the Constitution. It shows that the Constituent Assembly intended that Article 368 is both the source of power of amendment and the procedure for such amendment. Such a power also includes the power to amend any Fundamental Right.

(f) A Bill initiating ordinary legislation may be passed by a majority of members present and voting at a sitting of each House and if there is difference of opinion between the two Houses, there is provision for joint sitting of both the Houses. Again in passing ordinary laws, the quorum in each House is one tenth of the total members of that House.

(g) For a Constitutional amendment, the procedure is entirely different as a Bill to amend the Constitution must be passed by each House by a majority of total membership of that House and by a majority of not less tan two-thirds of members of that House present and voting. If certain specified Articles – including Article 368 – are sought to be amended, there is the requirement of ratification of the proposed amendment by at least one-half of the legislatures of States. Unlike for an ordinary Legislative Bill there is no provision for a joint sitting of both Houses of the Parliament to pass a Constitution Amendment Bill.

104. The majority of Judges in I.C. Golaknath case (AIR 1967 SC 1643) relied on a Privy Council decision in Mc. Cawley *versus* the King (AIR 1920 PC 21) to hold that an amendment to the Constitution is an ordinary legislative process; but a close scrutiny of Mc. Cawley's judgment does not support such a conclusion.

105. The majority of Judges in I.C. Golaknath case (AIR 1967 SC 1643) also held that the judgment of the Privy Council in Bribery Commissioner *versus* Ranasinghe (1965 AC 172) is an authority on the point that amendment to the Constitution is an ordinary legislative process. But a close scrutiny of the judgment does not support such a conclusion.

106. Justice K.N. Wanchoo – one of the Judges who wrote a minority judgment in I.C. Golaknath case (AIR 1967 SC 1643) – rightly said that the power to amend the Constitution is distinct from ordinary legislative power.

107. This view of Justice K.N. Wanchoo was adopted by the Parliament in the Constitution (Twenty-fourth Amendment) Act 1971, which stated that the Parliament has the constituent power under Article 368 to amend the Constitution by way of addition, variation or repeal.

108. As early as 1789, Thomas Jefferson had said that each generation has a right to determine the law under which it would live. As a matter of fact, an unamendable Constitution is the worst tyranny.

109. On behalf of the respondents, Niren De, the Attorney-General, cited several American decisions to say that under Article V of the U.S. Constitution, the amending power extends to every part of the Constitution.

110. The Constituent Assembly made no distinction between the essential and the non-essential features of our Constitution. Moreover, no one in the Constituent Assembly ever said that the Fundamental Rights can never be amended.

111. There can be no implied limitations on power of Parliament to amend any provision of the Constitution. In 1910, Lord Dunedin had said that express powers in an enactment shuts the door to any implied limitation.

112. The argument that if unlimited powers to amend the Constitution can be read into Article 368, the Constitution could be destroyed, is not supported by working of the Constitution in actual practice. To illustrate, from the year 1951, when in Sankari Prasad case (AIR 1951 SC 458), the Supreme Court did not impose any fetter on power of amendment of a Fundamental Right till the year 1967, when in I.C. Golaknath case (AIR 1967 SC 1643) the Supreme Court held that the Fundamental Rights cannot be amended under Article 368, no evidence is there that the full plenitude of power under Article 368 was used to subvert the Constitution. As held by the Privy Council "if the text is explicit, the text is conclusive, alike in what it directs and what it forbids".

113. In A.K. Gopalan *versus* the State of Madras (AIR 1950 SC 27), Chief Justice Harilal Kania held that to strike down a law on the basis of spirit of the Constitution would be, "to place in the hands of the judiciary powers too great and too indefinite either for its own security or for the protection of private Rights."

114. Chief Justice Harilal Kania also held that though a liberal interpretation should be given to provisions of the Constitution, it does not mean that the Courts are free to stretch the language of the Constitution in the interest of any legal or Constitutional theory. The Privy Council in Benoari Lal Sharma's case (AIR 1945 P.C. 48) also overturned the judgment of the Federal Court of India by observing that questions of policy or jurisprudence were not relevant for exercise of power conferred in an affirmative language and not restricted in any negative term.

115. The general rule is not to import into statues words which are not there. Words are not to be added by implications into language of a statute unless it is necessary to do so to give the words sense and meaning in the context.

116. N.A. Palkhivala has cited some essential features of the Constitution, which are beyond the power of amendment under Article 368. This argument is not valid as the Constitution does not make any distinction between the essential and the non-essential features.

117. The argument that the Judges, who have the power to pronounce on reasonableness of restrictions on a Fundamental Right, can be trusted to find out what are the basic features of the Constitutions is fallacious because in testing reasonableness of a restriction on

Fundamental Rights, the Judges are guided by the objective standard of reasonableness. In deciding what are the basic features of a Constitution, the Judges have no such objective standard to guide them.

118. There is considerable merit in Justice K.N. Wanchoo's observations in his dissenting Judgment in I.C. Golaknath case (AIR 1967 SC 1643) that any distinction between essential and non-essential features of our Constitution will introduce uncertainty.

119. It will be wrong to equate Fundamental Rights with Natural Rights as Natural Rights are nothing but a foundation of shifting sand.

120. In a democracy, determination of the right policies to be pursued can only be determined by a majority of elected representatives in the legislature. As Justice Oliver Wendell Holmes had said the underlying theory of democratic government is "the right of a majority to embody their opinion in law subject to the limitations imposed by the Constitution."

121. Therefore, the Constitution (Twenty-fourth Amendment) Act 1971 is valid.

122. The observation of Justice A.N. Ray regarding the *vires* of the Constitution (Twenty-fifth Amendment) Act 1971 may be summed up as follows:

(a) The Constitution (Twenty-fifth Amendment) Act 1971 introducing Article 31C is valid. By amending Article 31(2), the expression "amount" was substituted for the expression compensation for property acquired or requisitioned for a public purpose. It also provided that the law providing for acquisition of requisition of private property shall not be questioned on the ground that the whole or part of the amount is to be paid otherwise than in cash.

(b) The new Article 31C provided that notwithstanding anything in Article 13, no law giving effect to the policy of the state towards securing provisions of clauses (b) or (c) of Article 39 of the Directive Principles of State Policy shall be deemed to be void on the ground that it is inconsistent with or takes away or abridges any of the Rights conferred by Articles 14, 19 or 31 and no law containing a declaration that it is for giving effect to such a policy can be called in question in any Court on the ground that it does not give effect to such policy. It was also stipulated that if a state legislature passes such a law, it will not get the protection unless such a law, having been reserved for consideration of the President of India, receives his assent.

(c) Even after the Constitution (Fourth Amendment) Act of 1955 providing for "amount" for acquisition or requisition of private property and laying down that adequacy of the amount was not justiciable, in R.C. Cooper's case (AIR 1970 SC 564) it was held that "amount" meant equivalent sum for the property acquired or requisitioned. The Constitution (Twenty-fifth Amendment) Act 1971 was enacted to nullify the ratio of R.C. Cooper's case, popularly known as the Bank Nationalization case.

(d) Article 31C does not delegate the power of amendment to state legislatures. Article 31C merely removes the restrictions imposed by Fundamental Rights on any legislation – either by Parliament or by a State Legislature – provided such legislation promotes the objectives of clauses (b) and (c) of Article 39.

(e) The Constitution (Twenty-fifth Amendment) Act 1971 is valid.

(f) The inclusion of the two Kerala land reforms Acts of 1969 and 1971 in the Ninth Schedule by the Constitution (Twenty-ninth Amendment) Act 1971 is valid.

123. Justice Jaganmohan Reddy delivered a separate judgment which could be summarized as follows:

(a) The validity of the Constitution (Twenty-fourth Amendment) Act 1971 would depend upon interpretation of the expression "law" in Article 13 and "amendment" in Article 368.

(b) In I.C. Golaknath case (AIR 1967 SC 1643) five Judges, viz. Chief Justice K. Subba Rao, Justice J.C. Shah, Justice S.M. Sikri, Justice J.M. Shelat and Justice C.A. Vaidialingam, held that the power to amend the Constitution was to be found in Articles 245, 246 and 248 read with Entry 97 of the Union List. They also held that Article 368 contained the provision only for procedure of amendment. Justice M. Hidaytullah, however, did not agree with them and held that the power of amendment in Article 368, is a legislative power but is *sui generis* and is outside the Union List, the State List and the Concurrent List in the Seventh Schedule of the Constitution. Justice K.N. Wanchoo, Justice R.S. Bachawat and Justice V. Ramaswami found the power to amend the Constitution in Article 368 itself. Thus a majority of six out of the eleven Judges in the Constitution Bench in I.C. Golaknath case (AIR 1967 SC 1643) did not find the power to amend the Constitution in Entry 97 of the Union List.

(c) In I.C. Golaknath case (AIR 1967 SC 1643) a majority of six judges held that "subject to provisions of the Constitution" in Article 245 meant subject to Article 13(2), which stipulates that the state shall not make any law which takes away or abridges Fundamental Rights.

(d) Having regard to importance of the amending power, if a constitutional amendment would have meant "law" in Article 13(2) of the Constitution, it should have been specifically included in Article 13 itself. Surely, framers of the Constitution would not have applied the bar of Article 13(2) to any constitutional amendment by implication when in respect of minor instruments as ordinance, order, bye-law, rule, regulation, notification, custom or usage, they made a specific mention that the expression "law" shall include any or all of them.

124. Moreover, if amendment of the Constitution would be "law", the Constitution itself will be also a "law". But in several places in the Constitution of India, the expression "Constitution" has been used as distinguished from the expression "law".

125. While it may be right not to refer to debates in the Constituent Assembly to interpret provision of the Constitution, it is permissible to ascertain intention of framers of the Constitution by referring to various stages through which the Draft Constitution had to pass in the Constituent Assembly.

126. In the Constituent Assembly, amendments were proposed by K. Santhanam to clarify that the embargo imposed by Article 13(2) did not apply to constitutional amendments. But the Drafting Committee for reasons, which have not been recorded, did not accept the proposed amendment of K. Santhanam.

127. It may not be helpful to rely on foreign judgments on constitutional law as our Constitution has been framed keeping our heritage in view.

128. The seed of the Constitution is sown in a particular soil. It is the nature and quality of the soil and the climatic conditions which will ensure its growth and determine the benefits it can confer. The same seed cannot be planted in a different soil and the same growth and the same benefit therefrom cannot be expected.

129. Not relying fully on foreign judgments to interpret provisions of our Constitution "is not a case of shutting out light that could possibly enlighten and benefit us. The concern is rather to safeguard against the possibility of being blinded by it."

130. Sir Maurice Gwyer, a Chief Justice of the Federal Court of India, had said that since no two Constitutions are in identical terms, it is extremely unsafe to assume that a decision on one of them can be applied without qualification to another. The observation of Sir Maurice Gwyer has been endorsed by the Chief Justice P.B. Gajandragadkar in the advisory opinion in Special Reference of 1964 (AIR 1965 SC 745).

131. Provision for amendment of a Constitution is made in the Constitution itself as otherwise, the Constitution can be wrecked by extra-constitutional methods. As Woodrow Wilson said in his monumental work "Constitutional Government in the United States":

"A constitutional government, being an instrumentality for the maintenance of liberty, is an instrumentality for maintenance of a right adjustment and must have a machinery for constant adaptation."

132. A comparison of Article V of the U.S. Constitution, with Article 368 of our Constitution shows no similarity in the procedure for amendment of the Constitution even in the two major democracies.

133. Members of the Constituent Assembly were not elected through universal adult suffrage. They were elected on the basis of very limited franchise under the Cabinet Mission plan of May 1946. Voting right for electing members of the Constituent Assembly was restricted by the property, educational and other qualifications. The representatives of the princely states in India were not elected by the people of the princely states as the Rulers sent only their nominees to the Constituent Assembly.

134. When the Objective Resolution was adopted by the Constituent Assembly, legal sovereignty over India still rested with the King-in-Parliament. The legal sovereignty over India was transferred to the Constituent Assembly by the India Independence Act 1947 passed by the British Parliament. The Constitution of India was not ratified by the people of India. Article 395 of the Constitution repealed the Government of India Act 1935 and the Indian Independence Act 1947.

135. Even in the United Kingdom, where there is no written Constitution, it is not correct to say, that the King-in-Parliament is supreme. The basic principles, which King-in-Parliament, cannot violate as the legal sovereign, are four in number. They are:

(a) no man is above the law;

(b) those who govern Great Britain do so in a representative capacity and are subject to change as, an immortal government is an immoral government;

(c) freedom of speech and thought and assembly are an essential part of democratic governance;

(d) independence of the judiciary from control of the Executive or the Legislature.

136. It is not disputed by Niren De, the Attorney-General for India, and H.M. Seervai counsel for the respondent that an amendment of the Constitution does not mean abrogation of the Constitution and by the process of amendment, the Constitution cannot be substituted by a new Constitution.

137. If a Constitution is considered as a mechanism, or as an organism or as a piece of constitutional engineering, it must stand on some pillars or props and must have a basic structure. The edifice of the Indian Constitution stands on several props as

(a) Sovereign Democratic Republic.

(b) Justice, Social, Economic and Political.

(c) Liberty of Thought, Expression, Belief, Faith and Worship.

(d) Equality of Status and of Opportunity.

138. If any one of the props is removed, the basic structure of the Constitution will collapse and it will not be the same Constitution. Therefore, to quote N.A. Palkhivala, the Constitution has a basic structure and is "not a jelly-fish."

139. The Drafting Committee did not agree with the suggestion of Sir B.N. Rau, the Constitutional Adviser, to make the Fundamental Rights subservient to the Directive Principles of State Policy.

140. It is implicit in the Constitution that there is a duty cast upon the Courts to interpret the Constitution and the laws to implement the Directive Principles.

141. Justice Jaganmohan Reddy summed up his conclusions as follows:

(a) Article 13(2) does not place any embargo on Article 368 for amending any of the Fundamental Rights. But by such amendment, the Parliament cannot either abrogate the Constitution or alter its basic structure.

(b) The power of amendment of the Constitution is to be found in Article 368 as held by the six judges in I.C. Golaknath case (AIR 1967 SC 1643).

(c) Even though the power of amendment is wide enough, it is not wide enough to totally abrogate or emasculate or damage the basic structure of the Constitution so as to destroy its identity. The Constitution (Twenty-fourth Amendment) Act 1971 is valid as it has not drastically changed scope of the amending power under Article 368.

(d) In the Constitution (Twenty-fifth Amendment) Act 1971, the expression "amount" has been substituted for the expression compensation for acquisition of private property. This amendment is perfectly valid. The expression "amount" is not a legal concept. It only means that the "amount" could be in cash and has to be fixed on the basis of some relevant principles. Once Courts are satisfied that the amount or the manner of its payment is neither arbitrary nor illusory or the principles for fixation of the amount have reasonable relationship to value of the property acquired, Courts cannot go into the question of adequacy of the amount.

(e) Article 31C is valid if the portion that "no law containing a declaration that it is for giving effect to such policy shall be called in question in Court on the ground that it does not give effect to such policy" is severed from the proposed amendment introduced by Article 31C.

(f) Regarding the Constitution (Twenty-ninth Amendment) Act 1971 it has to be seen whether the two Kerala Land Reforms Acts – one of 1969 and the other of 1971 – damage or destroy any of the Fundamental Rights.

142. Justice D.G. Palekar delivered a separate judgment upholding validity of the Constitution (Twenty-fourth), the Constitution (Twenty-fifth) and the Constitution (Twenty-ninth) Amendment Acts.

143. The salient points in Justice D.G. Palekar's judgment are as follows:

(a) The Constitution of India is not an indigenous product. Those who framed it were aware of the provisions in Constitutions in other countries.

(b) The Constitution of India has provided for a quasi-federal polity. It has adopted the parliamentary system of government based on adult franchise.

(c) The expression "flexible" and "rigid" in relation to the Constitution was first coined by Lord Bryce to describe the British and the American Constitution respectively.

(d) A.V. Dicey in his book, *Law of the Constitution* (1885) popularized the expression "flexible" and "rigid" Constitutions. The Privy Council in Mc Cawley *versus* The King (AIR 1920 PC 91) used the expression "uncontrolled" and "controlled" for the expression flexible and rigid respectively.

(e) The three lists viz. the Union List, the State List and the Concurrent List in the Seventh Schedule do not mention 'amendment of the Constitution' as one of the items on which either the Parliament or State Legislatures are competent to legislate. On the other hand, Article 368 is provided in a separate chapter to deal with Parliament's power to amend the Constitution and the procedure thereof.

(f) In Article 368, a special procedure is provided for passing a Constitution Amendment Bill in each House by a majority of total membership of each House and by a two-third majority of members of each House present and voting.

(g) There is no provision in Article 368 to provide for a joint sitting of both the Houses in case there is a difference of opinion between the Houses about provisions of a Constitution Amendment Bill.

(h) Articles 245 and 248 – dealing with distribution of legislative powers between the Union and the States – do not vest the two Houses of the Parliament with the Constituent power under Article 368 to amend the Constitution.

(i) In other Articles of the Constitution viz. Article 4, Article 169, paragraph (7) of the Fifth Schedule and paragraph (11) of the Sixth Schedule which empower the

Parliament to amend specific provisions by ordinary legislation are not constitutional amendments under Article 368.

(j) If the framers of the Constitution had regarded the power to amend the Constitution as no better than a legislative power of the Parliament they could have provided for it by an entry in the Union List in the Seventh Schedule instead of leaving it to be located in an omnibus residuary power in Entry 97 of the Union List.

(k) Article 245 of the Constitution opens with the expression, "subject to the provisions of the Constitution". No such limitation is there on exercise of constituent power by Parliament under Article 368.

(l) There are several constitutional authorities to support that the power of amendment of a Constitution is a constituent power. In his book, *Amending of the Federal Constitution* (1942), Orfield says that in the United States of America, the amending body is sovereign both in law and in fact. Herman Finer in his book, *The Theory and Practice of Modern Governments* (1961) also supports such a view. Such a view is also expressed by Geoffrey Marshal in his book, *Constitutional Theory* (1971).

144. The Indian Parliament cannot be a constituent body as ultimate power to amend the Fundamental Rights resides with the people of India, who are sovereign. Constitutional experts have not read into the power of amendment of the U.S. Constitution as limited in its scope. The experts have not also said that the power of amendment of the Bill of Rights of the U.S. Constitution is with the people of USA.

145. So far as Article V of the U.S. Constitution is concerned, it does not provide for any ratification by the people of the USA. It only provides for ratification by the people acting through their representatives either in three-fourths of legislatures or by special Convention of representatives of the people in three-fourth of the states.

146. Except for equal representation of each of the states in the Senate other provisions including the Bill of Rights can be amended under Article V of the U.S. Constitution.

147. The Attorney-General for India has furnished to the Court extracts from nearly 71 modern constitutions of different countries. Constitutions of more than fifty countries show that the Constitution itself contains power of amendment of the Constitution.

148. West Germany has constitutional provisions regarding Human Rights, which cannot be taken away by amendment of the Constitution.

149. The *raison d'etre* for making provision in a Constitution for amendment is the basic need for orderly change.

150. Grant of power of amendment under Article 368 is plenary, unqualified and without any limitations.

151. Amending powers in a Constitution in the modern world – where rapid changes are taking place in society – must be wide enough to reach all provisions, whether essential or inessential. Such an argument has the support of judgments of the U.S. Supreme Court.

152. So far as Article 368 is concerned, there is nothing in it which limits the power of amendment expressly or by necessary implications. Admittedly, it is not the function of the Court to invent limitations on such power.

153. As stated in *Corpus Juris Secundum*, amendment of the Constitution is not an ordinary legislative function. Burdick also says in his book, *The Law of the American Constitution* that under Article V of the U.S. Constitution, the proposal for amendment and the power of ratification are not legislative powers.

154. Amendment of the Constitution not being liable to be voided with reference to a superior law is not "law" within the meaning of Article 13(2) of the Constitution.

155. The oath of office for the President of India and the oath of office for Governor of a state of the Indian Union makes a distinction between the Constitution and the law.

156. In Webb *versus* Outrim (1907), the Privy Council expressly rejected the doctrine of "implied limitation" against exercise of a power if such power is derived from the express provisions of the Constitution.

157. The U.S. Supreme Court has also rejected the doctrine of implied limitation on power of amendment of the Constitution.

158. If N.A. Palkhivala's contention that the Parliament cannot amend the basic features of the Constitution is accepted, it will mean that Article 368 of the Constitution has to be redrafted as follows:

"Nothing in the above amendment will be deemed to have authorized an amendment of the Constitution, which has the effect of damaging or destroying the core of the essential features, basic principles and fundamental elements of the Constitution as may be determined by the Courts."

159. The Constitution (Twenty-fifth Amendment) Act 1971 introduces abridgement of the Fundamental Right to property. Henceforth, there shall be no Right to receive compensation judicially interpreted as just equivalent of the property acquired but there is only the Right to receive an amount as fixed by law or according to principles prescribed in the law.

160. By inserting Article 31A and 31B by the Constitution (First Amendment) Act 1951, it was ensured that zamindaris and Estates were to be abolished. By the Constitution (Fourth Amendment) Act 1955 the expression "amount" was substituted for the expression compensation.

161. If the core or the basic features of the Constitution are set out in the Preamble to the Constitution, it must be noted that the Right to property is nowhere mentioned in the Preamble. Therefore, Justice M. Hidaytullah was right when he held in I.C. Golaknath case (AIR 1967 SC 1643) that Right to Property is one of the weakest of Fundamental Rights.

162. When concepts of social or economic justice are offered for scrutiny by the Courts in their interaction with the Right to Property, the Courts are bound to flounder "in labyrinths".

163. Article 31C, introduced by the Constitution (Twenty-fifth Amendment) Act 1971, provides that a law of a particular description shall not be deemed to be void on the ground that it affects Fundamental Rights under Articles 14, 19 and 31(b) if such a law contains a declaration that it is to secure provisions of clauses (b) and (c) of Article 39.

164. But Article 31C does not prevent the Courts from examining whether in pith and substance, the law was for some other objective but not to implement the policies contained in Article 39(b) and (c) of the Constitution.

165. Justice D.G. Palekar summed up his conclusions as follows:

(a) Article 368 contains both the power and the procedure for amendment of the Constitution.

(b) A constitutional amendment under Article 368 is not "law" which can be hit by Article 13(2) of the Constitution.

(c) The decision of the majority of Judges in I.C. Golaknath case (AIR 1967 SC 1643) is not correct as the Parliament can amend any Fundamental Right.

(d) There was no implied limitation on power of amendment in Article 368 before the Constitution (Twenty-fourth Amendment) Act 1971. *Pro tanto*, there can be no limitation whatsoever after such amendment.

(e) The Constitution (Twenty-fourth Amendment) Act 1971, the Constitution (Twenty-fifth Amendment) Act 1971 and the Constitution (Twenty-ninth Amendment) Act 1971 are valid.

166. Justice H.R. Khanna delivered a separate judgment whose main points are in the following paragraphs:

167. The question whether a Fundamental Right can be amended under Article 368 was first considered in Sankari Prasad's case (AIR 1951 SC 458).

168. By a unanimous judgment in Sankari Prasad case (AIR 1951 SC 458), the Supreme Court upheld validity of the Constitution (First Amendment) Act 1951.

169. Power of the Parliament to amend Fundamental Rights under Article 368 of the Constitution was again upheld in Sajjan Singh's case (AIR 1965 SC 845) though by a majority of Judges.

170. In I.C. Golaknath case (AIR 1967 SC 1643), the Supreme Court by majority of six out of eleven judges overturned the 'ratio' in Sankari Prasad case (AIR 1951 SC 458) and Sajjan Singh's case (AIR 1965 SC 845).

171. Justice M. Hidayatullah, who was in the Constitution Bench of eleven Judges in I.C. Golaknath case (AIR 1967 SC 1643), agreed with the above and said that for amending Fundamental Rights, a new Constituent Assembly will have to be convoked.

172. The minority of five Judges (Justice K.N. Wanchoo, Justice R.S. Bachawat, Justice V. Ramaswami, Justice Vasisth Bhargava and Justice G.K. Mitter) upheld the ratio in Sankari Prasad Singh Deo's case (AIR 1951 SC 458) and Sajjan Singh's case (AIR 1965 SC 845).

173. The words in Article 368 of the Constitution that the constitution shall stand amended in terms of the Bill clearly indicate that both the power and the procedure of amendment are contained in Article 368. The marginal note to Article 368 namely the procedure for amendment of the Constitution cannot control the express provisions in Article 368.

174. By the very nature of things, the power to amend the Constitution cannot be located in the residuary entry in item 97 of the Union List as the power to amend the Constitution also includes the power to amend the entries covered in the three lists (i.e. the Union List, State List and Concurrent List in the Seventh Schedule).

175. Moreover, in the Constituent Assembly, in the initial stages, it was proposed to give the residuary power to the states of the Indian Union but in the final draft constitution the residuary power was included in the Union List at Entry 97.

176. The decision of the Privy Council in Queen *versus* Burah (1868) is also applicable in case of interpretation of Article 368. In Queen *versus* Burah (1868), it was held that if the question is whether the legislature has exceeded its limit, it must be decided by examining the instrument by which affirmatively the legislative powers were created and by which, negatively they were restricted. If the legislation comes within the limits of the affirmative words, which gave the power and if it violates no express condition or restriction by which the power was limited, it was not for the Courts to enlarge those conditions or restrictions.

177. Before the Constitution of India was enacted, Sir B.N. Rau, the Constitutional Adviser to the Drafting Committee, had circulated a set of questions to members of the Constituent Assembly. Question 27 of the set of questions stipulated what should be the provision for amendment of the Constitution. The note of Sir B.N. Rau contained exhaustive material on the existing provisions for amendments of the U.S., British, Canadian, Australian, South African, Swiss and the Irish Constitutions. Since in some foreign constitutions, there were express limitations on powers of amendment, it is unlikely that the Constituent Assembly would not have provided for such a limitation in Article 368 if they wanted to do so. As a matter of fact, the speeches of Dr. B.R. Ambedkar, nowhere mentioned that the power of amendment – which finally took shape in Article 368 – was subject to any limitation.

178. There is a clear distinction between statutory provisions made in exercise of legislative power and constitutional amendment made in exercise of constituent power.

179. Before entering upon office, the form of oath by the President of India in Article 60 of the Constitution, makes a clear distinction between the "Constitution" and the "law".

180. Article 61 of the Constitution, mentions that the President of India could be impeached only for violation of the Constitution. There is no mention of the expression "law" in Article 61, which shows that the Constitution has itself put "law" in a separate category.

181. If the preservation of Fundamental Rights was too vital, it is logical that a provision should have been made in the Constitution expressly guaranteeing "the continued existence of Fundamental Rights in unabridged form". This was not done by framers of the Constitution.

182. Harold Laski has said that: "The American Constitution compels the Twentieth-Century American to move in the swaddling cloth of his ancestor's ideas."

183. Laski also held that the American Constitution must be moulded to fit new needs and new necessities.

184. Sir Ivor Jennings has said in his book, *Some Characteristics of the Indian Constitution* that a Constitution has to work not only in the environment it was drafted, but also centuries later.

185. The machinery of amendment is a safety-valve, which should not be operated with too great felicity nor be set in motion, on accumulation of force sufficient to explode it.

186. An unamendable Constitution is the worst tyranny. "It places the scepter over a free people in the hands of dead men, and the only office left to the people is to build thrones out of the stones of their sepulchre."

187. Thomas Jefferson had said that each generation should be considered as a distinct nation. He also said that the earth belongs in its usufruct to the living and the dead have neither the power nor the Right over it.

188. It cannot be said – as the Swiss experience has shown – that the method of amendment of the Constitution through popular referendum is a difficult method. In Switzerland, out of 64 amendments proposed for amending the Federal Constitution, as many as 49 were ratified by popular referendum.

189. Justice Oliver Wendell Holmes of the U.S. Supreme Court has said that legislatures are the ultimate guardians of the liberties and welfare of the people in quite as great a degree as the Courts.

190. As Justice Learned Hand of the U.S. Supreme Court has said, "liberty lies in the hearts of men and women; when it dies there, no Constitution, no law and no Court can save it."

191. Adolf Hitler destroyed the Weimar Constitution of Germany not by amending it but by invoking Article 48 of the Weimar Constitution dealing with emergency powers.

192. There should be no unnecessary apprehension that if under Article 368 there is no limitations on power of amendment – including power of amendment of Fundamental Rights – calamity will be the result because from 1951 till 1967 Parliament did not want to only exercise its power of amendment to take away vital Fundamental Rights of the people of India.

193. Carl J. Friedrich, has said that amending power, however unlimited, cannot be invoked to change the pillars fundamental to the Constitutional structure. Therefore, there should be no provision for amendment of a Constitution, which authorizes drafting of a fundamentally different Constitution with a different basic structure.

194. When individual Rights clash with the larger interest of the society, the state must acquire power to subordinate the individual Rights to the larger interest of society for social justice. The famous jurist, Roscoe Pound, is a supporter of subordination of individual Rights to larger social goals.

195. In his book, *The Indian Constitution: Cornerstone of a Nation*, Granville Austin has said that in India, with achievement of independence, the national revolution was completed but the social revolution commenced with the commencement of the Constitution on 26 January 1950.

196. The Constitution (Twenty-fifth Amendment) Act 1971 has to be viewed in the context of the social revolution in India. It limits the Right to Property by prescribing payment of an amount for requisition and acquisition of private property. Though the Courts cannot inquire into adequacy of the amount, they can step in if the amount is illusory and expropriatory. The Courts can also step in if the principles for fixing the "amount" are not relevant to determine the "amount".

197. The Constitution (Twenty-fifth Amendment) Act 1971 is valid except Article 31C. Article 31C stipulates that if a law contains a declaration that it is for implementing the provisions in clauses (b) and (c) of Article 39, the law cannot be challenged on the ground that it does not give effect to such a policy.

198. It is well-known that state legislatures are quite often swayed by local or regional considerations and do not safeguard the larger public interest. It is not difficult to conceive of laws by state legislatures against citizens of India, who have come from other states and have settled down in the state to which they originally did not belong. A law enacted by a state legislature may mandate that as the old residents of the state are economically backward, those who have come from other states and have not been in the state in question for more than three generations, their property will be acquired for distribution among the original backward residents of the State. Such a law passed by a state legislature, if it contains a declaration that it seeks to implement provisions in clauses (b) and (c) of Article 39, cannot be challenged for being violative of Articles 14, 19 and 31. Thus highly inequitable results will follow if Article 31C is retained as a piece of valid amendment. It is highly likely that Article 31C might sow the seeds of national disintegration.

199. Article 31C, departs from the scheme of Article 31A because Judicial Review is permissible under Article 31A but not permissible under Article 31C.

200. The second part of Article 31C is liable to be quashed on the following grounds:

(a) It gives a "*carte blanche*" to the Parliament and the state legislatures to enact a law violative of Articles 14, 19 and 31.

(b) The power of the legislature – including a state legislature – to exclude even limited Judicial Review, violates the basic structure of the Constitution.

201. The Constitution (Twenty-fourth Amendment) Act 1971 is valid subject to the stipulation that the power of amendment in Article 368 does not alter the basic structure of the constitution.

202. The Right to Property does not relate to the basic structure of the Constitution.

203. The Constitution (Twenty-ninth Amendment) Act 1971 is valid.

204. Justice K.K. Mathew wrote a separate judgment. He called it a healthy practice rendered impossible by increasing volume of work of the Court.

205. The points dealt with by Justice K.K. Mathew are as follows: the argument of N.A. Palkhivala that the word amendment in Article 368, did not confer the power to make any change in the Constitution by way of addition, variation or repeal, is without

substance. Similarly, N.A. Palkhivala's argument that the expression amendment in Article 368 only meant improvement in the text of the Constitution is also not valid.

206. In Rhode Island *versus* Palmer (1919) – known as the National Prohibition Judgment – the U.S. Supreme Court overruled the argument that under Article V of the U.S. Constitution, only alteration or improvement of the Constitution could be made to provisions already contained in the Constitution. The U.S. Supreme Court also overruled the contention that any amendment cannot change basic features of the U.S. Constitution.

207. In Ryan's case (1935), the Irish Supreme Court held that the expression amendment in the Irish Constitution was of the widest amplitude.

208. Sir Maurice Gwyer, Chief Justice of the Federal Court of India, had held that a broad and liberal spirit should inspire those whose duty it is to interpret the provisions of a Constitution. He also observed that a Court should avoid either a narrow or pedantic approach and when a power is granted to the Parliament such power can be limited by only some express provision.

209. The basic principle of construction of a statute – which is the same as the basic principle for interpretation of a Constitution – as laid down by the Privy Council in Queen *versus* Burah (1878) – is that when a question arises whether the limits of power have been exceeded, it has to be decided by looking at language of the instrument by which affirmatively, the power was vested and by which negatively it was restricted. In other words, if the text of the Constitution is explicit, the text is conclusive of what it directs and what it forbids.

210. The Constitution has roots in the past but is designed primarily for the unknown future. Justice Oliver Wendell Holmes of the U.S. Supreme Court had said in Missouri *versus* Holland (1920) that development of a Constitution – as the Constitution of the United States of America – could not have been foreseen completely by the most gifted of its begetters.

211. Carl J. Friedrich has said that every well-known Constitution will provide for its own amendment in such a way as to forestall revolutionary upheavals.

212. No Constitution has reached its final form and shape and has become a fixed thing incapable of further growth. The Constitution of a country must respond to the deep pulsation for change. As Justice Holmes said in Abrams *versus* the United States (1918), "a constitution is an experiment as all life is an experiment". If the experiment fails, there must be provision for making a new experiment by amending the Constitution.

213. Thomas Jefferson has said that "a Constitution is not ark of the covenant, too sacred to be touched." Dr. B.R. Ambedkar had said in the Constituent Assembly that what Thomas Jefferson said is absolutely true.

214. The power to amend under Article 368 includes the power to add any provision to the Constitution, to alter any provision, to substitute any other provision in its place and to delete any provision.

215. Article 368 as it stood before the Constitution (Twenty-fourth Amendment) Act 1971 contained not only the procedure but also the power of amendment.

216. Hans Kelsen has said in his book *General Theory of Law and State* that as the basic norm, the Constitution is not created by a legal procedure by a law-creating organ. The Constitution – as a positive legal norm – is valid not because it is created in a certain way by a legal act but it is valid because it is presumed to be valid. The validity of the Constitution is meta-legal.

217. In I.C. Golaknath case (AIR 1967 SC 1643) Chief Justice of India, K. Subba Rao and four other Judges located the power of amendment not in Article 368 but in Articles 245, 246 and 248 read with Entry 97 of the Seventh Schedule. They argued that as the Constitution could be amended by a law enacted by Parliament in exercise of its legislative power, an amendment of a Fundamental Right is "law" within the meaning of Article 13(2). They also held that a constitutional amendment amending any Fundamental Right is void. But they failed to notice that Article 245 begins with the expression, "subject to provisions of the Constitution". It is a logical fallacy to hold that an amendment of the Constitution can be made in exercise of powers under Article 245, which opens with the expression, "subject to provisions of the Constitution".

218. In I.C. Golaknath (AIR 1967 SC 1643) Chief Justice of India, K. Subba Rao has relied on the Privy Council's Judgments in Mc Cawley *versus* The King (AIR 1920 PC 1921) and the Bribery Commission *versus* Ranasinghe (1965 AC 172) in support of the proposition that the power to amend a constitution is a legislative power. Unfortunately, these two judgments do not support his contention.

219. Mc Cawley's case (AIR 1920 PC 1921) was in the context of a flexible Constitution where the Constitution could be amended by the same procedure as prescribed for ordinary legislation. But in our Constitution, the procedure of amendment in Article 368 is different than the procedure of enacting any ordinary law. Therefore, Mc Cawley's case is not relevant to hold that amendment of any provision of our Constitution is a legislative process and the power to amend is a legislative power.

220. Ranasinghe's case (1965 AC 172) is also no support for the proposition that in our Constitution, power of amendment is a legislative power because in Ranasinghe's case, only constitutionality of the Bribery Commission was decided and no decision was pronounced regarding whether power of amendment of the Constitution was a legislative power.

221. N.A. Palkhivala has argued that Parliament is a creature of the Constitution and sovereignty resides with the people of India, who gave themselves the Constitution. But this argument is rather weak. Historically, the people of India did not adopt, enact and gave unto themselves the Constitution. The Constituent Assembly was indirectly elected on the basis of a limited franchise. As Granville Austin says, the Constituent Assembly at best represented about 28.5 percent of adult population of the British provinces in the Indian subcontinent. The princely states did not send their representatives to the Constituent Assembly after conducting a popular election. They only sent their nominees to the Constituent Assembly.

222. The Constituent Assembly derived its legal competence to frame the Constitution under the India Independence Act 1947.

223. There are Constitutions which provide for active participation by the people in the mechanism of amendment either by way of "initiative" or "referendum" as in Switzerland, Australia and Ireland. But in our Constitution, there is no such mechanism.

224. Some French political philosophers have said that the nation alone possesses the constituent power and an agency as a legislature has no constituent power but only a power to amend the Constitution within the original scheme of the Constitution.

225. It is unnecessary to enter the arid tract of what Abraham Lincoln called pernicious abstraction where no green things grow or resolve the metaphysical niceties because in our Constitution, there is no scope for the people of India to exercise the constituent power.

226. N.A. Palkhivala has said that there are implied limitations on power of amendment under Article 368 because the Preamble to the Constitution sets out the essential features of the Constitution, which cannot be amended without destroying the identity of the Constitution.

227. Even though in the U.S. Constitution, there is a Preamble, the Supreme Court of the USA has never read into the Preamble implied limitations on the power to amend the Constitution.

228. In Rhode Island *versus* Palmer (1919), popularly known as the National Prohibition Case, the U.S. Supreme Court held that in Article V of the U.S. Constitution there was no limitation on power of amendment of the Constitution except the express limitation provided therein i.e. without their consent, the states may not be deprived of equal representation in the Senate of the U.S. Congress.

229. Eminent Constitutional experts have held that there are no implied limitations whatsoever on the power of amendment in the U.S. Constitution and that an amendment of the U.S. Constitution can change the form of government or the Bill of Rights and the framers of the Constitution did not intend to lay down an unalterable framework of Government.

230. The doctrine of implied limitation against exercise of power was rejected by the Privy Council in Web *versus* Outrim (1907).

231. Leading authors on the Constitution of Australia have been of the view that all provisions of the Australian Constitution can be amended and there are no implied limitations on the power of amendment.

232. N.A. Palkhivala has argued that if power of amendment under Article 368 is unlimited, it would give rise to far-reaching changes as the Parliament can extend its life, make India a satellite of a foreign country, do away with the Supreme Court and the High Courts, abolish the Parliamentary system of Government and make the Constitution virtually unamendable by making the process of amendment extremely difficult. In reply, it can be said that if there is power to amend in Article 368, "the fact that it may be abused is no ground for cutting down its width".

233. In Ex Parte Crossman (1924), the U.S. Supreme Court has held that presumption is that every organ of a state will act in coordination and that though one organ of the state can paralyze the functions of other organs and make the Constitution come to a standstill,

yet "no Constitution proceeds on the assumption that one organ will act in such a way as to defeat the action of the other".

234. In India, we have a democratic Republic. Democracy proceeds on the assumption that representatives of the people in Parliament will reflect the will of the people. The effective remedy for gross abuse of power by the Parliament is in the ballot boxes.

235. N.A. Palkhivala has argued that Fundamental Rights are the rock upon which the Constitution has been built. They are extensions, combinations and permutations of the Natural Rights of Life, Liberty and Equality possessed by the people. The implied limitation on power of amendment stems from the character of those Rights. The counsels for the respondents, have argued that the contention that Fundamental Rights are transcendental, primordial and sacrosanct in the sense that they are "not of today or yesterday but live eternally and none can date their birth", smacks of sentimentalism. All Natural Rights are liable to be limited or even taken away for common good is itself a principle recognized by all writers on Natural law.

236. Despite attacks on the theory of Natural Rights – and the ebb and flow in its fortune – there has been a revival of the Law of Natural Rights in the 20th century. The doctrine of Natural Rights as the bulwark of the Rights of man has been incorporated in the Universal Declaration of Human Rights (1948). Harold Laski said in his *magnum opus* "A Grammar of Politics" that Man has Rights which are inherent in him as a member of society and the state is to be judged by the manner in which it seeks to secure for men the substance of those Rights.

237. In the Chapter on Fundamental Rights, there are provisions as Articles 33, 34, and 35 which give Parliament the power to modify these Rights. (Article 33 lays down the power of the Parliament to modify implementation of Fundamental Rights in their application to members of the Armed Forces of the Union, members of the forces charged with maintenance of public order i.e. members of the police and para-military force and employees of the Intelligence Bureau.)

238. Article 34 stipulates indemnification of any person for acts done by the person for restoration of public order when Martial law is in force in any part of the territory of India. If the Fundamental Rights would have been inalienable because they are Natural Rights, Article 33 and Article 34 of the Constitution would not have found a place in the chapter on Fundamental Rights.

239. Article 29(2) of the Universal Declaration of Rights of Men (1948) stipulates that every Right contained in the Declaration can be subject to limitations for the common good.

240. The history of amendments to the Constitution under Article 368 demonstrates that the apprehension of N.A. Palkhivala that catastrophic consequences will arise if there are no implied limitations on power of amendment is wholly unjustified.

241. H.M. Seervai, pointed out that there is no objective standard for the Courts to locate the core of a Fundamental Right. He further submitted that the task of finding a core of a Fundamental Right is like the quest for the "philosopher's stone" and the Amending Body would be left without a chart or a compass when it proceeds to amend the Constitution under Article 368.

242. H.M. Seervai also submitted that the framers of our Constitution deliberately omitted the expression due process of law and substituted it with the expression procedure established by law in Article 21 of the Constitution to avoid flirtation by Courts with any gossamer concepts drawn from higher law to annul laws enacted by the legislature. Even in USA, invalidation of law for violation of substantive due process has become practically obsolete.

243. Substantive due process means testing an Act or Legislation on the touchstone of reason. The reason why the expression due process has not been defended is that it embodies a concept of fairness which has to be decided with reference to facts and circumstances in each case. As Justice Felix Frankfurter, a former judge of the U.S. Supreme Court, has said due process is not a technical conception with a fixed content unrelated to time, place and circumstances.

244. For imposing reasonable restrictions by legislation, the Indian Courts also adopt the same standard of reasonableness adapted by the courts in USA under the due process clause.

245. Even though in Municipal Committee *versus* the State of Punjab (AIR 1969 SC 1100), the Supreme Court held that the due process clause has no application in India, the concept of due process enters into the meaning of reasonableness of restrictions in clauses (2) to (6) of Article 19 of our Constitution.

246. Though our Supreme Court said in Collector of Customs *versus* Sampathu (AIR 1962 SC 316) that even though clauses (2) to (6) in Article 19 of our Constitution might in great part be relevant for judging due process, reasonable restrictions in Article 19 of our Constitution and "due process" in the American Constitution are not identical.

247. But it is not clear how the expression reasonable restrictions is more definite than the expression due process.

248. To quote Thomas Jefferson, a Constitution, as an unalterable framework, cannot bind the succeeding generations. Dr. B.R. Ambedkar has quoted the observation of Jefferson approvingly in debates in the Constituent Assembly.

249. There is no sacredness about the theory of basic structure of the Constitution as history has shown that Mankind has changed its opinion about the best form of government. Even eminent political philosophers have not agreed about the best form of government. Plato advocated rule by the Guardians, who will have no family and no property. His own disciple, Aristotle differed from him and advocated a mixed form of government.

250. From a juridical point of view, the Directive Principles of State Policy do form a part of the Constitutional law of India. The Directive Principles are in no way subordinate to the Fundamental Rights. The only limitation is that no citizen can claim specific performance of any Directive Principles whereas a citizen can seek specific performance of a Fundamental Right. But if the state makes a law embodying a Directive Principle, the Courts must enforce the law.

251. Judicial function is a process of creation and application of the law. The law-creating function of the Courts is specially manifest when the judicial decision has character of a precedent, which becomes a judicial norm. Within such a legal system, Courts are legislative organs in the same way as the legislature is a law-making organ.

252. Lord Reid had said in his address, "The Judges as Law Makers" (1972) that no one is prepared to accept the theory of Blackstone that the law declared by the Courts has an ideal existence before it is expounded by the Judges. John Chipman Gray has said that in the ultimate analysis, the Courts also make our statute law and quoted Bishop Hoadly that whoever has absolute power to interpret the law, it is he who is the law-giver, not the one who originally enacted the law.

253. Nobody doubts today that within the confines of vast spaces, a judge moves with freedom. As Benjamin N. Cardozo said in his book, *The Nature of the Judicial Process*, the law which is the resultant product is not found, but made. The process being legislative demands the legislator's wisdom.

254. In building up a just social order, it is sometimes imperative that the Fundamental Right should be subordinated to the Directive Principles.

255. Fundamental Rights themselves have no fixed contents; most of them are merely empty vessels into which each generation must pour its content in the light of its experience. At what stage, a Fundamental Right should have priority over the Directive Principles of State Policy, must be left for each generation to decide. Judicial Review of a constitutional amendment on the ground that it seeks to abrogate a Fundamental Right to implement a Directive Principles is impermissible as the Parliament – being the Amending Body in the Constitution – has passed the Constitutional amendment to implement the Directive Principles.

256. Justice K.K. Mathew summed up his conclusions as follows:

(a) The Constitution (Twenty-fourth Amendment) Act 1971 is valid and there is no implied limitation on power of amendment.

(b) The Constitution (Twenty-fifth Amendment) Act 1971, including Article 31C introduced by it, is valid. The expression "amount" in Article 31(2) does not convey the idea of any norm. The fixation of the amount or the principle for determining the amount is a matter within the absolute discretion of the Parliament or the State legislatures. The Court cannot go into the question whether the amount fixed by law or the principles laid down for determining the amount is either adequate or relevant to determine the amount to be paid for acquisition of private property. [**N.B.:** In the text of the Judgment, Justice K.K. Mathew gave the example of abolition of slavery by law in the USA in the middle of the 19th century, when the slave-owners were not paid full market value of the slaves they owned. Similarly, in the early part of the 20th century, when prohibition of possession and consumption of alcoholic beverage was made illegal in USA, the owners of breweries and distilleries got no compensation].

(c) The Court can go into the question whether a law to give effect to provisions of Article 39(b) and (c) of the Constitution does indeed give effect to such a policy.

(d) The Constitution (Twenty-ninth Amendment) Act 1971 is valid.

257. Justice M.H. Beg delivered a separate judgment agreeing with some of the observations of brother Judges and disagreeing with some others.

258. A brief summary of the judgment of Justice M.H. Beg is as follows: the task of a modern Judge in a democratic country is increasingly complex as he has to carefully evaluate conflicting values and interests. The great Judges have not given infallible answers to all legal problems.

259. As stated by N.A. Palkhivala, the issue before the Judges is scope of the amending power under Article 368.

260. The Preamble, the Chapter on the Fundamental Rights and the Chapter on the Directive Principles of State Policy make it clear that the Constitution of India seeks to express the principle, "salus populi suprema lex" (the good of the people is the supreme law).

261. The Constituent Assembly, which drafted and enacted the Constitution of India was not elected on the basis of universal adult suffrage.

262. Section 8 of the Indian Independence Act 1947, passed by the British Parliament, was the legal mandate of the Constituent assembly to enact the Constitution of free India. Thus historically the legal power to enact the Constitution of India was not with the people of India.

263. N.A. Palkhivala is not right in stating that the Fundamental Rights are the means and the Directive Principles are the ends to be achieved to fulfill the objectives in the Preamble of the Constitution. The correct view would be that both the Fundamental Rights and the Directive Principles are the means of achieving the objectives in the Preamble of the Constitution. The mandate of Article 37 of the Constitution in the Chapter on the Directive Principles is that it shall be the duty of the State to apply the Directive Principles in making laws. Primarily, the mandate of Article 37 is to the Parliament and the State Legislatures but in so far as Courts of Justice can indulge in some judicial law-making either within the interstices of the Constitution or any statute, the Courts too are bound by the mandate of Article 37 of the Constitution.

264. Sovereignty is not vested in any one organ of the state but is divided among them. A feature of sovereignty is the possession of "constituent power", which under Article 368 vests in the Parliament. Control of the judiciary over the constituent power in Article 368 is limited to ensuring that the form and manner of amendment as laid down in Article 368 is properly observed.

265. The framers of our Constitution – some of them being eminent jurists – must have been familiar with our ancient law-givers, Manu and Parasara who said that the Fundamental Law may differ from one Age to another. Pandit Ganganath Jha, in his treatise on Hindu Law has cited the original passages from Manu and Parasara in this regard.

266. Power of amendment in our Constitution must include the power to change the Fundamental Rights to suit the needs of each age and generation. Justice Holmes of the U.S. Supreme Court had rightly observed that the life of law has not been logic but the felt necessities of the times.

267. The expression "law" in Article 13(2) deals only with ordinary law and not constitutional amendments. Even before the Constitution (Twenty-fourth Amendment) Act 1971, under

Article 368, Parliament had full powers to amend any part of the Constitution including the Fundamental Rights. Therefore, the Constitution (Twenty-fourth Amendment) Act 1971, is only declaratory in nature.

268. It has been argued that draft Article 13(2) of the Constitution contained a specific exemption that a constitutional amendment would not be "law". There is no reason recorded by the Drafting Committee why in the final draft of the Constitution, Article 13(2) was incorporated without specific mention that a constitutional amendment would not be "law". Perhaps, the Drafting Committee did not consider it necessary.

269. The Constitution uses the expression "Constitution" as distinct from ordinary "law" in several places.

270. The only implied limitation on power of amendment under Article 368 is that in exercise of the amending power, the Parliament in one stroke cannot abrogate the Constitution.

271. Niren De, the Attorney-General, has rightly conceded that the scope of amendment of the Constitution under Article 368 is not so wide as to create a vacuum by abrogating the Constitution.

272. Similarly, the theory of implied limitations on powers expressly granted by the Constitution was rejected in Privy Council's decision in Mc Cawley *versus* the King (AIR 1920 PC 1921). In Web *versus* Outrim (1907), the theory of implied limitations on powers expressly conferred by an Act of Parliament was also rejected by the Privy Council. No support for the theory of implied limitation on powers under the Constitution could also be found in the Canadian and Irish decisions cited by N.A. Palkhivala.

273. The judgment of the Privy Council in Bribery Commissioner *versus* Ranasinghe (1965 AC 172) does not also support the theory of implied limitations on powers of amendment.

274. N.A. Palkhivala referred to the theories of Natural Law and Natural Rights to justify the theory of implied limitations on powers of amendment under Article 368 of the Constitution. But the history of Natural Law is a tale of failure of the search for absolute justice.

275. Courts have no power to control a power expressly sanctioned by the Constitution. Checks on possible abuse of such a power do not lie through the Courts of law: pressure of public opinion and fear of revolt are the only possible checks if such contingencies arise.

276. Justice M.H. Beg summed up his views as follows:

(a) The majority view in I.C. Golaknath *versus* State of Punjab (AIR 1967 SC 1643) was erroneous and is overruled.

(b) The Constitution (Twenty-fourth Amendment) Act 1971 is valid. There are no implied limitations on power of amendment of the Constitution.

(c) The Constitution (Twenty-fifth Amendment) Act 1971 is valid. Article 31C included by the Constitution (Twenty-fifth Amendment) Act is valid as it seeks to implement provisions in clauses (b) and (c) of Article 39 of the Directive Principles of State Policy. Article 31C only protected any law from alleged violation of Articles 14, 19 and 31 of the Constitution; but if there was a colourable piece of legislation with the pretence of merely protecting the law by the stipulated declaration in the law itself, the Courts can examine whether in substance – and not merely in form – the law actually implements provisions in clauses (b) and (c) of Article 39.

(d) The expression "amount" for acquisition or requisition of private property in Article 31(2) does not convey the idea of any prescribed norm. By the Constitution (Twenty-fifth Amendment) Act 1971, fixation of the amount is within the exclusive jurisdiction of the Parliament or the state legislature. The Courts cannot pronounce on the relevance of the principles of fixation of the amount or the adequacy of the amount in exercise of power of Judicial Review.

(e) The Constitution (Twenty-ninth Amendment) Act 1971 is valid.

277. Justice S.N. Dwivedi delivered a separate judgment agreeing with conclusions of Justice A.N. Ray. He, however, held that in view of importance of the case, he preferred to cite reasons why he agreed with Justice A.N. Ray.

278. At the outset, Justice S.N. Dwivedi said that ideas, which failed to win the minds of the Englishmen in the Stuart period, are now seeking transmigration into the Constitution of India through the arguments of N.A. Palkhivala.

279. In the Stuart period, the following ideas were in circulation in the English society but they were not accepted.

(a) Acts of Parliament can take away flowers and ornaments of the crown but not the crown itself.

(Almost on similar lines, N.A. Palkhivala, has argued that in exercise of powers under Article 368, the Parliament cannot abridge or abrogate the basic structure of the Constitution).

(b) The Parliament cannot deliver the free people of England to a foreign government or to laws imposed by foreigners.

(N.A. Palkhivala's argument was that Parliament cannot so amend the Constitution as to make India a satellite of a foreign country).

(c) Right to Property is foundation of the Constitutions and not the Constitutions of the Right to property. Law of Nature gives every man a Right of property of what he has or may have which is not another man's.

(N.A. Palkhivala has argued that the Right to Property is a Human Right required for enjoyment of every other Right. As Right of Property is based on Natural Law, it cannot be taken away by amendment of the Constitution.)

(d) A representative that makes laws is merely a creature of the fundamental law.

(N.A. Palkhivala's argument was that Parliament, which is a creature of the Constitution, cannot destroy or damage the core of the Fundamental Rights and thus rise above the creator.)

(e) When an Act of Parliament is against the Rights of the common man, common law will control it and adjudge such an Act as void.

(N.A. Palkhivala has argued that amending powers in Article 368 are limited by the Natural Law and an amendment in violation of the principles of Natural law will be void.)

(f) Cases which concern the life or inheritance or goods or fortunes of subjects are not to be decided by natural reason but by artificial reason and judgment of law.

(N.A. Palkhivala's argument is that the inherent and implied limitations to the amending power in Article 368 will be determined by Judges possessing a trained judicial mind.)

280. In the Stuart Period in English history, there were three contenders for power viz., the King, the Parliament and the Common Law. Finally, the Parliament won and the King and votaries of the common law accepted the supremacy of Parliament. In the Stuart Period, England was passing through a period of transition, similar to the period India is passing through at present.

281. At bottom, the controversy is such that the Court is called upon to decide whether our polity is a prison-house or a free country and whether it speaks for the few or for the many. These issues can hardly be decided with the aid of decisions of either foreign Courts or opinion of foreign jurists.

282. Since no two Constitutions are identical, it would be unsafe to assume that a decision in one of them can be applied without qualification to another. This may be so even when the 'words' and 'expressions' used are the same in both the cases for a 'word' or 'expression' may take a colour from its context and bear different meanings.

283. Justice Vivian Bose has rightly observed in Re Delhi Laws Act 1912 (AIR 1951 SC 332) that our Constitution is unique and it is useless to try and look at our Constitution through the eyes of another country or other Courts.

284. The Constitution of India reflects hopes and aspirations of the people of India emerging from colonialism in the second half of the Twentieth century. Constitutions of the past cannot be a safe guide for interpreting the provisions of the Constitution of India meant to achieve social and economic democracy.

285. Constitutions from the Seventeenth to Nineteenth century gave a lot of importance to the Right to Property. Jurists have said how the French Revolution allowed the exclusive Right to Property to remain and how politics dealt mainly with the alterations to be made to uphold the Right to Property.

[**N.B.:** The French Revolution was against privileges and not against property.]

286. The ancient law-givers of India did not believe in acquisition of things for pleasure. Instead, the law-givers stood for the good and the wholesome. The King in ancient India was to secure the welfare of all. Their Rule of Law – or Dharma – was intended to help the power-minus to keep the power-plus in check.

287. If procedure in Article 368 is followed, the Constitution shall stand amended in terms of the Constitution Amendment Bill.

288. Power to amend the Constitution is in Article 368 and not in Entry 97 of the Union List read with Article 248.

289. Entry 97 in the Union List which deals with residuary powers, provides for matters, which could not be foreseen by framers of the Constitution. But amendment of the Constitution, which was clearly foreseen by the framers of the Constitution, could not have been located in Entry 97 of the Union List.

290. The framers of our Constitution were familiar with the meaning of legislative and constituent power. They put Article 368 in a separate chapter dealing with constituent power.

291. Our Constitution is partly controlled like the American Constitution and partly uncontrolled like the British Constitution. It is controlled in respect of provisions which may be amended by following the procedure in Article 368. It is uncontrolled with respect to those provisions of the Constitutions which can be amended by passing an ordinary law in exercise of legislative power.

292. No provision of the Constitution can claim immunity from the sway of the amending power under Article 368.

293. The Constituent Assembly was not fully representative of the people of India as its members were not elected on the basis of universal adult suffrage. After commencement of the Constitution on 26 January 1950, in the first General Election (1952) the Parliament was elected on the basis of universal adult suffrage. Thereafter, General Elections to the Parliament have been held from time to time under provisions of the Constitution and the Representation of the People's Act. Hence Parliament, is fully competent to amend any provision of the Constitution under Article 368.

294. The Constitution of India through a process of amendment can adapt itself to the changing political, social and economic conditions. As Immanuel Kant has said: "One Age cannot enter into an alliance on oath to put the next Age in a position when it would be impossible for it to extend or correct its knowledge or to make any progress whatsoever. This would be a crime against human nature whose original destiny lies precisely in such progress."

295. Power of the Constituent Assembly to frame the Constitution was unlimited. The nature of the power conferred on the Parliament by Article 368 is similar to the power of the Constituent Assembly. It may be said that by virtue of Article 368, the Parliament of India acts as a continuing Constituent Assembly.

296. The nature, object and history of the amending power and the context of Article 368 leave little room for doubt that the power of amendment includes the power to repeal or abrogate any provision of the Constitution. It may be that Parliament may not be able to annihilate the entire Constitution by a stroke of pen. But Article 368 empowers the Parliament to amputate any part of the Constitution for good health of other parts. Article 368 empowers the Parliament to not only apply the physician's needle but also the surgeon's saw.

297. There is a distinction between the 'Constitution' and the 'Law'. A Constitution is a politico-legal document. Woodrow Wilson, a former President of USA, has said that the American Constitution is a political document and not merely a lawyer's document.

298. There are many provisions in the Constitution, where the expressions the 'Constitution' and the 'law' are used separately.

299. When the prescribed legislative procedure is followed, the end product is a 'law'. When the procedure prescribed under Article 368 is followed, the end product is a constitutional amendment.

300. In our Constitution, if there is difference of opinion between the House of the People and the Council of states regarding an ordinary legislative bill, there is provision for a joint sitting. But no provision for joint sitting of both Houses is provided for a constitutional amendment under Article 368.

301. Legislative power in the Indian Constitution under Article 245 is subject to provisions of the Constitution. But Article 368 does not contain any such expression.

302. Fundamental Rights in the Indian Constitution are not sacrosanct and inviolate. When a Proclamation of Emergency has been made by the President of India under Article 352, Fundamental Rights under Article 19 of the Constitution are automatically suspended. Article 359 empowers the President to suspend the Right to constitutional remedies in Article 32 of the Constitution when a proclamation of Emergency is in operation so that all Fundamental Rights may be made quiescent.

303. According to N.A. Palkhivala, Natural Law is the higher law, which limits the power of Parliament under Article 368. This may not be correct as even though Natural Law has been the religion with many constitutional and political thinkers, votaries of Natural Law have never believed in a single Godhead. The Gods of Natural Law are locked in constant internecine conflict. The bewildering variety of exponents of Natural Law has led Hans Kelsen to observe that the principles of Natural Law are not only highly conflicting but they also represent the highly subjective value judgment of different exponents.

304. In A.K. Gopalan *versus* State of Madras (AIR 1950 SC 27), the majority of Judges acknowledged omnipotence of the legislative power to deprive a person of his life and personal liberty according to procedure established by law. The Court thus displayed humility and self-restraint in acknowledging legislative supremacy. But a complete departure was made in I.C. Golaknath case (AIR 1967 SC 1643) when a majority of judges held that the Parliament cannot amend any Fundamental Right. "From Gopalan to Golaknath, the Court has shifted from one end to the other end of the diagonal – from Parliament's supremacy to its own supremacy".

305. Justice S.R. Das has said in State of West Bengal *versus* Subodh Gopal (AIR 1954 SC 92) that it is futile to cling to notions of absolute sanctity of individual liberty or private property of Hugo Grotius in the 16th century or Blackstone in the 18th century or to ideas when the U.S. Constitution was framed. Emphasis has now shifted from individual to the community. Establishment of a welfare state – which is the objective of the Constitution – mandates social control by the State. It should be left to the State to decide when and how and to what extent, social control should be exercised for common good.

306. The Indian Constitution has not set up a government of Judges in the country. It has entrusted the Parliament to determine the paramount norms. Courts are permitted to make limited value choices within the parameters of constitutional value choices. The Courts cannot gauge the urgency of an amendment and the danger to the State for want of it.

307. The Constitution is not meant to be an arena of legal quibbling for men with long purses. The Constitution, which is meant for the people of India should be so interpreted that the people will understand and appreciate it. The more they love it, the more they prize it.

308. An apprehended abuse of power would not be a legitimate reason for denying to the Parliament wide and unrestricted power of amendment under Article 368. There is a general presumption in favour of an honest and reasonable exercise of power.

309. In State of West Bengal *versus* Bela Banerjee (AIR 1954 SC 170) the Supreme Court held that compensation in Article 31(2) meant market value of the property.

310. To overcome the problem following the judgment, the Parliament enacted the Constitution (Fourth Amendment) Act 1955 to lay down that no law providing for acquisition of private property shall be called into question on the ground that the "amount" paid to the owner for acquisition of the property was not adequate.

311. The effect of the Constitution (Fourth Amendment) Act 1955 was neutralized by the Supreme Court in P. Vajravelu's case (AIR 1965 SC 1017). The ratio of P. Vajravelu's case was reiterated in Metal Corporation case (AIR 1967 SC 637).

312. In the subsequent judgment in Shantilal Mangaldas (AIR 1969 SC 634), the Supreme Court overruled the ratio in the Vajravelu case (AIR 1965 SC 1067) and the Metal Corporation case (AIR 1967 SC 637).

313. Though Shantilal Mangaldas case (AIR 1969 SC 634) transfused blood into the Constitution (Fourth Amendment) Act 1955 made anemic by Vajravelu case (AIR 1965 SC 1017) and Metal Corporation case (AIR 1967 SC 637), in R.C. Cooper's case (AIR 1970 SC 564) the Court overruled the ratio in Shantilal Mangaldas case (AIR 1969 SC 634). Therefore, Parliament had no other option but to enact the Constitution (Twenty-fifth Amendment) Act 1971.

314. The Constitution (Twenty-fifth Amendment) Act 1971 also introduced a new provision in Article 31C which protected from Judicial Review any legislation seeking to implement provisions in Article 39(b) and (c) of the Directive Principles of State Policy.

315. Justice S.N. Dwivedi summed up his views as follows:

(a) The majority opinion in I.C. Golaknath Case (AIR 1967 SC 1643) that Parliament cannot amend any Fundamental Right, is not correct and is overruled.

(b) The word amendment in Article 368 is broad enough to authorize the varying, repealing and abrogating each and every provision of the Constitution including Fundamental Rights.

(c) There are no implied limitations on the power of amendment in Article 368.

(d) The Constitution (Twenty-fourth Amendment) Act 1971, the Constitution (Twenty-fifth Amendment) Act 1971 and the Constitution (Twenty-ninth Amendment) Act 1971 are valid except that the new Article 31C cannot oust the jurisdiction of the Courts to examine whether the impugned law containing a declaration that it seeks to implement provisions of clauses (b) and (c) of Article 39 is indeed such a law or is a mere colourable legislation for some other purpose.

316. Justice Y.V. Chandrachud delivered a separate judgment bemoaning the fact that counsels took a lot of time to argue and the judges had hardly any time to discuss the issues among themselves.

[**N.B.:** Chief Justice S.M. Sikri, who presided over the 13-Judge Bench was due to demit office on 25 April 1973 on attaining the age of 65 years. The counsels took 65 days before the Bench of 13-Judges and the Judges could not get enough time to discuss the issues among themselves. If Judgments in Kesavananda Bharati case would not have been delivered on 24 April 1973 (the last working day of Chief Justice S.M. Sikri), a new Bench would have been constituted by the new Chief Justice, and the long period of 65 days spent by the Counsels would have become infructuous and *de novo* hearing of the case before a new Bench would have become necessary].

317. Justice Y.V. Chandrachud acknowledged the brilliance, industry, scholarship and precision of N.A. Palkhivala, counsel for the petitioner, Niren De, the Attorney-General for India and H.M. Seervai, the Advocate-General for Maharashtra, who represented the state of Kerala.

318. The salient points in the judgment of Justice Y.V. Chandrachud are as follows: Orfield, an authority on the U.S. Constitution, has described the power of amendment as "*sui generis*". Borrowing the expression from Orfield, it can be said that the whole matter before the 13-Judge Constitution Bench is indeed *sui generis*.

319. The 13-Judge Bench to hear the Kesavananda Bharati case (AIR 1973 SC 1461) is the largest Bench which sat for the longest period to decide momentous issues not merely for future of Indian democracy but for future of democracy itself.

320. Even though eminent counsels debated and discussed before the Bench provisions for amendment of Constitutions of as many as 71 countries, the utility of those discussions were limited as there is no international yardstick to measure the width of the amending power.

321. At one end is the view that an unamendable Constitution is the worst tyranny of time and such a Constitution constitutes government by the graveyard.

322. At the other end, the view is that any amending power, cannot change the fundamental pillars supporting its constitutional authority and the power to amend the Constitution – however unlimited – cannot contain the power to destroy it.

323. Some theories of political science, sociology, economics and philosophy contained a valiant defence of the Right to Property and some other theories stated that the Right to Property is the weakest of the Fundamental Rights. The decision on this vexed question must depend upon the philosophy of our Constitution, which aims at a synthesis between the Fundamental Rights and the Directive Principles by giving to the former a pride of place and to the latter a place of prominence. Together they form the core of the Constitution.

324. The U.N. Charter of 1945, the Universal Declaration of Human Rights of 1948 and the European Convention of 1950, show that the Rights of individuals have received international recognition. The correct answer will depend upon the urgency of striking a balance between the Rights of individuals and the good of the society.

325. Some political philosophers as Hugo Grotius (1583-1645), Thomas Hobbes (1588-1679), John Locke (1632-1704), Jean Jacques Rousseau (1712-78), William Blackstone (1723-80), Immanuel Kant (1724-1804); Jeremy Bentham (1748-1832) and George Hegel (1770-1831) have been exponents of Natural Law and Natural Rights. They have said that as a moral and rational being, man has some inherent and inalienable Rights and these Rights guaranteed by the Constitution cannot be destroyed.

326. The validity of the argument in favour of Natural Right will depend upon whether there is such a Right and whether it was recognized by the Constitution of India and whether such a Right was reserved for the people of India.

327. Jawaharlal Nehru had said that even though the Constituent Assembly wanted the Constitution to be as solid and as permanent a structure, it had to be acknowledged that there was no permanence in a Constitution. He rejected the idea of an unchanging and static Constitution.

328. In the battle for defence of fundamental freedoms, it may not be possible to say, as Justice Mc Reynolds of the U.S. Supreme Court has said in the National Prohibition case regarding validity of the 18th Amendment of the U.S. Constitution, that he was unable to come to any conclusion. There is also no use for the argument that since there could be no freedom to end freedom even if the people desire to enslave themselves, the Supreme Court must act to preserve freedom.

329. It would be difficult to accept the argument that where legislators have not provided adequate safeguards for protection of civil liberties, the Courts must preserve individual Rights.

330. Judges are not law-givers. It is relevant to mention that the Constituent Assembly had rejected the due process clause of the U.S. Constitution. In USA, there was a time when the Supreme Court used to invalidate laws because such laws were thought to be incompatible with due process of law. In Lochner *versus* New York (1904), the U.S. Supreme Court invoked the due process clause to strike down a law, which restricted work in Bakeries to ten hours per day and sixty hours per week. It was considered as undue interference with the Right of adult workers to contract with respect to their means of livelihood.

331. The framers of our Constitution chose the expression "procedure established by law" in Article 21 of the Constitution in preference to "due process of law".

332. There is difference between the power of amendment of the U.S. Constitution contained in Article V of the Constitution and power of amendment of our Constitution contained in Article 368.

333. Sir Henry Maine has said that the U.S. Supreme Court is a unique creation. The history of the United States has been written not only in the halls of the Congress or the fields of battle but to a great extent in the chambers of the Supreme Court. Though from time to time, the U.S. Supreme Court was urged to declare that there were certain inherent limitations on power of amendment in Article V of the U.S. Constitution, the argument of implied limitations on power of amendment of the Constitution has been brushed aside by the U.S. Supreme Court as unworthy of serious attention.

334. As Sir Maurice Gwyer, a Chief Justice of the Federal Court of India, said in the advisory opinion in The Central Provinces and Berar Act of 1938 (AIR 1939 F.C.), that a broad and liberal spirit should inspire those whose duty it is to interpret the Constitution. He also said that in exercise of power of Judicial Review, the Courts should not act as a check of the hoary past on the present and the future. As Schwartz said in his book, *A Basic History of The U.S. Supreme Court*, it is the present that represents the will of the people and it is that will that must ultimately be given effect in a democracy.

335. 'Law' is not, in the phrase of Justice Holmes, a brooding omnipotence in the sky. In the Republic of India, "Law" is a flexible instrument of social order.

336. Words as "law" and "amendment" are not occurring in a textbook prescribed for students of a secondary school so that one can find their meaning by consulting a dictionary and a book of grammar. "Law" & "amendment" occurring in a Constitution occur in a single complex instrument in which one part may throw light on another so that the Constitution must hold a balance of all its parts. As Justice Holmes of the U.S. Supreme Court said in Towne *versus* Eisner (1917),

"a word is not a crystal, transparent and unchanged; it is the skin of living thought and may vary greatly in colour and content according to circumstances and the time in which it is used."

337. The main questions which arise for decision are:

(a) What is the ratio of I.C. Golaknath case (AIR 1967 SC 1643) and whether it deserves to be upheld?

(b) If judgment of the majority in I.C. Golaknath case (AIR 1967 SC 1643) is incorrect, what is the extent of the implied limitations, if any, on power of the Parliament to amend the Constitution?

338. In Sankari Prasad Singh Deo case (AIR 1951 SC 458), Justice Patanjali Sastri delivered the unanimous judgment for the Court and held that though "law" would ordinarily include Constitutional amendment, there was a clear demarcation between ordinary law, made in exercise of legislative power and constitutional amendment made in exercise of constituent power. Justice Patanjali Sastri also held that in absence of a clear indication to the contrary, Fundamental Rights are not immune from amendment under Article 368.

339. The next important landmark was the Constitution (Seventeenth Amendment) Act 1964 which was challenged in Sajjan Singh *versus* State of Rajasthan (AIR 1965 SC 845). By majority judgment – delivered by Chief Justice P.B. Gajendragadkar – it was held that the expression 'amendment of the Constitution' includes the power to amend under Article 368 all provisions of the Constitution. It was held that Article 13(2) of the Constitution applied to ordinary law and not to constitutional amendments.

340. In I.C. Golaknath case (AIR 1967 SC 1643) the majority of judges – including Chief Justice K. Subba Rao – overruled the earlier two judgments.

341. Justice M. Hidaytullah agreed with the majority judgment in I.C. Golaknath case (AIR 1967 SC 1643) with some reservations. His views are summed up as follows:

(a) The power of amendment of the Constitution must be with the State.

(b) Article 368 outlines a procedure, which, if followed, can result in amendment of the Constitution.

(c) Procedure of amendment laid down in Article 368 – if at all can be called a power – is a legislative power; but it is *sui generis*.

(d) Constitutional Amendments are "law" within the meaning of "law" in Article 13(2) of the Constitution.

(e) Only Fundamental Rights are outside the power of amendment of the Parliament. Otherwise any provision of the Constitution can be amended under Article 368.

(f) For amendment of Fundamental Rights, Parliament may convoke another Constituent Assembly by enacting a law under the 'residuary power' in Entry 97 of the Union List.

(g) Parliament has no power to amend Article 368 so as to confer on itself power to amend the Fundamental Rights.

(h) The earlier Amendments of the Constitution which abridged Fundamental Rights can be protected by not invoking the doctrine of prospective overruling but by invoking the principle of acquiescence in those Amendments for a long time.

342. Justice K.N. Wanchoo, who delivered the leading minority judgment in I.C. Golaknath case (AIR 1967 SC 1643) came to the following conclusions:

(a) Both the procedure and the power of amendment of the Constitution are contained in Article 368 and not in Entry 97 of the Union List.

(b) The expression 'amendment' must be given a wide meaning to include addition, deletion and substitution of existing provisions in the Constitution.

(c) Under Article 368, the Parliament can amend any provision in our Constitution.

(d) The expression "law" in Article 13(2) includes ordinary law passed by the Parliament or the State legislatures in exercise of their legislative power but not constitutional amendments under Article 368.

(e) The power to amend the Constitution, being a constituent power, is not subject to any implied limitation.

343. Justice R.S. Bachwat agreed with Justice K.N. Wanchoo but held that whether basic feature of the Constitution as the federal form of Government or the Republican form of Government could be amended need not be gone into as these issues did not arise for a decision in I.C. Golaknath case (AIR 1967 SC 1643).

344. Justice V. Ramaswamy broadly agreed with Justice K.N. Wanchoo and Justice R.S. Bachawat and held that the expression "law" in Article 13(2) did not include 'constitutional amendment'. Justice V. Ramaswamy also held that the Preamble could be amended under Article 368. The power of amendment also extended to amending some of the basic features of the Constitution as the distribution of legislative power between the Union Government and the State Governments and the Parliamentary form of Government. There is no implied limitation on power of amendment under Article 368 of the Constitution.

345. The majority of Judges in I.C. Golaknath Case (AIR 1967 SC 1643) including Chief Justice K. Subba Rao and Justice M. Hidaytullah held that the expression "law" in Article 13(2) also includes constitutional amendment and there is no distinction in this regard between ordinary law and Constitutional law.

346. Chief Justice K. Subba Rao speaking for the majority of Judges in I.C. Golaknath case (AIR 1967 SC 1643) held that if the Constitution had to be radically altered, the residuary power in Entry 97 in the Union List could be invoked to convene a new Constituent Assembly.

347. Justice M. Hidaytullah took a different view and held that to make radical alternation in the Constitution so as to abridge the Fundamental Rights, a new Constituent Assembly could be called after passing a law under Entry 97 of the Union List.

348. It is significant to note that the Court in I.C. Golaknath case (AIR 1967 SC 1643) agreed that Fundamental Rights in the Constitution could be amended and taken away but they suggested different methods for achieving it.

349. The petitioners in I.C. Golaknath case (AIR 1967 SC 1643) won only a Pyrrhic victory. They came to the Court not for a decision on an academic issue but to obtain a declaration that the laws, which offended their Fundamental Rights were unconstitutional. These laws were upheld by the Court by applying the doctrine of prospective overruling. The petitioners left the Court with the satisfaction that the posterity will enjoy the fruit of the walnut tree planted by them. But it looked as if a storm was brewing threatening the very existence of the tree.

350. Six out of eleven judges in I.C. Golaknath case (AIR 1967 SC 1643) held that Article 368 contained not only the procedure but the power to amend the Constitution. These six Judges did not agree with Chief Justice K. Subba Rao and his four brother Judges that Article 368 merely dealt with the procedure of amendment of the Constitution.

351. Justice Y.V. Chandrachud also held that Article 368 must deal both with the procedure and the produce of that procedure. The marginal note to Article 368, "procedure for Amendment of the Constitution" was only a catchword and was partially correct.

352. The history of the residuary power since the days of the Government of India Act 1935, and the scheme of distribution of legislative power in the present Constitution show that if a subject of legislative power was prominently present in minds of the framers of the Constitution, it would not have been relegated to a residuary matter in Entry 97 of the Union List.

353. The legislative power in Entry 97 of the Union List belongs to the Parliament exclusively. The power to amend the Constitution cannot be located in Entry 97 of the Union List as in regard to matters falling within proviso to Article 368, Parliament does not possess exclusive power to amend the Constitution.

354. Entry 97 in the Union List has to be read with Article 245 of the Constitution. Article 245 starts with the sentence, "subject to the provisions of the Constitution". Therefore, under Entry 97 in the Union List read with Article 245, no amendment could be made to any part of the Constitution, as any amendment is bound to be inconsistent with provisions of the unamended Constitution.

355. Justice Y.V. Chandrachud posed the question whether power to amend under Article 368 is unfettered or is there any implied limitation on the power?

356. In answering the question, Justice Y.V. Chandrachud held that the word amendment is not a term of art and has no precise meaning. He also held that the power to amend the Constitution has some implied limitation, which does not empower the Parliament to damage or destroy any of its essential features. In other words, Article 368 should not be understood to express the death-wish of the Constitution. Parliament, in exercise of powers under Article 368, cannot arrogate to itself the role of an Official Liquidator of the Constitution.

357. The Indian Constitution is neither the first written Constitution of the world nor of course the last. Since the American Constitution – the first written Constitution in the world framed in 1787 – the word amendment has found place in many written Constitutions.

358. In all written Constitutions, including the American Constitution, the word 'amendment' has been used as an expression of the widest import.

359. The history of the Government of India Act 1935 also leaves no scope to doubt the wide sweep of the expression 'amendment'. By the Government of India (Third Amendment) Act 1939, Section 291 of the Government of India Act 1935 was repealed and the new Section 291 was substituted. Therefore, 'amendment' in the Government of India (Third Amendment) Act 1939 included the power of addition, alteration and repeal of the existing provisions.

360. Amendment in Article 368 connotes a power of the widest amplitude to make additions, alterations or variations. The proviso to Article 368 confers the power to amend the amending power in Article 368 itself. Thus, there can be no better evidence of width of the power under Article 368.

361. As a Nation works out its destiny, new horizons unfold themselves, new challenges arise and therefore, new answers have to be framed to meet the new challenges. The power of amendment is a safety valve. As Carl J. Friedrich has said in his book, *Constitutional Government and Democracy*, the Constituent power bears an intimate relation to Revolution. When the amending provisions fail to work in adjusting the constitutional document to altered needs, Revolution may occur.

362. The rule of strict construction, which applied to a penal or a taxing statute is out of place in interpreting a constitutional provision. As the Privy Council had observed a construction most beneficial to the widest possible amplitude must be adopted in interpretation of a Constitution.

363. The word 'law' in Article 13(2) does not include a constitutional amendment. Article 368 avoids with scrupulous care the use of the word "law". As Sir Ivor Jennings says in his book, *The Law and the Constitution*, the term "constitutional law" is never used in the sense of laws made under the Constitution. Constitutional law is the fundamental, superior or paramount law. As A.V. Dicey has said in, *Introduction to the Study of the Laws of the Constitution*, the legislature in a Federal Constitution is a subordinate law-making body whose laws are in the nature of bye-laws within the authority conferred by the Constitution.

364. It has been urged by the petitioners that several constitutional laws of the former princely states were in force at commencement of the Constitution on 26 January 1950 and the object of Article 13(1) was to protect these constitutional laws of the former princely states. The answer is: it is doubtful if the former princely states had a proper Constitution. But even assuming that such Constitutions were at one time in force in the princely states, they ceased to be constitutional law on integration of the princely states with the Indian Union. Article 13(1) of our Constitution, therefore, does not include any constitutional law.

365. Article 13(3)(a) of the Constitution contains a definition of "law" as including any ordinance, order, bye-law, rule, regulation, notification, custom or usage having the force of law. If the framers of the Constitution wanted to include 'constitutional amendment' within the meaning of 'law' in Article 13(2), they would have included it in the inclusive definition of 'law' in Article 13(3)(a) of the Constitution.

366. The Corpus Juris Secundum makes it clear that under Article V of the U.S. Constitution, the Congress makes a proposal for amendment of the Constitution and if the states ratify it, neither the Congress nor the States are legislating. Therefore, a constitutional amendment in the U.S. is not ordinary law.

367. There is a fundamental distinction between constitutional law and ordinary law. In case of a constitutional law, its validity is inherent whereas in case of an ordinary law, it has to be tested on the touchstone of the Constitution. The majority judgment in I.C. Golaknath case (AIR 1967 SC 1643) overlooked this vital distinction between constitutional law and ordinary law.

368. There is also a fundamental distinction between the procedure for enacting an ordinary law and the procedure for passing a constitutional amendment under Article 368. In case of an ordinary law, the special two-thirds majority required for an amendment of the Constitution is not necessary. In case of disagreement between the two Houses, there is a provision for joint sitting where the legislative Bill can be passed by ordinary majority. In case of Constitutional Amendment Bill, there is no provision for a joint sitting of both Houses of Parliament. Moreover, the process of ratification by at least half of the state legislatures in case of an amendment to matters contained in the proviso to Article 368 cannot be possibly called an ordinary legislative power.

369. The Indian Constitution is rigid because for amendment of the Constitution, the special procedure in Article 368 has to be followed.

370. The distinction between rigid and flexible constitution brings into sharp focus the true distinction between legislative and constituent power. In a rigid constitution, the power to make laws is the genus of which the legislative and constituent powers are the species, the differentia being the procedure of amendment. If the procedure is ordinary, the power is legislative; if it is special, it is constituent. This distinction was not appreciated by the majority of judges in I.C. Golaknath case (AIR 1967 SC 1643).

371. On close scrutiny, the argument of implied limitations on power of amendment in our Constitution cannot be sustained. It has been argued that implied limitations are those which are implicit in the scheme of the Constitution. It has been argued that most of the

adequate. The Madras Act was however struck down by the Court presided over by Chief Justice K. Subba Rao on the ground of equality before law in Article 14 of the Constitution as for land required for other public purpose full monetary compensation as per the market value of land had to be paid under the Land Acquisition Act 1894, whereas it was not so in the Madras Act.

399. In Union of India *versus* Metal Corporation (AIR 1967 SC 637), the Supreme Court made some changes in their earlier pronouncement in P. Vajravelu Mudaliar's case (AIR 1965 SC 1017) by stating that if the principles for fixing the amount are relevant to the fixation of compensation and are not arbitrary, the Court shall not question adequacy of the amount.

400. Two years later, in State of Gujarat *versus* Shantilal Mangaldas (AIR 1969 SC 634) the Court overruled its earlier decisions in both P. Vajravelu case (AIR 1965 SC 1017) and the Metal Corporation case (AIR 1967 SC 637). The Court held that the amount of compensation could not be challenged on the ground that it was not the just equivalent. Further, the Court held that the principles for determining the amount also could not be challenged on the ground that the principles for determining the amount would not result in payment of just equivalent for private property acquired. But this did not mean that the amount paid for acquisition of private property would be illusory. Therefore, the principles for determining the compensation could be challenged on the ground that they were irrelevant to determination of compensation but not on the ground that the amount awarded as a result of the specified principles was not just or fair compensation.

401. In R.C. Cooper *versus* Union of India (AIR 1970 SC 564) – popularly known as the Bank Nationalization Case – ten out of eleven Judges of the Constitution Bench virtually overruled the decision in Shantilal Mangaldas case (AIR 1969 SC 634). The Court held that if a law providing for acquisition of private property provided for compensation in form of "Bonds" and the present value of what was determined to be given was thereby substantially reduced, the law infringed the constitutional guarantee and was *ultra vires*.

402. In the Constitution (Twenty-fifth Amendment) Act 1971, Parliament has taken care to remove the uncertainty of law relating to compensation for acquisition of private property to give effect to Article 39 of the Directive Principles of State Policy and substituted the word "amount" in Article 31(2) and provided that nothing in Article 19(1)(f) (i.e. Right to acquire, hold and dispose of property) shall affect any law referred to in Article 31(2) of the Constitution. This immunity of attack on the ground of violating the since repealed Article 19(1)(f) was provided in the Constitution (Twenty-fifth Amendment) Act 1971 as the Judgment in R.C. Cooper's case (AIR 1970 564) overruled a long line of decisions that Article 19(1)(f) and Article 31(2) were mutually exclusive. In other words, R.C. Cooper's case, overruled the first major decision of the Supreme Court on Fundamental Rights in A.K. Gopalan *versus* State of Madras (AIR 1950 SC 27) that each Fundamental Right in the Constitution is exclusive and self-contained and there is no interrelationship among the Fundamental Rights.

403. N.A. Palkhivala mounted a virulent attack on provision in Article 31C of the Constitution introduced by the (Twenty-fifth Amendment) Act 1971. His arguments are as follows:

(a) Article 31C destroys the Rule of Law by subverting the supremacy of the Constitution. It gives a blank charter to the Parliament and the state legislatures to amend the Constitution.

(b) By enacting Article 31C, Parliament has resorted to the procedure of maintaining the Fundamental Rights unamended but authorizing the enactment of laws, which are void for offending the Fundamental Rights, by validating them by a legal fiction that they shall not be deemed to be void.

404. Though Fundamental Rights constitute the ark of the Constitution, it cannot be denied that to achieve the objectives in the Preamble, the Directive Principles are fundamental in governance of the country. What is fundamental for governance cannot be less significant than what is fundamental in the life of an individual. That one is justiciable and the other is non-justiciable may show the intrinsic difficulties in making the latter enforceable through legal process but that distinction does not bear on their relative importance. As Granville Austin has said in his book, *The Indian Constitution – Cornerstone of a Nation* both Fundamental Rights and Directive Principles together constitute, the conscience of the Constitution.

405. Article 31(2), however, does not authorize a legislature to confiscate or expropriate private property.

406. The specific obligation to pay an amount or to fix principles to pay an amount means that the amount fixed for acquisition of private property cannot be illusory.

407. As long as the Right to Property has a place in the Constitution, none can mock at the private property owner and ridicule his Right by saying that his fortune will be taken for a farthing.

408. But the amount fixed for payment cannot be challenged on the ground that it is inadequate and falls short of market value of the property acquired. Even the principles for fixation of the amount for acquisition of private property cannot be challenged on the ground that they have no relationship with market value of the property.

409. But as stated earlier, the amount can be challenged as illusory and the principles for fixation of the amount on the ground that they are not relevant for such fixation. But if the principles for fixation of the amount are shown to be principles bearing on social good, it may not be possible to say that the principles are irrelevant.

410. As stated earlier, constitutional amendments partake of the vitality of the Constitution itself. The exclusion of challenge under Article 19(1)(f) – the Right to acquire, hold and dispose of property – in regard to a law passed under Article 31(2) cannot, therefore, be deemed as unconstitutional.

411. It is not open to the Judge to cut the Gordian Knot in Article 31C. [**N.B.:** King Gordius of Phrygia had tied a knot which an Oracle had said can only be untied by the future Master of Asia. Alexander The Great, failing to untie the knot, cut it with his sword.]

412. Article 31C does not delegate the power of amendment of the Constitution to the State legislatures. Article 31C only identified a class of legislation to exempt such legislation from operations of Articles 14, 19 and 31. Earlier by the Constitution (First Amendment)

Act 1951, some agrarian laws, providing for estate abolition, had been protected from attack on the ground of infringement of Articles 14, 19 and 31. Article 31C protects some other legislations – to implement policies in clauses (b) and (c) of Article 39 – from similar attack on ground of infringement of Articles 14, 19 and 31.

413. The provision of Article 31C that no law containing a declaration that it is for giving effect to such policy shall be called in question in any Court on the ground that it does not give effect to such policy, is also valid. Such a declaration only protects a law, which has a direct nexus with clauses (b) and (c) of Article 39.

414. No Court can ever take upon itself the task of finding out whether a law in fact gives effect to its stated policy. If such a latitude was open to the Judges, laws prohibiting sale, consumption and storage of alcoholic drinks and laws prohibiting gambling should have lost their place in the statute book long ago.

415. Validity of Article 31B has been accepted in a decision of the Supreme Court viz. State of Bihar *versus* Kameswar Singh (AIR 1952 SC 252) where Chief Justice Patanjali Sastri spoke for the Court. Even Chief Justice K. Subba Rao upheld the vires of Article 31B in Jeejeebhoy *versus* Assistant Collector, Thane (AIR 1965 SC 1096).

416. The opening words of Article 31B that 'without prejudice to the generality of the provisions contained in Article 31A, none of the Acts and Regulations in the Ninth Schedule shall be deemed to be void on ground of infringement of any Fundamental Right, shows that even a law not covered under Article 31A shall be protected if it finds a place in the Ninth Schedule. In other words, Article 31B is not governed by Article 31A and hence the Constitution (Twenty-ninth Amendment) Act 1971, which has placed two Kerala Land Reforms Amendment Acts in the Ninth Schedule, is valid.

417. Records of debates in the Constituent Assembly and in the Provisional Parliament are not admissible as aids to interpretation of the Constitution.

418. H.M. Seervai, Advocate-General for Maharashtra, who represented the respondent State of Kerala, said that in the Privy Purse case (AIR 1971 SC 530) and in H.S. Dhillon case (AIR 1972 SC 1061), the Supreme Court has relied upon Parliamentary debates to interpret legal provisions.

419. But a close scrutiny of the two judgments referred to shows that his contention is not correct. In the Privy Purse case (AIR 1971 SC 530), Justice J.C. Shah referred to the speech of Sardar Patel in the Constituent Assembly to indicate the circumstances in which certain guarantees were given to the former Rulers of Princely States on their integration with the Indian Union.

420. In the Privy Purse case (AIR 1971 SC 530) Justice G.K. Mitter referred to the Parliamentary debates to interpret Article 363 of the Constitution, which bars jurisdiction of Courts in disputes arising out of certain treaties and agreements with former Rulers of Indian states but he did so without discussing whether such speeches were admissible in interpreting a provision of the Constitution.

421. In H.S. Dhillion's case (AIR 1972 SC 1061) the Supreme Court did not refer to Parliamentary debates for interpretation of the Constitution.

422. It may not be expedient to depend upon records of Parliamentary Debates to interpret provisions of the Constitutions. Parliamentary Debates might be used for the limited purpose of whether a phrase or expression in the Constitution was at all discussed in the Constituent Assembly.

423. Justice Y.V. Chandrachud summed up his separate judgment as follows:

(a) The decision of the majority of Judges in I.C. Golaknath case (AIR 1967 SC 1643) that Article 368 only lays down the procedure for amendment of the Constitution whereas the power of amendment may be located in Entry 97 of the Union List in the Seventh Schedule of the Constitution read with Articles 245, 246 and 248, is not correct.

(b) The decision of the majority of Judges in I.C. Golaknath case (AIR 1967 SC 1643) and the decision of Justice M. Hidaytullah who delivered a separate judgment in that case that there was no distinction between an ordinary law and a law amending the Constitution is not correct. Article 13(2) only refers to ordinary law and not amendment of the Constitution under Article 368.

(c) The decision of majority of Judges in I.C. Golaknath case (AIR 1967 SC 1643) and Justice M. Hidaytullah, who delivered a separate judgment in that case that Parliament has no power to amend any Fundamental Right is also not correct.

(d) Article 368 confers wide and unfettered power of amendment of the Constitution and such power can reach every part and each provision of the Constitution.

(e) Preamble to the Constitution is a part of the Constitution and can be amended under Article 368.

(f) There are no implied limitations on power of amendment of the Constitution.

(g) The Constitution (Twenty-fourth Amendment) Act 1971 is valid as it only declares the true legal position as it existed even before the amendment.

(h) Clauses (2)(a) and 2(b) of the Constitution (Twenty-fifth Amendment) Act 1971 are valid. Though the Courts have no power to question a law on the ground that the amount fixed for acquisition of private property is not adequate or that the whole or any part of the amount is to be given otherwise than in cash, Courts have power to question such a law, if the amount fixed is illusory or if the principles adopted for determining the amount are wholly irrelevant for its fixation.

(i) Clause (3) of the Constitution (Twenty-fifth Amendment) Act 1971 – which introduced Article 31C – is valid. Inspite of the declaration in the law for acquisition of property that it seeks to implement provisions in clauses (b) and (c) of Article 39 in the chapter on the Directive Principles of State Policy, the Courts can examine whether there is direct nexus between the law and provisions in Article 39(b) and (c). If there is no direct nexus, the law for acquisition will not be immune from an attack, for violation of Articles 14, 19 and 31 of the Constitution.

(j) The Constitution (Twenty-ninth Amendment) Act 1971, which put two Kerala Land Reforms Amendment Acts in the Ninth Schedule of the Constitution, is valid.

Chapter 10

Indira Gandhi *versus* Raj Narain (AIR 1975 SC 2299)

[CHIEF JUSTICE A.N. RAY, JUSTICE H.R. KHANNA, JUSTICE K.K. MATHEW, JUSTICE M.H. BEG AND JUSTICE Y.V. CHANDRACHUD]

Case Summary

In Civil Appeal number 887 of 1975 before the Supreme Court, the Appellant is Indira Nehru Gandhi and the respondent is Raj Narain. Raj Narain also filed a cross-objection, which is listed as Civil Appeal number 909 of 1975. The Court directed that both the appeals would be heard together. The appeals arise out of the judgment dated 12 June 1975 of Justice J.M.L. Sinha of the Allahabad High Court. Justice J.M.L. Sinha had held Indira Gandhi guilty of corrupt practice under the Representation of the People Act 1951 and debarred her from holding any elected office for six years from date of the judgment.

1. Chief Justice A.N. Ray, who presided over the five judge Constitution Bench delivered a separate judgment. The salient points in the judgment of Chief Justice A.N. Ray are as follows.

2. The Constitution (Thirty-Ninth Amendment) Act 1975 passed by the Parliament – after the judgment of Justice J.M.L. Sinha of the Allahabad High Court – contained features, which are as follows:

   (i) Article 71 of the Constitution has been replaced by a new Article 71. The new Article stipulated that Parliament may by law regulate any matter relating to election of the President and the Vice President of India.

   (ii) Article 329A – a new Article – was inserted in the Constitution. There are six clauses in the new Article 329A. They are as follows:

      (a) No election to either House of Parliament of any person, who holds the office of Prime Minister or Speaker of the House of the People, shall be called in question except before an Authority to be set up by law.

      (b) The validity of any such law to be enacted and the decision of the Authority to be set up shall not be called in question in any Court on any ground.

(c) If an election petition is pending against the Prime Minister or the Speaker, such election petition shall abate and their election may be challenged under the new law under Article 329A.

(d) Clause (4) of Article 329A, which directly concerns the present appeal by Indira Gandhi, stipulates that no law enacted by Parliament before commencement of the Constitution (Thirty-Ninth Amendment) Act 1975 shall apply to any election of the Prime Minister or the speaker of the House of the People and notwithstanding any order of any Court declaring such election to be void, such election shall continue to be valid in all respects.

(e) Clause (5) of Article 329A stipulated that any appeal or cross-appeal pending before the Supreme Court shall be disposed off in accordance with provisions of clause (4) of the new Article 329A.

(f) The provisions of the Article 329A shall have effect notwithstanding any provision of the Constitution.

3. By Article 329A, the Representation of the People Act 1951, the Representation of the People (Amendment) Act 1974 and the Election Laws (Amendment) Act 1975 are included in the Ninth Schedule of the Constitution to protect their constitutionality.

4. Shanti Bhusan, Counsel for Raj Narain, contended that the Representation of the People Act 1951 and the other two Acts do not enjoy constitutional immunity by being included in the Ninth Schedule as these Acts destroy the basic structure of the Constitution. The counsel also argued that clause (4) of Article 329A is exercise of a purely judicial power by Parliament and it is not a part of the constituent power of the Parliament under Article 368.

5. The counsel argued that clause (4) of Article 329A is also subversive of the Rule of Law and the principle of Judicial Review.

6. Chief Justice A.N. Ray held that power of the legislature to validate matters, which have been held as illegal by the Courts has been a fairly well-known practice. The Sales Tax validation cases and the Election validation cases are illustrations in this regard. The effect of validation is to change the law with retrospective effect so as to alter the basis of any judgment, which might have been delivered by the Courts on the basis of the old law and thus make the judgment of the Court ineffective.

7. When invalid elections by reason of corrupt practice have been declared as valid by the legislature changing the definition of corrupt practice with retrospective effect, the Supreme Court have upheld the election. The leading case in this regard is Kanta Kathuria *versus* Manak Chand Surana (AIR 1970 SC 694).

8. Clause (4) in article 329A has made the following changes:

(i) First, it has wiped out judgment of any Court on election of the Prime Minister as a Member of the House of the People. It has also made infructuous any pending election petition in this regard.

(ii) The constituent power in its legislative judgment has validated an invalid election.

9. Chief Justice A.N. Ray held that a decision on an election petition has to be based on a law. Parliament has powers to enact a law and apply the same. But in this case because

of clause (4) of Article 329A, Parliament has not applied any law to decide validity of the election of the Prime Minister as a Member of the House of the People. Such an approach offends the Rule of Law. By clause (4) of Article 329A, Parliament has passed not a law but a declaratory judgment in exercise of judicial power. Such a course of action is not permissible under the scheme of separation of powers in the Constitution. [N.B.: After exhaustive discussion on the nature of corrupt practice by Indira Gandhi, Chief Justice A.N. Ray delivered a rather lengthy judgment setting aside the judgment of the Allahabad High Court dated 12 June 1975 and dismissed the cross-objection of the Respondent, Raj Narain. Chief Justice A.N. Ray had also declared clause (4) of the Article 329A of the Constitution – inserted by the Constitution (Thirty-Ninth Amendment) Act 1975 – as *ultra vires*.]

10. Justice H.R. Khanna also delivered a separate judgment. The salient point in the judgment are as follows.

11. The question is whether under clause (4) of Article 329A, it is open for the Parliament as the Constituent Authority under Article 368 to declare a judgment of a High Court as void or whether such a judgment can be challenged only before the Supreme Court.

12. Although in the Indian Constitution, there is no provision supporting a rigid theory of separation of powers, by and large, the spheres of judicial and legislative functions have been demarcated. The Constitution does not permit the legislature to encroach upon the judicial sphere and exercise adjudicatory functions in a disputed election.

13. The judgments of the Supreme Court lay down that whereas a legislature is competent to change with retrospective effect the provisions of a law, which formed the basis of a judgment, it is not competent to declare a judgment of a Court or a Tribunal as void.

14. It has been held by constitutional experts that a legislation may not destroy, annul, set aside, vacate, reverse, modify or impair a judgment of a Court so as to take away private Rights vested by the judgment. A statute attempting to do so is a violation of the constitutional guarantee of the procedure established by law.

15. It was argued by counsel of Indira Gandhi that a Constituent Authority in exercise of its power – as the Indian Parliament in exercise of its power of amendment under Article 368 – can declare a judgment of the Court as void.

16. In reply, it has been argued by counsel for Raj Narain that a Constituent Authority cannot declare a judgment of a Court as void and act as a super Court in the same way as a Court cannot operate as a super legislature.

17. In Kesavananda Bharati case (AIR 1973 SC 1461) the majority of judges held that Parliament has no powers to alter the basic structure of the Constitution by an amendment under Article 368. The democratic form of government was held to be a part of the basic structure of the Constitution.

18. Democracy postulates that there should be free and fair elections at periodic intervals and disputes relating to any election should be adjudicated by a fair and impartial machinery.

19. In the United Kingdom, any dispute regarding election to the House of Commons is tried by two judges on the rota for trial of election petitions. In the United States of America, the Constitution provides that each House of the Congress shall be judge of the election returns and the qualification of candidates for election to the House of the Representatives or the Senate as the case may be. Major countries as Australia, Japan and the Federal Republic of Germany have similar provisions.

20. If validity of an election to the Parliament is challenged on some ground, the said election can be declared as valid only if there is a prescribed forum for adjudicating the matter according to law.

21. To confer absolute validity upon the election of a particular candidate would necessarily mean that however gross might be the impropriety or irregularity which might have vitiated election of a candidate, the gross impropriety or irregularity would not be questioned and the candidate would be deemed to have been validly elected.

22. The vice of declaration of validity of election of the Prime Minister as per clause (4) of Article 329A is aggravated by the fact that such a declaration is made after the Allahabad High Court has declared the election of the Prime Minister to the House of the people as void.

23. In the famous judgment of Marbury *versus* Madison (1803), the U.S. Supreme Court – speaking through Chief Justice Marshall – held that the government of the United States has been emphatically termed a government of the law and not of men. The U.S. Supreme Court has also held that no man is so high as to be above the law. This principle also applies in the context of the Indian Constitution.

24. Justice H.R. Khanna however observed that election dispute concerning the office of the Prime Minister and the Speaker need not be always decided by Courts of Law. In France, Japan and the United States of America, determination of such disputes is vested in authorities other than the Courts of law. But the question is whether it is permissible in a Democracy that a dispute with regard to validity of an election shall not be raised before any forum and shall not be governed by any law.

25. Law prescribes the abstract principles for adjudication of individual cases. Roscoe Pound has said law is the authoritative material for guiding action in a politically organized society. Law is not the same as judgment. Law lays down the norm in abstract terms with sanction against the guilty. Judgment represents the decision arrived at by application of the law to facts of a case.

26. The net result is that clause (4) of Article 329A is struck down as violative of free and fair election – an essential postulate of a Democracy and a part of the basic structure of the Constitution.

27. After an exhaustive discussion of merits of the appeal of Indira Gandhi in regard to the allegations of corrupt practice Justice H.R. Khanna set aside the judgment of Justice J.M.L. Sinha of the Allahabad High Court.

28. Justice K.K. Mathew also delivered a separate judgment. The salient points of his judgment are in the following paragraphs.

29. Raj Narain, filed an election petition against Indira Gandhi in which he made seven charges of corrupt practice out of which only two charges were held as proved by Justice J.M.L. Sinha.

30. The consequence was that Indira Gandhi incurred the disqualification under Section 8A of The Representation of People Act 1951.

31. On 10 August 1975, Parliament under Article 368 passed the Constitution (Thirty-Ninth Amendment) Act 1975. By this Amendment, Article 71 of the Constitution was replaced by a new Article 71, which stipulated that:
    (a) Parliament may by law regulate any matter relating to election of the President of India or the Vice-President of India including the grounds on which such election might be challenged.
    (b) All disputes relating to election of the above high constitutional functionaries shall be decided by an Authority in such manner as shall be laid down by the Parliament by law.
    (c) The new Article 71 also provided that the decision of such Authority shall not be called into question by any Court.

32. By the Constitution (Thirty-Ninth Amendment) Act 1975, Article 329A was inserted in the Constitution which provided that the election to the House of the People of the Prime Minister and the Speaker of the House of the People shall not be called into question except before an Authority set up by law. Article 329A also provided that validity of any law to be enacted and the decision of the Authority referred to regarding disputes to the election of the Prime Minister and the Speaker shall not be called into question in any Court.

33. Clause (4) of the Constitution (Thirty-Ninth Amendment) Act 1975 provided that no law enacted by the Parliament before the Constitution Amendment Act 1975 shall be deemed to have applied to any election of the Prime Minister or the Speaker of the House of the People and "such election shall not be deemed to be void or ever to have become void" notwithstanding any order made by any Court.

34. Any appeal or cross-appeal against any such order of any Court pending before the Supreme Court immediately before commencement of the Constitution (Thirty-Ninth Amendment) Act 1975 shall be decided in accordance with clause (4) of the Amendment Act 1975.

35. Counsel for Raj Narain argued that by declaring the invalid election of the Prime Minister as valid without changing the basis of the law the Constitution (Thirty-Ninth Amendment) Act 1975 has damaged the system of free and fair election to high elective offices and free and fair election of such functionaries is a part of the basic structure of the Constitution.

36. The majority of Judges have held in Kesavananda Bharati *versus* State of Kerala (AIR 1973 SC 1461) that though under Article 368, the Parliament can amend any Fundamental Right and any other provision of the Constitution, by such amendment, Parliament cannot alter the basic structure of the Constitution.

37. Clause (4) of the Constitution (Thirty-Ninth Amendment) Act 1975 damages the democratic and republican polity visualized by the Constitution and hence clause (4) of Article 329A is *ultra vires*.

38. It was contended by the Counsel for Indira Gandhi that in England, originally the House of Commons decided the election disputes of its Members. It was only in the year 1770, the power for deciding an election dispute was delegated to Committees of the Parliament.

39. It was pointed out that at present, even in England, the adjudication of election petitions to the House of Commons is done by a panel of judges. The Judges make a report to the House of Commons when a charge of electoral malpractice is proved. The report has to be accepted by the House of Commons to establish the charge.

40. The U.S. Constitution stipulates that each House of the Congress shall be the judge of the election returns and qualifications of its Members. But in whichever body or authority, the jurisdiction to adjudicate election dispute is vested, exercise of the jurisdiction must be judicial in character. It has been held by the Supreme Court of India as early as the year 1955 that any Authority adjudicating an election dispute was performing a judicial function.

41. Justice Oliver Wendell Holmes had said about an adjudication as follows:

"A judicial inquiry investigates, declares and enforces liabilities as they stand on present or past facts and under laws which exist."

42. As contrasted to adjudication, legislation is concerned with making a binding rule of conduct to be enforced in future.

43. The Privy Council, had held that judicial power is concerned with existing Rights which parties had at the inception of the suit.

44. In Kanta Kathuria *versus* Manak Chand Surana (AIR 1970 SC 694) a new law was enacted by the legislature to remove the basis of electoral disqualifications. In this case, the judgment of the Court setting aside the election was not held as void but only basis of the judgment was changed by the legislature amending the law with retrospective effect.

45. Counsel for Raj Narain also challenged the Parliament's constituent power to make a void election valid as it was against the doctrine of separation of powers – a part of the basic structure of the Constitution.

46. The exception to the doctrine of separation of powers are only a few which are as follows:
    (i) when the legislature passes a resolution to impeach a Judge of the High Court or the Supreme Court for proven misbehavior;
    (ii) when the executive exercises a veto over any legislation – as in the United States of America – and
    (iii) when in exercise of power of Judicial Review, the High Courts and the Supreme Court strike down laws passed by the legislature as *ultra vires*.

47. Whereas in USA and Australia, judicial power is vested exclusively in the Supreme Court, in India judicial power is not vested exclusively in the Supreme Court. But the Parliament cannot exercise judicial power by declaring a void election as valid.

48. Clause (4) of the Constitution (Twenty-Ninth Amendment) Act 1975 is like a Bill of Attainder and is invalid as it gives the Parliament the power to declare a judgment of a competent court as a nullity.

49. Even though in Kesavananda Bharati's case (AIR 1973 SC 1461) the Supreme Court did not specifically mention Article 14 – guaranteeing Equality before Law – as a part of the basic structure of the Constitution, in the aforesaid judgment, Rule of Law has been identified as a part of the basic structure of the Constitution.

50. Lord Dicey had defined the Rule of Law as supremacy of the law as opposed to arbitrary power. The Rule of Law mandates that decisions should be made by application of known principles of law. An arbitrary decision is the anti-thesis of the Rule of Law.

51. The legislature must fix some point of time before which a person cannot be a candidate in an election and a wide latitude be given to the Legislature in fixing this point. It has been held by the Supreme Court that choice of a date as a basis for classification cannot be arbitrary even if no particular reason is forthcoming unless the choice of date is shown to be either capricious or whimsical.

52. Even if it is assumed that between 07 January to 24 January 1971 Indira Gandhi obtained or procured the assistance of Yashpal Kapur, a government servant, she shall not be deemed to have committed "corrupt practice" under the Representation of the People Act 1951 as she became a candidate for the election only on 01 February 1971.

53. In view of the foregoing, Justice K.K. Mathew allowed the appeal of Indira Gandhi and set aside the judgment of Justice J.M.L. Sinha of the Allahabad High Court.

54. **N.B.:** Justice M.H. Beg delivered a separate judgment, which is rather lengthy and highly repetive.

55. The following facts were stated by Justice M.H. Beg before framing issues regarding the two Election Appeals before the Supreme Court.

56. Before the election petition against Indira Gandhi could be decided, an "explanation" was added to Section 77(1) of the Representation of the People Act 1951 having some bearing on Indira Gandhi's election expenses in the 1971 Parliamentary Election from the Rae Bareilly constituency. However, on findings of facts the "explanation" to section 77(1) of the Representation of the People Act 1971 became immaterial.

57. By his judgment, Justice J.M.L. Sinha held Indira Gandhi guilty of having used service of Yashpal Kapur in her election campaign before Yashpal Kapur ceased to be a government servant. The factual position is that though Yashpal Kapur resigned as a government servant on 14 January 1971, the acceptance of his resignation was notified on 25 January 1971. The records also indicate that Indira Gandhi became a candidate when she filed her nomination on 01 February 1971. The Notification dated 25 January 1971 made resignation of Yashpal Kapur effective from 14 January 1971 and he received no pay as a government servant from that date.

58. It is on record that Indira Gandhi became a candidate for the Parliamentary Election only on 01 February 1971 when she filed her nomination. Therefore, she could not be accused of "corrupt practice" under the Representation of the People Act 1951 for having availed herself of service of a Government Servant as a candidate for the General Election of 1971.

59. As regards appraisal of evidence in an election dispute, what Justice Krishna Iyer said in Rahim Khan *versus* Khurshid Ahmed (1974 (2) SCC 660) is relevant. Justice Krishna Iyer said that, "An election is a politically sacred public act, not of one person or one official but of the collective will of the whole constituency. Courts must respect the public expression .... and show extreme reluctance to set aside or declare as void an election which has already been held unless clear and cogent testimony compelling the Court to uphold the corrupt practice against the returned candidate is adduced. Indeed election petitions where corrupt practices are imputed must be regarded as proceedings of a quasi-criminal nature where strict proof is necessary."

60. After an elaborate discussion of implication of Article 329A, Justice M.H. Beg struck down the judgment of Justice J.M.L. Sinha declaring the election of Indira Gandhi as void and dismissed the cross-appeal of Raj Narain.

61. Justice M.H. Beg further held that the purpose of clause (4) of Article 329A was to meet the political needs of the country. It was not meant to oust the Court's jurisdiction under clause (5) of Article 329A. Briefly put, Justice M.H. Beg held that clause (4) of Article 329A does not stand on the way of consideration of appeals before the Supreme Court under the Representation of the People Act 1951.

62. Like his brother judges, Justice Y.V. Chandrachud delivered a separate judgment upholding the election of Indira Gandhi. Justice Y.V. Chandrachud also struck down clauses (4) and (5) of the new Article 329A as unconstitutional.

63. The salient points in the judgment of Justice Y.V. Chandrachud are summed up in the following paragraphs.

64. Raj Narain, who lost to Indira Gandhi from the Rae Bareilly Parliamentary Constituency in March 1971 by a margin of 1,11,810 votes, filed an election petition before the Allahabad High Court challenging the election of Indira Gandhi on several grounds. Justice J.M.L. Sinha held her guilty of corrupt practice under Section 123(7) of the Representation of the People Act 1951 on two grounds viz.,

(i) Indira Gandhi obtained assistance of officials of the Government of Uttar Pradesh for furthering her prospects in the election;

(ii) Indira Gandhi also obtained for the election campaign assistance of Yashpal Kapur, an officer of the Government of India, who was officer on special duty to the Prime Minister.

(iii) By his judgment dated 12 June 1975, Justice J.M.L. Sinha also disqualified Indira Gandhi under the Representation of the People Act 1951 for holding any elected office for a period of six years from the date of the judgment.

65. Justice J.M.L. Sinha however rejected the other five grounds urged by Raj Narain which are as follows:

(i) Indira Gandhi got assistance of flight by aeroplanes and helicopters of the Indian Air Force;

(ii) Yashpal Kapur, election agent of Indira Gandhi and her other supporters, distributed clothes and liquor to induce the voters of Rae Bareilly to vote for her;

(iii) Indira Gandhi and her supporters made appeal to the religious symbol of the cow and the calf – the election symbol of the Congress party.

(iv) Indira Gandhi and her supporters arranged vehicles to transport voters to the election booths on the day of the poll.

(v) Indira Gandhi and her supporters violated the ceiling of expenditure on election fixed under provisions of the Representation of the People Act 1951 read with Rule 90 of the Conduct of Election Rules 1961.

66. As Justice J.M.L. Sinha did not accept the aforesaid five grounds against the election of Indira Gandhi, Raj Narain filed before the Supreme Court a cross appeal against the judgment of Justice J.M.L. Sinha.

67. Both the appeal of Indira Gandhi and the cross appeal of Raj Narain were heard together by the Court.

68. Raj Narain's contention before the Court was that expenditure incurred by the Congress party in Indira Gandhi's election – including the expenditure incurred by Indira Gandhi herself – was in excess of the ceiling of authorized expenditure of Rs. 35,000/- (Rupees Thirty five thousand) for a Parliamentary candidate.

69. The aforesaid contention of Raj Narain had legal basis in a judgment of the Supreme Court in Kanwarlal Gupta *versus* Amarnath Chawla (AIR 1975 SC 308).

70. To remove the legal hurdle following the judgment in Kanwarlal Gupta's case (AIR 1975 SC 308), the President of India promulgated an Ordinance amending the Representation of the People Act to the effect that notwithstanding any judgment or order of any Court, any expenditure incurred by any political party – or by an individual or by an association of individuals – shall not be deemed to be an expenditure incurred by a candidate for a Parliamentary election.

71. The Ordinance was replaced by the Representation of the People (Amendment) Act which was to have retrospective operation from date of promulgation of the Ordinance in October 1974.

72. When the appeal of Indira Gandhi was pending before the Supreme Court, Parliament passed the Election Laws (Amendment) Act of 1975. It incorporated a new Section 8A in the Representation of the People Act 1951 empowering the President of India to decide whether a person guilty of corrupt practice shall be disqualified and if so what was the period for which such disqualification could be incurred.

73. The Election Laws (Amendment) Act of 1975 amended the Representation of the People Act 1951 to lay down that pre-nomination expenses shall not be counted towards election expenses of a candidate. It also defined a candidate as one who has been duly nominated as such. It also laid down that no symbol allotted to a candidate would be considered a religious symbol. These provisions were to take effect retrospectively and govern election appeals of Indira Gandhi and Raj Narain pending before the Supreme Court.

74. *Inter alia*, Article 329A deprives the courts of powers to try election petitions in which election to Parliament of the Prime Minister or Speaker of the House of the People is challenged.

75. Clause (4) of Article 329A frees the disputed election of the Prime Minister and the Speaker from the restraints of all elections laws. It declares such elections as valid notwithstanding any judgment to the contrary. It also stipulates that any appeal or cross-appeal pending before the Supreme Court shall be disposed off on the assumption that the judgment, under appeal, is void. In other words, the election of Indira Gandhi declared as void by Justice J.M.L. Sinha, shall continue to be valid in all respects.

76. Shanti Bhusan, appearing for Raj Narain, argued that the Thirty-Ninth Amendment of the Constitution has destroyed the separation of powers which is a part of basic structure of the Constitution. Shanti Bhusan also argued that (i) because of the Thirty-Ninth Amendment, the Legislature has adjudicated upon an election dispute, which is not permissible; (ii) because of the Thirty-Ninth Amendment, free and fair election to the House of the People of the person, who is elected by the ruling party as the Prime Minister, has been given a body blow as such election, though declared void by the High Court, is nevertheless made valid by a legislative fiat; (iii) because of the Thirty-Ninth Amendment, Judicial Review of the election of the Prime Minister as a Member of House of the People could not be possible and such an Amendment of the Constitution is *ultra vires* as Judicial Review has been upheld as a part of basic structure of the Constitution.

77. The Attorney-General for India, argued that the ratio of the judgment in Kesavananda Bharati case (AIR 1973 SC 1461) was not an authority for the proposition that without the higher judiciary exercising the power of Judicial Review, there could be no free and fair election. Continuing his arguments, the Attorney-General pointed out that several major countries have entrusted the power of deciding upon election disputes to the Legislature itself and have kept such elections out of the purview of the Judiciary.

78. Justice Y.V. Chandrachud also observed that until the Representation of the People Amendment Act of 1966, which empowered the High Courts to try election petitions concerning elections to the state legislatures and the Parliament, the jurisdiction to try election petitions was vested in a Tribunal of three Members and later in a Tribunal of a single Member, who was a District Judge. The decisions of these Tribunals could be challenged before the Supreme Court under Article 136 of the Constitution.

79. In the United Kingdom, prior to the year 1770, disputed elections were tried by the House of Commons. Erskine May's 'Parliamentary Practice' states that in the year 1770, the House of Commons divested itself of the privilege of trying election petitions and entrusted trial of such petitions to a Tribunal composed of its Members. In the year 1868, a law was passed to transfer the trial of election petitions to the courts of law. At present, in U.K., a Parliamentary election petition is tried by two judges of the Queen's Bench Division chosen by rotation. The decision of the two judges becomes final on confirmation by the speaker of the House of Commons. No appeal lies against the decision of the Election Court save by leave of the Court and if leave is granted, the decision of the Court of Appeal is final.

80. Under the Constitution of the United States of America, each House is the judge of the election, returns and qualifications of its members. While deciding election petitions, each House acts as a Judicial Tribunal. There is no provision for an appeal against decision of a House on an election petition.

81. In view of the aforesaid, clauses (4) and (5) of Article 329A are not unconstitutional on the ground that election of the Prime Minister as a member of the House of People is placed beyond purview of the Courts. It also cannot be urged that the Thirty-Ninth Amendment to the Constitution is in total derogation of "political justice". The concept of "political justice" in the Preamble is too vague and nebulous and in any case, the Preamble cannot be a source of power.

82. Moreover, the Thirty-Ninth Amendment Act 1975 has only ensured immunity of the Prime Minister and the Speaker from any challenge to their election to the House of the People. But no such immunity can be claimed by other democratically elected functionaries in the Republic of India. It would be futile to argue that such isolated immunity to the Prime Minister or the Speaker has destroyed the democratic character and the basic structure of the Constitution. One swallow does not make a summer. The swallow with its pointed wings, forked tail, a curving fling and twittering cry is undoubtedly a harbinger of summer but to see all these in the Thirty-Ninth Amendment and to argue that the summer of a totalitarian rule is knocking at the door is to take an unduly alarmist view of the political scene. As Sir Frederick Pollock said, "if there is any real danger it is of the alarmist's own making."

83. Clause (4) of Article 329A makes the existing Election Laws retrospectively inapplicable to election to the House of the People of the Prime Minister and the Speaker. The inapplicability of such laws creates a legal vacuum because the repeal is a step-in-aid to free the election of the Prime Minister and the Speaker from the restraints of all election laws, indeed of all laws. The impact of clause (4) of Article 329A is that the election of the Prime Minister to the House of the People could not be declared void as there was no law to apply to that Election; the judgment of the Allahabad High Court declaring the Election as void is itself void and the Election of the Prime Minister continues to be valid.

84. These provisions are an outright negation of the Right to Equality under Article 14 of the Constitution. Article 14 which prohibits class legislation however permits reasonable classification so that the same law may not apply to all persons alike if these persons have some distinguishing attributes or features, which demarcates them from the others similarly situated.

85. Since the judgment in The State of West Bengal *versus* Anwar Ali Sarkar (AIR 1952 SC 75), the Supreme Court has taken the view that for the purpose of reasonable classification under Article 14 of the Constitution, the classification must be founded on an intelligible differentia, which distinguishes those who are grouped together from those who are left out. Further for reasonable classification, the differentia must have a reasonable nexus with the object of the law sought to be achieved.

86. In the present case, the first test, as aforesaid, may be assumed to be satisfied as in our political system, the Prime Minister has a unique position. But what about the second test that the law must have a reasonable nexus with the object of the law sought to be achieved? What is the rational explanation for the provision in Article 329A that the election to the House of the People of the Prime Minister and the Speaker will be above

all laws and that the election will be governed by no norms or standard applicable to all others, who contest Parliamentary elections. What is the rational basis for the proposition that an election of the Prime Minister to the House of the People declared as void by the Allahabad High Court shall be deemed to be valid and the judgment of the High Court itself is void? "Such is not the doctrine of classification." It is the common man's sense of justice which sustains democracies and the Thirty-Ninth Amendment does offend the sense of justice of the common man.

87. It follows that clauses (4) and (5) of Article 329A are arbitrary and are calculated to destroy the Rule of Law. Admittedly by the year 1975, Constitutional law had undergone many changes since Lord Dicey delivered his lectures in the year 1885 as the Vinerian Professor of English law at Oxford. Dicey had given three attributes of the Rule of Law viz. (i) absence of arbitrary power; (ii) equality before law; and (iii) administration of law by ordinary law courts. Dicey's fondness for ordinary law arose out of his distrust of Droit Administratif which was the administrative law of France. Dicey considered Droit Administratif as the "misfortune" of the "folk across the channel". So pervasive was Dicey's distrust of Droit Adminstratif that as late as the year 1935, Lord Hewart, the Lord Chief Justice of England, dismissed Droit Adminstratif as a continental jargon.

88. Unlike the American and the Australian Constitution, in the Indian Constitution, there is no rigid application of the theory of Separation of Powers. It is, however, conceded that the function of the Indian Parliament is to legislate and not to adjudicate upon disputed cases. The British Parliament – which is legally supreme – may enact a law to enable a Parliament to settle a dispute, which was hitherto settled by ordinary courts of law. The British Parliament with impunity may legislate for "boiling the Bishop of Rochester's cook". As a contrast, the Indian Parliament, which has constitutional mandate for its functions, cannot direct that an accused in a pending criminal case shall stand acquitted or that a civil suit shall stand decreed in favour of one of the contesting parties.

89. Madison wrote in The Federalist that all power is of an encroaching nature. The encroaching power, which the Federalist was afraid of, was legislative power. Encroachment of power by the Legislature is an inherent danger in all Republics. The history of USA and France has shown on many occasions that such fear was not wholly unjustified.

90. No Constitution can survive without a conscious adherence to a system of fine checks and balances. Just as Courts should not enter into the political thicket, Parliament must also respect the adjudicatory functions of the Courts.

91. Harold. J. Laski says that exercise by the legislature, what is primarily a judicial function, is impossible to sustain in the context even of co-operative federalism, which contains no rigid separation of powers.

92. Justice Y.V. Chandrachud concluded his judgment by holding clauses (4) and (5) of Article 329A as unconstitutional. He upheld the appeal filed by Indira Gandhi against the judgment of Justice J.M.L. Sinha of the Allahabad High Court. He also dismissed the Civil Appeal which is the cross-objection filed by Raj Narain.

93. The Supreme Court also unanimously dismissed a Review Petition against their judgments delivered in the matter.

Chapter 11

Additional District Magistrate, Jabalpur *versus* S.S. Shukla and Others (AIR 1976 SC 1207)

[CHIEF JUSTICE A.N. RAY, JUSTICE H.R. KHANNA, JUSTICE M.H. BEG, JUSTICE P.N. BHAGWATI AND JUSTICE Y.V. CHANDRACHUD]

Case Summary

In this case, a majority of four Judges including Chief Justice A.N. Ray, Justice M.H. Beg, Justice Y.V. Chandrachud and Justice P.N. Bhagwati held that in view of the Presidential Order dated 27 June 1975 under clause (1) of Article 359 of the Constitution, no person has any *locus standi* to move a writ petition under Article 226 for *Habeas Corpus* or any other writ or order or direction to challenge the legality of an order of detention on the ground that the order is not in compliance with the provisions of the Constitution or is vitiated by *mala fides*.

1. Justice H.R. Khanna is the only judge who wrote a dissenting judgment. [**N.B.:** Justice H.R. Khanna's dissenting judgment has been hailed as an important landmark in affirmation of the Rule of Law in a Democracy.]
2. The judgment of Chief Justice A.N. Ray may be summed up as follows: Shivkant Shukla and others filed writ petitions in different High Courts challenging the Proclamation of Emergency under Article 352 of the Constitution on 27 June 1975 and the legality of the orders of detention of the respondents including Shivkant Shukla.
3. Chronologically speaking, on 03 December 1971, the President of India in exercise of powers under Article 352(1) of the Constitution issued a Proclamation that a grave emergency exists whereby the security of India is threatened by external aggression. On 25 June 1975 the President of India in exercise of the same powers under Article 352(1) issued a fresh Proclamation that a grave emergency exists whereby the security of India is threatened by internal disturbance. The only difference between the two Proclamations is that the earlier Proclamation was on ground of external aggression and the latter Proclamation was on ground of internal disturbance.

4. On 27 June 1975, in exercise of powers conferred by Article 359(1) of the Constitution, the President passed an order that Right of any person, including a foreigner, to move any Court for enforcement of Rights under Article 14, Article 21 and Article 22 of the Constitution and all proceedings pending in any Court for enforcement of the above mentioned Rights shall remain suspended for the period during which the proclamation of Emergency shall remain in force.

5. On 08 January 1976, there was a Notification that in exercise of powers under Article 359(1), the Right of any person to move any Court for enforcement of the Fundamental Rights under Article 19 shall also remain suspended during the period the Proclamation of Emergency shall remain in force.

6. *Niren De*, the Attorney-General for India, argued that grant of special powers to the Executive is justified during the period a proclamation of emergency is in force. He also argued that during the aforesaid period, neither any law nor any executive action can be challenged for violation of the Fundamental Rights.

7. The Attorney-General also argued that during the period when proclamation of Emergency is in force, challenge to Executive actions either on the ground that they are arbitrary or unlawful has been negatived in England in Liversidge *versus* Anderson (1942 AC 206) and Greene *versus* Secretary of State for Home Affairs (1942 AC 284). Our Supreme Court has followed the ratio of these judgments in Makhan Singh *versus* State of Punjab (AIR 1964 SC 381).

8. The arguments of the counsel for the respondents have been as follows:
   (i) It cannot be the case of the State that during the period of Emergency under Article 352(1), there is no Right to Life and all liberties are put on hold.
   (ii) The object of Article 359(1) is to bar the Right to move the Supreme Court under Article 32; but it does not bar the enforcement of common law Rights and statutory Rights to personal liberty.
   (iii) Article 359(1) does not permit unlimited power to the Executive in violation of the system of checks and balances of the Constitution.
   (iv) The proclamation of Emergency does not widen the power of the Executive under Article 162 of the Constitution to take any illegal action.
   (v) The power to arrest without trial is conferred on the Executive by Section 3 of the Maintenance of Internal Security Act 1971 and if an arrest is made in violation of Section 3, the courts can strike it down as illegal.

9. Chief Justice A.N. Ray did not accept the arguments of the counsels for the Respondent and held that in England during the Emergency arising out of the First World War (1914-18), the Defence of the Realm Act was passed empowering the Executive to frame Regulations by order-in-Council. The House of Lords had held that a Regulation framed by the Secretary of the State under the Defence of the Realm Act to detain a British subject without trial on grounds of his hostile origin or hostile association was perfectly valid. This was the ratio of the famous judgment of the House of Lords in The King *versus* Halliday ex parte Zadiq (1917 AC 260).

10. Similar powers were conferred on the Executive in England to detain a person without trial under the Emergency Powers (Defence) Act 1939 during the Second World War (1939-45).

11. In Liversidge *versus* Anderson (1942 AC 206), the House of Lords took the view that in view of the Emergency Powers (Defence) Act 1939, the Courts could not question detention without trial. The House of Lords, however, ruled in Liversidge *versus* Anderson (1942 AC 260) that the Courts could intervene in case of *mala fides* or mistaken identity.

12. Lord Dicey held that the objective of the *Habeas Corpus* Suspension Act which enabled the British Government to do acts, which were expedient for the defence of the Realm though these acts of the Government might not be strictly legal.

13. The Liversidge Case (1942 AC 260) is an authority on the point that however precious personal liberty may be, it can be sacrificed by legal enactment, for "national success in the war or escape from national plunder or enslavement. In other words, liberty itself is the gift of law and may by law forfeited or abridged."

14. Speaking for the majority of four Judges, Chief Justice A.N. Ray held that four issues are required to be considered which are as follows:
   (i) Is the Presidential order under Article 359 a bar to the Courts at the threshold?
   (ii) Is Article 21 the sole repository of Right to Life and Personal Liberty?
   (iii) Is the Presidential Order under Article 359(1) subject to the rubric of the Rule of Law?
   (iv) Is Section 16A(9) of the Maintenance of Internal Security Act 1971 a rule of evidence?

15. The answer to the first issue is that the effect of the Presidential order suspending enforcement of any Fundamental Right bars the *locus standi* of any person to move either the High Courts under Article 226 or the Supreme Court under Article 32. This position was made clear in Makhan Singh *versus* State of Punjab (AIR 1964 SC 381) and Dr. Ram Manohar Lohia *versus* State of Bihar (AIR 1966 SC 740).

16. Article 359(1) makes no distinction between threat to the security of India by war or external aggression on the one hand and threat to security of India by internal disturbance on the other. In fact, both situations are covered by the expression "grave emergency" in Article 352(1).

17. The Maintenance of Internal Security Act 1971 is the law validly enacted. Any allegation that order of arrest without trial under the aforesaid Act is not made according to the law shall not rob the order of arrest and detention the protective umbrella of Article 359(1).

18. The next issue is whether Article 21 of the Constitution is the sole repository of the Right to life and the Right of personal liberty. The answer is that before Article 21, there was no pre-existing common law remedy of *Habeas Corpus*. Moreover no common law Right corresponding to a Fundamental Right can co-exist as a distinct Right apart from the Fundamental Right. Section 491 of the Code of Criminal Procedure 1898 contained the statutory provision for *Habeas Corpus*. This provision has been repealed in the new Code of Criminal Procedure 1973. It establishes that the only source of the Right to Life and personal liberty in India is Article 21 itself and not any common law or statute law.

19. The third issue is whether the Presidential order under Article 359(1) is subject to the rubric of the Rule of Law? The answer is that the Presidential order does not violate any law as it is based on a constitutional provision and the Constitution is the fundamental law.

20. The Rule of Law is a normative as well as a descriptive term. It expresses an ideal as much as a juristic fact.

21. In Ram Jawaya Kapoor *versus* State of Punjab (AIR 1955 SC 549) it was decided that for every action of the Executive, there need not be always a law to support it; but if Executive action operates to the prejudice of any person, such action must have the authority of law.

22. Article 358 of the Constitution permits executive action under a law which may violate a Fundamental Right in Article 19 but if the law is void or if there is no law at all, the executive action will not be protected by Article 358.

23. The suspension of the Right to enforce any Fundamental Right has the effect that emergency provisions in the Constitution by themselves constitute the Rule of Law during the period when a Proclamation of emergency by the President is in force.

24. Regarding the final issue whether Section 16(A)(9) of the Maintenance of Internal Security Act 1971 permits implied exclusion of Judicial Review on the ground of *mala fide* order of detention, it may be mentioned that when allegations of *mala fide* is made by any person, who has been detained, the Courts can ask the state to satisfy them that grounds did exist to detain the person; but beyond that it does not permit the detenue to see the grounds of detention as Article 22 of the Constitution has been suspended by a Presidential order under Article 359(1) of the Constitution.

25. It is not possible for the High Courts or the Supreme Court to adjudicate on allegations of *mala fides*.

26. De Smith in his book *Judicial Review of Administrative Action* (1973) has said that review of a case of bad faith is hardly more than a formality. This is because a detenue has to discharge the impossible burden of proof that the Detaining Authority did not genuinely believe that it had reasonable grounds for detention of the detenue.

27. When enforcement of Fundamental Rights has been suspended because of the Presidential order under Article 359(1), it is not open for the Courts to question the discretion of the lawful Authority in having exercised the power of arrest under the Maintenance of Internal Security Act 1971.

28. To sum up:
   (i) In view of Presidential order dated 27 June 1975 under Article 359(1), no person has *locus standi* to move any High Court for the writ of *Habeas Corpus* under Article 226 of the Constitution to enforce any Right of personal liberty in Article 21 on the ground that the order of detention is not under any valid law or is *mala fide*.
   (ii) Article 21 is the sole repository of the Right to Life and the Right to Personal Liberty against the state. A writ of *Habeas Corpus* is therefore barred by the Presidential order.

(iii) Section 16(A)(9) of the Maintenance of Internal Security Act 1971 is valid. It is a rule of evidence. It is not open for either the detenue or the Courts to ask for grounds of detention as Article 22 has been suspended by the Presidential order of 27 June 1975.

(iv) It is not competent for the Courts to go into question of *mala fides* of the order of detention or *ultra vires* character of the order or that the order was not passed on satisfaction of the Detaining Authority.

29. The result is that the orders of the High Courts of Allahabad, Bombay (Nagpur Bench) Delhi, Karnataka, Madhya Pradesh and Punjab & Haryana that the High Courts could examine the order of detention under the Maintenance of Internal Security Act 1971 to decide whether it is *ultra vires* or *mala fide* are set aside.

30. Justice M.H. Beg agreed with the majority of judges but chose to write a separate judgment.

31. Justice M.H. Beg stated that Niren De, the Attorney-General has posed two issues viz.

(i) Whether in view of the Presidential order dated 27 June 1975 it is open to a detenue to file a writ of *Habeas Corpus* before any High Court on the ground that his detention is not in compliance with the Maintenance of Internal Security Act 1971?

(ii) If a writ of *Habeas Corpus* can be filed before a High Court what is the scope and extent of judicial scrutiny in view of suspension of enforcement of the Fundamental Right under Article 226 and in view of Section 16(A)(9) of the Maintenance of Internal Security Act 1971.

32. Neither Article 136 nor Article 226 of the Constitution are meant to answer pure questions of law unrelated to facts of a case. Therefore, purely hypothetical questions will not be answered by the Court.

33. The Attorney-General has conceded that the risks of misuse of power by the Detaining Authority must be presumed to be over-ridden by the higher claims of national security. If there is misuse of power the detenue can always approach the higher authorities in the Government for redressal.

34. Justice M.H. Beg stated that Counsels for the respondents have invoked the common law to interpret Article 359(1) of the Constitution. The mere assertion of the respect for the Rule of Law without an understanding what it meant in the past and what it should mean to-day is "another name for obfuscation of thought." Even Ivor Jennings has criticized Lord Dicey's theory of the Rule of law in its application to functions of the modern state. According to modern thinkers, Dicey's Rule of Law was "idealistic rosy optimism, reflecting the whig tradition of minimum interference with individual freedom". It was destined to be displaced by more "down to earth" pragmatism of the Twentieth Century. Dicey did not anticipate the myriad functions of a Welfare State.

35. In USA, the power of Judicial Review was asserted by Chief Justice Marshall in Marbury *versus* Madison (1803). In USA, the "due process" clause introduced by the Fifth Amendment (1791) and by the Fourteenth Amendment (1868) of the Constitution became the most prolific source of judge-made law. The Indian Constitution has not given the Courts amplitude of power for judicial legislation by incorporating "procedure established

by law" in Article 21 of the Constitution instead of the "due process of law" of the American Constitution.

36. Chief Justice Harilal Kania has held in A.K. Gopalan *versus* State of Madras (AIR 1950 SC 27) that the constitution has to be read as a whole without giving undue weightage to the chapter on Fundamental Rights.

37. In India, the Constitution, being the fundamental law, provides the validity for all other laws. "The wider the sweep of the provisions of Articles 21 and 22 of the Constitution, the more drastic must be the effect of suspending their enforcement. Suspension of Article 21 and Article 22 does not mean their retention under a disguise."

38. Our Constitution is the embodiment of the highest "positive law". It is not open to appeal to some "spirit of the Constitution" to frustrate its express provisions.

39. Even in England, after Lord Coke's judgment in Dr. Bonham's case, when common law was invoked to declare a statute *ultra vires*, common law has not been invoked to strike down a statute.

40. In Kesavananda Bharati's case (AIR 1973 SC 1451), the majority of judges rejected the argument that Natural Rights could be enforced to limit express powers of amendment in Article 368 of the Constitution. Justice S.N. Dwivedy, who was one of the judges in the Kesavananda Bharati case, said that though Natural Law has been a sort of religion with many political and constitutional thinkers, "it has never believed in a single Godhead" and the pantheon of Gods of Natural Law have been locked in constant internecine conflict.

41. Justice M. Hidaytullah observed in I.C. Golaknath case (AIR 1967 SC 1643) that a distinction must be made between the possession and exercise of those Rights. "The first is fixed and the latter is controlled by Justice and Necessity".

42. It will be clear from a reading of A.K. Gopalan's case (AIR 1950 SC 27) and Kharak Singh's case (AIR 1963 SC 1295) that all aspects of freedom of a person are covered by Articles 19, 21 and 22 of the Constitution. If during proclamation of Emergency, these Rights cannot be enforced by the Courts because they are suspended, the Courts cannot also inquire whether any of the aforesaid Rights has been violated by the executive.

43. Reliance has been placed by counsels for the respondents on Halsbury's Laws of England which says, that the power to issue a writ of *Habeas Corpus* exists at common law independent of any statute.

44. The contention of the Counsels of the respondents has no force. In India, unlike in England, there are no King's or Queen's Bench or any prerogative of a monarch. In India, only High Courts and the Supreme Court have powers to issue writs as provided for in the Constitution. If the Constitution prescribes that during proclamation of Emergency, the writ of *Habeas Corpus* shall remain suspended, no other prerogative power can be invoked to issue the writ.

45. Provision of preventive detention in itself is a departure from the ordinary norms. In Haradhan Shah *versus* The State of West Bengal (AIR 1974 SC 2154) it was held that

Preventive Detention is to be distinguished from punitive detention. But whether it is preventive or punitive detention, it necessarily imposes constraints.

46. Preventive detention is generally resorted to in times of war when the country's security and defence are badly threatened. The Indian Constitution has also provided for preventive detention in peace time.

47. The proclamation of emergency following the Chinese attack in October 1962 did not specifically suspend enforceability of Article 14 of the Constitution but the proclamation of emergency of June 1975 was followed by a Presidential order suspending the Right to Equality before law in Article 14.

48. The Presidential order following the proclamation of emergency in 1962 expressly hedges the suspension of Fundamental Rights in Article 21 and Article 22 with the condition that the detenue could be deprived of his Rights under the Defence of India Act 1962 or the Rule framed thereunder. In other words, during the proclamation of emergency in 1962, the Courts could inquire whether the requirements of the Defence of India Act 1962 and the Rule framed thereunder have been satisfied whereas the June 1975 proclamation of emergency has been followed by the Presidential order suspending enforcement of the Fundamental Rights under Articles 14, 21 and 22 of the Constitution. In view of the aforesaid, the Courts are prohibited from examining whether deprivation of these Fundamental Rights conforms to any statutory requirement.

49. The Presidential order following the proclamation of emergency in 1962 refers to no pending proceedings before the High Courts under Article 226 and the Supreme Court under Article 32 where enforcement of specified Fundamental Rights will remain suspended. But the Presidential order following the June 1975 proclamation makes specific mention of pending proceedings before the High Courts and the Supreme Court.

50. The proclamation of emergency in June 1975 was clearly aimed at suspending the ordinary process of law in those cases where persons complain of infringement of their Fundamental Rights. It is clear from the provisions of 16(A)(9) of the Maintenance of Internal Security Act 1971, introduced with retrospective effect from 25 June 1975 by Act 14 of 1976, which received assent of the President of India on 25 January 1976. [N.B.: Section 16(A)(9) provided that once a declaration was made as stipulated in sub-section (2) or (3) of Section 16(A), the provisions of Section 8 to 12 of the Act of 1971 would not apply and the grounds of detention would not be communicated to the detenue.]

51. The term Rule of Law is not a magic wand to remove all difficulties. It is not an Alladin's lamp to fulfill any desire. The Rule of Law means laws at a particular time in a particular country. In other words, the Rule of Law must differ in shades, meaning and emphasis from time to time and from country to country. It could not be rigid, unchanging and inflexible like the laws of the Medes and the Persians. It cannot be like some brooding omnipotence in the sky.

52. If the *locus standi* of a person to move the Court is gone because of a Presidential Notification following a proclamation of emergency, it is no use appealing to a particular concept of the Rule of Law to get legal remedy for deprivation of a Right, which remains suspended by the Presidential Notification.

53. It is also not correct to hold that a writ of *habeas corpus* can be issued in view of section 491 of the Code of Criminal Procedure 1898, which was incorporated in the Code in 1923. The sweep of the Notification under Article 359(1) taking away the power of "any court" is wide enough to include denial of any kind of relief by Courts to enforce a Fundamental Right.

54. No evidence could be led before any Court regarding illegality of an order of preventive detention because of the amended Section 16(A)(9) of the Maintenance of the Internal Security Act 1971.

55. In Liversidge *versus* Anderson (1942 AC 206), Lord Atkin said that,

"However precious the personal liberty of the subject may be, there is something for which it may well be, to some extent sacrificed by legal enactment, namely national success in the war or escape from national plunder or enslavement."

56. The opinion of the overwhelming majority of Law Lords of England in Liversidge case (1942 AC 206) was that jurisdiction of the courts is ousted by a statutory rule that the subjective satisfaction of the Secretary of State was adequate to detain a person whose activities were prejudicial to national safety.

57. Erskine May has said in his book, *Constitutional History of England* that though the writ of *Habeas Corpus* is the first security of civil liberty, it has been suspended from time to time in periods of public danger or apprehension of such danger.

58. During the First World War (1914-19) and the Second World War (1939-45), even though the Habeas Corpus Act was not suspended, the courts supported the Defence of the Realm Act and did not interfere with the executive's power to detain a person, whose activities were prejudicial to war efforts.

59. Even in Halsbury's Laws of England, the Crown's common law prerogative power during an Emergency has been defended. The passage in Halsbury's Laws of England, which is relevant, is as follows:

"The Crown has the same power as a private individual of taking all measures which are absolutely and immediately necessary for the purpose of dealing with an invasion or other emergency."

60. The Crown in UK has also emergency powers under the Emergency Powers Act 1964. Though the proclamation of an Emergency under the Act of 1964 has validity for only a month the period of emergency can be extended by "another proclamation at or before the end of that period."

61. The Presidential order of 27 June 1975 stipulated that under clause (1) of Article 359 of the Constitution, the President declared that the Right of any person – including a foreigner – to move any Court for enforcement of Rights conferred by Article 14, Article 21 and Article 22 shall remain suspended for the period of proclamation of emergency made on 25 June 1975. It also stipulated that all pending proceedings in Court for enforcement of the aforesaid Articles shall remain suspended during the period the Proclamation of Emergency was in force.

62. It may be noted that the Presidential order of 03 November 1962 – following the proclamation of Emergency on 26 October 1962 in the wake of the Chinese invasion – did not suspend Article 14 of the Constitution. Secondly, the Presidential order of November 1962 stipulated that Article 21 and Article 22 shall remain suspended if a person is deprived of his freedom under the Defence of India Act 1962 or any Rule or order made thereunder.

63. On the other hand, the Presidential Order of 27 June 1975 unconditionally suspends the Right of any person to move any Court for enforcement of Article 14, Article 21 and Article 22 of the Constitution. The result is that the Courts are not obliged to test the validity of detention of a person to decide whether the detention was in pursuance of any statutory requirement.

64. Moreover, the Presidential order of November 1962 did not cover pending proceedings in Courts whereas the Presidential order of 27 June 1975 covered the pending proceedings also.

65. The above analysis makes it clear that the Presidential order of 27 June 1975 expressed in no uncertain terms that the ordinary process of law shall remain suspended to enforce Fundamental Rights. This is also clear from provision of Section 16A(9) of the Maintenance of Internal Security Act 1971 introduced by Act 14 of 1976, which received assent of the President of India on 25 January 1976 making Section 16A(9) operate retrospectively.

66. But if a detention order has been passed by a person, who did not have the power to detain, such detention can be challenged as it has been ordered by a private person without any semblance of authority. But in the present batch of cases – including the detention of the respondent Shivkant Shukla – orders of detention have been passed by duly authorized officers.

67. Counsel cited the judgment of the Supreme Court in Dr. Ram Manohar Lohia *versus* State of Bihar (AIR 1966 SC 740) in support of the contention that the detention of Shivkant Shukla was bad in law. But the case of Dr. Ram Manohar Lohia (AIR 1966 SC 740) does not support the contention of the counsel as the detention order in that case was held as bad in law as it was made for activities prejudicial to "law and order" and not prejudicial to "public order".

68. In Dr. Ram Manohar Lohia's case (AIR 1966 SC 740) Justice M. Hidaytullah said that one has to imagine three concentric circles. Law and order represents the largest circle within which is the next circle representing public order and the smallest circle represents security of the state. Thereafter, an act may affect law and order but not public order and an act may affect public order but not security of the state.

69. An argument has been advanced by counsel that vesting powers on the Executive to pass order of detention during the validity of a Proclamation of Emergency violates the principle of separation of powers. A suitable answer could be that the Indian Constitution has not recognized the doctrine of separation of powers in its absolute rigidity. This is the ratio of the judgment of the Supreme Court in Rai Saheb Ram Jawaya Kapur *versus* the State of Punjab (AIR 1955 SC 549).

70. A maxim of justice, "Let the Heavens fall but justice must be done" when applied to "Judicial Justice" means that Justice must accord with the highest standards of objective, impartial, unruffled dictates of a clear judicial conscience working "without fear or favour, affection or ill-will". It fully recognizes the legal validity of the principle expounded in Liversidge *versus* Anderson (1942 AC 206) of *Salus Populi Est Supreme Lex* (regard for the public welfare is the highest law).

71. There are enough safeguards in the provisions of the Maintenance of Internal Security Act 1971 against arbitrary detention of a person. Section 3 of the Act stipulates that the Detaining Authority has to submit a report forthwith to the State Government with the grounds for detention. If within 12 days, the detention order is not approved by the State Government, it automatically lapses. Section 14 of the Act of 1971 provides for revocation of the order of detention either by the Detaining Authority or by the State Government or the Central Government. Section 15 of the Act of 1971 provides for temporary release of the detenue to avoid undue hardship or to meet special circumstances. Means of redress in cases of mistaken identity or misapprehension of facts or detention of a person due to malicious information circulated by the enemy are open to a detenue by approaching the executive authorities. What is not possible is to secure the release of a detenue by a Court in exercise of its writ of *Habeas Corpus*.

72. An argument was advanced by counsel of the respondent that the High Courts can exercise their power under Article 226 of the Constitution to enforce the Rule of Law, which has been held as the basic structure of the Constitution.

73. The argument has no merit as the theory of basic structure cannot be used to build into the Constitution an imaginary part, which may be in conflict with the express provisions of the Constitution relating to Promulgation of Emergency.

74. If a person inflicts an injury on another person in contravention of the law, he cannot claim that he did it with an innocent mind. This is what in jurisprudence is called "malice in law". "Malice in fact" means actual malicious intention of a person who inflicted an injury on another person.

75. No question of "malice in law" can arise in a *Habeas Corpus* proceeding because the Right to move the Court for enforcement of any named Fundamental Right is suspended during the period of validity of Promulgation of Emergency.

76. As regards 'malice in fact', it cannot be subject of scrutiny in a *Habeas Corpus* proceeding during the period of validity of Promulgation of Emergency though it may be possible to try it in a regular suit the object of which is not to enforce a Right of personal freedom but to claim damages for an intentional wrong of the Detaining Authority.

77. The possibility of such a suit claiming damages for a malicious order of detention is a deterrent against dishonest use of power.

78. While concluding his separate judgment agreeing with the majority judgment, Justice M.H. Beg compressed into one the two issues raised by him and stated that a prima facie valid detention order – duly authenticated by an officer authorized to issue it – is a complete answer to a detenue's petition for a writ of *Habeas Corpus*. Once a valid detention order is shown to exist, the High Courts cannot enquire into it on grounds of mala fides or on

ground of non-compliance with the Maintenance of Internal Security Act 1971. In view of the aforesaid, Justice M.H. Beg allowed the appeal and set aside the judgments of the High Courts.

79. Justice H.R. Khanna was the only judge in the five-judge Constitution Bench, who did not agree with the majority of judges and wrote a dissenting judgment.

80. The judgment delivered by Justice H.R. Khanna may be summed up in the following paragraphs.

81. Law of Preventive Detention is anathema to all those who love personal liberty. The contrary view is that the love of personal liberty and opposition to any order of detention without trial should not stand on the way of ensuring public order and security of the state, which are threatened during war and internal disturbance.

82. The issue before the Supreme Court is whether in view of the Presidential order dated 27 June 1975, any petition before a High Court under Article 226 to enforce personal liberty of a person by issue of a writ of Habeas Corpus, is maintainable. It may be mentioned that petitions of persons detained under the Maintenance of Internal Security Act 1971 was pending before some High Courts when the matter came up before the Supreme Court.

83. The order issued by Fakhruddin Ali Ahmed, the President of India, on 27 June 1975 under clause (1) of Article 359 suspended during the period of proclamation of emergency was in operation – the right of any person (including a foreigner in India) – to move any Court for enforcement of the Fundamental Right under Article 14, Article 21 and Article 22 of the Constitution.

84. In October 1975, an ordinance was issued by the President of India to insert, *inter alia*, clause 16A(9) in the Maintenance of Internal Security Act 1971, which provided that the grounds of detention of a detenue shall be treated as confidential and shall be deemed to refer to matters of state and to be against the public interest to disclose. It was also stipulated that save as provided under the Maintenance of Internal Security Act 1971, no one shall communicate or disclose any such ground, information or method or any document containing such ground, information or method.

85. In Makhan Singh *versus* State of Punjab (AIR 1964 SC 381), the Supreme Court had considered the Presidential order under Article 359(1) of the Constitution of India, which was issued in November 1962 following the Chinese attack in October 1962.

86. In the aforesaid judgment, Justice P.B. Gajendragadkar who spoke for the majority of six out of seven judges of the Supreme Court, held as follows:

(i) in spite of the Presidential order of November 1962, if the detenue was pleading enforcement of any Right outside the Rights suspended by the Presidential order, his Right to move any Court in that behalf was not suspended. To put it briefly, if a detenue would file a petition under Article 226 or Article 32, that the mandatory provisions of the Preventive Detention law were not followed by the Detaining Authority, the High Court under Article 226 or the Supreme Court under Article 32 could strike down the order of detention in spite of the Presidential order under Article 359(1) of the Constitution.

(ii) A detenue can also move the Court on the ground that the order of detention was mala fide. It was, however, necessary for the detenue not only to allege mala fides but to prove it.

87. It was held by the Supreme Court that whereas detention of any person was *intra vires* on the ground of activities prejudicial to public order, the Detaining Authority in Ram Manohar Lohia's case (AIR 1966, SC 740) detained the detenue for activities prejudicial to law and order, which was not as serious as activities prejudicial to public order. The Supreme Court, therefore, struck down the detention order as not being in conformity with the law of Preventive Detention.

88. It was urged by the Attorney-General that Article 21 is the sole repository of the Right to Life and personal liberty guaranteed to both citizens and non-citizens alike.

89. Justice H.R. Khanna did not agree with contention of the Attorney-General as the Right to Life and the Right of Personal liberty are the most important of all Fundamental Rights. Blackstone, the celebrated jurist, has held that the absolute Rights of Englishmen were the Rights of personal security, personal liberty and private property. The American Declaration of Independence (1776) stated that all men were created equal and among their inalienable Rights are the Right to Life, liberty and pursuit of happiness. In 1959, the International Commission of Jurists adopted the Universal Declaration of Human Rights in which respect for the supreme value of human personality was stated to be the basis of all laws.

90. Justice H.R. Khanna also held that even in absence of Article 21 of the Constitution, the state has no power to deprive a person of his life and personal liberty without the authority of law. No case has been cited before the Supreme Court that before commencement of the Constitution of India, the state could deprive a person of his life or personal liberty without a valid law bestowing on the state such a power.

91. In Eleko *versus* Officer Administering the Government of Nigeria (AIR 1931 Privy Council 248), Lord Atkin held that it is a fundamental principle of British Jurisprudence that no member of the Executive could interfere with the liberty or property of a British subject except on condition that he could support the legality of his action before a Court of Justice.

92. Even though vast powers can be assumed by the Government in the interest of the security of the state, there is no antithesis between the power of a state to detain a person without trial in the interest of the security of the State and the power of the Courts to examine whether the order of detention was passed according to the law of preventive detention. As held in the famous judgment of Liversidge *versus* Anderson (1942 AC 206), the fact that the Nation is at war is no justification for relaxation of vigilance of the Courts in ensuring that the law is duly observed especially in a matter so fundamental as personal liberty.

93. In India, there was no absolute bar to approach the Courts during the Proclamation of Emergency following the Chinese attack on India in October 1962 and the Indo-Pak wars of 1965 and 1971.

94. The Detaining Authority must apply its mind to the facts regarding a person's prejudicial activities in relation to security of the State before honestly deciding that the person deserves to be detained without trial. As held by Lord Halsbury in Sharpe *versus* Wakefield (1891) discretion must be exercised by the Authority according to rules of reason and justice and not according to private opinion...according to law and not humour. It is to be not arbitrary, vague and fanciful but legal and regular. Therefore, the Courts might interfere if the order of detention under the Maintenance of Internal Security Act 1971 is issued not in good faith but is exercised mala fide for an ulterior purpose. The Notification issued by the President of India on 27 June 1975 will not protect an order of detention not strictly according to law or for an ulterior purpose.

95. A Presidential order under Article 359(1) of the Constitution can suspend during the period of Emergency, only the Right to move any Court for enforcement of the Fundamental Rights mentioned in the order. But the Presidential order does not suspend any statutory Right.

[**N.B.:** Both Justice Y.V. Chandrachud and Justice P.N. Bhagwati have agreed with the majority of Judges in A.D.M. Jabalpur *versus* S. Shukla (AIR 1976 SC 1207) that the Presidential Order dated 27 June 1975 bars any investigation or inquiry into the question whether the order of detention is vitiated by mala fide, factual or legal or whether it is based on extraneous considerations. They have also agreed with the majority of judges that the Presidential Order of 27 June 1975 bars any inquiry by the Courts as to whether the Detaining Authority has reached his subjective satisfaction validly on proper and relevant material.]

[**N.B.:** It has been widely acknowledged that the judgment in A.D.M. Jabalpur *versus* S. Shukla (AIR 1976 SC 1207) marks the lowest watermark of the Supreme Court of India as a defender of Fundamental Rights under the Constitution. It is indeed a serious matter that the majority of four judges of the Supreme Court – with only Justice H.R. Khanna dissenting – decided that even the Courts cannot question the vires of a mala fide order of detention in view of the Presidential Notification referred to.]

CHAPTER 12

Maneka Gandhi *versus* Union of India (AIR 1978 SC 597)

[CHIEF JUSTICE M.H. BEG, JUSTICE Y.V. CHANDRACHUD, JUSTICE P.N. BHAGWATI, JUSTICE V.R. KRISHNA IYER, JUSTICE N.L. UNTWALIA, JUSTICE MURTAZA FAZL ALI AND JUSTICE P.S. KAILASHAM]

Case Summary

This is a landmark judgment where it was held, *inter alia*, that the principle of reasonableness – which legally and philosophically is an essential element of the Right to Equality in Article 14 of the Constitution – pervades Article 14 like "a brooding omnipresence." It was also held that the "procedure established by law" in Article 21 of the Constitution must answer the test of reasonableness to be in conformity with Article 14. In other words, the "procedure established by law" in Article 21 must be "right, just and fair" and not "arbitrary, fanciful or oppressive." Further, it was held that even if there is no requirement in a statute that the adversely affected party must be heard before an order is passed, justice of the common law will supply the omission of the legislature. In other words, the principle of *Audi Alteram Partem* – the Right to be heard – is an integral part of the principle of Natural Justice. The principle also applies to administrative decisions likely to adversely affect a party.

1. The facts of the case are as follows: Maneka Gandhi filed a writ petition before the Supreme Court challenging the order dated 02 July 1977 of the Government of India impounding her passport "in the interest of the general public". The grounds for challenge advanced by Maneka Gandhi are as follows:
   (a) The Passport Act of 1967 is violative of Article 14 of the Constitution as it authorizes the Government to impound a person's passport "in the interest of the general public". Such a provision confers vague and undefined power and is violative of Article 14 of the Constitution;
   (b) The Passport Act of 1967 does not provide for a hearing of the person before his passport is impounded and hence is violative of the principle of *Audi Alteram Partem* and is contrary to the principles of Natural Justice;
   (c) The Passport Act of 1967 is violative of Article 21 of the Constitution as it does not prescribe "a procedure" for impounding a passport;

(d) Even if it is held that the Passport Act of 1967 lays down a procedure, the procedure is arbitrary and unreasonable and violative of Article 14 of the Constitution;

(e) The Passport Act of 1967 is violative of Article 19(1)(a) and Article 19(1)(g) of the Constitution.

2. Even though the order dated 02 July 1977 stipulated that Maneka Gandhi's passport was impounded in the public interest, the Government of India in its counter-affidavit admitted that the passport was impounded as Maneka Gandhi's presence was required in connection with proceedings before a Commission of Inquiry set up under Chairmanship of Justice J.C. Shah, a former Chief Justice of India.

3. During the hearing, the Attorney-General for India gave an undertaking that Maneka Gandhi could make a representation against impounding of her passport and the representation would be considered expeditiously and even if the order impounding the passport was confirmed by the Government, it would be only in force for a period of six months from date of the order.

4. As per the majority decision of the Supreme Court – Chief Justice M.H. Beg dissenting – it was not necessary to strike down the impugned order dated 02 July 1977 in view of the undertaking of the Attorney-General for India. Chief Justice M.H. Beg was however of the view that as the order dated 02 July 1977 was neither fair nor proper, it deserved to be quashed.

5. The majority judgment in this case was delivered by Justice P.N. Bhagwati on behalf of himself, Justice N.L. Untwalia and Justice Murtaza Fazal Ali. Three other judges, viz. Justice Y.V. Chandrachud, Justice V.R. Krishna Iyer and Justice P.S. Kailasham delivered separate judgments agreeing with the majority judgment. [**N.B.:** In these pages only the separate judgment of Justice Y.V. Chandrachud has been summarized.] As mentioned earlier, Chief Justice M.H. Beg delivered the sole dissenting judgment.

6. In his dissenting judgment, Chief Justice M.H. Beg, not only struck down the order impounding the passport of Maneka Gandhi but also observed that the impounded passport be returned to her. The important observations of Chief Justice M.H. Beg are in the following paragraphs.

7. In view of the wide amplitude of the expression "personal liberty", the Right to go abroad is an integral part of "personal liberty" guaranteed by the Indian Constitution.

8. Article 21 of the Constitution states that no person shall be deprived of his life or personal liberty except according to the procedure established by law.

9. On the face of it, Article 21 appears as a shield operating negatively against executive encroachment over something covered by the shield. As a matter of fact, Article 21 is "legal recognition of both the protection of the shield as well as what it protects which lies beneath the shield."

10. Article 19 of the Constitution cannot be considered as the only Article safeguarding personal liberty. If it was so, several well-recognized Rights as for instance, the Right to eat or drink, the Right to work, play and swim and several other Rights will not be deemed as protected under the Constitution. Therefore, Chief Justice Harilal Kania in

A.K. Gopalan *versus* State of Madras (AIR 1950 SC 27) held that Article 19 was a separate and self-contained constitutional provision.

11. Justice Fazl Ali, however, did not agree with the views of the Chief Justice Harilal Kania, even though the opinion of Chief Justice Harilal Kania was the view of the majority of judges in A.K. Gopalan *versus* State of Madras (AIR 1950 SC 27). Justice Fazl Ali did not think that each Article in the chapter on Fundamental Rights was a complete and self-contained code as Articles 19, 20, 21 and 22 of the Constitution, to some extent, overlap each other.

12. The Constitution must be read as an integral whole with possible overlapping of provisions relating to Fundamental Rights. The earlier view that Article 19 and Article 21 are mutually exclusive and hence water-tight compartments – a view held by the majority of judges in A.K. Gopalan *versus* State of Madras (AIR 1950 SC 27) – has been already negatived by a larger Bench of the Supreme Court in R.C. Cooper *versus* Union of India (AIR 1970 SC 564).

13. As pointed out in A.D.M. Jabalpur *versus* S. Shukla (AIR 1976 SC 1207), the ambit of personal liberty protected by Article 21 is both wide and comprehensive. In both A.K. Gopalan *versus* State of Madras (AIR 1950 SC 27) and A.D.M. Jabalpur *versus* S. Shukla (AIR 1976 SC 1207), it was held that Article 21 of the Constitution includes the substantive Right of personal liberty and the procedure for its deprivation.

14. Both the Rights of Personal Security and the Right of Personal Liberty recognized by Blackstone, in his "commentaries of the Laws of England as 'Natural Law', have been embodied in Article 21 of the Constitution."

15. The reasonable restrictions on Article 19(1) set out at clauses (2) to (6) do not suggest that these restrictions do not operate when an Indian citizen goes abroad.

16. The total effect and not the mere form of a restriction will determine which Fundamental Right is really involved in a particular case and whether a restriction upon its exercise is reasonably permissible on facts of the case.

17. A scrutiny of the Passport Act 1967 would indicate that each of the orders, which could be passed by the Passport Officer, requires the officer's satisfaction on certain objective conditions before the officer can pass an order impounding or revoking a passport. The Passport Act 1967 provides for an appeal to the Central Government from an order of a Passport Officer.

18. Following the ratio in the judgment in State of Orissa *versus* Dr. Binapani Dei (AIR 1967 SC 1269) (where it was laid down that if there is power in any authority to decide a matter against a person, duty to act judicially would be implicit in exercise of such power) the Passport Officer has to give an opportunity to an affected party to be heard before the officer decides to impound or revoke his passport. In an emergent situation, the Passport Officer may pass an order adverse to the holder of a passport but after the order is passed, the person affected may be given an opportunity to show cause why the passport should not have been impounded at the first instance.

19. If the essentials of justice are ignored and an order to the prejudice of a person is made, the order is a nullity. That is a basic concept of the Rule of Law.

20. The Central Government while impounding the passport of Maneka Gandhi did not communicate to her the reason for such action. The Government also did not give an opportunity to her to be heard before the passport was impounded. In the counter-affidavit filed in the Supreme Court, the Government had indicated that her passport was impounded because of the possibility of her being called before a Commission of Inquiry to give evidence. The whole episode gives an impression of existence of some prejudice against Maneka Gandhi. She has to be protected against such a prejudice.

21. As even by the admission of the Attorney-General before the Supreme Court, the order impounding the passport of Maneka Gandhi is neither fair nor procedurally proper, the order is quashed and the passport be returned to Maneka Gandhi, who is also entitled to her costs.

22. Justice Y.V. Chandrachud delivered a separate judgment agreeing with the majority judgment delivered by Justice P.N. Bhagwati. The salient observations of the judgment of Justice Y.V. Chandrachud are in the following paragraphs.

23. Under Section 10(5) of the Passport Act 1967, the Passport Officer refused to communicate to Maneka Gandhi the reasons why her passport was impounded. The power to refuse to disclose the reasons as in the relevant provision of the Passport Act is of an exceptional nature. It ought to be exercised fairly, sparingly and only when fully justified by the exigencies of an uncommon situation. Law cannot permit exercise of a power to keep the reasons undisclosed if the sole reason for doing so is to keep the reason away from judicial scrutiny.

24. In Satwant Singh Sawhney *versus* D. Ramarathnam, Assistant Passport Officer (AIR 1967 SC 1836), it was held that "personal liberty" in Article 21 of the Constitution includes the Right to travel abroad and that no person can be deprived of that Right except according to procedure established by law. The Passport Act 1967 was enacted by the Parliament following the judgment. It laid down a procedure for granting, impounding and revoking a passport.

25. The mere provision in a law of some "procedure" by itself cannot meet the mandate of Article 21. The "procedure prescribed by law" must be fair, just and reasonable and not fanciful, oppressive or arbitrary.

26. In R.C. Cooper *versus* Union of India (AIR 1970 SC 564) – popularly known as the Bank Nationalization case – the majority of judges held that the ratio in A.K. Gopalan's case (AIR 1950 SC 27) that certain Articles in the chapter on Fundamental Rights exclusively deal with specific freedoms cannot be accepted as correct. The Supreme Court reiterated the above decision in Shambhu Nath Sarkar *versus* State of West Bengal (AIR 1973 SC 1425) where it held that a law of Preventive Detention has to meet the challenge of not only of Article 21 and Article 22 but also of Article 19(1)(d) of the Constitution, i.e. the Right to move freely throughout the territory of India.

27. In view of the interpretation of the Supreme Court on interrelationship of different Fundamental Rights, the inquiry whether the Right to travel abroad is a part of any of the freedoms in Article 19(1) of the Constitution cannot be shut out at the threshold.

28. In A.K. Gopalan's case (AIR 1950 SC 27), the test of directness of the impugned law – as contrasted with its consequences – was thought to be the true approach to determine whether a Fundamental Right was infringed. An illustration of this approach was the judgment of the Supreme Court in Naresh Mirajkar's case (AIR 1967 SC 1) where the Court upheld a decision of the Bombay High Court prohibiting publication of evidence of a witness in a defamation case on the ground that such prohibition would ensure that the witness would give truthful evidence. It was held by the Supreme Court that the decision of the High Court in Naresh Mirajkar's case on the Right of Freedom of Speech and Expression guaranteed in Article 19(1)(a), was only incidental as the objective of the High Court was to ensure that the witness deposed truthfully.

29. In Express Newspapers case (AIR 1958 SC 578), the Court evolved the test of proximate effect of a statute to ascertain whether the statute violated any Fundamental Right. This test was applied by the Court in Sakal Newspaper case (AIR 1962 SC 305) where the Court gave precedence to the direct and immediate effect of the statute over its form and object and struck down the Daily Newspaper (Price & Page) Order.

30. The direct effect of a statute on an individual's Fundamental Right was also adopted as the test in R.C. Cooper *versus* Union of India (AIR 1970 SC 564) and in Bennett Coleman case (AIR 1970 SC 106) where the Court held that "the action may have a direct effect on a Fundamental Right although its direct subject-matter may be different."

31. Against the background of these judicial pronouncements, one has to ascertain whether Section 10(3)(c) of the Passport Act 1967 violates the Right of Freedom of Speech and Expression guaranteed in Article 19(1)(a) of the Constitution.

32. There is nothing in the language of Article 19(1)(a) that the Right of Freedom of Speech and Expression is limited to the geographical boundary of India. Thus, the Right of Freedom of Speech and Expression can be exercised by an Indian citizen on a foreign soil subject to the limitations contained in clause (2) of Article 19. The Right of free speech and expression of an Indian citizen is, however, subject to the laws of the foreign country in which the Right is sought to be exercised.

33. The Right of Freedom of Speech and Expression does not necessarily comprehend the Right to go abroad. The facility to go abroad by an Indian citizen may facilitate his Right to Freedom of Speech and Expression but it does not mean that the Right to go abroad is a constituent of the Right of Freedom of Speech and Expression.

34. Some decisions of the U.S. Supreme Court have been cited to give an expanded meaning to certain Fundamental Rights under the Indian Constitution. But the U.S. Supreme Court interprets the Rights of the U.S. citizens in the background of the "due process clause".

35. The Indian Supreme Court's approach to the Fundamental Rights is certainly not influenced by the due process clause. In the All-India Bank Employees' Association case (AIR 1962 SC 171), the Court rejected the contention that the freedom to form associations or unions guaranteed in Article 19(1)(c) does not carry with it the stipulation that a Worker's

Union could do everything required to make that Right effective. The Court rejected the theory that "one Right could lead to another and that another to still another" as such an approach could produce "grotesque result."

36. As mentioned earlier, the majority view contained in the judgment of Justice P.N. Bhagwati which he delivered on behalf of himself, Justice N.L. Untwalia and Justice Murtaza Fazal Ali was agreed to by other Judges in the Bench as Justice Y.V. Chandrachud, Justice V.R. Krishna Iyer and Justice P.S. Kailasam. The salient points in the majority judgment delivered by Justice P.N. Bhagwati are in the following paragraphs.

37. Before the judgment of the Supreme Court in Satwant Singh Sawhney *versus* D. Ramarathnam, Assistant Passport Officer (AIR 1967 SC 1836), there was no law governing issue of passports to Indian citizens. The Supreme Court held in the aforesaid case that personal liberty in Article 21 included the Right of locomotion and travel abroad. Against this background, Parliament enacted the Passport Act 1967.

38. In A.K. Gopalan *versus* State of Madras (AIR 1950 SC 27), it was held that the freedoms under Articles 19, 21, 22 and 31 are mutually exclusive. In other words, each of the aforementioned Rights is a self-contained code relating to protection of a distinct Right. But this ratio was overturned in R.C. Cooper's case (AIR 1970 SC 564) where Justice J.C. Shah, speaking for the majority, said that "Part III of the Constitution weaves a pattern of guarantees on the texture of basic human Rights. The guarantees delimit the protection of those Rights in their allotted fields: they do not attempt to enunciate distinct Rights."

39. After the judgment in R.C. Cooper's case (AIR 1970 SC 564) the Court has consistently taken the view that "the procedure established by law" in Article 21 of the Constitution must not only satisfy the test of Article 19 but also of test of Article 14 of the Constitution.

40. The great equalizing principle enunciated in Article 14 is a founding faith of the Constitution. Therefore, interpretation of the Rights to Equality in Article 14 should not be subjected to a narrow pedantic or lexicographic approach.

41. In E.P. Royappa *versus* State of Tamilnadu (AIR 1974 SC 555), it was laid down that from a positivistic point of view Equality is antithetical to arbitrariness. Equality and Arbitrariness are sworn enemies – one belongs to the Rule of Law in a Republic while the other to the whims and caprices of an absolute monarch. Article 14 ensures fairness and equality of treatment. The principle of reasonableness – an essential element of Equality – pervades Article 14 like the "brooding omnipresence". The "procedure established by law" in Article 21 must answer the test of reasonableness to be in conformity with Article 14 of the Constitution. In other words, the procedure must be right, just and fair and not arbitrary or fanciful.

42. The procedure for impounding a passport under the Passport Act of 1967 is not a fair procedure and cannot stand the scrutiny of non-arbitrariness as it did not mandate that the holder of the passport must be heard before the Passport is impounded, confiscated or revoked. This is against the principle of Natural Justice or principle of *Audi Alteram Partem*. Natural Justice is only "fair play in action". Justice Byles, the English Jurist, has called it "the justice of the common law." It is as Justice Megarry has called "a distillate of due process of law."

43. In the beginning, the view was that the Right of the affected party for a hearing before a decision adverse to his interest is taken belongs to the category of judicial and quasi-judicial decisions. It was held that the Right of a hearing did not apply to purely administrative decisions of the Executive. This erroneous view gained acceptance because in the year 1928, Lord Hewart misinterpreted an earlier observation of Lord Atkin. But after the epoch-making English decision in Ridge *versus* Baldwin (1964), it has been held that if an Authority is vested with power to decide a matter to the prejudice of any person, a duty to act judicially is implicit in the exercise of such power.

44. In A.K. Kraipak *versus* Union of India (AIR 1970 SC 150), it was held that the concept of quasi-judicial power has been undergoing radical change and the dividing line between administrative power and judicial power is being gradually obliterated.

45. As observed by the Supreme Court in A.K. Kraipak *versus* Union of India (AIR 1970 SC 150) proliferation of administrative law has provoked considerable fresh thinking on the subject and it has come to be recognized that even in administrative proceeding, the doctrine of Natural Justice must be applicable. The aim of the Rules of Natural Justice is to secure justice or to put it negatively to prevent miscarriage of justice. These Rules can only operate in area not covered by law validly made. In other words, the principles of Natural Justice do not supplant the law but only supplement it.

46. As observed by the Supreme Court in Suresh Koshy George *versus* The University of Kerala (AIR 1969 SC 198), the principles of Natural Justice are not always contained in a set of embodied Rules. What particular Rules of Natural Justice should apply must depend to a great extent on facts and circumstances of the case, the framework of the law under which the Enquiry is held and the constitution of the Tribunal set up for the purpose. Ultimately, it has to be decided whether observance of any principle of Natural Justice was required for a just decision in the case.

47. There are however situations when an Authority may have to act urgently and dispense with the principle of Natural Justice of being heard by the affected party. De Smith has mentioned in his book, *Judicial Review of Administrative Action* that the requirement of prior notice can be dispensed with where prompt action – specially action of a preventive nature – has to be taken by the Authority in the public interest.

48. The Right of being heard prior to the decision can be dispensed with where such a course would prevent the Administration to act promptly. The *Audi Alteram Partem* Rule may undergo situational modifications to ensure that Administration does not get paralysed due to inability to act promptly. But the core of the Rule of Natural Justice in relation to the Right of the affected party to present his case must remain, even though it is either a minimal hearing or a post-decisional hearing.

49. The Passport Officer can impound a passport in a special case where prompt action is required. This he can do without prior hearing of the affected party. After the passport is impounded, the Passport Officer must quickly give an opportunity to the party to represent. If such a procedure can be read into the Passport Act 1967 by implication, the procedure in the Passport Act to impound a passport in emergent cases – with an implied Right to the affected party to represent against the impounding – would be "right, fair

and just" and would not suffer from the vice of arbitrariness or unreasonableness. Hence, the procedure in the Passport Act 1967 for impounding a passport – and by implication giving a post-decisional hearing – conforms to the requirements of "procedure established by law" in Article 21 of the Constitution.

50. Section 10(3)(c) of the Passport Act 1967 where, *inter alia*, a passport can be impounded in the interest of the general public is not violative of Article 14 of the Constitution as it does not confer vague and undefined power on the Passport Officer. It has to be noted that the Passport Officer is obliged to give a brief statement of the grounds for which a passport is being impounded and send it to the passport holder so that he can prefer a statutory appeal to the Central Government.

51. Though the order dated 02 July 1977 impounding the passport of Maneka Gandhi is bad in law for violation of the *Audi Alteram Partem* Rule, the undertaking given by the Attorney-General before the Supreme Court has cured the impugned order of the vice of non-compliance with a salutary principle of Natural Justice.

CHAPTER 13

Minerva Mills Limited *versus* Union of India (AIR 1980 SC 1789)

[CHIEF JUSTICE Y.V. CHANDRACHUD, JUSTICE P.N. BHAGWATI, JUSTICE A.C. GUPTA, JUSTICE N.L. UNTWALIA AND JUSTICE P.S. KAILASHAM]

Case Summary

Minerva Mills is a company dealing in textiles. As substantial fall in production of the Mills was apprehended, in August 1970, Government of India appointed a committee under the Industries (Development and Regulation) Act 1951 to make a comprehensive investigation into affairs of the Minerva Mills. In January 1971, the committee submitted a report. In pursuance of the report, Government of India passed an order under the Industries (Development and Regulation) Act 1951 authorizing the National Textiles Corporation Limited to takeover management of the Minerva Mills. Subsequently, Minerva Mills was nationalized under the Sick Textile Undertakings (Nationalization) Act 1974. The petitioner challenged the constitutional validity of the aforesaid Act and the Constitution (Thirty-ninth Amendment) Act 1975 which put the Act nationalizing the Minerva Mills in the Ninth Schedule of the Constitution. The petitioner also challenged the constitutional validity of Section 4 and Section 55 of the Constitution (Forty-second Amendment) Act 1976.

1. The Supreme Court by majority (Chief Justice Y.V. Chandrachud, Justice A.C. Gupta, Justice N.L. Untwalia and Justice P.S. Kailasham) held that Sections 4 and 55 of the Constitution (Forty-second Amendment) Act 1976 are void as they are beyond the amending powers of the Parliament under Article 368. Justice P.N. Bhagwati did not agree with the majority of judges and wrote a dissenting judgment.
2. The following are the main points in the majority judgment delivered by Chief Justice Y.V. Chandrachud.
3. In Kesavananda Bharati *versus* Union of India (AIR 1973 SC 1461), the Supreme Court held by majority that under Article 368, the Parliament cannot amend the basic structure of the Constitution. The issue before the Court is whether Sections 4 and 55 of the

Constitution (Forty-second Amendment) Act 1976 transgress the limitations on amending power of the Parliament under Article 368?

4. In Kesavananda Bharati *versus* Union of India (AIR 1973 SC 1461), Chief Justice S.M. Sikri held that the Fundamental Rights cannot be abrogated by amendment under Article 368 though in the public interest reasonable abridgment of the Rights can be done by a constitutional amendment. Therefore, amendment of a Fundamental Right has to be within the broad contours of the Preamble to carry out the basic objectives of the Constitution.

5. Justice J.M. Shelat and Justice A.N. Grover had held in Kesavananda Bharati case (AIR 1973 SC 1461) that the Preamble contains essence of the Constitution. They also held that the Fundamental Rights have to be balanced and harmonized with the Directive Principles of State Policy. This balance and harmony constitute a component of basic structure of the Constitution, which cannot be altered by any amendment. In other words, there are some implied limitations on power of the Parliament to amend the Constitution.

6. Justice K.S. Hegde and Justice B.K. Mukherjee also held similar views regarding the Preamble. They held that for building a Welfare State, Parliament could not abrogate the fundamental freedoms.

7. Justice Jaganmohan Reddy also agreed with the Chief Justice S.M. Sikri and the two brother judges. The same view was of Justice H.R. Khanna, who held that any amendment must ensure that the Constitution survives without loss of identity as the Parliament has no power to abrogate the basic structure of the Constitution.

8. Briefly put, nine out of the 13 judges in the Bench held in Kesavananda Bharati case (AIR 1973 SC 1461) that power of amendment does not extend to abrogating the basic structure of the Constitution.

9. Section 4 of the Constitution (Forty-second Amendment) Act 1976 amended Article 31C. The amended Article 31C reads as follows:

"31C: Notwithstanding anything contained in Article 13, no law giving effect to the policy of the state towards securing all or any of the principles laid down in Part IV (i.e. Directive Principles of State Policy) shall be deemed to be void on the ground that it is inconsistent with, or takes away or abridges any of the Rights conferred by Article 14, Article 19 or Article 31; and no law containing a declaration that it is for giving effect to such policy shall be called in question in any court on the ground that it does not give effect to such policy;

Provided that where such law is made by the legislature of the state, the provisions of this Article shall not apply thereto unless such law, having been reserved for consideration of the President has received his assent."

10. Section 55 of the Constitution (Forty-second Amendment) Act 1976 inserted two new sub-sections (4) and (5) into Article 368. These two new sub-sections (4) and (5) read as follows:

"(4): No amendment of this Constitution including the provisions of Part III (i.e. Fundamental Rights) made or purporting to have been made under this Article (whether before or after the commencement of Section 55 of the Constitution (Forty-second Amendment) Act 1976 shall be called in question in any Court on any ground."

"(5): For the removal of doubts, it is hereby declared that there shall be no limitation whatever on the constituent power of the Parliament to amend by way of *addition*, *variation* or *repeal* the provision of this Constitution under this Article."

11. The new clause (5) of Article 368 confers upon the Parliament vast and undefined power to amend the Constitution even so as to distort it out of recognition.

12. The theme song of the majority decision in Kesavananda Bharati case (AIR 1973 SC 1461) is as follows: "Amend as you may even this solemn document, which the Founding Fathers have committed to your care, for you know the best the needs of your generation. But the Constitution is a precious heritage; therefore, you cannot destroy its identity."

13. It is, therefore, obvious that the Constitution had conferred a limited amending power on the Parliament.

14. The Constitution (Forty-second Amendment) Act 1976 amended the Preamble and by this amendment, the Preamble, which before the amendment read as "sovereign democratic Republic" became after the amendment, "sovereign, socialist, secular, democratic, republic." Similarly, an amendment was made to the Preamble to change, the expression "unity of the nation" to "unity and integrity of the nation." These amendments to the Preamble show how the Parliament can exercise its power of amendment consistently with "the creed of the Constitution". These amendments do not destroy the basic features of the Constitution as they "offer promise of more; they do not scuttle a previous heritage."

15. In Indira Nehru Gandhi *versus* Raj Narain (AIR 1975 SC 2299), Justice H.R. Khanna struck down clause (4) of Article 329A of the Constitution which abolished the forum for adjudicating upon a dispute relating to an election on the ground that the particular Article violated the principle of free and fair election – a part of the basic structure of the Constitution. Two other judges, viz. Justice K.K. Mathew and Justice Y.V. Chandrachud also struck down the Constitutional amendment on ground of violation of the "basic structure".

16. Clause (5) of Article 368 – introduced by the Constitution (Forty-second Amendment) Act 1976 – confers on the Parliament unlimited power of amendment of the Constitution including any Fundamental Right. Thus, clause (5) enables the Parliament to destroy the identity of the Constitution by an amendment. Clause (4) of Article 368 – also introduced by the Constitution (Forty-second Amendment) Act 1976 – stipulated that no amendment of the Constitution could be questioned on any ground in any Court. In other words, all amendments of the Constitution – including amendment of any Fundamental Right – were made immune to Judicial Review. Therefore, the Constitution (Forty-second Amendment) Act 1976 inserting clause (4) in Article 368 violated the doctrine of Judicial Review, a component of the basic structure of the Constitution.

17. Article 31C – introduced by the Constitution (Forty-second Amendment) Act 1976 – provided that any law giving effect to Directive Principles of State Policy shall not be

deemed to be void on the ground that it is inconsistent with or takes away or abridges any of the Rights conferred by Articles 14, 19 and 31.

18. It is relevant to mention that the unamended Article 31C, i.e. Article 31C as it was before the Constitution Amendment Act 1976 – protected laws to implement provisions in clause (b) and clause (c) of Article 39 of the Constitution. This was upheld in Kesavananda Bharati case (AIR 1973 SC 1461).

19. It has to be seen whether the new Article 31C, introduced by the Constitution (Forty-second Amendment) Act 1976, can be justified on the same grounds on which Article 31C before its amendment in 1976 was upheld by the Supreme Court.

20. The basic structure of the Constitution rests on the foundation that whereas the Directive Principles of State Policy stipulate the mandatory objectives of Government, those ends can be attained consistent with the Fundamental Rights. The new Article 31C introduced by the Constitution (Forty-second Amendment) Act 1976 completely subordinates the Fundamental Rights to the Directive Principles of State Policy. The new Article 31C will confer an unrestricted license on the legislature – both at the centre and in the states – to destroy democracy and establish an authoritarian regime.

21. N.A. Palkhivala has argued that it is not correct to say that the Fundamental Rights have to be destroyed to achieve some of the important objectives in the Directive Principles. He gave examples of free legal aid, organization of village Panchayats, living wages for workers, just and humane conditions of work, free and compulsory education for children, organization of agriculture and animal husbandry and protection of the environment and wild life. Briefly stated, what the Constituent Assembly had rejected by creating a harmonious balance between the Fundamental Rights and the Directive Principles has been brought back by the new Article 31C introduced by the Constitution (Forty-second Amendment) Act 1976.

22. Admittedly, Fundamental Rights can be suspended by a Presidential Order during the Emergency under Article 359 of the Constitution. The new Article 31C, however, can abrogate them even in normal times.

23. In reply to N.A. Palkhivala's argument, the Attorney-General for India, Lal Narayan Sinha has argued that the new Article 31C enables a legislature to implement any provision of the Directive Principles. He also argued that a law to implement any Directive Principle is basically a reasonable restriction on Fundamental Right in the public interest. Hence, the new Article 31C has to be upheld.

24. It was also argued on behalf of the Union of India that Judicial Review is not strictly excluded by the amended Article 31C because it will still be open to the Court to consider the following:

(i) Whether the impugned law has direct and reasonable nexus with any of the Directive Principles;

(ii) Whether the provisions in the impugned law encroaching upon the Fundamental Rights are essential for implementation of any of the Directive Principles;

(iii) Whether the Fundamental Rights encroached upon are an essential feature of the basic structure of the Constitution.

25. The petitioners have challenged Sections 4 and 55 of the Constitution (Forty-second Amendment) Act 1976. The question is whether in view of the majority decision in Kesavananda Bharati (AIR 1973 SC 1461) the Parliament can amend the Constitution so as to give precedence to the Directive Principles over the Fundamental Rights. The answer will depend upon whether Article 14 and Article 19 in the chapter on Fundamental Rights are a part of the basic structure of the Constitution.

26. Article 14 and Article 19 confer Rights which are elementary for a democracy. If Articles 14 and 19 are put out of operation in regard to bulk of the laws, Article 32 will be drained of its life-blood.

27. Article 32 stipulates that the Right to move the Supreme Court for enforcement of any Fundamental Right is guaranteed and cannot be suspended except as provided for by the Constitution. Section 4 of the Constitution (Forty-second Amendment) Act 1976 has found an easy way to circumvent Article 32 by withdrawing protection of Article 14 and Article 19 in respect of a large category of laws so that there would be no violation to complain of in regard to which redress can be sought under Article 32. Article 14 forbids class legislation; but because of Section 4 of the Constitution (Forty-second Amendment) Act 1976, there would be no constitutional check on class legislation. The nature and quality of Section 4 of the Constitution (Forty-second Amendment) Act 1976 are such that they virtually tear away the heart of basic fundamental freedom.

28. Article 31C, introduced by the Constitution Amendment Act 1976 speaks of laws giving effect to Directive Principles of State Policy. Even if a state legislature passes a law for giving effect to policy of a local authority towards securing a Directive Principle, the law passed by the state legislature will enjoy immunity from attack for violation of Articles 14 and 19. The state legislatures are thus given unfettered discretion to deprive people of their civil liberties. It is, however, relevant to mention that such a law of a state legislature must secure assent of the President before becoming a valid law.

29. The Attorney-General argued that Article 31C should be read down to save it from the challenge of unconstitutionality. He urged that it should be read into Article 31C that only such laws would be immune from challenge under Article 14 and Article 19 if they do not damage the basic structure of the Constitution.

30. The principle of reading down the provisions of a law for saving it from constitutional challenge is well known. But, in this case, the principle of reading down a provision such as Article 31C cannot be invoked as the principle of reading down is invoked when words of width are incorporated inadvertently in a law.

31. The device of reading down is not to be resorted to save the susceptibility of the law-makers. It cannot also be used to imagine law of one's liking to have been passed. One must take the Parliament at its word when it undertakes a constitutional amendment as Article 31C.

32. N.A. Palkhivala read out before the Court an extract from the speech of the then Union Law Minister, who while speaking on the amendment to Article 31C pointed out that the amendment has become necessary as Government did not want the "let and hindrance" of the Fundamental Rights to frustrate a socio-economic regime envisaged by the Directive Principles. In other words, if the Parliament has manifestly a clear intention to exercise an unlimited power of restricting Fundamental Rights by Article 31C, it would be impermissible to read down the amplitude of that power so as to make it limited.

33. In the history of constitutional law, no constitutional amendment has ever been read down to mean the exact opposite of what it says and intends.

34. It was argued on behalf of the Union of India that Article 31C has been amended to provide that no law shall be deemed to be void on the ground of violation of Articles 14 and 19 if such law gives effect to policy of the state towards securing all or any of the principles laid down in the chapter on Directive Principles. But the Attorney-General argued that even after such amendment, the Court can ask the following questions:

(i) Does the law secure any of the Directive Principles of State Policy?

(ii) Is it necessary to encroach upon Fundamental Rights to secure the object of the Directive Principles?

(iii) Does the encroachment upon Fundamental Rights violate the basic structure of the Constitution?

35. Chief Justice Y.V. Chandrachud speaking for the majority of judges held that reading the existence of an extensive Judicial Review into Article 31C is really to permit distortion of Article 31C itself, which provides expressly that no law of a particular description shall be deemed to be void on the ground that it violates Article 14 or Article 19. It would be sheer adventurism for the Courts to undertake a judicial inquiry, which the Attorney-General has argued the Courts are free to undertake. The Courts can at best decide whether there is a nexus between the law enacted under Article 31C and Article 39B and 39C of the Directive Principles of State Policy. Briefly stated, the Courts can enquire into the reasonableness of the nexus and not reasonableness of the law. The attempt to drape Article 31C into the democratic outfit under which the Courts can undertake an extensive Judicial Review must, therefore, fail.

36. Article 31C gives protection to an uncatalogued variety of laws to be enacted by the Parliament. If this happens, fundamental freedom will become "a parchment in a glass case" to be viewed as a matter of historical curiosity.

37. Articles 14, 19 and 21 stand between the heaven of freedom into which Rabindranath Tagore wanted the country to awake as contrasted with the abyss of unrestrained power. Article 31C has removed two sides of the golden triangle, which gives an assurance to the people of the country that the promise set forth in the Preamble to the Constitution will be performed.

38. In view of the aforesaid, Section 4 of the Constitution (Forty-second Amendment) Act 1976 is void as it destroys the basic structure of the Constitution by putting certain laws beyond Judicial Review. Similarly, Section 55 of the Constitution (Forty-second Amendment) Act

1976 which removes all limitations on power of the Parliament to amend the Constitution is also void as it destroys the power of Judicial Review and clothes the Parliament with sweeping power of amendment, which is against the basic structure of the Constitution.

39. Justice P.N. Bhagwati wrote a dissenting judgment in the Minerva Mills case (AIR 1980 SC 1789).

40. The salient points in the judgment of Justice P.N. Bhagwati are as follows: there was hardly any time to exchange draft judgment by the majority of judges as the majority judgment was to be pronounced by Chief Justice Y.V. Chandrachud within two days before the summer vacation commenced on 11 May 1980. Hence, there was no scope for discussion among the judges.

41. As hearing of the arguments in the case had commenced from 22 October 1979 and concluded on 16 November 1979 and the arguments had been concluded nearly five and a half months ago, there should have been free and frank exchange of views before the Chief Justice and the brother judges decided to deliver the majority judgment.

42. As there were as many as eleven separate judgments delivered by the 13-Judge Constitution Bench in Kesavananda Bharati case (AIR 1973 SC 1461) after delivery of judgments, a summary of the judgments was signed by nine judges to indicate the *ratio decidendi*. But as the Bench of 13 judges had become *functus officio* after the judgment was delivered, the summary of judgments signed by nine out of 13 judges cannot lay down the law under Article 141 of the Constitution.

43. The correct import of the ratio in Kesavananda Bharati's case (AIR 1973 SC 1461) is to be found in the later judgment of the Supreme Court in Indira Nehru Gandhi *versus* Raj Narain (AIR 1975 SC 2299) where it was held that in Kesavananda Bharati's case, the majority of the judges held that the amending power in Article 368, though wide in its sweep, did not confer power on the Parliament to alter the basic structure of the Constitution.

44. In Kesavananda Bharati's case (AIR 1973 SC 1461), it was held that any Fundamental Right could be amended by the Parliament under Article 368 but by such amendment, the basic structure of the Constitution cannot be altered.

45. Justice H.R. Khanna was of the view that the Right to Property guaranteed as a Fundamental Right was not a part of the basic structure but so far as other Fundamental Rights were concerned, he left the issue open.

46. In Kesavananda Bharati's case (AIR 1973 SC 1461), some judges including Chief Justice S.M. Sikri, identified some features of the basic structure of the Constitution. They, however, mentioned that what they have identified as the basic structure was merely illustrative and not exhaustive.

47. In Kesavananda Bharati's case (AIR 1973 SC 1461), six out of 13 judges held that though Article 368 conferred the power to amend the Constitution, there were implied limitations on such power and Parliament cannot amend the Constitution to destroy its basic structure. The six judges also held that though in the public interest a reasonable abridgement of the Fundamental Rights could be done by the Parliament under Article 368, the Fundamental

Rights could not be either emasculated or abrogated under Article 368. Out of the other seven judges, Justice H.R. Khanna did not agree that the Fundamental Rights could not be amended under Article 368; but he held that by such amendment, Parliament cannot abrogate or alter the basic structure of the Constitution.

48. After the Kesavananda Bharati judgment in April 1973, the Supreme Court had the opportunity of considering in Indira Nehru Gandhi *versus* Raj Narain (AIR 1975 SC 2299) what was the ratio in the eleven separate judgments in the 13-judge Bench in Kesavananda Bharati case (AIR 1973 SC 1461). The Court held that though the power of amendment in Article 368 has a very wide sweep, it cannot be invoked to abrogate the basic structure of the Constitution.

49. In Indira Nehru Gandhi *versus* Raj Narain (AIR 1975 SC 2299), the Constitution (Thirty-ninth Amendment) Act 1975, which introduced a new Article 329A, was held to be *ultra vires* as it forbade any challenge to election of the Prime Minister of India to the House of People. The Court considered it as violative of the Right to Equality and the basic structure of free and fair election to the legislature.

50. Whether a particular feature of the Constitution constitutes its basic structure can be ascertained from a thorough analysis of the specific provision supposed to constitute the basic structure.

51. Justice K.K. Mathew in Indira Nehru Gandhi *versus* Raj Narain (AIR 1975 SC 2299) held that "to be a basic structure, it must be a terrestrial concept having its habitat within the four corners of the Constitution." He also said that the basic structure is not like "a twinkling star up above the Constitution."

52. Justice K.K. Mathew also held that it is "impossible to spin out any concrete concept of the basic structure out of the gossamer concepts set out in the Preamble." He held that only from the specific provisions of the Constitution one can get "the stuff from which basic structure is woven."

53. In Minerva Mills case (AIR 1980 SC 1789), N.A. Palkhivala challenged amendment made to Article 31C of the Constitution by Section 4 of the Constitution (Forty-second Amendment) Act 1976. He argued that the amendment to Article 31C made the Directive Principles supreme over the Fundamental Rights and thereby destroyed the basic structure of the Constitution.

54. The argument of N.A. Palkhivala can be called an argument of despair. In order that a law to be enacted by the Parliament or a state legislature to give effect to any of the Directive Principles, there must be a real or substantive connection between the law and the particular Directive Principle sought to be implemented. If there is no substantive connection, the Courts could strike down the particular law.

55. Article 37 of the Constitution enjoins upon the state to make laws by applying the provisions in the chapter on the Directive Principles of State Policy. Granville Austin in his book, *The Indian Constitution: Cornerstone of a Nation,* has said that both the Directive Principles and the Fundamental Rights constitute "the conscience of the Constitution." If the state fails to create conditions in which the Fundamental Freedom is to be enjoyed

by all, "the freedom of the few will be at the mercy of the many and then all freedom will vanish."

56. It could be incongrous to hold the amended Article 31C invalid when the unamended Article 31C has been held to be valid by the majority of judges in Kesavananda Bharati case (AIR 1973 SC 1461) and in Waman Rao's case (AIR 1981 SC 271).

57. In view of the aforesaid reasons, Section 4 of the Constitution (Forty-second Amendment) Act 1976 which amended Article 31C is valid.

58. The arguments advanced by Justice P.N. Bhagwati in the Minerva Mills Case (AIR 1980 SC 1789) are applicable to the judgment in Waman Rao's case (AIR 1981 SC 271) in which Justice P.N. Bhagwati was in the Bench. In other words, Justice P.N. Bhagwati wrote a common judgment in Minerva Mills case (AIR 1980 SC 1789) and Waman Rao's case (AIR 1981 SC 271).

CHAPTER 14

Union of India *versus* Tulsiram Patel (AIR 1985 SC 1416)

[CHIEF JUSTICE Y.V. CHANDRACHUD, JUSTICE V.D. TULZAPURKAR, JUSTICE R.S. PATHAK, JUSTICE D.P. MADON AND JUSTICE M.P. THAKKAR]

Case Summary

This is a judgment of a five-Judge Constitution Bench of the Supreme Court in which Justice D.P. Madon, on behalf of majority of Judges delivered the judgment while Justice M.P. Thakkar delivered a dissenting minority judgment on the scope of Articles 309, 310 and 311 of the Constitution.

1. Justice D.P. Madon, who delivered the majority judgment, made an elaborate survey of history of the Civil Service in India. He quoted from the book, *The Common Law* by Justice Oliver Wendell Holmes to affirm that law, which embodies story of a nation's development can be fully understood if we know what it has been and what it tends to become. Justice Oliver Wendell Holmes also said that law cannot be dealt with as if it contained only the axioms and corollaries of a mathematical treatise.
2. The main points in Justice D.P. Madon's judgment are in the following paragraphs.
3. In the ordinary law of master and servant, if the contract of service contains a stipulation of termination of service by notice, the master can always dispense with service of a servant after giving him notice of termination. If, however, the contract of service is not for a fixed period, employment of a servant can be terminated by the master by giving him notice of a reasonable period.
4. Under the ordinary law of master and servant, if a contract is wrongfully terminated, the servant can sue the master for damages.
5. The ordinary law of master and servant, however, is not applicable to a Civil Servant.
6. The Civil Service of India has followed the British pattern though in some respects there are important differences between the Civil Service in the two countries.
7. In U.K., except when otherwise provided in a statute, public officers and servants of the Crown hold office during pleasure of the Crown (*durante bene placito*) as opposed to an office held during good conduct (*dum bene se gesserit*).

8. In U.K., since the 18th century, Parliament has imposed legal restrictions on pleasure of the Crown by providing for disciplinary procedure to dismiss or remove a civil servant.
9. In U.K., a Civil Servant can bring an action for unfair dismissal against the Crown. But just as a servant, under the ordinary law of master and servant, can sue the master for damages on account of wrongful dismissal, but cannot insist on continuing in employment, so also a Civil Servant in U.K. can sue the Crown for damages for wrongful dismissal or removal but cannot insist on continuing in service of the Crown.
10. When the East India Company was administering parts of India known as British India, any person in the Company's employment could be removed from service by the Court of Directors of the Company. Provisions to this effect were in the Charter Act of 1793 and the Charter Act of 1833.
11. After the Sepoy Mutiny (1857), the Government of India Act 1858 vested administration of British India in the Crown and conferred power on the Secretary of State-in-Council to frame Regulations for the Civil Service of India.
12. In 1861, the Indian Civil Service was given statutory recognition by the Indian Civil Service Act.
13. For the first time, the Government of India Act 1919 provided that every person in the Civil Service in India holds office during pleasure of His Majesty and may not be dismissed from service by an Authority inferior in rank than the Appointing Authority.
14. The Government of India Act of 1919 also provided for setting up of a Public Service Commission of India. The Commission was set up on 01.10.1926.
15. Section 240 of the Government of India Act 1935 reiterated the provisions of the Government of India Act 1919 that every Civil Servant holds office during pleasure of the Crown. It also reiterated that no Civil Servant or person holding a civil post in British India could be dismissed by an authority lower in rank than the Appointing Authority.
16. Section 240 of the Government of India Act 1935 also stipulated that no Civil Servant or person holding a civil post can be dismissed or reduced in rank until he has been given a reasonable opportunity of showing cause against the proposed punitive action.
17. The stipulation of reasonable opportunity of showing cause against punitive action as dismissal or reduction of rank did not apply if:
    - (i) A person was dismissed or reduced in rank on ground of conduct which has led to his conviction on a criminal charge, or
    - (ii) Where the authority empowered to dismiss or reduce in rank a person is satisfied that for reasons to be recorded in writing it would not be reasonably practicable to give the delinquent civil servant a reasonable opportunity of showing cause in relation to charges against him.
18. The stipulation in Section 240 of the Government of India Act 1935 that the delinquent Civil Servant would have a reasonable opportunity of showing cause in relation to charges against him did not exist in the earlier Government of India Act 1919.
19. The Constitution of India in regard to provisions for the Civil Services and Civil posts has broadly adopted the provisions of the Government of India Act 1935.

20. Article 311(2)(c) of the Constitution contains a stipulation that a reasonable opportunity to be heard in regard to charges of misconduct against a delinquent official would not be given to him if the President or the Governor, as the case may be, is satisfied that in the interest of the security of the state, it is not expedient to hold an Inquiry against the delinquent official. A similar provision did not exist in the Government of India Act 1935.

21. Article 311(2) of the Constitution, as originally enacted, provided as follows:

"No such person as aforesaid shall be dismissed, removed or reduced in rank until he has been given a reasonable opportunity of showing cause against action proposed to be taken in regard to him."

22. By the Constitution (Fifteenth Amendment) Act 1963, *inter alia*, clause (2) of Article 311 was amended to provide for a new clause (3) as follows:

"No such person as aforesaid shall be dismissed, removed or reduced in rank except after an Inquiry in which he has been informed of the charges against him and given a reasonable opportunity of being heard in respect of those charges:

Provided that where it is proposed after such Inquiry, to impose upon him any such penalty, such penalty may be imposed on the basis of evidence adduced during such Inquiry and it shall not be necessary to give such person any more opportunity of making representation against the penalty proposed."

23. Article 311(3) of the Constitution stipulates that if a question arises whether it is reasonably practicable to hold an Inquiry, the decision thereon of the authority competent to dismiss, remove or reduce in rank the delinquent Civil Servant shall be final. A similar provision was not there in the Government of India Act 1935.

24. Another point of difference between Article 311 of the Constitution and clause (240) of the Government of India Act 1935 is that Article 311 extends the protection and safeguards to not only dismissal from service and reduction in rank but also to "removal" from service whereas Section 240 of the Government of India Act 1935 extended the protection and safeguard to "dismissal" from service and "reduction in rank" only but not to "removal from service."

25. It has been contended on behalf of delinquent Government Servants that the "Pleasure Doctrine" is a relic of Feudalism and has no place in interpreting the provisions relating to Civil Servants in the Constitution of India. The counsel for the Union of India stated in reply that the "Pleasure Doctrine" was based on sound public policy.

26. Lord Hobhouse has said in Shenton *versus* Smith (1895) that the "Pleasure Doctrine" was necessary to be invoked to get rid of delinquent Civil Servants in the public interest.

27. In State of Uttar Pradesh *versus* Baburam Upadhya (AIR 1961 SC 651) and in Moti Ram Deka *versus* General Manager N.E. Railways (AIR 1964 SC 600), the Supreme Court held that the "Pleasure Doctrine" is not based on any special prerogative but on sound principles of public policy.

28. The relationship between Government and the Civil Servants is not an ordinary contract of service between a master and a servant. The legal relationship is in the nature of a status. The duties of a person having a status are fixed by law.

29. If a law or rule framed under Article 309 of the Constitution regulating recruitment or conditions of service of Government Servants violates constitutional guarantees under Article 311 or violates any Fundamental Right, the law or the Rule can be struck down by the Courts.

30. In Kameswar Prasad *versus* the State of Bihar (AIR 1962 SC 1166), the Bihar Government Servants' Conduct Rule which prohibited even peaceful demonstration by Government Servants, was struck down as violative of the Fundamental Right to assemble peaceably and without arms guaranteed under Article 19(1)(b) of the Constitution.

31. But at one time it was thought that a Government Servant could not sue the Government for arrears of salary as such salary was a bounty and subject to the "Pleasure Doctrine". Relying on an earlier decision of Lord Blackburn, the Privy Council decided in I.M. Lall's case (AIR 1948 P.C. 121) that though I.M. Lall's dismissal was quashed as being violative of Section 240(3) of the Government of India Act 1935, he could not sue Government for arrears of salary as a public servant, denied arrears of salary, could only pray to the Crown for the Crown's benevolence.

32. Happily, the ratio of I.M. Lall's case was not good law after judgment of the Supreme Court in State of Bihar *versus* Abdul Majid (AIR 1954 SC 245).

33. In India, for the first time, a fetter was imposed on the "Pleasure Doctrine" by Section 96B of the Government of India Act 1919. Under the aforesaid provision, only the Appointing Authority could dismiss a Government Servant. There were no other safeguards in the Government of India Act 1919 for a Government Servant regarding termination of service.

34. The Government of India Act 1935 provided several safeguards regarding tenure of a Government Servant even though he still held office during pleasure of the Crown.

35. Article 310(1) of the Constitution adopts the same "Pleasure Doctrine" as provided in Section 240 of the Government of India Act 1935.

36. A question arose whether Pleasure of the President or Governor of a State under Article 310(1) of the Constitution is to be exercised personally by the President or the Governor or by any other authority empowered by the Act or Rules under Article 309 of the Constitution.

37. A majority of Judges in a Constitution Bench decided in Babu Ram Upadhya's case (AIR 1961 SC 751) that power to dismiss, remove or reduce in rank a Civil Servant is not an executive power vested on the Governor of the State and hence cannot be delegated by the Governor to a subordinate officer and has to be exercised by the Governor personally as mandated by the Constitution.

38. The ratio of Babu Ram Upadhya's case (AIR 1961 SC 751) was overruled by a larger Constitution Bench of the Supreme Court in Moti Ram Deka *versus* General Manager N.E. Railway (AIR 1964 SC 600).

39. In Sardari Lal *versus* Union of India (AIR 1971 SC 1547), it was held that when a person is dismissed because in the interest of security of the State, it is not expedient to hold an Inquiry, it must be the personal satisfaction of the President or the Governor as the case may be.

40. But the ratio in Sardari Lal's case was overruled by a larger Bench in Shamsher Singh *versus* the State of Punjab (AIR 1974 SC 2192).

41. Clause (2) of Article 311 of the Constitution gives a mandate to one of the important principles of Natural Justice, i.e. the *Audi Alteram Partem* Rule. It stipulates that a person holding a civil post under the Union or the State shall not be dismissed or removed from service or reduced in rank until after an Inquiry in which he has been informed of the charges against him and has been given a reasonable opportunity of being heard in respect of the charges.

42. The safeguard provided for in clause (2) of Article 311 is, however, taken away:
   (a) where a person is dismissed, removed or reduced in rank on the ground of conduct which has led to his conviction on a criminal charge; or
   (b) where the authority empowered to dismiss or remove or reduce in rank a person holding a civil post is satisfied that for reasons to be recorded in writing it is not reasonably practicable to hold such Inquiry; or
   (c) where the President or the Governor as the case may be is satisfied that in the interest of security of the state it is not expedient to hold such Inquiry.

43. It was argued that even though the second proviso to Article 311(2) operates in specified cases and a full-fledged Inquiry can be dispensed with in such cases, there is nothing to prevent the Disciplinary Authority from holding a minimal Inquiry as no prejudice can be caused in doing so.

44. The above argument is devoid of substance. If a Government Servant, who has not been convicted of a serious offence by a Court but because of mistaken identity is either dismissed or removed from service or reduced in rank, the extremely active service grapevine would reveal identity of the real culprit and to that extent the Competent Authority can correct its error.

45. The expression in the second proviso to Article 311(2) that Article 311(2) would not apply in circumstances mentioned in sub-clauses (a), (b) and (c) of the second proviso to Article 311(2) is mandatory. It is a prohibitory injunction in the Constitution to the Disciplinary Authority from holding an Inquiry.

46. It might appear harsh but the second proviso to Article 311(2) has been provided as a matter of public policy and for public good just as the "Pleasure Doctrine" has been incorporated in Article 310(1).

47. It is relevant to mention that sympathy and commiseration cannot be allowed to outweigh considerations of public policy, concern for public interest and regard for public good.

48. Even after a Government Servant has been dismissed or removed from service or reduced in rank without any Inquiry, the aggrieved Government Servant has the remedy of appeal to the Appellate Authority and the constitutional remedy of Judicial Review.

49. "Reasonable Opportunity" in Article 311(2) has been discussed in Khem Chand *versus* Union of India (AIR 1958 SC 300). The Court have held that "reasonable opportunity" includes:

(i) An opportunity to the charged official to deny his guilt and establish his innocence which can only be done if the charged official is formally communicated the charges against him and the imputations on which such charges are based;

(ii) An opportunity to the charged official to defend himself by cross-examining the witnesses produced against him before the Inquiring Authority and by examining himself or any other witness in his defence;

(iii) And finally an opportunity to make his representation as to why the proposed penalty should not be imposed on him. He can only make such representation after the Inquiring Authority, on due application of mind to the charges held proved communicates to the charged official the penalty to be imposed on him.

50. The Constitution (Fifteenth Amendment) Act 1963 was both a declaratory as well as a clarificatory amendment. The declaratory part made it clear that no additional opportunity was to be given to a Government Servant beyond what was originally conferred by Article 311. It was also clarificatory as it allowed the charged official to submit his representation against the proposed penalty only on the basis of evidence adduced during the Inquiry.

51. The Constitution (Fifteenth Amendment) Act 1963 was necessary because as pointed out by the Supreme Court, an erroneous impression prevailed that every Disciplinary Proceeding must consist of two Inquiries, one before issuing a show cause notice to a charged official and another Inquiry thereafter.

52. By the Constitution (Forty-second Amendment) Act 1976 (which came into effect from 01.01.1977) the charged official's Right of representation against penalty proposed to be imposed by the Competent Authority was deleted.

53. It is relevant that both the Constitution (Fifteenth Amendment) Act 1963 and the Constitution (Forty-second Amendment) Act 1976 did not make any change in the second proviso to Article 311(2) of the Constitution.

54. It was submitted on behalf of the delinquent Government Servants, who were imposed penalties of dismissal and removal from service by dispensing with inquiry that the principle of Natural Justice of *Audi Alteram Partem* must be read into the second proviso to Article 311(2). It was argued that an order of dismissal or removal from service might be valid under the second proviso to Article 311(2) but might be void because of violation of Natural Justice that the official was not heard before such dismissal or removal.

55. The principles of Natural Justice are not the creation of Article 14 of the Constitution but Article 14 is their constitutional guardian.

56. The principles of Natural Justice traces its origin to the *Jus Naturale* of Roman Jurists of ancient times.

57. Natural Law was also invoked to put a check on supremacy of the Parliament in the 17th century. In 1610 A.D., Lord Coke said in Dr. Bonham's case that when an Act of Parliament was against the common Right or reason, the common law would control it and adjudge such parliamentary enactment as void. In his *magnum opus*, *Commentaries on the Laws of England*, Blackstone said that the Law of Nature, dictated by God was superior to any human law.

58. Judges have defined Natural Justice in different ways.

(i) Following the judgment of the Queen's Bench in Ridge *versus* Baldwin (1964 AC 40) Justice P.N. Bhagwati called Natural Justice as "fair play in action" in Maneka Gandhi *versus* Union of India (AIR 1978 SC 597).

(ii) In 1967, Lord Parker called "Natural Justice" as a duty to act fairly.

(iii) In 1976, Lord Russell of Killowen described "Natural Justice" as "a fair crack of the whip".

(iv) Lord Reid has said in Ridge *versus* Baldwin (1964 AC 40) that Natural Justice is what a reasonable man would regard as fair procedure in particular circumstances.

59. In Re the Special Court Bill 1978 (AIR 1979 SC 479), Chief Justice Y.V. Chandrachud divided Article 14 into two parts. He said that the first part of Article 14 relating to equality before law enshrines the basic principle of Republicanism. The second part of Article 14, owed its inspiration to the Fourteenth Amendment of the American Constitution. The second part of Article 14 guarantees equal protection of the laws throughout the territory of India. A facet of Article 14 is that if a person is penalized in violation of the principles of Natural Justice, it would be an arbitrary action and violative of the guarantee in Article 14.

60. In State of Andhra Pradesh *versus* Nalla Raja Reddy (AIR 1967 SC 1458), the Supreme Court, speaking through Chief Justice K. Subba Rao, held that

"Official arbitrariness is more subversive of the doctrine of equality than statutory discrimination" as "the wand of official arbitrariness can be waved in all directions indiscriminately."

61. Justice P.N. Bhagwati has held in E.P. Royappa *versus* State of Tamilnadu (AIR 1974 SC 555) that:

(i) Article 14 is the genus while Article 16 is the species.

(ii) Equality is a dynamic concept with many aspects and dimensions.

(iii) Equality and arbitrariness are sworn enemies.

(iv) "Equality" belongs to the Rule of Law in a Republic while arbitrariness reflects the whims and caprice of an absolute monarch.

(v) Where an Act is arbitrary, it is unequal both according to political logic and constitutional law and hence violative of Article 14.

(vi) *Mala fide* exercise of power and arbitrariness are different lethal radiations emanating from the same vice.

(vii) The principle of reasonableness which legally as well as philosophically is an essential element of equality or non-arbitrariness pervades Article 14 like a brooding omnipresence.

(viii) The principles of Natural Justice apply equally to administrative and quasi-judicial inquiries because both inquiries seek to help a person to get justice.

62. The nature of the hearing to be given to a delinquent Government Servant under Clause (2) of Article 311 has been set out elaborately in Khem Chand *versus* Union of India (AIR 1958 SC 300).

63. After Khem Chand's case (AIR 1958 SC 300), the only change in the concept of "reasonable opportunity" to the delinquent Government Servant to defend himself was made by the Constitution (Forty-second Amendment) Act 1976, which stipulated that a Government Servant has no right to be intimated the penalty proposed against him so that he could represent against the penalty.

64. In A.K. Kraipak's case (AIR 1970 SC 150), it has been held that what particular Rules of Natural Justice would apply would depend to a great extent on facts and circumstances of a case.

65. In Union of India *versus* Colonel J.N. Sinha (AIR 1971 SC 40), it was held that the Rules of Natural Justice do not supplant but supplements the law. Therefore, if a statutory provision either specifically or by necessary implication excludes the application of any of the principles of Natural Justice, the Court cannot ignore the mandate of the legislature and read into the concerned provisions the principle of Natural Justice.

66. The settled position of law with regard to Natural Justice are as follows:

 (i) Where an Authority functions under a statute and the statute provides for observance of Natural Justice, Natural Justice will be observed only in the manner provided for in the statute.

 (ii) No wider Right of Natural Justice than that provided by the statute can be claimed by an aggrieved party. Conversely, Natural Justice provided for in the statute cannot be interpreted narrowly.

 (iii) Where a statute is silent about observance of the principles of Natural Justice, such silence is taken to imply compliance with the principles of Natural Justice.

 (iv) The principles of Natural Justice cannot only be modified but in exceptional cases, they can even be excluded. The principle of Natural Justice that no one can be a judge in his own case is subject to the Doctrine of Necessity and yields to it as pointed out in J. Mohapatra & Co. *versus* State of Orissa (AIR 1984 SC 1572).

 (v) So far as the *Audi Alteram Partem* Rule is concerned, both in England and India, it is well-established that where the aforesaid Rule would obstruct prompt action, such a Right can be excluded as pointed out in Maneka Gandhi *versus* Union of India (AIR 1978 SC 597).

67. There is no case for introducing the *Audi Alteram Partem* Rule by a side door to provide once again for the same Inquiry which the second proviso to Article 311(2) has expressly prohibited.

68. Where the second proviso to Article 311(2) applies, though a Government Servant, who is dismissed, removed or reduced in rank has no prior opportunity to defend himself, he has the Right of appeal under the relevant Service Rules.

69. In Maneka Gandhi *versus* Union of India (AIR 1978 SC 597), and in Liberty Oil Mills *versus* Union of India (AIR 1984 SC 1271), the right to make a representation after action was taken (i.e. a post-decisional representation) was held to be adequate compliance with Natural Justice.

70. It was argued that even though the second proviso to Article 311(2) of the Constitution excludes any Right of being heard by the Civil Servant or person holding a civil post, the Right of hearing is available under Article 14 of the Constitution.

71. The above argument was supported by the ratio in R.C. Cooper's case (AIR 1970 SC 564) which overruled the majority view in A.K. Gopalan *versus* State of Madras (AIR 1950 SC 27) that each Fundamental Right operated exclusively without having any inter-relationship with any other Fundamental Right. Justice M.H. Beg elaborated this ratio in R.C. Cooper's case (AIR 1970 SC 564) when he said that Fundamental Rights do not represent entirely separate streams of Rights which do not mingle at many points as they are all parts of an integrated scheme in the Constitution.

72. But, in this case, the second proviso to Article 311(2) is being considered where the Constitution has expressly excluded the *Audi Alteram Partem* Rule.

73. In this connection, Justice Meggary has rightly observed that the principles of Natural Justice must not be allowed to run wild. To put it differently, Natural Justice is a magnificent thoroughbred and must not be allowed to be an unruly one.

74. Sometimes Service Rules under Article 309 of the Constitution have been interpreted to provide for the principle of Natural Justice even in cases where the second proviso to Article 311(2) operates. Such interpretation of Service Rules is not permissible as Article 309 of the Constitution under which Service Rules are framed, opens with the expression, "subject to the provisions of the Constitution". Therefore, the Rules framed for different services under Article 309 have to be in conformity with Article 310(1) and Article 311.

75. There cannot be an exercise of power unless such power exists in law. Even the mention of a wrong provision or omission to mention the provision which contains the source of power will not invalidate an order where the source of power exists.

76. Where a Disciplinary Authority finds that a Government Servant has been convicted of a criminal charge, he must consider whether the conduct which has led to the conviction was such that it warrants imposition of a penalty and if so, what would be an adequate penalty.

77. If the Disciplinary Authority comes to the conclusion that the conduct of the Government Servant, which led to his conviction by a criminal court, was such that the Government Servant deserved either dismissal or removal from service or reduction in rank, he would first decide which of the three penalties has to be imposed. In passing that order he is not required to give a hearing to the Government Servant.

78. If the Government Servant on whom a penalty has been imposed following conviction in a criminal court does not succeed after invoking administrative remedies of appeal, revision or review, he can invoke the Court's power of Judicial Review. The Court will examine whether the penalty imposed has been arbitrary or grossly excessive and out of all proportion to the offence for which the Government Servant has been convicted.

79. In Shankar Das *versus* Union of India (AIR 1985 SC 772), the Supreme Court set aside the impugned order of penalty of dismissal from service on the ground that the penalty of dismissal was whimsical.

80. It is not necessary that when a Court sets aside the penalty of dismissal or removal from service, it has to necessarily order reinstatement of the Government Servant with full back wages. Instead the Court can substitute a penalty which in its opinion would be just and fair in circumstances of the case.

81. The earlier decision of the Supreme Court in T.R. Challapan's case (AIR 1975 SC 2216) that even when under clause (b) of the second proviso to Article 311(2) service of a Government Servant was dispensed with, a show cause notice to the Government Servant was necessary is hereby overruled as Challapan's case was wrongly decided.

82. Clause (b) of the second proviso to Article 311(2) lays down that satisfaction of the Competent Authority that it is not reasonably practicable to hold an Inquiry is the condition precedent to dispense with the Inquiry and impose a penalty. According to the *Oxford Dictionary*, "practicable" means capable of being put into practice. It is not absolute or total impracticability which is the requirement of Clause (b) of the second proviso to Article 311(2). If the witnesses or the official appointed to hold the Inquiry are threatened, intimidated or terrorized, it can be assumed that it would not be reasonably practicable to hold the Inquiry. It is not material whether the delinquent Government Servant is or is not a party to the atmosphere of violence or general indiscipline. At the same time, the Competent Authority is not to dispense with an Inquiry lightly, arbitrarily or with ulterior motive.

83. It is laid down in Article 311(3) that if a question arises whether it is reasonably practicable to hold an Inquiry, the decision thereon of the Authority empowered to dismiss or remove such person from service or reduce him in rank shall be final.

84. But a case, where Article 311(3) has been invoked can also be amenable to Judicial Review as held by the Supreme Court in Arjun Chaubey *versus* Union of India (AIR 1984 SC 1356).

85. It is not necessary that a situation where it is not reasonably practicable to hold an Inquiry must exist before Disciplinary Inquiry is initiated against a Government Servant. Such a situation could also arise after service of the chargesheet or at any subsequent stage of the Inquiry.

86. It would not also be reasonably practicable to afford a delinquent Government Servant an opportunity of hearing when at the commencement of an Inquiry or pending the Inquiry, the Government Servant absconds and does not participate in the Inquiry. In such cases, the Inquiry may proceed ex-parte.

87. Therefore, even when a part of an Inquiry has been held and the rest is dispensed with as it is not reasonably practicable to hold the Inquiry any further the Government Servant cannot take a valid stand that he has been dismissed, removed or reduced in rank in violation of safeguards in Article 311(2) of the Constitution.

88. It would be better for the Competent Authority to record the reasons why it is not reasonably practicable to hold the Inquiry in the body of the order of penalty of dismissal, removal or reduction in rank.

89. Sometimes a situation might arise when it would not be possible to give detailed reasons why it was not reasonably practicable to hold an Inquiry. This would not, *per se*, invalidate the order of penalty. But each case may be judged on its facts to decide whether the reasons recorded by the Disciplinary Authority was sufficient to hold that it was not reasonably practicable to hold an Inquiry.

90. The constitutional obligation is that the Competent Authority must record in writing that it is not reasonably practicable to hold an Inquiry because of facts and circumstances contained in the order but it is not a mandatory requirement that a copy of the order recorded must be communicated to the concerned Government Servant.

91. In exercise of the power of Judicial Review, the Court will interfere on well-established legal grounds to question administrative discretion. The Court will examine the relevance of circumstances which led the appropriate authority to decide that it was not reasonably practicable to hold an Inquiry. If the reasons recorded are totally irrelevant, the Court will invalidate the impugned order of penalty, as an instance of abuse of power.

92. Sometimes not taking prompt action against a delinquent Government Servant may result in the situation becoming uncontrollable. Not taking prompt action may also be construed as a sign of weakness of the Disciplinary Authority.

93. Clause (b) of the second proviso to Article 311(2) stipulates a situation where it is not reasonably practicable to hold an Inquiry and not where it is impossible to hold an Inquiry. What is required is that the holding of an Inquiry is not practicable in the opinion of a reasonable man taking a reasonable view of the prevailing situation. Some instances by way of illustration are as follows: it is not reasonably practicable to hold an Inquiry if the delinquent Government Servant by himself or in association with others, threatens, intimidates or terrorizes the Disciplinary Authority or member of family of the Disciplinary Authority so that he is afraid to hold the Inquiry or direct it to be held. Similar situation would arise if witnesses are threatened, intimidated or terrorized by the delinquent Government Servant. It would also not be reasonably practicable to hold an Inquiry where there is an atmosphere of violence, general indiscipline or insubordination. It is immaterial whether the delinquent Government Servant is a party to such an atmosphere.

94. The extent of the power of Judicial Review in this regard has been laid down by the Supreme Court in Arjun Chaubey *versus* Union of India (AIR 1984 SC 1356). In this case, the appellant, Arjun Chaubey, was working as a senior clerk in office of the Chief Commercial Superintendent, Northern Railway. He was called upon to submit his explanation to twelve charges of gross indiscipline mostly relating to the Deputy Chief Commercial Superintendent. Arjun Chaubey, submitted his explanation. The very next day the Deputy Chief Commercial Superintendent served a notice on Arjun Chaubey that his explanation was not satisfactory and he was being given another chance to explain his conduct in regard to the same twelve charges. The day after Arjun Chaubey submitted his further explanation, the Deputy Chief Commercial Superintendent passed an order that Arjun Chaubey, was not fit to be retained in service and the order of dismissal from service was served upon him. The Supreme Court struck down the order on the ground

that seven of the twelve charges related to conduct of Arjun Chaubey in relation to the Deputy Chief Commercial Superintendent. If an Inquiry was to be held, the principal witness for the Railways would have been the Deputy Chief Commercial Superintendent himself resulting in the same person being the main accuser, the chief witness and also the judge of the matter.

95. In considering relevance of the reasons recorded by the Disciplinary Authority that it was not reasonably practicable to hold an Inquiry, the Court will not sit in judgment over the order of the Disciplinary Authority as the Court of Appeal. The Court must put itself in place of the Disciplinary Authority and consider what in the then prevailing situation a reasonable man, acting in a reasonable way, would have done. When two views are possible whether it was reasonably practicable to hold an Inquiry, the Court will necessarily agree with the view which the Disciplinary Authority took in the then prevailing situation.

96. It is to be noted that clause (b) of the second proviso to Article 311(2) of the Constitution requires the reasons to be recorded in writing by the Disciplinary Authority why an Inquiry was not reasonably practicable whereas clause (c) of the second proviso to Article 311(2) does not stipulate that the President or the Governor is required to record reasons for such satisfaction.

97. The expression "security of the State" in clause (c) of the second proviso of Article 311(2) is to be interpreted as the gravest threat to the State and has to be distinguished from 'public order' or "law and order". It is difficult to enumerate the various ways in which security of the State can be threatened. Amongst the more obvious ways in which the security of the State can be threatened would be disaffection in the armed forces or para-military forces.

98. The police also stands on the same footing as the military or para-military force as the police is also charged with maintenance of public order. Because of the need for discipline among the armed forces, the para-military force and the police, Article 33 of the Constitution has provided that Parliament may by law abrogate or restrict exercise of any Fundamental Right by members of such forces including any member of an organization in Government charged with the duties of collection of intelligence.

99. While exercising powers to dispense with an Inquiry against a Government Servant in interest of security of the State, the President or the Governor, as the case may be, can also act on the basis of secret information. Moreover, there can be no appeal or revision against the order of the President or the Governor when he is satisfied that it will not be expedient to hold an Inquiry into conduct of Government Servant in interest of security of the State. In exercise of the power of Judicial Review, the Courts will also not question the satisfaction of the President or the Governor unless it can be shown that such satisfaction has been vitiated by *mala fides*.

100. Coming to the facts of the present case, the respondent, Tulsiram Patel, was an auditor of the Military Engineering Department at Jabalpur. An order was issued by the Controller of Defence Accounts that Tulsiram Patel's increment of pay was to be stopped for a year as a measure of penalty in a Disciplinary Inquiry. In July 1976, Tulsiram Patel went to

the office of the MES at Jabalpur and questioned the Audit Officer, Raj Kumar Jairath as to why his increment was stopped for a year. When Jairath replied that the increment of Tulsiram was not stopped by him, Tulsiram lost his temper and hit Jairath with an iron rod. Jairath fell down from his chair bleeding. The Magistrate at Jabalpur convicted Tulsiram Patel under Section 332 of the Indian Penal Code (grievous hurt) and released him on executing a bond for good behavior under the Probation of Offender's Act 1958. The appeal against the conviction by the Magistrate was dismissed by the District Judge of Jabalpur. The Disciplinary Authority of Tulsiram Patel imposed on him the penalty of compulsory retirement from service. The Madhya Pradesh High Court, set aside the order of compulsory retirement imposed on him following the ratio in T.R. Challappan's case (AIR 1975 SC 2216) that the principle of Natural Justice has been violated as Tulsiram Patel was not served a notice against the penalty. The Supreme Court held that after conviction for an offence, a Government Servant need not be served a show cause notice as stipulated in T.R. Challappan's case (AIR 1975 SC 2216). The Court overruled its earlier judgment in T.R. Challappan's case (AIR 1975 SC 2216) and held that it is no longer good law.

101. Writ petitions were also filed by some Railway Servants against the Union of India challenging imposition of major penalty on them by dispensing with a Disciplinary Inquiry on the ground that it would not be reasonably practicable to hold an Inquiry. It can be said that the Railway Servants who were imposed major penalties without Inquiry, had participated in an All-India strike where the Railway Service was paralyzed and loyal workers and superior officers were assaulted and the country was virtually held to ransom. Public Interest required immediate action against striking Railway Employees – who had taken part in an illegal strike – to restore normalcy in operation of the Railways. In these circumstances, it was rightly held that no Inquiry was reasonably practicable and imposition of a major penalty was justified by dispensing with the Inquiry.

102. Similarly, action of the Governor of Madhya Pradesh dismissing some striking policemen was justified as the Governor held that a Disciplinary Inquiry was not expedient in the interest of the security of the State. The facts and circumstances why the Governor was so satisfied are not amenable to Judicial Review unless *mala fides* are attributed to the Governor.

103. The material disclosed to the Court by the State of Madhya Pradesh revealed horrendous acts of lawlessness by the constables of the Madhya Pradesh police at Gwalior in January 1981. The constables went berserk and attacked the police station and created chaotic scenes. The Supreme Court was, therefore, satisfied that it would not have been expedient in the interest of the security of the State to hold an Inquiry before passing orders of dismissal against a few delinquent police constables.

104. Similarly, imposition of major penalties on members of the Central Industrial Security Force at Bokaro and Hosangabad was justified in terms of sub-clause (b) of the second provision to Article 311(2) of the Constitution.

105. Justice M.P. Thakkar did not agree with the majority judgment in Tulsiram Patel's case (AIR 1985 SC 1416) and delivered a minority judgment. He bemoaned the fact that when the ratio laid down in T.R. Challappan's case (AIR 1975 SC 2217) had held the field for a long period, there was no reason to overrule it and the five judges constituting the Bench in Tulsiram Patel's case (AIR 1985 SC 1416) should have met and discussed the issues before overruling the ratio in Challappan's case. Justice M.P. Thakkar also held that a delinquent Government Servant has a right to be heard in regard to the quantum of the penalty before a major penalty is sought to be imposed on him by dispensing with an Inquiry.

106. Thus as per the majority judgment, the Supreme Court held that no inquiry is required once the Disciplinary Authority is of the view that it is not reasonably practicable to hold an Inquiry and the President of India or the Governor of a State is satisfied that it would not be expedient to hold an Inquiry in the interest of security of the state.

CHAPTER 15

Supreme Court Advocates-On-Record Association and Another *versus* Union of India (AIR 1994 SC 268)

[JUSTICE S. RATNAVEL PANDIAN, JUSTICE A.M. AHMADI, JUSTICE KULDIP SINGH, JUSTICE J.S. VERMA, JUSTICE M.M. PUNCHHI, JUSTICE YOGESHWAR DAYAL, JUSTICE G.N. RAY, JUSTICE A.S. ANAND AND JUSTICE S.P. BHARUCHA]

Case Summary

In this judgment of a Nine-Judge Constitution Bench, the Supreme Court by a majority of seven judges held that the opinion of the Chief Justice of India must have primacy in matter of appointment of judges of the High Courts and the Supreme Court.

1. The judgment known popularly as the second S.P. Gupta judgment overruled an earlier judgment of the Supreme Court in S.P. Gupta and Others *versus* Union of India (AIR 1982 SC 149) known as the first S.P. Gupta Judgment.
2. In the Second S.P. Gupta Judgment (AIR 1994 SC 268) seven judges viz. Justice S. Ratnavel Pandian, Justice Kuldip Singh, Justice J.S. Verma, Justice Yogeswar Dayal, Justice G.N. Ray, Justice A.S. Anand and Justice S.P. Bharucha delivered the majority judgment whereas Justice A.M. Ahmadi and Justice M.M. Punchi delivered the minority judgments.
3. Justice Ratnavel Pandian, commenced his Judgment by alluding to King Solomon of The Old Testament. He said that Solomon's Throne was supported by two Lions on either side but the moot question is whether the present day Solomon's Throne – symbolizing majesty of our System of Justice – is supported by the two Lions under the Throne – one Lion symbolizing the Executive and the other Lion symbolizing the Legislature.
4. The issue is whether the Lions in modern times are supporting the throne of Solomon and whether it is for the Lions to pronounce the name of Solomon and his successor to occupy the Throne.

5. Arising out of the main issue whether the lions i.e. the Executive and the Legislature are still under the Throne (the Judiciary) the ancillary issues are whether the Lions can propose constitution and composition of the Kingdom of Solomon and completely ignore the suggestion of Solomon in this regard.
6. As Justice Ratnavel Pandian put in his colourful prose, "whether under the present scheme and procedure Solomon is made to sit on 'the Chair of the Handicapped' and not 'on his own Throne'".
7. The main issue is to give primacy to the opinion of the Chief Justice of India in all matters relating to appointment of Judges to the superior Judiciary so that independence and integrity of the Judiciary are maintained.
8. Although frequent change of its earlier decision by the Supreme Court will give rise to uncertainty regarding what the law is, it is imperative for the Court to review its earlier decision and overrule any incorrect decision taken in the past.
9. The Supreme Court has inherent powers to review its earlier Judgment if it is satisfied that it is in the interest of Justice to do so.
10. There have been a number of judgments of the Supreme Court when earlier Judgments have been re-considered and have been either modified or overruled. The most leading Judgment in this regard is Kesavananda Bharati *versus* State of Kerala (AIR 1973 SC 1461).
11. In Constitutional Law, the need for Review of the Supreme Court's earlier Judgments arises frequently as the words and phrases in Constitutional Law have to express new concepts. As held by the Court "Words are but framework of concepts and concepts may change more than words themselves".
12. In the first S.P. Gupta case (AIR 1982 SC 149), the majority of Judges held that the ultimate power of appointment of Judges of High Courts and the Supreme Court is with the President of India, who acts according to aid and advice of his Council of Ministers.
13. But Justice P.N. Bhagwati who delivered the majority judgment upholding the Right of the President to make the appointment of Judges of High Courts and the Supreme Court, had himself made some suggestions to improve the modalities of appointment. He had suggested that to ensure the widest consultation and to make recommendation of names of persons for appointment of Judges more broad-based, a Collegium must be involved in making recommendations of suitable names to the President of India.
14. Justice P.N. Bhagwati also said that the Collegium should have members, who must have intimate knowledge of persons qualified and suitable for appointment as Judges. He also stated how in Australia and New Zealand there has been a move to entrust appointment of persons to the higher judiciary to a high-level Judicial Commission.
15. Not only Justice P.N. Bhagwati but also Justice Y.V. Chandrachud who remained as Chief Justice of India for nearly eight years and Justice D.A. Desai have recommended constitution of a Collegium or a National Judicial Commission to make final recommendation to the President for appointment of Judges of the High Courts and the Supreme Court.

16. Even Dr. B.R. Ambedkar was not quite happy that the Judges would be appointed by the President merely on advice of the executive Government of the day.

17. In several countries, where power of appointment of Judges vests with the Executive, in recent years, some drastic reforms have been suggested to check the power of the executive in this regard. In U.K., it was suggested as early as 1972 that while the Lord Chancellor, a member of the British Cabinet, should continue to retain the power to advise His Majesty about high judicial appointments, he might be assisted by an Advisory Committee appointed by the Judiciary.

18. In USA, the President has constituted a "Circuit Judges Nomination Commission" to recommend names for appointment to the U.S. Court of Appeal. In USA though the President appoints Judges of the U.S. Supreme Court, each case of appointment has to be confirmed by the Judiciary Committee of the Senate through a hearing when the nominee of the President for office of judge of the U.S. Supreme Court appears before the Committee to answer questions regarding his track record and his legal philosophy.

19. In May 1990, the Constitution (Sixty-seventh Amendment) Bill was introduced in the Lok Sabha empowering the President of India to constitute a high-level National Judicial Commission for recommending names of suitable persons as Judges of the Supreme Court, Chief Justice of High Courts and transfer of a Judge of a High Court from one High Court to another. The Bill was introduced in the Lok Sabha pursuant to recommendation of the Law Commission of India.

20. The Constitution (Sixty-seventh Amendment) Bill of 1990 however lapsed on dissolution of the Ninth Lok Sabha.

21. A battery of eminent counsels as F.S. Nariman, Ram Jethmalani, Kapil Sibal, P.P. Rao and Shanti Bhushan argued for re-consideration of "ratio" of the decision in the first S.P. Gupta's case (AIR 1982 SC 149), where the Executive had the primacy in selection and appointment of Judges, which has resulted in politicization of such appointments.

22. As against the above argument, the Attorney-General for India, Milon K. Banerjee and Senior Counsel, K. Parasaran argued that there was no need for re-consideration of the ratio in the first S.P. Gupta's case (AIR 1982 SC 149). In the colourful language of K. Parasaran, the decision in the first S.P. Gupta's case (AIR 1982 SC 149) does not require to be taken to the legal smithy for either mending or tinkering.

23. It has been held in Union of India *versus* Sankal Chand Himatlal Seth (AIR 1977 SC 2388) that independence of the Judiciary is a fighting faith of our Constitution.

24. It has also been held in Shamsher Singh *versus* State of Punjab (AIR 1974 SC 2192) that Justice can become fearless and free only if institutional immunity and autonomy are guaranteed.

25. Justice P.N. Bhagwati in the first S.P. Gupta's case (AIR 1982 SC 149) had said that the concept of independence of the judiciary is not limited only to independence from executive pressure. Independence of the judiciary is a much wider concept which takes within its sweep independence from many other pressures and prejudices. Justice P.N. Bhagwati also said that judges should be of stern stuff and tough fibre unbending before power and they must uphold the Rule of Law, which says, "Be you ever so high, the law is above you".

26. The persons to be appointed to the higher judiciary must be of the highest reputation for independence, uncommitted to any prior interest, loyalty and obligations and prepared under all circumstances to pay any price, bear any burden and meet any hardship. They must always be wedded to the Constitution and the Rule of Law.

27. If a person to be appointed as a Judge of the High Court or the Supreme Court bows to the decision of the Appointing Authority, the independence of the Judiciary cannot be secured notwithstanding the constitutional safeguards for the Judges as fixed tenure of office, rights and privileges, conditions of service and immunities.

28. M.C. Setalvad, the first Attorney-General for India and Chairman of the Fourteenth Law Commission, has brought out in his Report how there was widespread criticism of appointment of Judges in High Courts through influence exerted by the Executive. Ram Jethmalani, a distinguished jurist, has been also of the view that the Executive tended to corrode judicial independence in making appointments of Judges.

29. Justice P.N. Bhagwati in Sankal Chand case (AIR 1977 SC 2328) quoted Granvile Austin to say that Article 50 of the Constitution stipulating separation of the judiciary from the executive in the public services of the state is the conscience of the Constitution. Article 50 of the Constitution embodies the intention of framers of the Constitution to immunize the judiciary from any form of executive control or interference.

30. The concept of separation of the judiciary from the executive cannot be confined only to the subordinate judiciary. It extends to the concept of insulating appointments to the higher judiciary from executive interference.

31. The debates and discussions focus on key issues as follows:
   (i) Where the power of appointment of Judges of the High Courts and the Supreme Court is to be located?
   (ii) Who is the final authority to make appointments of judges of the High Courts and the Supreme Court?
   (iii) Whether there are recognized guidelines for making these appointments?
   (iv) Whether the power of appointment of judges vested in the constitutional functionaries is unfettered and uncircumscribed?
   (v) Whether the opinion of the Chief Justice of India, has primacy over opinion of other constitutional functionaries?

32. The constitutional task assigned to the judiciary is no way less than that of other functionaries – the legislature and the executive. It is the role of the judiciary to keep a vigilant watch over the functioning of democracy in accordance with imperative commands of the Constitution by checking excessive authority of other constitutional functionaries. In that sense, the judiciary has to act as a sentinel on the *qui vive*.

33. There are some intractable problems connected with judicial administration starting from initial selection of candidates to be judges of the Supreme Court and the High Courts leading to the present malaise.

34. In trying to tackle the issues regarding appointments of Judges of the High Courts and the Supreme Court, the judiciary is not attempting to get itself locked up in a power struggle either for social aristocracy or for judicial imperialism or for any vainglory in establishing judicial supremacy. The purpose is only to demand recognition of the primacy of the Chief Justice of India in the matter of appointments of judges of the High Courts and the Supreme Court.

35. The Indian judicial system, being pyramidic in character is an integrated one in contradistinction to the dual system in USA and Australia. Our judicial system is vertically structured with the Supreme Court at the apex.

36. The process of Indianization of the judiciary started with the Government of India Act 1919. Under the Act, the judges of the High Court were appointed by His Majesty. The qualifications for appointment of Judges of the High Court were such that Indians could get appointed.

37. Under the Government of India Act 1935, a judge of the Federal Court was appointed by His Majesty by warrant under the Royal Sign Manual and held office till he attained the age of 65 years. The High Court Judges were appointed by His Majesty in similar manner and held office till the age of 60 years.

38. In the Constituent Assembly, there was a suggestion that the judges of the Supreme Court should be appointed with concurrence of the Chief Justice of India but the suggestion was not accepted.

39. The power to appoint a Judge of the Supreme Court or to a High Court vests with the President of India under Articles 124(2) and 217(1) respectively. It is obligatory for the President before making an appointment of a Judge of the Supreme Court, other than the Chief Justice of India, to consult the Chief Justice of India. Under Article 124(2), the President before making an appointment of Judge of the Supreme Court may consult such judges of the Supreme Court and the High Courts as he considers necessary. For appointment of a judge of the High Court, the President is required to consult the Chief Justice of India, the Government of the State and the Chief Justice of the High Court.

40. The procedure for appointment of the Chief Justice of India and judges of the Supreme Court prior to the first S.P. Gupta judgment (AIR 1982 SC 149) was as follows: Whenever a permanent vacancy was expected to arise in the office of the Chief Justice of India, action was taken by the Union Minister of Law and Justice through the personal channel. Whenever a permanent vacancy was expected to arise in the office of a Judge of the Supreme Court, the Chief Justice of India did intimate the fact to the Union Minister of Law and Justice. At the same time, the Chief Justice of India intimated to the Minister of Law the manner in which the vacancy should be filled up. Unless the Minister of Law and Justice considered that the recommendations of the Chief Justice of India should be accepted straightaway, the Minister might consult such judges of the Supreme Court and the High Courts he considered necessary. If after such consultation, the Minister considered it desirable to bring any point to the notice of the Chief Justice of India or to suggest consideration of claim of any other person, he might write to the Chief Justice of India accordingly. On receiving the final recommendation of the Chief Justice, the Ministry of

Law and Justice with concurrence of the Prime Minister advised the President of India as to who should be appointed as a Judge of the Supreme Court.

41. The procedure of appointment of the Chief Justice and the Judges of the High Court before the first S.P. Gupta's Judgment in 1982 was as follows: When a permanent vacancy was expected to arise in the office of a Judge of the High Court, the Chief Justice of the High Court communicated to the Chief Minister of the State his views about the persons to be appointed as a judge of the High Court. The Chief Minister, in consultation with Governor of the State, did forward his recommendation to the Minister of Law and Justice of the Union Government. When the Chief Minister or Governor of a state recommended name of a person other than the person recommended by the Chief Justice of the High Court, the comments of the Chief Justice were invited. The comments of the Chief Justice of the High Court was forwarded by the Chief Minister along with his recommendation to the Minister of Law and Justice of the Union Government. The Minister in consultation with the Chief Justice of India and the Prime Minister would then advise the President as regards the appointment to the vacancy of the judge of the concerned High Court.

42. S.P. Gupta, a senior Advocate practising in the Allahabad High Court filed a writ petition challenging the circular letter dated 18 March 1981 of the Union Minister of Law and Justice to the Chief Ministers of the states and the Governor of Punjab [**N.B.:** The State of Punjab was then under the President's Rule]. V.M. Tarkunde, a senior Advocate of the Supreme Court also filed an analogous petition before the Supreme Court. These petitions were heard together by a seven judge bench of the Supreme Court presided over by Justice P.N. Bhagwati. In the first S.P. Gupta's (AIR 1982 SC 149) Justice P.N. Bhagwati, who gave the leading judgment held that:

(i) It would be open to the Central Government to override the opinion of the constitutional functionaries required to be consulted and to arrive at its own decision in regard to appointment of a judge of the High Court or the Supreme Court so long as decision of the Central Government is based on relevant considerations and is not otherwise *mala fide*.

(ii) Even if the opinion by all the constitutional functionaries consulted by the Union Government is identical, the Central Government is not bound to act in accordance with such opinion though being a unanimous opinion of all the constitutional functionaries consulted, it would have great weight.

(iii) If an appointment is made to the Supreme Court or the High Court in defiance of the unanimous opinion of the constitutional functionaries, it may be *prima facie* vulnerable to attack on the ground of *mala fide*.

43. The above view in the first S.P. Gupta's case (AIR 1982 SC 149) created a lot of dissatisfaction and the need for a change in the mode of appointment appears to be the provocation for filing the present petition.

44. The grievance of the petitioners is that the Executive is given primacy in matter of appointment of judges of the High Courts and the Supreme Court and the Executive is thus the "Lord of the Lords" and the Chief Justice of India is reduced to the position of a passive by-stander. The petitioners have urged that if the opinion of the Chief Justice of

India is not accorded primacy in the matter of appointment of judges of the High Court and the Supreme Court, the majesty of the judicial system would be eroded.

45. K. Parasaran opposed the above arguments by stating that the submissions made for primacy of views of the Chief Justice of India in matter of appointments to the superior judiciary are only verbal gymnastics and nothing more than mere verbiage. He stated that there is no grey area in the present procedure of appointment of judges, which needs to be altered. He also said that the present procedure which has stood the test of time is the only procedure in conformity with the constitutional mandate. As K. Parasaran said there is no riddle wrapped up in a mystery inside of an enigma in the present mode of selection of judges. K. Parasaran concluded his argument by saying that he was second to none in upholding the dignity and independence of the judiciary.

46. The Supreme Court is anxious to dispose of this hotly debatable issue with the avowed object of rejuvenating the judiciary so that "the stability of the system for ages to come may have support because if the system is either weak-kneed or crippled or becomes impotent or sterile, it will lose its strength and authority." Resultantly the other constitutional functionaries will try to prevail upon the justice delivery system because "when the eagle of empire falls each sparrow takes a feather."

47. John Marshall, former Chief Justice of the U.S. Supreme Court, has said that in interpreting a constitution, the courts must remember that it is a Constitution which is meant to endure for ages and to be adapted to various crises in human affairs. The Constitution need not be so rigidly interpreted that amendments and revisions of the Constitution would be constantly required to ensure smooth functioning of Government.

48. Under Article 124 of the Constitution, at the time of commencement of the Constitution, the Supreme Court comprised the Chief Justice and not more than seven judges. Subsequently, in different years, the Parliament increased the number of Judges of the Supreme Court to twenty-five. [**N.B.:** In the year 2008, the number of judges of the Supreme Court has been further increased to thirty-one. It is significant to note that the U.S. Supreme Court comprises only nine judges including the Chief Justice and there has been no change in the number of judges of the Court since the commencement of the U.S. Constitution nearly 240 years ago.]

49. Article 124(2) stipulates as follows:

"Every Judge of the Supreme Court shall be appointed by the President by warrant under his hand and seal after consultation with such of the Judges of the Supreme Court and the High Courts as the President may deem necessary for the purpose...."

50. Proviso to Article 124(2) stipulates that in case of appointment of a Judge of the Supreme Court other than the Chief Justice of India, the Chief Justice of India shall always be consulted.

51. Article 217(1) of the Constitution contains the provision for appointment of Judges of High Courts. A Judge of the High Court is appointed by the President of India by warrant under his hand and seal after consultation with the Chief Justice of India, Governor of a State and in case of a Judge of a High Court other than the Chief Justice of the High Court, the Chief Justice of the High Court to which a Judge will be appointed.

52. The word "Consultation" has come up for judicial interpretation before the Supreme Court, the High Courts and even the foreign courts. In Fletcher *versus* Minister of Town Planning (1947) it was laid down as follows:

(i) "Consultation" which is in general use is well-understood.
(ii) No useful purpose would be served by defining "Consultation".
(iii) It would not also be appropriate to lay down the manner in which "Consultation" must take place.
(iv) If a complaint is made of failure of consultation, it will be for the Courts to examine the facts of a particular case to decide whether "Consultation" took place.

53. In C. Prasad *versus* Patna High Court (AIR 1970 SC 370), the Supreme Court interpreted the word "Consultation" in Article 233 of the Constitution as follows:

(i) Consultation with the High Court under Article 233 of the Constitution is not an empty formality.
(ii) The High Court is the most suitable institution to adjudge the claims and merits of persons to be promoted as District Judges.
(iii) The Governor of a state cannot discharge his functions under Article 233 of the Constitution if he appoints a person as a District Judge without consulting the High Court.
(iv) "Consultation" is not complete before the parties thereto make their respective points of view known to the other and discuss the relative merits of their views.

54. If one party makes a proposal to the other, who has a counter-proposal in his mind which is not communicated to the proposer, the direction to give effect to the counter-proposal without anything more, cannot be said to have been issued after consultation.

55. In Shamsher Singh *versus* The State of Punjab (AIR 1974 SC 2192), Justice Krishna Iyer held that the opinion of the Chief Justice of India, after consultation with him, should be accepted by the Government of India and the Courts are entitled to examine if any extraneous matter has entered into the decision of the Minister/Prime Minister in departing from the advice of the Chief Justice of India.

56. In Sankal Chand case (AIR 1977 SC 2328) the Supreme Court speaking again through Justice Krishna Iyer reiterated the stand taken by the Court in Shamsher Singh's case.

57. Fali S. Nariman argued that the expression, "after consultation with" must be determined in the constitutional context and conditioned by the true object of such consultation. He argued that for appointment of other high-ranking constitutional functionaries – other than the judges of the higher judiciary – the President is not required to consult any authority before making an appointment. But as the President is required to consult such of the Judges of the Supreme Court and the High Courts as "the President may deem necessary" and for appointment of a Judge of the Supreme Court other than the Chief Justice of India mandatorily the Chief Justice of India, the process of "Consultation" has a particular significance and it means something more than merely seeking the advice of such high judicial functionaries. According to Fali S. Nariman, the advice tendered by

the constitutional authority for appointment of a Judge of the higher judiciary is binding in character though the Constitution does not say so in as many words.

58. Ram Jethmalani also argued that the judgment in the first S.P. Gupta's case (AIR 1982 SC 149) giving primacy in matter of appointment of judges of the higher judiciary to the President of India was rendered per incuriam and the expression "Consultation" being a flexible one can also mean "Consent" or "Concurrence".

59. K. Parasaran, refuted the arguments of F.S. Nariman and Ram Jethmalani by pointing out the following:

(i) When the Constitution mandates that the President may consult such judges of the Supreme Court and the High Courts as the President may deem necessary and mandatorily the Chief Justice of India in case of appointment of judges of the Supreme Court, it is not necessary that the opinion of the Chief Justice in regard to such appointment has to be accepted by the President of India.

(ii) Under the Constitution, the Supreme Court has no administrative control over the High Courts. Therefore, the Chief Justice of a High Court is as much an independent authority as the Chief Justice of India. Under Article 217(1), the Chief Justice of a High Court is to be consulted by the President in case of appointment of judge of a High Court.

(iii) The Executive has also an important role to play in the process of consultation since the Executive may have knowledge as to the qualities and personal integrity of the person to be appointed as a judge of the High Court or the Supreme Court.

(iv) Debates in the Constituent Assembly about certain proposed amendments to the draft Articles would show that "Consultation" does not mean "Consent" or "Concurrence". In the Constituent Assembly amendments to the draft Articles expressly providing for concurrence of the Chief Justice to appointment of High Court and Supreme Court judges was rejected. There is no justification for the argument that consultation with the Chief Justice of India must be given primacy over consultations with other constitutional functionaries. If an interpretation is given to give primacy to the "Consultation" with the Chief Justice of India, it would be tantamount to re-writing the Constitution with regard to appointment of judges of High Courts and the Supreme Court.

(v) While replying to the debates in the Constituent Assembly, Dr. B.R. Ambedkar said that as the Chief Justice of India, though a very eminent person, is likely to have "all the failings, all the sentiments and all the prejudices which we common people have", it would not be proper to allow the Chief Justice of India practically a veto on all appointments to the higher judiciary.

(vi) If intention of the framers of the Constitution that the opinion of the Chief Justice of India regarding appointment of a Judge of the High Court or a Supreme Court would be final, Article 124(2) providing for Consultation by the President of India "with such of the judges of the Supreme Court and of the High Courts in the States as the President may deem necessary for the purpose" would become redundant. In Uttar Pradesh *versus* Radhe Shyam Nigam (AIR 1989 SC 682), the Supreme Court have held that it is a settled rule of the interpretation of statutes that provisions of an Act should be interpreted in such a manner as not to render any of its provisions otiose unless there are compelling reasons to resort to that extreme contingency.

60. The controversy raised by different arguments boils down to the correct interpretation of the expression "Consultation".

61. The Constitution of India is structured with a wealth of "choice words, measured phrases and expressions" where the real meaning and message are sometimes missed and on many occasions are either hidden or unforeseen.

62. In Chapter Four of the treatise, "The Loom of Language" it has been stated that:

"Words are not passive agents meaning the same thing and carrying the same value at all times and in all contexts. They do not come in standard shapes and sizes like coins from the mint, nor do they go forth to all the world that they shall mean only so such, no more and no less." Each word has a penumbra of meaning which no draftsmen can entirely cut away. A word refuses to be used as a mathematical symbol.

63. In Town *versus* Eisner (1917), Justice Holmes of the U.S. Supreme Court has said that,

"a word is not a crystal, transparent and unchanged; it is the skin of a living thought and may vary greatly in colour and content according to the circumstances and the time when it is used."

64. The Privy Council in Minister of Home Affairs *versus* Fisher (1979) has held that a constitutional instrument is a document sui generis, to be interpreted according to principles suitable to its particular character and not necessarily according to the rules and presumptions of statutory interpretation.

65. The word "consultation" is used in the context of appointment of Judges to the Supreme Court under Article 124(2) and to the High Courts under Article 217(1). In the first S.P. Gupta's case (AIR 1982 SC 149) there was a consensus of opinion that "consultation" did not mean concurrence. It was also held that the Central Government, which advises the President, can override opinion of the constitutional functionaries required to be consulted and to arrive at its own decision in regard to appointment of judges of the High Courts and the Supreme Court "so long as such decision is based on relevant considerations and is not otherwise mala fide."

66. As to the nature of "consultation", the Constitution does not lay down any specific mode and no guideline. But three pre-conditions are necessary for effective consultation, which are as follows:

(i) The President of India must disclose all the facts necessary for due deliberation by the Chief Justice of India;

(ii) The Chief Justice of India must express his opinion on full consideration of the relevant facts before him;

(iii) The quintessence of consultation is that the two parties must exchange their views and examine the merits of the proposals and counter-proposals.

67. The Fourteenth Report of the Law Commission under Chairmanship of M.C. Setalvad, the first Attorney-General for India, has expressed dissatisfaction over the present mode

of appointment of judges and recommended that the opinion of the Chief Justice of India be given primacy.

68. The person to be selected for appointment as a Judge of the Supreme Court or a High Court must have high integrity, skill, high order of emotional stability, firmness, serenity, legal soundness, ability and endurance. The most important personal attributes for appointment of a Judge of the Supreme Court or the High Court is moral vigour, ethical firmness and imperviousness to corrupting and venal influences, humility, lack of affiliations, judicial temperament and zeal for work.

69. Winston Churchill had said that the service rendered by the Judges demands the highest qualities of learning, training and character.

70. The Chief Justice of India and the Chief Justice of the High Courts alone can speak of a candidate's professional attainments and his knowledge of law. The Executive, however, can give its views on other qualities such as affiliation, personal integrity, antecedents and background of a candidate.

71. The Chief Justice of India, as the Head of the judiciary in India, is the pater familias of the judicial family. He has to be vigilant in protecting the integrity and guarding the independence of the judiciary. He alone can judge the merit of a candidate in regard to his professional attainments and legal ability.

72. As held by a three judge Bench of the Supreme Court in All India Judges Association *versus* Union of India (AIR 1993 SC 2493), the judicial service is not a service in the sense of employment. As members of the judiciary, they exercise the sovereign power of the state. They are holders of public offices in the same way as the members of the Council of Ministers and the members of the legislature.

73. Though the judges of the Supreme Court in USA are appointed by the President, the process of appointment is a lengthy one as each Presidential nominee has to face a hearing before the Judiciary Committee of the Senate. The "confirmation hearing" before the Judiciary Committee usually extends over a few days when the President's nominee is subjected to incisive and searching questions regarding his constitutional philosophy, his legal knowledge and his background. The hearings before the Judicial Committee is broadcast live so that the Americans know the merit of the candidate proposed to be appointed as a judge of the Supreme Court. If the judiciary committee confirms the appointment then only he is appointed by the President as a Judge of the Supreme Court.

74. In U.K. the Lord Chancellor, who is a Member of the British Cabinet as well as the Head of the judiciary advises the crown on all appointments to judicial office from Justice of the Peace to the higher offices of the judiciary. Since 1972, the Lord Chancellor is advised by an Advisory Appointment Committee in regard to all judicial appointments.

75. In the first S.P. Gupta's case (AIR 1982 SC 149) the Supreme Court speaking through Justice P.N. Bhagwati referred to the argument that the opinion of the Chief Justice of India must have primacy in case of difference of opinion among constitutional functionaries regarding a particular candidate's selection for appointment as a Judge of the Supreme Court or the High Courts.

76. The decision in the first S.P. Gupta's case (AIR 1982 SC 149) overlooks the fact that members of the judiciary are not employees of the state. They cannot be placed on par with members of other services. For other Constitutional appointments – except members of the higher judiciary – the President is not bound to have prior consultation with any functionary.

77. The expression "shall always be consulted" in the first proviso to Article 124(2) and the expression "shall be appointed...after consultation" in Article 217(1) indicates the mandatory character of the "consultation".

78. To place the opinion of the Chief Justice of India on par with other constitutional functionaries is not in consonance with the spirit of the Constitution. Against the factual and constitutional background, the meaning of "consultation" cannot be confined to its ordinary lexical definition. The contents of the word "consultation" greatly vary according to the circumstances and context in which the word is used in the Indian Constitution.

79. Like the Pope enjoying supremacy in the ecclesiastical and temporal affairs, the Chief Justice of India being the highest judicial authority has the right of primacy – if not supremacy – to be accorded to his opinion concerning the "Temple of Justice". "It is a right step in the right direction and that step alone will ensure optimum benefits to the society."

80. The President of India is, however, not a figurehead or a glorious cipher. As Justice Krishna Iyer has said in Shamsher Singh *versus* The State of Punjab (AIR 1974 SC 2192) the President of India has the right to be consulted, to encourage and to warn the Council of Ministers as Walter Bagehot had said about the crown in England.

81. Even though in India constitutional functionaries have their roles in making appointment of judges of the higher judiciary, the judiciary has the highest responsibility in this regard. An independent judiciary is essential for a healthy democracy. If the opinion of the Executive in matters of appointment of judges of the higher judiciary is to prevail over the opinion of the Chief Justice of India, it will mean end of an independent judiciary.

82. Reports of the Law Commissions of India – particularly the Fourteenth, Eighteenth and the one hundred and twenty-first Commissions have indicated that a need has arisen to curb the power of the Executive in making appointments of judges of the Supreme Court and the High Courts. In view of the aforesaid, the Executive will not be justified in enjoying supremacy over the opinion of the Chief Justice of India in matter of appointment of judges.

83. The merit of a candidate with regard to professional attainment, legal acumen, ability and skill can only be properly assessed by Chief Justice of a High Court with regard to appointment of judges of the High Court. Similar assessment can be done by the Chief Justice of the Supreme Court in regard to appointment of a person as a judge of the Supreme Court. The Government, with resources and machinery at its command, can check the antecedents and background of a candidate. When the recommendation of the Chief Justice of the High Court with views of the Governor of the State concerned comes to the Chief Justice of India, he will be in a better position to assess the suitability of the candidate for appointment as a judge of the High Court. Therefore, in all circumstances,

the opinion of the Chief Justice of India, is entitled to have the right of primacy in selection of judges to the Supreme Court as well as to the High Courts.

84. In order to have a pragmatic approach to matters relating to appointment of judges of the Supreme Court, it would be "a healthy practice that the Chief Justice of India gives his opinion on a consultation process by taking into account views of two senior-most judges of the Supreme Court" and the views of any other Judge or Judges of the High Court whose opinion is likely to be significant in adjudging suitability of the candidate. Similar exercise may be undertaken by the Chief Justice of a High Court in regard to suitability of a candidate for appointment as a judge of the High Court.

85. The Chief Justice of India while adjudging the suitability of a candidate for appointment as a Judge of a High Court may consult his colleagues in the Supreme Court, who have been elevated from such High Courts and who are expected to be familiar with performance of the candidate recommended for appointment as a Judge of the High Court. This has been also the suggestion of Justice J.S. Verma, who delivered a separate judgment in this case.

86. The crucial issue is whether the President of India can veto the proposal of the Chief Justice of India made after consultation with his two senior-most colleagues and other Judges after recording his reasons? In such a case, the methods which weighed with the President not to accept advice of the Chief Justice of India and his collegiums shall be communicated to the Chief Justice of India and if after re-consideration, the Chief Justice and his collegium reiterate their earlier advice the President must accept such advice and appoint the candidate.

87. The Executive has no right to propose name of any candidate for being appointed as a Judge of the Supreme Court or the High Courts.

88. But in view of the pluralistic society of India where each section and class in society may have "equality of status and of opportunity", it may be permissible for the Executive to make its recommendation in regard to appointment of Judges of High Court and the Supreme Court such persons, who might not be appearing before the High Court or the Supreme Court but may be appearing before some other judicial or quasi-judicial Authority.

89. The distribution of Judges in 18 High Courts of the country as on 01.01.1993 shows that only 13 Judges belong to the Scheduled Castes and seven Judges belong to the Scheduled Tribes. There are only 13 lady Judges and 42 OBC Judges in the High Courts, whose total sanctioned strength is 512. If the vulnerable section of the people is completely neglected, in India we cannot claim to have participatory democracy.

90. The next important question is whether the Supreme Court can give direction to the Executive to increase the number of Judges in different High Courts and the Supreme Court for better disposal of pending cases.

91. Article 124 of the Constitution deals with establishment and constitution of the Supreme Court of India. At the commencement of the Constitution, there was a Chief Justice and seven other Judges of the Supreme Court. By the Supreme Court (Number of Judges)

Amendment Act 1960, the number of Judges was increased from seven to thirteen. By an Amendment Act of 1977, the number of Judges was increased to seventeen. In the year 1986, by another Amendment Act, the number of Judges was increased to twenty-five. [**N.B.:** In the year 2008, by an Amendment Act, the number of judges has been increased to 31.]

92. Article 216 dealing with the constitution of High Courts stipulates that a High Court shall consist of a Chief Justice and such other Judges as the President may from time to time deem it necessary to appoint.

93. The legislative power to constitute a High Court belongs to the Parliament in view of item 78 in the Union List of the Seventh Schedule.

94. The following issues arise in relation to strength of Judges in High Courts and the Supreme Court:

(i) Whether there are norms on the basis of which the President (i.e. the Government of India) can fix the strength of the Judges?

(ii) Whether request of the Chief Justice of India to the President of India to review and re-fix the strength of Judges of a High Court deserves great weight?

(iii) Whether the issue of fixation of strength of Judges is justiciable?

95. Even though successive Law Commissions have recommended increase of strength of Judges of the High Courts, their recommendations have been either implemented slowly or have been completely ignored.

96. In the One Hundred Twentieth Report of the Law Commission, Justice D.A. Desai, Chairman of the Commission, has bemoaned the fact that over the years adequate manpower planning for the judiciary has not been done.

97. By the Constitution (Forty-second Amendment) Act 1976, Articles 323A and 323B have been inserted into the Constitution to enable the Parliament to set up Tribunals for specified disputes. In all matters in which the Tribunals have jurisdiction, the appeal lies not to the High Courts but to the Supreme Court only. [**N.B.:** In L. Chandrakumar's case (AIR 1997 SC 1125) it has been held that the ouster of writ jurisdiction of the High Courts in matters within the purview of the Tribunals – set up under Articles 323A and 323B – is against the basic structure of the Constitution and the final order of the Tribunals is subject to writ jurisdiction of the High Courts under Article 226 read with Article 227 of the Constitution.]

98. Laws and rules and regulations under the laws have been multiplying very fast. With increase of laws, volatile issues arise which the Executive finds it too hot to handle. As the judiciary is being increasingly relied upon to solve intricate legal issues, the judiciary is playing the role of a "lightning arrester".

[**N.B.:** The minority judgments of Justice A.M. Ahmadi and Justice M.M. Punchi have not been summarized in this book.]

CHAPTER 16

Managing Director E.C.I.L. *versus* B. Karunakara (AIR 1994 SC 1074)

[CHIEF JUSTICE M.N. VENKATACHALIAH, JUSTICE P.B. SAWANT, JUSTICE K. RAMASWAMY, JUSTICE S. MOHAN AND JUSTICE B.P. JEEVAN REDDY]

Case Summary

This is a landmark judgment in service law where a Constitution Bench of five Judges, including Justice M.N. Venkatachaliah, the Chief Justice of India, interpreted provisions of Article 311 of the Constitution. The issue was whether it was mandatory to furnish a copy of the Report of Inquiry to the Charged Official to enable him to submit his representation to the Disciplinary Authority against findings of the Inquiry Officer. The Court held that furnishing of a copy of the Report to the Charged Official was required as a part of "reasonable opportunity" before the Disciplinary Authority made up its mind regarding the findings of the Inquiry Officer and the penalty to be imposed.

1. There are also the following incidental questions, which are dealt with in the judgment. These questions are:

   (i) Whether the Report of the Inquiry Officer is to be furnished to the Charged Official even when the Statutory Rules governing the Inquiry are either silent about it or specifically prohibit it?

   (ii) Whether the Report of Inquiry is to be furnished to the Charged Official even when the penalty proposed to be imposed is neither dismissal nor removal nor compulsory retirement from service?

   (iii) Whether the obligation to furnish a copy of the Report of Inquiry arises only on the Charged Official's request for such a copy?

   (iv) Whether the law laid down in Mohammed Ramzan Khan's case (AIR 1991 SC 471) would apply to all employees, whether in government or in the public and the private sectors?

   (v) Since the ratio of the judgment in Mohammed Ramzan Khan's case (AIR 1991 SC 471) is to apply to all Departmental Proceedings – where an Inquiry Officer has been appointed – where penalty is to be imposed prospectively from 20 November 1990 (the day the judgment was delivered by the Supreme Court), what was the law before 20 November 1990 regarding furnishing a copy of the Inquiry Report to the Charged Official?

2. Historically speaking, for the first time, the Public Servants Inquiry Act 1850, regulated the conduct of inquiry against public servants not removable from their appointments without sanction of the Government.

3. The next landmark in service law was Section 96(B) of the Government of India Act 1919. It authorized the Secretary of State-in-Council to make Rules for regulating classification of the Civil Servants, the methods of their recruitment, their conditions of service including pay and allowances and their discipline and conduct.

4. The Civil Service Classification Rules framed in the year 1920 provided that, without prejudice to the Public Servants (Inquiry) Act 1850, in all cases where dismissal, removal or reduction in rank of an official is ordered, the order shall – except in cases where the guilt of the official is established in a judicial trial – be preceded by "a properly recorded departmental inquiry".

5. There was, however, no stipulation in the Civil Services Classification Rules 1920, that the Charged Official would be heard before any specific penalty was imposed on him. The 1920 Rules, however, stipulated that any Charged Official, aggrieved by an order of penalty, can prefer an appeal to the higher departmental authorities.

6. The next landmark was Section 240(3) of the Government of India Act 1935. It stipulated that a delinquent Civil Servant is not to be either dismissed or reduced in rank unless he has been given a "reasonable opportunity" to show cause against action proposed to be taken against him. It was provided in the Government of India Act 1935, that the Charged Official would be furnished a copy of the Report of Inquiry to enable him to get "a reasonable opportunity" to defend himself if it was proposed to dismiss him from service or reduce him in rank. In view of interpretation of the provision of the Government of India Act 1935 by the higher Judiciary, a copy of the Inquiry Report was also to be furnished to the Charged Official if it was proposed to remove him from service.

7. Article 311 of the Constitution incorporated the provisions of Section 240(3) of the Government of India Act 1935, with the further stipulation that removal from service would attract the same safeguard as reduction in rank and dismissal from service.

8. By the Constitution (Fifteenth Amendment) Act 1963 – which came into force from 06 October 1963 – Article 311 of the Constitution was amended. Before the Amendment, it was stipulated that "reasonable opportunity" to the Charged Official to defend himself in a Departmental Inquiry meant:

   "until he has been given reasonable opportunity of showing cause against action proposed to be taken in regard to him".

   The aforesaid stipulation in Article 311(2) was amended to read as follows:

   "Except after an Inquiry in which he has been informed of the charges against him and given a reasonable opportunity of being heard in respect of those charges and where it is proposed after such Inquiry to impose on him any such penalty until he has been given reasonable opportunity of making representation against penalty proposed but only on the basis of evidence adduced during the Inquiry".

9. Article 311(2) was further amended by the Constitution (Forty-second Amendment) Act 1976. The Amendment of 1976 stipulated that it shall not be necessary to give a charged official an opportunity of making representation against the proposed penalty.

10. In Khem Chand *versus* Union of India (AIR 1958 SC 300), the Court held that "reasonable opportunity" in Article 311(2) of the Constitution meant:
   (i) An opportunity to the Charged Official to deny his guilt and establish his innocence by communicating to him the Articles of Charge and the imputations on which such charges are based.
   (ii) An opportunity to the charged official to defend himself by examining his defence witness and to cross-examine the witnesses produced against him.
   (iii) An opportunity to represent against the proposed penalty of dismissal, removal or compulsory retirement from service.

11. The Court also held in Khem Chand case (AIR 1958 SC 300) that an opportunity to show cause against the proposed penalty be given to the Charged Official after the Disciplinary Authority applies his mind to the evidence in support of Articles of Charge held as proved and tentatively decides about the proposed penalty.

12. Before the commencement of the Constitution, the Privy Council had held in I.M. Lal's case (AIR 1948 PC 121) that the findings of the Inquiry Officer in his Report are not final and binding on the Disciplinary Authority. It was also held that for valid reasons, to be recorded in writing on basis evidence adduced during the Inquiry, the Disciplinary Authority may fully or partially disagree with the findings of the Inquiry Officer.

13. After commencement of the Constitution, the Supreme Court reiterated the ratio in I.M. Lal's case (AIR 1948 PC 121) in Khem Chand *versus* Union of India (AIR 1958 SC 300).

14. In State of Gujarat *versus* R.G. Teredesai (AIR 1969 SC 1294), it was held that the requirement of giving a "reasonable opportunity" to the Charged Official would not be satisfied unless a copy of the Report of Inquiry was furnished to him by the Disciplinary Authority.

15. In Tulsiram Patel *versus* Union of India (AIR 1985 SC 1416), the Court noted that the Constitution (Forty-second Amendment) Act 1976, dispensed with the need for giving an opportunity to the Charged Official to show cause against the proposed penalty. But the aforesaid judgment did not discuss the issue whether the Disciplinary Authority was required to give an opportunity to the Charged Official to represent against findings of the Inquiry Officer in his Report. In other words, after the Forty-second Amendment Act 1976, the Charged Official was not entitled to represent against the proposed penalty and was also deprived of the Right to represent against the findings of the Inquiry Officer.

16. The Supreme Court held in Mohammed Ramzan Khan's case (AIR 1991 SC 471) that though following the Constitution (Forty-second Amendment) Act 1976, it was not

mandatory for the Disciplinary Authority to furnish a copy of the Report of Inquiry to the Charged Official before imposing a penalty, furnishing a copy of the Report of Inquiry Officer was mandatory to fulfill the requirement of "reasonable opportunity" in Article 311(2) of the Constitution.

17. Even though the ratio of the decision in Mohammed Ramzan's case (AIR 1991 SC 471) was to apply prospectively from 20 November 1990 (the day the judgment was delivered) unfortunately, the Court committed a mistake and allowed all appeals pending before it and set aside the penalty imposed by the Disciplinary Authority on the ground of non-furnishing a copy of the Report of Inquiry to the Charged Official. This anomaly was noticed by the Court at a later stage whereupon the Chief Justice of India referred the issue to a larger Bench. The larger Bench decided the matter in the present case of Managing Director ECIL *versus* Karunakara (AIR 1994 SC 1074).

18. The issues can be viewed in the light of the judgment in A.K. Kraipak *versus* Union of India (AIR 1970 SC 150) where it was held that the Rules of Natural Justice operate in areas not covered by any law. In other words, the Rules of Natural Justice do not supplant the law but only supplement it. The Rules of Natural Justice are not embodied Rules and their aim is to secure Justice or to prevent miscarriage of Justice. It was also held that in recent years the concept of Natural Justice has undergone a great deal of change and what particular Rule of Natural Justice would apply in a case would greatly depend upon facts and circumstances of the case.

19. Since the Constitution (Forty-second Amendment) Act 1976, dispensed with the requirement of issue of notice to the Charged Official against the proposed penalty, some High Courts took the view that the Charged Official also was no longer entitled to a copy of the Report of Inquiry. The error occurred because of failure to distinguish the two Rights, i.e. the Right to represent against the proposed penalty and the Right to represent against the findings of the Inquiry Officer. The Court has held in Managing Director ECIL's case (AIR 1994 SC 1074) that these two Rights are distinct and independent of each other.

20. In Chairman Board of Mining Examination *versus* Ramjee (AIR 1977 SC 965), the Court held that Natural Justice is not an unruly horse, no lurking landmine nor a judicial cure-all. If fairness is shown by the decision-maker to the person proceeded against, the form, the features and the fundamentals of procedure being conditioned by the facts and circumstances of each case, no breach of the principle of Natural Justice can be complained of.

21. The catena of judgments of the Supreme Court has established the proposition that the principles of Natural Justice must be applied in the unoccupied interstices of the statute.

22. The Right of the Charged Official to represent against findings in the Report of Inquiry is part of the "reasonable opportunity" during the first stage of a Departmental Enquiry. The Right to show cause against the proposed penalty belongs to the second stage of the Inquiry after the Disciplinary Authority has come to a conclusion regarding the guilt of the Charged Official. The first stage of a Departmental Enquiry must give a Charged Official reasonable opportunity to defend himself and prove his innocence. The second stage of

a Departmental Enquiry is to represent against the proposed penalty if it is dismissal, removal or reduction in rank. It is this Right of the Charged Official at the second stage of the Departmental Enquiry, which has been taken away by the Constitution (Forty-second Amendment) Act 1976.

23. The findings of an Inquiry Officer in his Report of Inquiry has to be based on evidence which are a part of the case records of the Inquiry. The principles of Natural Justice require that the Charged Official should have a fair opportunity to meet, explain and controvert the findings of the Inquiry Officer before he is penalized.

24. The legal position in the matter of "reasonable opportunity" to a Charged Official may be looked at from a different angle. The findings on the charges by an Inquiry Officer, if arrived at without any evidence in support thereof or by misconstruing the evidence, could themselves constitute an unwarranted imputation. Therefore, by the Constitution (Forty-second Amendment) Act 1976, what is dispensed with is the Right to represent against the penalty proposed and not the Right to represent against the findings of the Inquiry Officer.

25. The law laid down in Mohammed Ramzan Khan's case (AIR 1991 SC 471) being a facet of Natural Justice, should apply to employees in all Establishments – whether Government or non-Government, public or private.

26. What is the effect on order of penalty on a Charged Official when the Report of Inquiry is not furnished to him? The answer to this question depends largely on facts and circumstances of each case. In some cases, non-furnishing of the Report of Inquiry may have prejudiced the Charged Official gravely while in some other case, it would have made no difference to the penalty imposed on the Charged Official. Therefore, in all cases, where a Charged Official is penalized without furnishing him a copy of the Report of Inquiry, the order of penalty need not be set aside lest the Rules of Natural Justice are reduced to a mechanical ritual.

27. The theory of reasonable opportunity and the principles of Natural Justice have been evolved to uphold the Rule of Law and to assist an aggrieved party to vindicate his just Rights. They are not incantations to be invoked on all occasions.

28. If the Court or the Tribunal – after hearing the parties – comes to the conclusion that non-supply of the Report of Inquiry would have made no difference to the penalty imposed on the Charged Official, the Court or the Tribunal should not interfere with the order of penalty.

29. Where the Court or the Tribunal sets aside the penalty imposed on the Charged Official, the proper relief is to order reinstatement of the Official with liberty to the Employer to proceed with the Inquiry by placing the official under suspension and to continue the Inquiry from the stage of furnishing him with a copy of the Report of Inquiry.

30. If the Charged Official succeeds in the fresh Inquiry and is reinstated in service, the Employer should be at liberty to decide according to law how to treat the period from the date of dismissal to the date of reinstatement and to what financial benefit, if any, the reinstated official would be entitled to.

31. As already stated, the ratio in Mohammed Ramzan Khan's case (AIR 1991 SC 471) was to apply prospectively by invoking the doctrine of prospective overruling, applied in I.C. Golaknath case (AIR 1967 SC 1643).

32. In Orissa Cement Ltd. *versus* State of Orissa (AIR 1991 SC 1676), the Court held that although the mining royalty and related charges for mining lease was illegal, it did not mean an automatic refund of collections of levy made earlier. The Court held that it was open for them to grant moulded or restricted relief in a manner most appropriate to the situation before it so as to advance the interest of justice.

33. Article 141 and Article 142 are couched in very wide terms. They enable the Supreme Court not only to declare the law but to give such direction or to pass such order as is necessary to do complete justice. Therefore, the Supreme Court can hold that the law they lay down can only operate prospectively in the interest of justice.

Chapter 17

S.R. Bommai *versus* Union of India (AIR 1994 SC 1918)

[JUSTICE S. RATNAVEL PANDIAN, JUSTICE A.M. AHMADI, JUSTICE KULDIP SINGH, JUSTICE J.S. VERMA, JUSTICE P.B. SAWANT, JUSTICE K. RAMASWAMY, JUSTICE S.C. AGRAWAL, JUSTICE YOGEHWAR DAYAL AND JUSTICE B.P. JEEVAN REDDY]

Case Summary

This is a landmark judgment where a Constitution Bench of nine Judges pronounced regarding Article 356 of the Constitution and the issue of Centre-State relations. The judgment also deals with the concept of secularism and the power of Judicial Review.

1. Justice S. Ratnavel Pandian delivered a separate judgment agreeing with four brother Judges, viz. Justice P.B. Sawant, Justice Kuldip Singh, Justice B.P. Jeevan Reddy and Justice S.C. Agarwal.
2. A summary of Justice Ratnavel Pandian's judgment is as follows:
   (i) The Indian Constitution, is both a legal and a social document and the machinery of Government is a means to achieve the constitutional ideals.
   (ii) During debates in the Constituent Assembly, the issue of Rights of the State Governments vis-à-vis the Rights of the Union Government cropped up mostly around two issues, viz.
      (a) What powers were to be taken away from the State Government and vested with the Union Government and
      (b) How could a Union Government be constituted without completely denuding powers of the State Governments?
   (iii) The final result was a compromise of a federal Government as opposed to a unitary Government.
3. The Constitution of India was framed by the people of India for themselves and not for individual States of the Indian Union. The Constitution derives its power from the people of India.

4. Up to the year 1991, on as many as 82 occasions since commencement of the Constitution, President's Rule has been imposed in states by invoking Article 356(1). During the same period, on as many as 13 occasions, President's Rule has been imposed on Union Territories. Of the total of 95 occasions when President's Rule was imposed on States and the Union Territories on 23 occasions, the State Assemblies were dissolved and on 13 occasions, the Assemblies, which remained suspended during President's Rule, got revived after President's Rule was over. Some of the states where Legislative Assemblies were dissolved took the matter to High Courts where they fought legal battles. They bled honorably in the battle, which they however lost pathetically.

5. Power of the President under Article 356(1) should be used sparingly only when the President is genuinely satisfied that Government of a State cannot be carried on in accordance with provisions of the Constitution. Frequent use of the power is likely to disturb the constitutional balance.

6. Justice A.M. Ahmadi delivered a separate judgment agreeing with his brother Judge K. Ramaswamy.

7. A summary of the Judgment of Justice A.M. Ahmadi is as follows: India is a vast country with a population of about 850 million. The people of India speak different languages, have different racial origins and profess different religions. In India, strong executive action is necessary to preserve the unity and integrity of the country. To enable the Central Government to take urgent action, there was provision in the Government of India Act 1935 to take over provincial governments. But when in the draft Constitution similar powers were sought to be vested in the President of India, there was resistance by some members of the Constituent Assembly. Dr. B.R. Ambedkar pacified the agitated members by saying that he shared their sentiments and hoped that Article 356(1) will "remain a dead letter". Dr. Ambedkar also said that the President will first issue a warning to the errant State Government that affairs of the Government were not being carried out in accordance with the Constitution.

8. Dr. Ambedkar hoped that Article 356(1) would be invoked only in the rarest of the rare cases. This hope was soon belied as, the power of the President under Article 356(1) had been invoked on numerous occasions.

9. There was considerable argument whether the Indian Constitution was federal in character. Lord Dicey calls federalism a political contrivance for States who desire Union but not unity. In a federation, several States come together to form a Union without sacrificing their fundamental political integrity. The essence of federation is distribution of powers between the Union and the States in a federal compact.

10. The oldest federal Constitution is that of the United States of America. In USA, the constituent states first formed a confederation and thereafter became a federation. Although the states in USA have their own Constitution, the federal Constitution is the supreme law and is binding on the states. In the American Constitution, without consent of the state no amendment to the Constitution can be made depriving the concerned state of its equal representation in the Senate. In the American Constitution, there is a single legislative list enumerating powers of the Union. Automatically, other subjects,

not in the legislative list of the Union Government, are within legislative competence of the States. The responsibility of protecting the States from foreign invasion is that of the Union Government. The States are prohibited from entering into any treaty with a foreign Government. In USA the federal laws are administered by the Federal Courts while the State laws are administered by the State Courts. The U.S. Supreme Court alone can interpret the provisions of the U.S. Constitution.

11. In USA, the Congress cannot alter the names and the boundaries of different States whereas in India, under Article 3 of the Constitution, the Parliament may change name of a State, alter its boundaries, create new States and abolish existing States.

12. While framing the Constitution, the Constituent Assembly transferred some of the subjects of common interest from the provincial list under the Government of India Act 1935 to the Union List in the Seventh Schedule of the Constitution. It is in this context that the Supreme Court observed in State of West Bengal *versus* Union of India (AIR 1963 SC 1241) that "powers of the States are not coordinate with the Union and are not in many respects independent."

13. Under the Government of India Act 1935, residuary power was not given either to the Union or to the provincial legislatures but in the Constitution of India, residuary power has been vested on the Parliament.

14. Under Article 256 of the Constitution, executive power of a State shall be so exercised as not to impede or prejudice executive power of the Union. Moreover, under Article 257, executive power of the Union extends to giving such direction to a State as may appear to be necessary for construction and maintenance of means of communication declared to be of national or of military importance and for protection of the Railways.

15. The States have to largely depend upon financial assistance by the Union Government. Under provisions of Articles 268 to 273 of the Constitution, the following arrangements have been made:

(i) States are allowed to collect and retain some duties imposed by the Union.

(ii) States are assigned some taxes levied and collected by the Union on behalf of the States.

(iii) In some cases, taxes levied and collected by the Union are shared by the Union with the states.

(iv) Under Article 275 of the Constitution, the Union Government can give grant-in-aid to States.

16. Under Article 282 of the Constitution, both the Union Government and the State Governments can give a grant for a public purpose.

17. Under Article 368, power to amend the Constitution is only with the Union Parliament. Only for some specific amendments as in proviso to Article 368, the Union Government requires a resolution supporting the amendment by legislatures of at least half the states.

18. The Indian Constitution is not truly federal as the U.S. Constitution. In State of Rajasthan *versus* Union of India (AIR 1977 SC 1361), Chief Justice M.H. Beg, observed that the extent of federalism in India has been watered down by needs of socio-economic development of the country.

19. The Indian Constitution has set up a Union Government which is amphibian in the sense that it can move in the federal or unitary plane according to needs.

20. Unlike the American Constitution, the Indian Constitution does not recognize dual citizenship. Unlike an American citizen, who owes allegiance to both the State and the federal Constitution, the Indian citizen has no such problem.

21. As the Indian Constitution is a mixture of both federal and unitary features, the noted constitutional expert, K.C. Wheare has called it quasi-federal.

22. The history of freedom struggle indicates that the leaders wanted a secular India where the State will not only guarantee freedom of religious worship but also would not have bias towards any religious denomination. Equality before law is a facet of secularism even though the Preamble was amended in 1976 by the Constitution (Forty-second Amendment) Act to insert the expressions "socialist" and "secular". Secularism has been very much embedded in our constitutional philosophy. Article 25 (freedom of conscience and freedom for profession, practice and propagation of religion); Article 28 (freedom as to attendance at religious instruction or religious worship in certain educational institutions); Article 29 (denial of admission to an educational institution maintained wholly or partly out of State funds solely on ground of religion) and Article 30 (Rights of the minorities to establish and administer educational institutions of their choice) are part of the basic structure of the Constitution.

23. The Fundamental Duties in Article 51A of the Constitution, introduced by the Forty-second Amendment Act 1976 bring out the dual concepts of secularism and democracy.

24. As stated by brother judges Justice P.B. Sawant, Justice K. Ramaswamy and Justice B.P. Jeevan Reddy, secularism is a basic feature of the Constitution.

25. In a federal Constitution due to periodic elections, a particular political party may come to power in the Centre while a different political party may be in power in a State or in more than one state. A change of political party forming the Union Government in India does not give the Union Government the mandate to advise the President to promulgate President's Rule in those States of India where a different political party is in power.

26. Where a State Government in India is functioning in accordance with provisions of the Constitution, the Union Government would not be justified in resorting to President's rule.

27. Milon K. Banerji, the Attorney-General for India and K. Parasaran counsel for the Union of India, have conceded that President's Rule under Article 356(1) in a state is amenable to judicial review. The controversy, therefore, narrows down to determination of scope and ambit of judicial review of Presidential Proclamation.

28. Both Milon K. Banerji and K. Parasaran argued that the law laid down in State of Rajasthan *versus* Union of India (AIR 1977 SC 1361) was correct regarding scope and ambit of judicial review of a Presidential Proclamation and did not require re-consideration. The counsels for different State Governments, which were taken over by proclamations

under Article 356(1), however argued to the contrary and urged a reconsideration of the decision.

29. Before deciding on the controversy regarding scope of power of judicial review of a Presidential Proclamation, it may be necessary to decide whether in exercise of power of judicial review, the Court can scrutinize what advice the Council of Ministers of the Union Government gave to the President to invoke Article 356(1).

30. Article 74(2) only bars advice of the Council of Ministers to the President from scrutiny of the Courts. It does not bar scrutiny by Courts of the materials and the circumstances which formed basis of the advice of the Council of Ministers. Of course, the privilege available under Sections 123 and 124 of the Indian Evidence Act would stand on a different footing and can be claimed by the Union of India even without invoking Article 74(2) of the Constitution.

31. What is the scope and ambit of judicial review of subjective satisfaction of the President under Article 356(1) of the Constitution? The answer is: exercise of power under Article 356(1) depends on satisfaction of the President on receipt of report of the Governor of the state or otherwise that a situation has arisen in which Government of the State cannot be carried on in accordance with provisions of the Constitution. Article 356(1) confers extraordinary powers on the President which he must exercise sparingly and with great circumspection. The expression "otherwise" in Article 356(1) is of very wide import and cannot be restricted to materials capable of being tested on principles relevant to admissibility of evidence in Courts. Since the President is not expected to record reasons for his satisfaction, it would be difficult for the Court to enter the "political thicket" to ascertain what weighed with the President for exercise of power under Article 356(1). Since several imponderables would be under consideration of the President and result in his ultimate decision, "satisfaction" of the President cannot be put at par with satisfaction of a Government official in taking an administrative decision. The Court cannot question exercise of constitutional power of the President under Article 356(1) unless the same can be shown as a *mala fide* exercise of power. Therefore, there is considerable force in arguments of brother judges Justice K. Ramaswamy and Justice J.S. Verma that there is limited scope of judicial review of President's Proclamation under Article 356(1). The judgment of the Supreme Court in the State of Rajasthan *versus* The Union of India (AIR 1977 SC 1361) lays down the law correctly when it says that a Presidential Proclamation under Article 356(1) can only be subject to judicial review on the ground of *mala fide*.

32. Justice J.S. Verma who was in the Bench of nine judges, delivered a separate judgment for himself and on behalf of Justice Yogeswar Dayal. In the opinion of Justice J.S. Verma, scope of judicial review of exercise of powers of the President under Article 356(1) is narrower than what brother judges constituting the Bench have held.

33. Continuing the argument, Justice J.S. Verma held that the scope for judicial review of a Presidential Proclamation is rather narrow in view of nature of the power and the wide discretion which inheres in its exercise. This also appears from requirement of approval of the Proclamation by both Houses of Parliament, which is a check provided for in the Constitution. The verdict of the people in the Election that will follow is, however, the ultimate check against unjustified exercise of power by the President.

34. De Smith says in his book *Judicial Review of Administrative Action* that the Court should exercise judicial restraint and should be slow to read implied limitations into grant of wide discretionary power, which might have to be exercised by the President on broad considerations of national policy.

35. In the year 1986, Lord Brightman had said that "whenever existence or non-existence of a fact is left to the judgment and discretion of a public body and that fact involves a broad spectrum ranging from the obvious to the debatable to the just conceivable, it is the duty of the Court to leave that decision to the public body...save in a case where it is obvious that the public body, consciously or unconsciously has been acting perversely."

36. This principle is equally applicable to the present case to determine the extent to which a Proclamation under Article 356(1) is justiciable. The grounds for invalidity of a Presidential Proclamation under Article 356(1) have been correctly stated in the State of Rajasthan *versus* The Union of India (AIR 1977 SC 1361).

37. Justice J.S. Verma concluded his judgment by stating that even if Parliament has approved a Presidential Proclamation under Article 356(1), judicial review on the limited ground of *mala fide* exercise of power by the President is not excluded.

38. Justice P.B. Sawant delivered a separate judgment on behalf of himself and brother judge Justice Kuldip Singh.

39. The salient points in the judgment of Justice P.B. Sawant are as follows: the question whether the President has unfettered powers to issue a Proclamation under Article 356(1) can be answered by keeping in view the following three issues:
    (i) Is the Proclamation amenable to judicial review?
    (ii) If the Proclamation is amenable to judicial review, what is the scope of such review?
    (iii) What is the meaning of the expression in Article 356(i) that "a situation has arisen in which Government of a state cannot be carried on in accordance with provisions of the Constitution"?

40. Materials showing that Government of a State cannot be carried on in accordance with provisions of the Constitution is a condition precedent before the President can issue a Proclamation under Article 356(1).

41. Once materials are shown to exist, the satisfaction of the President based on such materials is not open to question by the Courts in exercise of the power of judicial review.

42. Appearing for the Union of India, K. Parasaran said that there is difference in nature and scope of power of judicial review in administrative law and constitutional law. He argued that in administrative law, the Court's power extends to legal control of public authorities in exercise of their statutory power. It also extends to scrutiny of irregular exercise of power. He, however, maintained that scope of judicial review in constitutional law is only for preventing actions *ultra vires* the Constitution.

43. Justice P.B. Sawant held that the contention of K. Parasaran may not be correct as many of the parameters of judicial review in administrative law are also equally applicable to judicial review of constitutional law.

44. Lord Brightman had said that judicial review is not appeal from a decision but a review of the manner in which a decision was made.

45. Lord Diplock, has also said in Council of Civil Service Union *versus* Minister for the Civil Service (1985) that judicial review of administrative action is permissible on four grounds, viz.:
   (i) Illegality;
   (ii) Irrationality; and
   (iii) Procedural impropriety.
   (iv) Proportionality (the principle of Proportionality has already been recognized by the European Economic Community as a possible ground for Judicial Review).

46. Donaldson L.J. has said that the power of judicial review is a supervisory or a "long step" jurisdiction.

47. Regarding President's powers, it can be said that satisfaction of the President to invoke Article 356(1) may be subjective but existence of materials for the "satisfaction must be demonstrable".

48. In Kehar Singh *versus* Union of India (AIR 1989 SC 653), it was held that President's powers under Article 72 of the Constitution dealing with grant of pardons, reprieves and remissions or commutation of sentence of persons convicted of any offence can be subject of judicial review within limits laid down in Maru Ram *versus* Union of India (AIR 1980 SC 2147). These limits are whether the powers under Article 72 of the Constitution are exercised on wholly irrelevant considerations or the exercise of powers is irrational, discriminatory or *mala fide*.

49. The Report of the Sarkaria Commission on Centre-State Relations cites several instances where it would be inappropriate to issue a Proclamation under Article 356(1) of the Constitution.

50. These instances in the Sarkaria Commission's Report, approvingly cited by Justice P.B. Sawant, are as follows:
   (i) A situation of maladministration in a state even when the party-in-power has support of the majority in the state legislature.
   (ii) Where following resignation of a Ministry in a State, the Governor without waiting for formation of an alternative government under a new leader enjoying support of the majority in the legislature, sends a Report to the President that a Proclamation be issued under Article 356(1).
   (iii) Where a Governor recommends to the President to issue a Proclamation under Article 356(1) without giving the party-in-power in the state time for "floor test" to prove its majority.
   (iv) Where Article 356(1) is sought to be invoked on the sole ground that the party-in-power in a State has suffered a massive defeat in a General Election to the Lok Sabha.

(v) Where there is internal disturbance in a State but the State Government has not abdicated due performance of its duties and the Union Government has not yet exhausted measures to contain the disturbance.

(vi) Where the President has given no prior warning to the State Government to correct itself.

(vii) Where a State Government either applies the corrective in response to an informal direction of the Union Government or in response to a formal direction under Articles 256 and 257 of the Constitution or where the State Government satisfies the Union Government that the Union Government had issued directions to State Government under Articles 256 and 257 on basis of incorrect facts.

(viii) Use of power under Article 356(1) to sort out internal differences or inter-party problems.

(ix) Invoking powers under Article 356(1) in view of stringent financial conditions in the state.

(x) Invoking powers under Article 356(1) on the ground that there are serious allegations of corruption against Ministers of the State Government.

(xi) Invoking powers under Articles 356(1) for a purpose extraneous or irrelevant to the one for which it has been conferred by the Constitution.

51. Article 74(2) of the Constitution only bars the Courts to scrutinize advice of the Council of Ministers to the President. It does not bar judicial scrutiny of the materials and circumstances on basis of which the Council of Ministers tendered advice to the President.

52. Even Section 123 of the Indian Evidence Act would not help the Union Government to successfully claim privilege against disclosure of the materials and the circumstances as the Court would examine such claim of privilege on merits.

53. Democracy and Federalism are part of the basic structure of the Indian Constitution. Any interpretation that the Court has to place on Article 356(1) must therefore help to preserve democracy and federalism.

54. The power under Article 356(1) vests *de jure* on the President and *de facto* on the Council of Ministers of the Union Government. Such power has the latent capacity to emasculate two basic features of the Constitution as democracy and federalism.

55. It is necessary for the higher judiciary to scrutinize closely the materials on the basis of which the President is satisfied in terms of Article 356(1) of the Constitution to take over the State Government. The acknowledged parameters of judicial review in such cases will be illegality, irrationality and *mala fide*.

56. Another salutary check on powers of the President will be that after the State Assembly is suspended following a Proclamation under Article 356(1), the State Assembly can be dissolved only after the approval of the Presidential Proclamation by resolution of both Houses of the Parliament.

57. In appropriate cases, the Court can grant interim relief to an aggrieved party by preventing fresh election to the State Assembly but it has to be ensured that the challenge to the Proclamation under Article 356(1) is heard by the Court and disposed of expeditiously.

58. It would however be wholly impermissible either to interdict the issue of the Presidential Proclamation or its operation till a final verdict on its validity is pronounced.

59. If a Proclamation under Article 356(1) is held to be invalid by the Court, notwithstanding the fact that the Proclamation has been approved by both Houses of the Parliament, it would be open to the Court to restore the *status quo ante*, revive the Legislative Assembly and re-install the dismissed Council of Ministers of the State Government.

60. While restoring the *status quo ante*, the Court can mould the relief and validate action by the President in relation to the concerned State Government till the date *status quo ante* was restored by the Court.

61. Justice K. Ramaswamy delivered a separate judgment regarding scope of judicial review of a Proclamation under Article 356(1). He endorsed the decision in State of Rajasthan *versus* Union of India (AIR 1977 SC 1361) and held that the Proclamation can be impugned either on ground of legal *mala fides* or high degree of irrationality in exercise of discretion to issue the Proclamation or because the Proclamation was issued by the President on totally irrelevant grounds.

62. Exercise of power under Article 356(1) is an extraordinary one and needs to be invoked sparingly.

63. It is not possible to exhaustively catalogue a complete set of situations when breakdown of constitutional machinery in a state may be justifiably inferred.

64. Article 365 of the Constitution has laid down that where a State has failed to comply with directions given by the Union Government in exercise of executive powers it shall be lawful for the President to hold that the Government of the State cannot be carried on in accordance with provisions of the Constitution. If the State Government fails to comply with direction to construct or maintain means of communication declared by the Union Government to be of national or military importance, it will be an infraction of Article 257(2) of the Constitution. Similar infraction may be inferred under Article 257(3) if the State Government fails to take measures for protection of Railways within its territory.

65. During Proclamation of Emergency under Article 352 of the Constitution, the Union Government can give direction to a State Government regarding the manner in which executive power of the State Government shall be exercised and failure on part of any State Government to do so would come within the ambit of Article 356(1) of the Constitution.

66. Similarly, because of Article 365 of the Constitution, Article 356(1) will be attracted if during the period of promulgation of financial emergency under Article 360 of the Constitution, a State Government fails to observe canons of financial propriety.

67. Conversely, on resignation of Chief Minister of a State, if Governor of the State without satisfying himself that no alternative Government in the state is possible, recommends to the President that Article 356(1) should be invoked and the President issues a Proclamation and dissolves the State Assembly, it would be a highly irrational exercise of power. Such an exercise of power is subject to judicial review.

68. Similarly, if a Governor of a State recommends promulgation of a Proclamation under Article 356(1) only because the Chief Minister of the State belongs to a particular religion,

caste or creed, and the President acts on such recommendation it will also be a highly irrational exercise of power.

69. Since federalism is a basic feature of the Constitution, the motive for invoking Article 356(1) should not be political gain for the party in power in the Union Government.

70. Power of the President under Article 356(1) can be exercised only with great deal of circumspection and in a non-partisan manner.

71. The guidelines recommended by the Sarkaria Commission on Centre-State Relations and the Rajamannar Commission have weight and may be discussed among the major political parties to evolve a consensus. But the recommendations of the two commissions cannot be adopted by the higher judiciary to decide the *vires* of a Presidential Notification under Article 356(1) as sometimes the recommendations "are beset with difficulties in implementation".

72. The power of judicial review in judging the *vires* of a Presidential Proclamation under Article 356(1) must be exercised with great caution. It can be exercised on rare occasions to nullify *ultra vires* orders.

73. Justice Felix Frankfurter of the U.S. Supreme Court has said that, "Independence of the judiciary is jeopardized when Courts become embroiled in passions of the day and assume primary responsibility in choosing between competing political, economic and social pressures."

74. A Chief Minister whose majority support in the State Assembly is under challenge must be given an opportunity to prove his majority on floor of the Assembly. But this salutary principle, has several pitfalls. It was, therefore, not found to be a sound principle to be enforced even as a convention in a parliamentary form of Government with a federal Constitution.

75. If some State Governments act in breach of secularism, which is a basic structure of the Constitution, there would be adequate justification for a Presidential Proclamation under Article 356(1).

76. The Preamble is an integral part of the Constitution. Democracy, federal structure, unity and integrity of the nation, social justice and judicial review are basic features of the Constitution.

77. The office of the Governor of a State is a vital link and a channel of impartial communication to the President of India on working of the Constitution by the State Government. The Governor is to ensure protection and sustenance of the constitutional process. By playing an impartial role, as Head of the Executive of the State Government, he is to act with high degree of responsibility when he sends a report to the President that there is enough reason to believe that a situation has arisen in the state when the Government cannot be carried on in accordance with provisions of the Constitution. The Governor's Report to the President must have requisite factual details in this regard.

78. Article 74(2) of the Constitution is not a barrier for Judicial Review. It only provides a protective canopy on the advice given by the Council of Ministers to the President.

The material on basis of which the advice was tendered by the Council of Ministers is, however, subject to judicial review.

79. When "Discovery Order nisi" is issued by the Court, the Union of India would act in aid of the Court and is enjoined to produce the material which the Council of Ministers duly considered to recommend President's Rule.

80. For production of the materials by the Union of India, the Court must find a strong *prima facie* case and the materials and records are to be scrutinized by the Court in camera.

81. Judicial review is to be distinguished from justiciability by the Court. The power of judicial review is a constituent power. The Court cannot scrutinize the justiciability of a decision of the President to invoke powers under Article 356(1).

82. Justice B.P. Jeevan Reddy delivered a separate judgment on his own behalf and on behalf of brother judge Justice S.C. Agrawal.

83. The salient points in the judgment of Justice B.P. Jeevan Reddy are as follows: No other Constitution of the world except the Constitution of Pakistan has a provision similar to Article 356 of the Constitution.

84. The Government of India Act 1935 had similar provisions as Article 356 of the Constitution of India.

85. Dr. B.R. Ambedkar, was of the view that the new Constitution of India must provide for breakdown of constitutional machinery in State Governments analogous to Section 93 of the Government of India Act 1935. Dr. Ambedkar also said that in exercise of the power to take over the administration of a State Government, the President is not expected to act in a wanton or arbitrary manner but on basis of a written report of the Governor of the State or on basis of other materials in his possession.

86. Dr. Ambedkar also said that the President is expected to first give a warning to a State Government before invoking power under Article 356(1). He also hoped that Article 356(1) would remain a dead letter.

87. To analyse implications of powers of the President under Article 356(1), it is necessary to examine the nature of the Indian Federation. The expression "Federation" has no fixed meaning. It broadly indicates a form of Government where there is a division of power between the Federation and the States.

88. In view of history of the sub-continent, the Founding Fathers of the Indian Constitution wanted to have a strong Union Government.

89. The bias towards a strong Union Government is evident from the fact that important heads of legislation are placed in the Union List and in the Concurrent List and Parliamentary enactment is given primacy over enactments by states. Residuary power of legislation is also vested on the Parliament. By the Constitution (Forty-second Amendment) Act 1976, quite a few entries in the State List in the Seventh Schedule were either omitted or transferred to the Concurrent List. Article 3 of the Constitution is a very powerful provision in favour of a strong Union Government as under its provision, the Parliament cannot only alter the area and the boundary of the existing states but can also change the name of any State. Powers under Article 3 can be exercised by the Parliament by passing

a law and such law is not to be considered as an amendment of the Constitution under Article 368.

90. By virtue of the States Re-organization Act 1956, 14 states and six Union Territories came into existence. In India, there is a single citizenship and a unified judiciary. Under Article 249, Parliament can also legislate on entries in the State List in the national interest though for a limited period. During operation of a Proclamation of Emergency under Article 352 of the Constitution, Parliament can enact any law on entries in the State List. Under Article 253 of the Constitution, Parliament can also pass a law to give effect to any international agreement. In terms of powers of taxation, the Union Government can legislate to levy tax on highly revenue-yielding items. Article 355 of the Constitution provides that it is the obligation of the Union to protect every state against external aggression and internal disturbance and to ensure that Government of a state is carried on in accordance with provisions of the Constitution. Provisions of Article 355 of the Constitution are both an obligation and a source of power of the Union Government.

91. But the States in the Indian Federation are not mere appendages of the Union. They are supreme in the spheres allotted to them. The Courts should also respect their allotted powers and not whittle them down.

92. Federalism in the Indian Constitution is not a matter of administrative convenience but is an outcome of the historical process and the ground realities. M.C. Setalvad, the first Attorney-General for India, had dealt with this aspect elaborately in his Tagore Law lectures in the year 1974.

93. The Sarkaria Commission on Centre-State Relations has made several recommendations regarding powers under Article 356 of the Constitution. One of the important recommendations is that Article 356(1) should be invoked very sparingly and that too as the last resort.

94. The Sarkaria Commission also recommended that Legislative Assembly of the concerned State should not be dissolved before the Proclamation under Article 356(1) is laid before the Parliament and the Parliament has an opportunity to consider it. Article 356 should be suitably amended to provide for it. Article 356 should also be amended to provide for similar safeguards contained in clauses (7) and (8) of Article 352 dealing with Proclamation of Emergency due to war, external aggression and armed rebellion.

95. As early as the year 1971, the Rajmannar Commission appointed by the Government of Tamil Nadu, and headed by P.V. Rajmannar, a former Chief Justice of the Madras High Court, had recommended that Article 356 and Article 357 be repealed. In the alternative, the Rajmannar Commission recommended suitable safeguards against arbitrary and unilateral action by the Union Government commanding majority in the Parliament.

96. In 1976, the Forty-second Amendment of the Constitution inserted the expression "Socialist and Secular" in the Preamble of the Constitution. But even before the amendment, "Secularism" has been a basic feature of the Constitution because of some expressions in the Preamble as "social justice" and "liberty of belief, faith and worship". Article 14 dealing with the Right to Equality is also an ingredient of a secular state. There are also other provisions in the Constitution as Articles 25, 26, 27, 28 and 30, which establish

secular character of the Constitution. Two landmark judgments of the Supreme Court, viz. Kesavananda Bharati *versus* State of Kerala (AIR 1973 SC 1461) and Indira Gandhi *versus* Raj Narain (AIR 1975 SC 2299) also affirm secular character of the Constitution.

97. It is absolutely erroneous to say that secularism is a vacuous word or a phantom concept.

98. Regarding scope and reach of judicial review, it may be mentioned that there cannot be a uniform rule in all cases. As stated in Indra Sawhney *versus* Union of India (AIR 1992 SC 3682), the extent and scope of judicial review depends upon

(i) nature of the subject matter;
(ii) nature of the Right affected;
(iii) character of the legal and constitutional provisions applicable.

99. The Court would respect discretion of the Executive, which is a co-equal wing. The political executive, representing the majority will of the people, is presumed to know the needs of the people and hence its judgment in matters within its powers and discretion will be entitled to due weight.

100. The judges will adapt the rules to protect the Rule of Law. There is no fixed Rule which requires the same answer in every case. The Courts have to wrestle with the distinction between mandatory and directory requirements, where the law has been described as inextricable tangle of loose ends. The same statutory provisions may be differently interpreted according to circumstances of a case. Lord Halisham has said that in view of the rapidly developing jurisprudence of administrative law, there is a spectrum of possibilities and the Courts are not bound to fit the facts of a particular case and a developing chain of events either into rigid legal categories or to stretch them to fit into a Procrustean bed.

101. By the Thirty-eighth Constitutional Amendment Act 1975, clause (5) was incorporated in Article 356. It stipulated that the satisfaction of the President in Article 356(1) shall be final and conclusive and shall not be questioned in any Court on any ground. The aforesaid clause (5) was deleted by the Forty-fourth Constitution Amendment Act 1978.

102. Even when clause (5) of Article 356 had not been replaced by a totally different clause by the Constitution Forty-fourth Amendment Act 1978, five of the seven judges held in the State of Rajasthan case (AIR 1977 SC 1361) that if the power of the President under Article 356(1) has been exercised *mala fide* or on wholly extraneous considerations, the Court can strike down the Presidential Proclamation. Not a single judge held that the exercise of power under Article 356(1) is immune from judicial review in spite of clause (5) of Article 356 by the Thirty-eighth Constitutional Amendment Act 1975, which was then in force.

103. The principle of subjective satisfaction of the Union Government in relation to a company registered under the Companies Act 1956 came to be examined in Barium Chemicals case (AIR 1967 SC 297). It was held in the judgment that the formation of opinion by the Union Government may be a subjective process but circumstances warranting such an opinion are not subjective but must be objective and relevant for the Union Government to form its subjective satisfaction.

104. To sum up: Justice B.P. Jeevan Reddy speaking for himself and Justice S.C. Agrawal held as follows:

(i) Power of the President under Article 356(1) can be exercised only when in opinion of the President, Government of the State cannot be carried on in accordance with provisions of the Constitution. The power actually belongs to the Union Council of Ministers with the Prime Minister as its head. The satisfaction of the President under Article 356(1) is subjective in nature.

(ii) Power under Article 356(1) is a conditional and not an absolute power. The satisfaction of the President must be based on relevant materials. The recommendations of the Sarkaria Commission with respect to exercise of power under Article 356 do merit serious consideration.

(iii) The power to dissolve the Legislative Assembly though implicit in clause (1) of Article 356 can be exercised having regard to the overall constitutional scheme after the Proclamation is approved by both Houses of the Parliament. Until such approval, the President can only suspend the Legislative Assembly of the concerned State.

(iv) There is no room for holding that the President can take over some of the powers and functions of the State Government while keeping the State Government in office for the rest of the powers and functions.

(v) If both Houses of Parliament do not approve of the Proclamation under Article 356(1), the State Government, which was dismissed, revives and the suspended Legislative Assembly gets activated. Since the Proclamation under Article 356(1) lapses if not approved by both Houses of Parliament, the action taken and laws enacted during the period do not become either illegal or void when the Proclamation lapses.

(vi) If the Proclamation is approved by both Houses of the Parliament, the State Government, which was dismissed does not revive on expiry of the stipulated period. The Legislative Assembly, which has been dissolved after approval of the Proclamation by both Houses of the Parliament also does not revive on expiry of the Proclamation or on its revocation.

(vii) Article 74(2) of the Constitution merely bars an inquiry into the question whether any, and if so what advice was tendered by the Ministers to the President. It does not bar the Court to call upon the Union of India to disclose to the Court the materials upon which the President had formed his satisfaction. If the Union of India claims privilege under Section 123 of the Indian Evidence Act against disclosure of such materials, the Court will decide the claim on merits.

(viii) The Proclamation under Article 356(1) is not immune from judicial review. The High Courts and the Supreme Court can strike down the Proclamation if it is *mala fide* or based on wholly irrelevant grounds. The Courts will however not go into the correctness of the material or its adequacy. The Courts can only sit on judgment on its relevance. If part of the material is irrelevant, the Courts cannot interfere if other part of the material is relevant for "satisfaction" of the President under Article 356(1).

(ix) If the Court strikes down the Proclamation, it has power to restore the dismissed State Government to office and to revive the suspended or dissolved Legislative Assembly. In such a case, the Courts have the power to declare that acts done, orders passed and laws made during the period the Proclamation was in force shall remain valid unless orders issued are reviewed, modified by the State Government or laws passed are repealed by the State Legislature.

(x) India has a Federal Constitution with a powerful Central Government. But in normal times the States in the Indian Union are supreme in their own spheres.

(xi) Secularism is a basic feature of the Indian Constitution. Any State Government, which pursues anti-secular policies or takes anti-secular course of action is liable for action under Article 356(i) of the Constitution.

(xii) In view of the aforesaid, Justice B.P. Jeevan Reddy – speaking on his own behalf and on behalf of Justice S.C. Agrawal – is in broad agreement with some of the observations of Justice P.B. Sawant, who delivered a separate judgment on behalf of himself and the brother judge Justice Kuldip Singh.

Chapter 18

Tata Cellular *versus* Union of India (AIR 1996 SC 11)

[CHIEF JUSTICE M.N. VENKATACHALIAH, JUSTICE M.M. PUNCHI AND JUSTICE S. MOHAN]

Case Summary

In this judgment, three judges – with Justice M. Venkatachaliah, the Chief Justice of India, presiding over the Bench – laid down some important parameters of judicial review of administrative action. On behalf of the Bench, Justice S. Mohan delivered the judgment.

1. (a) The facts of the case are as follows: the Department of Telecommunication, Government of India, issued Notice Inviting Tender (NIT) for high-value contracts to operate cellular mobile telephone service by Indian Companies in four cities, viz. Delhi, Mumbai, Kolkata and Madras.

(b) The procedure for the tender comprised two stages,

(i) technical evaluation of the bids offered followed by

(ii) financial evaluation of the bids.

2. After technical evaluation of the bids, as many as 14 Indian Companies were shortlisted for submission of financial bids. The financial bids were opened on 17 August 1992 and after due scrutiny four companies were considered for grant of license to operate cellular telephone service.

3. (a) Four writ petitions were filed before the Delhi High Court by Indian Companies, who were not considered suitable for grant of license to operate cellular telephone service.

(b) The Delhi High Court by judgment and order of 26 February 1993, decided that instead of Tata Cellular Private Ltd. and Indian Telecom Limited – two of the four Indian Companies who were granted license to operate cellular service for the city of Delhi – the contract for cellular service for the city would be awarded to BPL Projects and Systems Ltd. and Sterling Cellular Limited.

4. Aggrieved by the judgment of the Delhi High Court, Tata Cellular approached the Supreme Court under Article 136 of the Constitution.

5. The grounds urged by counsel for Tata Cellular, before the Supreme Court, are as follows:

   (i) the conditions laid down by clause 2:4:7 of the financial bid was ignored by the Competent Authority despite observations of the Chairman, Telecom Commission that Indian Companies, viz. Bharati Cellular, Modi Telecommunications and Mobile Telecom did not satisfy the stipulation in clause 2:4:7 that requirement of foreign exchange to provide cellular mobile service would be met by the foreign collaborator of the Indian Company.

   (ii) B.R. Nair, a Member of the Telecom Commission of Government of India had participated in the process of selection for award of contract even though his son was an Executive with BPL Projects and Systems Ltd. Hence, the grant of license to BPL Projects and Systems Ltd. was vitiated by the likelihood of bias.

   (iii) Certain criteria for selection of the Indian Company for award of the tender and grant of license were not disclosed in the Notice Inviting Tender; but these "hidden criteria" were applied to eliminate some Indian Companies.

   (iv) The bid of Tata Cellular was rejected without any hearing and without assigning any reason for such rejection.

6. The Supreme Court framed the following issues to dispose of the Special Leave Petition by Tata Cellular:

   (i) What is the scope of judicial review in matter of award of any contract;

   (ii) What is the merit of the contention that award of the contract to BPL Projects and Systems Ltd. has been vitiated by likelihood of bias;

   (iii) Whether adopting "hidden criteria" – not disclosed in the N.I.T. – to eliminate bidders was valid.

7. Regarding the scope of judicial review of administrative action, the Supreme Court held that in matters of contract, judicial review is permissible to prevent any arbitrary decision as such a decision is hit by Article 14 of the Constitution.

8. As the Government is guardian of finances of the State, Government is entitled to reject any tender if acceptance of such a tender is prejudicial to financial interest of the State. But such a decision of the Government must be based on cogent reasons.

9. In the year 1986, Lord Scarman had observed that judicial review is a potent power in hands of judges; but the judges must understand the limits on exercise of such power. Currently, the mood among English Jurists is that self-restraint on power of judicial review of administrative matters is desirable in the public interest.

10. As observed by Lord Brightman, judicial review is not an appeal from an administrative decision by the Executive but a review of the manner in which the Executive took the decision.

11. Unless the higher judiciary exercises the power of judicial review with self-restraint, the Judiciary will, in the guise of preventing the abuse of power will be guilty of usurping power.

12. Judicial review is not concerned with the merit of the decision under appeal. In exercise of power of judicial review, the Courts are not to substitute their decision for the decision of the Authority vested with the power to take a decision.

13. In exercise of the power of judicial review, the Courts have to ensure whether the Designated Authority:
    (i) exceeded its power;
    (ii) Committed an error of law while exercising power;
    (iii) Committed a breach of the Rules of Natural Justice;
    (iv) Reached a decision which no Authority, in exercise of its power reasonably, would have taken;
    (v) Abused its power for an ulterior purpose.

14. Broadly speaking, the grounds on which administrative action is subject to judicial review can be classified into the following categories:
    (i) Illegality: The Authority must correctly understand the law that regulates its powers;
    (ii) Irrationality: The Authority must guard against taking decisions, which are so unreasonable that they suffer from the vice of Wednesbury unseasonableness;
    (iii) Procedural Impropriety.

15. In the year 1991, Lord Diplock has referred to the possible recognition of the principle of proportionality as an additional ground for exercise of the power of judicial review.

16. In the year 1948, Lord Green has defined Wednesbury principle of unreasonableness as follows:

    "A decision of a public authority is liable to be quashed…in Judicial Review proceedings where the Court concludes that no authority properly directing itself on the relevant law and acting reasonably could have reached it."

17. Lord Diplock has said that the Wednesbury principle of unreasonableness applies to a decision by an Authority which is so outrageous in its defiance of logic that no sensible person could have arrived at such an irrational decision.

18. In exercise of the power of judicial review, it is not function of the higher Judiciary to act as an Appellate Authority.

19. A judge who is not an accountant, an engineer, a financer, a banker, a stockbroker or a management analyst is not competent to intelligently review a five thousand page record addressing the intricacies of Public Utility Operation and substitute his judgment for judgment of the Administrator or the Statutory Authority.

20. Moreover, the pressure of judicial calendar combined with the elephantine bulk of records in so many cases of judicial review compels the Courts to take a view regarding the narrow scope of judicial review of decisions of Administrators or Statutory Authorities.

21. Lord Denning has stressed upon the supervisory nature of the Court's power of Judicial Review. The Court will exercise its supervisory role to ensure that the Authority Competent to decide a matter has acted fairly.

22. The Court has to perform its role in exercise of the power of judicial review in the following manner:
   (i) The decision-making Authority acts according to law.
   (ii) If a decision is to be taken regarding interpretation of a provision of the law – which the decision-making Authority has invoked in taking the decision – the Court has to interpret the particular provision of the law.
   (iii) The Court has to also decide whether the decision-making Authority has considered the relevant aspects – and has not considered any extraneous matter – in taking the decision.
   (iv) The Court can also interfere if the decision-making Authority has decided on the basis of no evidence on record.
   (v) The Court can also strike down the decision of the Authority which is such that no reasonable person could have come to such a decision as stated in Wednesbury Corporation's case (1948).
   (vi) The Court can also strike down the decision if the Authority has taken the impugned decision either in bad faith for an ulterior purpose.

23. The ultimate reliance for fair operation of any standard is a judiciary of high competence and character. There should also be the constant play of an informed professional critique upon its work.

24. In the year 1992, Clive Lewis had stated that the higher Judiciary must realize that upsetting of decisions of Administrative Authorities, in exercise of power of judicial review imposes heavy cost on the Executive and leads to increased unbudgeted expenditure. This is more so when the challenge to an administrative decision in procedural rather than substantive.

25. The Supreme Court have observed in F. Chaudhury *versus* D.G. Doordarshan (1989 I SCC 89) that there must be fair play in action in award of a Contract and any award of a contract due to favouritism and nepotism can be challenged successfully. The Supreme Court has also held that fairplay in action is possible with free play at the joints lest the Administration would come to a grinding halt.

26. The Supreme Court have held in F.C.I. *versus* Kamdhenu Cattle Feed Industries (AIR 1993 SC 1601) that even in commercial matters – as award of contracts – action of the state has to be tested on the anvil of Article 14 of the Constitution.

27. The Supreme Court have also held that the state may not enter into a commercial contract with any party but if it does, it must do so by following a fair procedure.

28. Terms and conditions contained in the N.I.T. are not ordinarily open to scrutiny in exercise of the power of judicial review as those terms are in the realm of a commercial contract. Broadly speaking, decision to award a commercial contract is normally reached by a process of negotiation through several tiers. More often than not, such decisions in modern commercial contracts are made by experts and specialists.

29. One of the general conditions of contract in this case of award of license for operating cellular service in major cities was that an Indian Company will be preferred if it has minimum reliance on borrowings from Indian financial institutions. Whereas Indian Companies, who had borrowed substantially from public financial institutions, got the license for cellular service in major cities, Tata Cellular who had not borrowed from public financial institutions, got no credit for fulfilling such a criterion. Moreover, Indian Companies, who had foreign partners without substantial financial strength were preferred to Tata Cellular, whose annual turnover was rupees twelve thousand crore and whose foreign partner had an annual turnover of rupees fifty-one thousand crore.

30. Regarding the contention that award of the contract and the license to BPL Systems and Projects was vitiated because son of B.R. Nair, Member, Telecom Commission was employed by BPL Systems and Projects Ltd. as an Executive, it may be said that likelihood of bias can arise, *inter alia*, from family relationship or financial interests. It may also be said that in ninety-nine cases out of a hundred, it is enough for the Court to ask itself whether a reasonable person in view of the facts of the case could think that there was substantial likelihood of bias.

31. There is a good deal of shallow talk that the judicial robe does not change the man within it. In real life, the judicial robe changes the man. On the whole, judges lay aside private views while discharging their judicial functions. This is achieved through training, professional habits, self-discipline and the fortunate alchemy by which men are loyal to their obligations with which they are entrusted. But it is also true that reason cannot control the sub-conscious influence of feelings of which reason is unaware. When there are grounds for believing that such unconscious feeling may operate in the ultimate judgment or may lead others to believing that they are operating, judges do not sit in judgment and recuse themselves.

32. Turning to facts of the case to examine the real likelihood of bias, it is seen that B.R. Nair, as a Member of the Telecom Commission, only accepted the Report of the Tender Evaluation Committee that BPL Systems and Projects Ltd. and three other Indian Companies, who did not meet the criteria laid down in the N.I.T., may be condoned so far as these criteria are concerned. After condonation, the number of Indian Companies short-listed for grant of license to operate the Cellular System, was fourteen – not a small number for competitive bidding.

33. B.R. Nair did not ultimately decide which Indian Company would be awarded the contract. He was only a recommending authority in the process of decision-making. Moreover, B.R. Nair's son was well-qualified and got a job in BPL Systems and Projects on the basis of an open advertisement in the print media.

34. As B.R. Nair was the Director-General of Telecommunications and had statutory powers under the Indian Telegraph Act 1885, his association with the decision-making process as a recommending authority could be justified on the basis of the Doctrine of Necessity.

35. The Doctrine of Necessity has been dealt with in Halsbury's "Laws of England". It states that even if all Members of a Tribunal, competent to decide a matter, were subjected to disqualification on ground of "bias", they might still be obliged to hear the matter if

there was no scope to constitute another competent Tribunal comprising persons, who did not incur any disqualification on ground of "bias". It has also been stated in Halsbury's "Laws of England" that a single Adjudicator, who incurs a disqualification on ground of "bias" might still adjudicate if there is no other person competent to adjudicate or if a quorum would not be there without him.

36. Regarding the contention that "hidden criteria" – not contained in the N.I.T. – were applied to reject some Indian Companies it can be said that "Mobile Cellphone Service" was a new technological area where the Government of India was embarking for the first time. It would not have been possible in the circumstances to set out all criteria for evaluation of the bids in the N.I.T. The important question is whether the new criteria – called as "hidden criteria" – were uniformly applied in case of all Indian Companies, who had bid in response to the N.I.T.

37. Another limb of argument before the Court was that BPL Systems and Projects Ltd. were allowed to change their foreign collaborator after tender was opened by the Department of Telecommunications. On the basis of records, it can be said that BPL Systems and Projects had mentioned in their bid three foreign companies as their partners and collaborators of which only one was dropped after their tender was opened. This is a minor breech of the conditions of tender as two of the foreign collaborators still remained as Joint Venture partners of BPL Systems and Projects Ltd.

38. In Poddar Steel Corporation *versus* Ganesh Engineering Works (1991(3) SCC 273), the Supreme Court have held that an Authority inviting tender for award of a contract is not bound to give effect to every term in the N.I.T. It was also held that the Authority can waive conditions, which are minor in nature and even waive a technical requirement of little or no significance.

39. A clerical mistake in the proposal by a bidder, if it is promptly declared by the bidder before the bid is opened, can be rectified; but as held by the U.S. Supreme Court if the bid has been opened by the Authority the bid is held as if in "a grasp of steel" and there is no escape even if the bidder has agreed to do a work worth $1,000,000/- (one million U.S. dollars) for only a small amount of $10 (Ten U.S. dollars) due to an error by his clerk. The bidder must be held to the strict letter of the contract "while equity stands by with folded hands and sees him driven into bankruptcy."

40. On the basis of facts of the case and the law on the subject, the Supreme Court directed that Tata Cellular's case for grant of license to operate mobile cellular service in the city of Delhi has to be considered favourably.

Author's Information

Purna Chandra Hota (born in Odisha 9 September 1938), is a former Indian bureaucrat, former Chairman, Union Public Service Commission (2002-03). Prior to this, he was Member, Union Public Service Commission Secretary (1996-2002), Secretary, Ministry of Personnel, Public Grievances and Pension (Department of Personnel & Training) Ministry of Parliamentary Affairs (1995-96). Born and brought up in Odisha as the eldest son of Banchanidi Hota, an Excise Officer, P.C. Hota was educated in Ravenshaw College, Cuttack and University of Allahabad (1953). A meritorious student, he secured first division in Matriculation Examination, Onslow Institute, Chatrapur, Ganjam, Odisha (1955), First Class in the Intermediate Examination, Ravenshaw College (1957), First Class in B.A. Honors, Ravenshaw College (1959), First Class MA in Political Science, University of Allahabad (1962).

Hota served as lecturer in the Post-Graduate Department of Political Science of the Utkal University. He competed in the I.A.S. Examination held by the UPSC and was among the first ten candidates in order of merit. Hota was allotted Odisha Cadre of the I.A.S. (1962). From 1966-84, Hota served as Commissioner & Secretary to Govt. of Odisha in different departments, viz. Urban Development & Public Health Engineering, Health & Family Welfare, Harijan & Tribal Welfare, Irrigation & Power. From 1984-89, Hota was the Additional Secretary, Union Public Service Commission & Member Secretary of Dr. Satish Chandra Committee to review the scheme of Civil Services Examination (1988-89). As the Additional Secretary, Ministry of Labor, Government of India (1990) he was appointed the Chairman of the Tripartite Committee appointed by Government of India, for framing a pension scheme for workers, which has been implemented since 1995.

In February 2004, Hota was appointed by Government of India's Chairman of the Committee on Civil Services Reforms. He submitted the report of the Committee to the Government of India within six months. In January 2006, Hota was nominated by the Government of India to the court of the Banaras Hindu University. In May 2010, he was appointment by the Government of India as Chairman of a Committee of Experts, to suggest measures for expeditious disposal of disciplinary & vigilance enquiries. In July 2010, he submitted the report of the Committee to the Government of India. In August 2012, he was conferred the degree of D.Lit. (Honoris Causa) by Ravenshaw University in recognition of 'Outstanding Contribution to Public Service'. In July 2013, he was appointed by the Government of Karnataka to recommend measures for reform of the practices and procedures of the Karnataka Public Service Commission. In August 2013, he submitted the Report to the Government of Karnataka.

Hota studied law in the South Campus Law College of the University of Delhi while serving in the I.A.S. He was appointed as the Pro Vice-Chairman of Delhi Public Society (2014 till present).

International Delegations

- 1982: Member of a Delegation to the World Bank, Washington DC for negotiating a loan for a major river valley project in Odisha
- 1991: Led the Indian delegation to the International Labor Conference at Geneva
- 1991: Member of the Indian delegation to the Asian Productivity Council at Bangkok
- 1992: Led the Indian Delegation to the International Social Security Association at Acapulco, Mexico
- 1995: Member of the Indian delegation to the Eastern Regional Organization of Public Administration (EROPA) at Tokyo
- 1995: Member of the Indian delegation to the International Anti-Corruption Conference at Beijing
- 2001: Led a delegation of Union Public Service Commission for Study of Modalities of Recruitment to the Public Service in Singapore and Australia